Interdisciplinary Approaches to Human Services

Interdisciplinary Approaches to Human Services

edited by

Peter J. Valletutti, Ed.D.

Dean of Extension and Experimental Programs
and Professor and Chairperson
Department of Special Education
Coppin State College
Baltimore, Maryland

and

Florence Christoplos, Ph.D.

Professor of Education
Graduate College
Bowie State College
Bowie, Maryland

University Park Press
Baltimore • London • Tokyo

UNIVERSITY PARK PRESS
International Publishers in Science and Medicine
233 East Redwood Street
Baltimore, Maryland 21202

Typeset by American Graphic Arts Corporation and Alpha Graphics, Inc.
Manufactured in the United States of America by Universal Lithographers, Inc.
and the Optic Bindery Incorporated.

Library of Congress Cataloging in Publication Data:
Main entry under title:

Interdisciplinary approaches to human services.

Includes index.
1. Social service—Addresses, essays, lectures.
I. Valletutti, Peter J.   II. Christoplos, Florence

HV37.I57   361   77-11089
ISBN 0-8391-1164-9

Contents

Contributors

Viki S. Annand, M.T.R.S., Research Project Coordinator, Department of Recreation and Leisure Studies, Temple University, Philadelphia, Pa. 19122

Judith R. Bunney, D.T.R., President, American Dance Therapy Association; Assistant Professorial Lecturer, Department of Human Kinetics and Leisure Studies, The George Washington University, Washington, D.C. 20052

Marcia Pearce Burgdorf, J.D., Assistant Professor of Law and Director of the Developmental Disabilities Law Project, University of Maryland Law School, Baltimore, Md. 21201; Consultant to the President's Commission on Mental Retardation; Consultant to the White House Conference on Handicapped Individuals

Robert L. Burgdorf, Jr., J.D., Director of Training and Technical Assistance, Developmental Disabilities Law Project, University of Maryland Law School, Baltimore, Md. 21201; Co-chairman, Mental Retardation and Handicaps Committee, American Bar Association, Section of Family Law

Pat Nuse Carlsen, OTR, Assistant Professor, Department of Occupational Therapy, School of Allied Health Sciences, Medical College of Georgia, Augusta, Ga. 30902

Florence Christoplos, Ph.D., Professor of Education, Graduate College, Bowie State College, Bowie, Md. 20715

James P. Connaughton, M.D., Associate Professor of Psychiatry and Pediatrics, Associate Director, Division of Child Psychiatry, The Johns Hopkins School of Medicine, Baltimore, Md. 21205

Charles H. Dankmeyer, Jr., C.P.O., President, Dankmeyer, Inc., Baltimore, Md. 21218

Lawrence A. Fox, D.D.S., M.P.H., M.Ed., Associate Professor and Chairperson, Department of Pedodontics, Case Western Reserve University, Cleveland, Ohio 44106

Lewis J. Goldfine, M.B., D. Phys. Med., F.A.A.P.M.&R., Associate Professor of Rehabilitation Medicine, University of Maryland School of Medicine, Baltimore, Md. 21201; Consultant to the Veterans Administration; Diplomate, American Board of Physical Medicine and Rehabilitation; Fellow, American Academy of Physical Medicine and Rehabilitation

Mary T. Goodwin, B.S., C.P.H., Chief Nutritionist, Montgomery County Health Department, Rockville, Md. 20850

Karen Gordon-Davis, R.N.M.A., Instructor, Helene Fuld School of Nursing, Coppin State College, Baltimore, Md. 21216

William J. Hersey, Jr., M.S.W., Director of Social Services, Social Service Division, The John F. Kennedy Institute; Assistant Professor of Pediatrics, The Johns Hopkins University School of Medicine, Baltimore, Md. 21205

Audrey S. Hoffnung, Ph.D., CCC-Speech Pathology, Lic. N.Y.S., Assistant Professor, Department of Speech, Brooklyn College, Brooklyn, N.Y. 11210

Robert B. Johnston, M.D., Assistant Professor of Pediatrics, The Johns Hopkins University School of Medicine; Coordinator of Training, The John F. Kennedy Institute, Baltimore, Md. 21205

Edith Kramer, ATR, Associate Professor of Art Therapy, New York University; Assistant Professorial Lecturer, The George Washington University, Washington, D.C. 20052

Hanna Yaxa Kwiatkowska, ATR, Assistant Professor of Art Therapy, The George Washington University, Washington, D.C. 20052; Visiting Professor, The Catholic University, Rio de Janeiro, Brazil

Stella Gore Lansing, OTR, Public Health Analyst, United States Consumer Product Safety Commission, Bethesda, Md. 20207

Ruth M. Latimer, M.S., M.Ed., Associate Professor, Department of Physical Therapy, University of Maryland School of Medicine, Baltimore, Md. 21201

Bonnie Liebman, B.A., M.S., Nutritionist, Center for Science in the Public Interest, Washington, D.C. 20009

Alice Jeanne Ludwig, Ed.D., RMT, Associate Professor, Chairperson, The Graduate Studies Committee in Special Education, Jersey City State College, Jersey City, N.J. 07305

Elise Michael Ph.D., R.N., Associate Professor, The College of Nursing, University of Delaware, Newark, Del. 19711

David C. Park, M.T.R.S., Coordinator of Therapeutic Recreation, Department of Human Kinetics and Leisure Studies, The George Washington University, Washington, D.C. 20052

Brockman Schumacher, Ph.D., Coordinator of Rehabilitation Counselor Training, Professor, Rehabilitation Institute, Southern Illinois University, Carbondale, Ill. 62901

Judith Strasser, R.N.M.S., Instructor, Helene Fuld School of Nursing, Coppin State College, Baltimore, Md. 21216

Elinor Ulman, ATR, Assistant Professor, Coordinator of Training, Master's Degree Program in Art Therapy, The George Washington University, Washington, D.C. 20052; Editor and Publisher, American Journal of Art Therapy

Peter J. Valletutti, Ed.D., Dean, Division of Extension and Experimental Programs, Professor and Chairperson, Department of Special Education, Coppin State College, Baltimore 21216; Assistant Professor Special Education (Pediatrics), The Johns Hopkins University School of Medicine, Baltimore, Md. 21205

Alfred M. Wellner, Ph.D., Executive Officer, Council for the National Register of Health Service Providers in Psychology, Washington, D.C. 20036

Nancy Wilkey, Ph.D., R.N., Associate Professor, Helene Fuld School of Nursing, Coppin State College, Baltimore, Md. 21216

Acknowledgments

We are indebted to the contributors who have shared their invaluable knowledge and experiences in the preparation of this book. The authors were chosen as outstanding members of a selected number of disciplines that are providing service to people in need.

We especially express our deep appreciation to our spouses. Billie B. Valletutti's expert editorial assistance and constant support contributed immeasurably, while George Christoplos' culinary arts provided nourishment and support.

We extend our thanks to Albert R. Hartgrove, Administrator, Constance Shaffer, Executive Secretary, Advancement Office, and Kathleen Cloyd, Director, Advancement Relations of the Kennedy Institute for Handicapped Children, Baltimore, Maryland, for permission to use photographs taken by Richard Holden at the Institute and for assistance in their selection.

We are grateful to Mary K. Strawhorn and Sylvia Silver for their assistance in manuscript preparation and chapter review.

to my three mothers
 Emily Valletutti
 Mabel Stratton
 Pearl Hanlin
                    p.j.v.

to Chris, Laura, and Ian
                  f.c.

Interdisciplinary Approaches to Human Services

INTERDISCIPLINARY APPROACHES TO HUMAN SERVICES
An Introduction and Overview

Peter J. Valletutti
and Florence Christoplos

This book has a dual purpose: to clarify the nature and scope of the various professions serving people in need and to allow those in one discipline to appreciate more fully the contributions of other professionals working with the same clients. Outstanding members of a selected number of disciplines were asked to indicate what they believe other professions should know about their fields of expertise, to discuss those skills and services that other professions already are (or should be) utilizing, to consider how their own disciplines might influence the other professions, and to describe how they would like those other professions to interact with them.

Interdisciplinary communication is prerequisite to the interdisciplinary cooperation needed to identify goals for clients and to prescribe treatment priorities, sequences, strategies, implementation processes, materials, and evaluative procedures. Sharing interdisciplinary information is an initial step toward providing a mechanism through which the collective wisdom of individual interdisciplinary team members may be marshalled for the purpose of arriving at the most logical, productive, and efficient means to remediate the difficulties that clients experience.

Interdisciplinary teams may be separated by function into 1) those directly responsible for prescribing a client's treatment program and 2)

1

those responsible for providing consultative services to an intermediary who, in turn, provides direct treatment to the client. The first category usually includes cases in which the nature of the treatment is such that numerous professionals from different disciplines have frequent contact with the client. A case in point would be a hospitalized client who is chronically ill. Case-study conferences would be held periodically to include all those professionals having some relation to the case. Intervention decisions would be made by consensus, and the responsibility for treatment implementation would be assigned to appropriate team members.

The second category usually encompasses cases in which members of relevant disciplines confer to advise teachers, families, nurses, and/or other day-to-day attendants about the prolonged care of a handicapped person. Treatment of a learning-disabled child attending a public school is an example. Such a child does not ordinarily have frequent contact with a variety of professionals. Members of disciplines having pertinent information to contribute with regard to the understanding and handling of this child would meet in groups to address the central problem: assisting the teacher and parent in the treatment of the child. What the treatment should be and how it would be carried out remain the decision and the responsibility of the teacher and parent.

In the first type (direct treatment team), accountability for the outcome is shared equally by the team members. In the second type (consultative treatment team), the responsibility of the intermediary who delivers care directly to the client becomes crucial. The team members in cases of the second type are far removed from the client in comparison to the personal and often intimate relationship of the intermediary with the client. The goals, behavior styles, biases, and personality of the intermediary are factors that should influence the deliberations of the team. To ignore these factors is to reduce the likelihood that the intermediary will heed the team's suggestions, thereby negating the benefits of the team input. The intermediary must, in effect, become a member of equal standing on the interdisciplinary team. The remaining team members, on the other hand, must not only consider how best to serve a particular client, but how to develop, in the intermediary, the necessary skills of observation, treatment, and evaluation so that the intermediary may indeed function as an equal team member.

Interaction skills among team members are always critical but are probably more complex and demanding for teams that serve as consultants to an intermediary than for direct treatment teams. Interaction skills, however, rarely are incorporated into the training skills of professionals who participate on interdisciplinary teams. Those with experience in any type of group effort know full well the power of a single individual to sabotage an entire team's effectiveness. Development of awareness, knowledge, and skill in group dynamics, perhaps, should become a pre-requisite for participation on a team, particularly when the regular team members are expected to work together on a number of cases over extended periods of time. Good will, a sense of humor, and freedom from status biases among all members may be all that is needed but difficult to develop. Investment in workshops to foster group interaction skills, therefore, would be a wise expenditure of time, money, and professional effort.

The following needs-assessment procedures can be utilized in initiating workshops to develop interdisciplinary team-interaction skills. One discipline at a time may be selected for study. Each team member, including the member(s) from the selected discipline, would be asked to list the competencies that they wish members from that discipline to demonstrate. Parents, clients, and a wider institutional representation than the team may be included for this initial survey. These competencies then would be compiled and resubmitted to each team member for ranking. Ranking may be from the highest to the lowest or on a five- or seven-point scale. Competency items for which the greatest consensus and nonconsensus exist among disciplines can serve to clarify the commonalities and areas of disagreement among team members. This procedure can be replicated for each discipline in turn, and the results can be used for discussions that seek to develop greater understanding among the disciplines.

A further aspect of training personnel toward goals of interdisciplinary cooperation is the need to develop an understanding of how specialized treatments affect total developmental progress. For example, even a cross-disciplinary treatment such as hospitalization must be viewed with caution because of possible effects beyond the more immediate advantages of ease and control over medical treatments. Hospitalization for seven- to twelve-month-old infants, for example, may be more psychologically damaging than for younger infants. At about seven months, infants develop the ability to anticipate events. Consequently, they are frightened and disoriented by the sudden loss of familiar persons or places, and they do not possess sufficient receptive language skills to lessen the shock. Thus, it can be seen that ramifications of medical and other interventions may differ at specific stages of cognitive development and that treatment outcomes will be affected accordingly.

A further consideration in interdisciplinary efforts is the comparison of effectiveness of treatment rendered by teams vis-à-vis that rendered by individuals. Should teams or the single professional initially consulted by the client decide whether or not interdisciplinary efforts are pertinent? No guidelines exist for making such decisions, and no research results regarding the comparative effects of team and individual efforts are available. Hampered by this lack of clear support, decisions are, in effect, left to chance or to the inclinations and/or sophistication of the client.

Whether teams or individuals are the source of assistance or whether the teams render direct or indirect service, the concern is with service to the handicapped.[1] The problems of the handicapped, defined here in a broad sense as those seeking or having been referred for help, are, as a rule, sufficiently multifaceted to require services from a variety of sources. The means of coping with the complexity of individual problems have become increasingly analytical and specialized as opposed to holistic in nature. The resulting dehumanization and depersonalization of institutions and agencies offering only discrete and single services to individuals have been decried ubiquitously. Solutions, individual and collective, have ranged from ombudsmen to alternative schools, from drugs and dropouts to strikes and shutdowns of needed services and agencies. A holistic approach, on the other hand, has been demeaned as romantically idealistic at best and costly, ineffective, unmanageable, and misleading at worst. Inefficient and stumbling efforts to treat total individuals rather than their discrete problems, however awkward and cumbersome, may nevertheless remain the best available alternative.

The fact is that innumerable agencies offer a variety of services to individuals who need many of these services simultaneously. Without interdisciplinary cooperation, the needs of the individual are invariably separated into portions shaped to fit the organizational needs and biases of agencies. As bureaucratic specialization supersedes integration, a person's parts become more important than his/her whole self. When efficiency is thus given hegemony over effectiveness, at some further point even efficiency is lost. Clearly, efficiency is meaningless without effectiveness.

Furthermore, the somewhat cumbersome operations of an interdisciplinary approach prevent hasty decisions made by an individual professional who does not face peer accountability. However, the alternate possibility of unwieldy team procedures depressing or stifling creative and unorthodox approaches by gifted individuals also must be considered. As with other attempts to eliminate the most offensive or speculative practices, a concomitant limit on highly creative efforts is equally likely to occur. Accountability thus cuts both ways: while forcing all to conform to minimal levels of acceptability in practice, those capable and creative individuals who would forge new approaches and models of practice may be inhibited by its restrictions. Whether the possibility of mediocrity is preferable to the risks associated with creative freedom is a question not easily resolved.

Nevertheless, without interdisciplinary teams, services will overlap and confusion will arise as to responsibility for particular, specialized services.

---

[1] The person receiving services is referred to as the client, the handicapped, the child, the student, or the patient. The choice of label depends on the general milieu from which the services emanate or on the setting in which the interdisciplinary team functions.

In the absence of cooperative efforts, fear of encroachment on one another's expertise may become an excuse for needless and esoteric tests, language, and treatment. Esoteric practices and the predilection of experts to engage in disputes of territorial rights do not negate the serious problem of what is and what is not legitimate in the sharing of specific practices among professionals. Specialized language within a profession, for example, is sometimes necessary for greater clarity of communication. Language specialization, however, must not be used for obfuscation or hypocritical elitism. Specialized language must not be an indirect way of saying, "Stay out of my domain!"

To make any significant area of human endeavor or problems the exclusive domain of one discipline negates the advantages inherent in several disciplines working toward common objectives. In the interests of serving clients, members of each discipline should be willing, whenever possible, to relinquish certain roles and to teach their own specialized skills to others. The legal constraints on such behaviors are as yet to be clarified. The transfer or sharing of responsibilities, however, requires a substantial degree of self-confidence and minimal defensiveness among those cooperating in team efforts.

Several disciplines working cooperatively to develop a client's recreational and leisure skills, for example, may result in a client's more judicious pursuit of leisure time activity than if a recreational therapist were to work alone without considering the findings of psychologists, nutritionists, and educators. In the same way, teachers must not leave the development of communication skills solely to the ministrations of a speech therapist but must utilize the information from speech therapists and families in setting reasonable and desirable curriculum goals and instructional processes for the development of language skills.

More effective teamwork with less confusion and conflict among treatments and professions should result in better services to a large number of handicapped people. Clients themselves are more likely to have greater confidence in decisions arrived at by professional consensus than by the idiosyncratic biases of one individual.

A further characteristic of today's service professions that supports the need for interdisciplinary efforts is the ambiguity of professional boundaries. Emergent cross-disciplinary areas are requiring new packaging in service and training, and more and more intradisciplinary crises of identity are discussed in the literature. What do psychologists, teachers, nurses, or physicians do that is exclusively within their sphere? Few professionals have escaped asking themselves this question of domain. When disciplinary overlap leads to defensiveness and professional exclusivity, clients may be denied needed services, particularly if they are caught in bureaucratic referrals from one agency to another.

Consensus as to the responsibilities of disciplines and/or individual professionals is the ideal solution. Obtaining consensus within a profession as to specific disciplinary responsibility and scope is, however, extremely difficult. On a national level, professional organizations develop the needed criteria for disciplinary cohesion in broad terms only. These bases are deliberately broad to incorporate the wide variance in philosophy and programming exhibited among individual professional training institutions. Program variations among training institutions have both positive and negative aspects. In a positive sense, institutions can capitalize on the special strengths of faculties and facilities and thus develop a unique training process. The acceptance of widespread variance in programming implies acceptance of creative innovations within disciplines.

On the other hand, variations in training models result in ambiguity of expectations by hiring agencies. These agencies, therefore, need to know the philosophy and program components of specific training institutions in order to understand the probable variance in skills, knowledge, and professional values found among those with the same degree qualifications within the same discipline who are applying for the same professional positions. The existence of consistency within institutional programs and for relatively prolonged periods of time is an additional component in the problem of developing predictable judgments about training institutions and their graduates.

The problem of consistency in professional training is further compounded when professional people are expected to function on interdisciplinary teams. Consistency in disciplinary training, clearly, is not available; perhaps, it is not even desirable as an eventual goal. Interdisciplinary team members, therefore, should be viewed as individuals with insights and skills to contribute to the team rather than as representatives of a discipline. Team membership is thus envisaged as a state of mind and members as unique contributors to the whole team process.

Another aspect of professional training involves the tendency of professions to gradually increase training requirements and certification criteria. As the profession seeks greater acceptance, support, and justification by mandating more training, one of two developments occurs: 1) specified levels of professionalism or paraprofessionalism emerge to distinguish among levels within the discipline, or 2) professionals become overtrained for the positions they hold. In the latter case, higher and higher costs may be placed on consumers for services that may be rendered by less costly professionals. When this situation arises, perhaps interdisciplinary teams would function more efficiently, without loss of effectiveness, because regular team members could be those at a moderate level of training who could make decisions about when to involve the more costly services of more elaborately trained professionals within or overlapping that same discipline. For example, registered nurses, as regular team members, could determine when to involve physicians. Rehabilitation counselors could determine when psychiatric services are needed, and a dental assistant when a dentist's services are necessary.

Another extremely important factor associated with interdisciplinary approaches is the shared responsibility for the making of difficult ethical decisions. For example, the awesome responsibility associated with decisions concerning terminally ill patients is lessened when shared. The handling of profoundly handicapped newborn infants involves questions of life and death that should not be left to any one individual. Abortion, adoption, and drug usage are other key ethical issues facing those in the human service professions. Godlike responsibilities in decision making are more safely assumed by interdisciplinary teams than by individuals.

A further advantage of interdisciplinary approaches is that group discussions may generate more creative approaches and higher professional commitment to keeping abreast of professional developments in the various related fields. With increasing professional contact and support, the problems of professional isolation and loneliness, coupled with the possible consequences of insensibility and even cruelty ("burn-out"), are reduced in frequency and intensity. With team discussions and continued professional stimulation from peers, marked improvement in morale and performance are more likely to occur. Indeed, team approaches may be one of the most valuable mechanisms by which to enhance professional tolerances in working with handicapped clients and to delay the onset of disillusionment with career choice. Isolation of professional individuals can be a virulent way of destroying skills and preventing professional as well as client growth. Without opportunities to share professional issues and problems, severe anomie or sadistic callousness are real possibilities.

Furthermore, the increasingly pervasive philosophy of providing the least restrictive environment for handicapped individuals clearly necessitates cooperation among service agencies. Those groups traditionally providing direct services to the handicapped are now facing changes; they now increasingly assume the more indirect responsibilities of working with professionals in general service agencies for the purpose of integrating the handicapped into their programs. There are many arguments to support the greater integration of handicapped persons into the mainstream institutions and activities of society *provided that adequate preparation and training are given to those who have critical roles in the integration process.* Through greater contact with handicapped persons, the fears, myths, and prejudices that pervade public and professional attitudes are reduced. Techniques for coping with special needs are more efficiently handled in regular settings, as opposed to specialized settings, than is generally believed. Once the handicapped are appreciated for their qualities that resemble those of the general public, they can be accepted more easily with their differences. Encroachments on the time of professionals who are not accustomed to working with handicapped persons can be minimized by careful support and assistance from those whose training has been more specialized.

Schools in particular provide an example of a general service institution that increasingly is accepting severely and multiply handicapped students at younger and younger ages. Schools, more than ever before, provide a wider range of services to all students and their respective families. Teachers in regular classrooms, accustomed to working with nonhandicapped children, are now becoming members of an expanded interdisciplinary team in order to serve children with handicaps who are entering their classrooms. The team members serve in an essential role by providing training and experience for those who are working with handicapped persons for the first time, and those team members accustomed to working with the handicapped gain needed perspectives on normal expectations while working in institutions for the general, nonhandicapped public.

Of course, the differing role of the interdisciplinary team under circumstances in which the team serves an intermediary person, rather than rendering direct services to a client, must be kept in mind. As indicated earlier, the team's function is more complex and demanding when the goals, style of functioning, attitudes, and skills of the intermediary are crucial intervening variables in serving a client.

Given, then, the need for interdisciplinary cooperation, the parameters and components of interdisciplinary cooperation must be considered. Of prime importance is the complex nature of clients in their interaction with the environment. The client is someone who is having significant difficulty in adjusting to environmental demands. Difficulty in adjusting obviously results, in part, from the individual's physical and psychological status. This difficulty is further related to the client's perception of self and his/her self-expectation. The client who suffers from epilepsy, for example, may have difficulty adjusting not only to the physical and neurological symptoms of epilepsy but to the attitudes toward epilepsy and toward individuals who suffer from it. Another example is a given society's demand for oral expressive fluency and competency, which is believed to be a primary cause of stuttering, influencing its onset and development. A final example is the child who enters school and is shortly thereafter labeled as mildly retarded. Whereas the child's competence had not heretofore been questioned, continued failure to meet age/grade expectations in school encourages the handicapped label. Many students thus labeled, however, successfully adjust to the social, work, and recreational demands of adult life when they leave school. Society and its institutions thus play a critical role in assigning handicapped labels that invariably compound the handicap.

Family intolerance and expectations, too, are shaped by cultural and socioeconomic factors in addition to idiosyncratic and subcultural factors. The child with a mild mental handicap, functioning in a family in which the other members are at the same, or a lower, cognitive level, may face different pressures than the child with a similar cognitive deficit functioning in a family whose intelligence lies in the superior range. In addition, some families may view extrafamilial services as interference, while others may actively seek a wide range of services. Family characteristics, tolerances, and expectations thus may interfere with, or support, broad social adjustment and attempts to render a variety of services.

Handicapped individuals are affected not only by age, grade, family, and sociocultural factors, but by geographic ones as well. Occupational and recreational opportunities are determined by the type and size of the community in which a person lives. Living in an urban center requires different social and occupational skills and competencies than those required in a rural environment. Also to be considered is the uneven clustering of services and professional expertise in various geographic areas. Finally, the degree to which campaigns have been mounted to educate the public to the need for particular services affects the utilization of services. In many cases, the "public" includes those professionals with a limited awareness of the scope of available human services. For example, therapists from the fine arts fields or nutritionists are rarely considered in interdisciplinary conferences unless a more catholic view of available services prevails than is usually found among more traditionally oriented professionals who establish team selection procedures.

Parameters dealing with the composition of the interdisciplinary team also must be considered. A team requires the membership of at least two individuals directly involved in the client's treatment and/or educational program. If one views the client or his/her representative as an integral member of any treatment team, then a single client-professional relationship is, in a sense, a "mini-team." Excluding this limited team, however, an interdisciplinary team is generally considered any group of two or more professionals actively involved with the education/treatment of a client. The disciplines represented should be directly related to the client and his/her family's treatment needs. To be more relevant, professional skills and knowledge should be the basis for election to team membership. As indicated earlier, a professional label is not necessarily an indicator of a member's demonstrable skills, insight, or wisdom.

The individual members of the team, however, should perhaps be selected on the basis of other criteria as well. The potentially positive- or negative-interaction patterns of specific team members should be considered in selecting a specific person for membership on a team. Some thought should be given to selecting representatives with an understanding of group dynamics while avoiding individuals who assume false leadership by verbal monopoly, dictatorial attitudes, or by presumed superiority vis-à-vis an implicit professional pecking order. A partial solution may be to develop interaction procedures and constraints that prevent one discipline from totally directing the deliberations of an entire team. In doing so, however, other difficulties may arise such as how to give full weight to individual strengths, both professional and personal, regardless of disciplinary affiliation, without denigrating the role of other individuals or disciplines. Each interdisciplinary team must struggle with such issues on an individual team basis. As indicated earlier, team training in group dynamics as a prerequisite to case discussion may save much time and effort in the long run.

Another key issue in deciding the composition of the team is whether the client or his/her representative/advocate should be a member of the team. The related legal issues are yet to be decided. Aside from legal issues, however, do clients and/or, in the case of minors, family members, have the moral and ethical right to participate in the process by which critical decisions are made about the client's present and future status? What are the client's rights with regard to the acceptance or rejection of final decisions? The issue of inclusion of client and family on the team has major implications: Do the team's meetings become part of the treatment strategy when the client participates in the process? How may clients be prepared for their role on the team so as not to be overawed by the authority of the team, thus defeating the purpose of client inclusion? Does the presence of the client at team meetings threaten whatever anonymity or privacy the client cares to retain? Will professional team members be more circuitous in their deliberations in order to avoid making the client aware of treatment elements which professionals believe clients are better off not knowing? Simple answers to any of these questions have not been forthcoming, and only with greater experience in interdisciplinary operations will professionals be able to proceed in their work with more than educated guesses.

Another component to be considered is the interdisciplinary team setting. Interdisciplinary teams usually function within a formal physical setting, e.g., a hospital, a subunit of a hospital, a clinic, a rehabilitation center, or a school. When the varied services are located over a broad geographic area, however, problems may arise as to the most appropriate place for the team to function. Perhaps the most logical meeting place for a team should be determined on the basis of client needs. For example, the school is the logical team-meeting setting for school age children whose greatest problems are related to learning and/or to the learning environment. Direct observation of school procedures and constraints can be of inestimable assistance to team members in making decisions. For the client who suffers from a medical or psychiatric condition requiring intensive and/or extensive treatment, the logical site from which team members should operate is a medical facility.

Wherever the team operates, however, no single profession should assume constant hegemony over the team. Changing leadership should correlate with the changing needs and special nature of the client as well as with the team setting. Leadership in certain cases may be assumed by the professional who is required to work directly with the client during most or all of the client's treatment. In this type of case, the leader is not only the executor of the team's decisions but is the primary recipient of the team's advice. As discussed earlier, this intermediary's values, style of functioning, skills, and attitudes become critical factors in the team's deliberations.

No matter who assumes the responsibility for "hands-on" contact with the handicapped person, however, the importance of interpreting program decisions made by the team to the client is obvious. Unless a special rapport exists, successful implementation may be severely threatened. It is no small task to identify and establish the *modus operandi* for selecting the most effective leader(s) to structure organizational patterns, to develop the operating rules of the team, and to provide the most effective communication with the client. Clearly, such decisions must be made on an individual team basis and not by rigid or automatic rules.

In conclusion, this chapter has presented a broadly sketched survey of interdisciplinary team purposes, characteristics, and issues. It is hoped that the issues raised and the questions asked will provide a stimulating framework within which to explore the characteristics of each of the disciplines providing human services. The following chapters define and clarify the nature and scope of a selected number of disciplines providing key services to people in need. The material is presented in the hope that the insights gained when disciplines become more knowledgeable about one another will enhance the effectiveness and efficiency of interdisciplinary efforts.

ART THERAPY

Elinor Ulman, Edith Kramer
and Hanna Yaxa Kwiatkowska

The purposeful use of art to meet psychological needs is more than 30 years old; yet, today, the art therapist's role as a member of the psychiatric or educational team is still a subject of debate. The ensuing discussion suggests why definition of the art therapist's professional territory is likely to remain inconclusive.

The chapter opens with a brief exposition of the leading theoretical trends and then touches on the material and administrative conditions desirable for the effective development of art therapy programs in various situations. Activities typical of existing programs are described next, after which special applications of art therapy in work with children, in research, and in community mental health centers are delineated.

Finally, current problems affecting the use of art therapy are discussed. The ongoing development of art therapy theory and of professional training and organization may eliminate some difficulties, but the nature of the visual arts itself creates certain complications. Painting and sculpture are susceptible to such a broad range of therapeutic and educational applications that the boundaries between art therapy and other disciplines are inevitably blurred.

ART THERAPY THEORY AND ITS PRACTICAL APPLICATIONS

In the 1940s, Naumburg began to develop the use of *art as a tool* in a form of psychotherapy that she designated as "analytically" or "dynamically" oriented. The method is based "on releasing the unconscious by means of spontaneous art expression; it has its roots in the transference relation between patient and therapist, and on the encouragement of free association. . . . The images produced . . . constitute symbolic speech" (Naumburg, 1958).

13

In keeping with the times during which her method was developed, Naumburg stresses an extension of psychoanalytic, interpretive, uncovering techniques; her main focus is on intensive work with individual patients. Art therapy, as she defines it, can stand as a primary therapeutic method rather than as an auxiliary to other forms of treatment. Its practice does not demand previous art training; it can be used effectively by any "well-trained psychotherapist who has a sympathetic interest in . . . the creative arts." Art materials used are limited to those that can be easily and quickly manipulated (Naumburg, 1966).

Starting to develop theory a decade later than Naumburg, Kramer also relies on psychoanalytic concepts, including the later findings of Freudian ego psychology. Concentrating on the *therapeutic values inherent in art,* she states that the art therapist's

> "primary function is to assist the process of sublimation, an act of integration and synthesis which is performed by the ego. . . . The therapeutic relationship . . . is less intimate than in psychotherapy. . . . The transference . . . remains subordinate to the task of making the patient productive. . . . In the creative act, conflict is re-experienced, resolved, and integrated. . . . In the artistic product, conflict is formed and contained but only partly neutralized. . ." (Kramer, 1958).

Art therapy thus conceived does not stand alone; it complements psychotherapy by bringing unconscious material closer to the surface and by providing an area of symbolic experience wherein changes may be tried out and gains deepened and cemented. The art therapist must be "at once artist, therapist, and teacher. . . . He encourages a high artistic level of performance within the limitation of the patient's talent." In general, patients are not treated individually but are seen in groups, and their art activity and products become an integral part of the culture of the therapeutic milieu (Kramer, 1958).

Kwiatkowska is another therapist whose highly developed experience as an artist has been supplemented by clinical training. Her work in art evaluation and therapy with family groups implies a further development of the field in keeping with psychiatric trends of the 1960s and 1970s. The transactions of the session serve, of course, to illuminate psychodynamics, but primary emphasis is placed on the development of immediate relationships among family members (Kwiatkowska, 1967a).

This brief overview indicates that art therapy originated in connection with psychotherapy and that the leading concepts of art therapy derive from psychoanalytic theory. Efforts to make the most of the psychological benefits stemming from work in the visual arts, however, extend far beyond the psychiatric sphere. Art therapy has found a place not only in psychiatric hospitals and clinics but also in geriatric centers, rehabilitation programs for the physically disabled, residential centers and schools for the retarded, and penal or correctional institutions.

In special education, the same principles that have guided progressive art educators since the early 1900s were later adapted to the needs of the physically, mentally, and emotionally handicapped. Lowenfeld used the term "art education therapy" to designate "a therapy specific to the means of art education," saying that it deals with "neither the interpretation of symbols, nor a diagnosis reached by speculative inferences based on certain symbols." He pointed out that in this area the art teacher's methods differed from his/her more usual ones "*in degree and intensity but not in kind*" (Lowenfeld, 1957).

More recently, art has been enlisted in the widespread search for enriched life experience on the part of people who are not suffering from unusually severe mental or emotional handicaps. Rhyne purposely avoided the word *therapy* when she titled her book *The Gestalt Art Experience*. Like Naumburg, Rhyne uses art as a tool; the full development of the individual's capacity for formed expression is not emphasized. There is relatively little emphasis on the translation into words of formerly unconscious conflict. In Rhyne's practice, the immediate experience of making art works enhances self-perception and intensifies exchanges among members of a group (Rhyne, 1973).

With the aim of delineating the boundaries of the art therapy field, Ulman formulated a synthesis of the psychoanalytic approaches expounded by Naumburg and Kramer. With such a synthesis in mind, she defined the arts as "a way of bringing order out of chaos—chaotic feelings and impulses within, the bewildering mass of impressions from without . . . , a means to discover both the self and the world, and to establish a relation between the two." She limited *therapy* to "procedures . . . designed to assist favorable changes in personality or in living that will outlast the session itself" (Ulman, 1971).

In summary, Ulman views art therapy as covering a broad range of endeavors limited only by the requirement that they must genuinely partake of both art and therapy. The completion of the artistic process may at times be sacrificed to more immediate goals; communication and insight may take priority over development of art expression, as in Naumburg's practice. On the other hand, stereotyped, compulsive work used to ward off dangerous emotions must sometimes be permitted even by the therapist who, like Kramer, emphasizes the healing quality of the creative process per se. Where no fruitful consolidation of insight can be foreseen, the exposure of conflicts may be avoided deliberately in favor of artistic achievement, because artistic and therapeutic success may go hand in hand (Ulman, 1971). As Kramer later stated, there need be no "sharp division between therapeutic creative activities and art activities . . . indeed, insofar as the therapeutic situation fosters honesty, it is more conducive to true art than are situations where pretense is encouraged . . ." (Kramer, 1971, 1975b).

BASIC REQUIREMENTS FOR AN ART THERAPY PROGRAM

Physical Requirements

Art therapy needs a specifically designated room, a room in which running water is accessible, in which storage for both supplies and finished work is adequate, and in which the grubbiness characteristic of studios will not be resented or interfered with by people using the room for other purposes. Wall space for the informal display of pictures and shelves for showing sculpture are desirable. There should be a kiln with a firing chamber at least 18 inches in each dimension.

It is particularly important that art should be separated from other activities for which art materials are used. Art and craft can fulfill their functions best when each is accorded its own dignity and distinct realm. Because the element of self-confrontation is absent in crafts, an object produced can be a source of pride to persons who reject their art work because it contains too much evidence of pathology, or to those who cannot endure the regression and the relaxation of compulsive defenses, the occurrence of which is necessary in the creation of art. Obsessive perfectionism, a hindrance in art, can be an asset in many of the crafts. It follows that, because art makes greater emotional demands, it flourishes with difficulty in the immediate neighborhood of activities offering a less challenging alternative.

Materials must be plentiful, and they should be of sufficient quality so that expressive work is not discouraged by the need to fight an unresponsive medium. Nor should the materials be so delicate or so precious that they may not be distributed and used freely. For patients of all ages, basic media should include paper of various sizes and colors (among them, 36-inch rolls of brown wrapping paper for murals and other large work), sturdy brushes, poster paint, pastels, and clay. Young children should be supplied with wax crayons, while older children and adolescents should have materials for three-dimensional construction. Adults also use most of these materials, and, for them, casein paints are a good addition to the list. These paints are an effective medium, avoiding the connotation of childishness (Horowitz, 1965), and at the same time circumventing the technical hazards of oils or the gaudiness of acrylics.

Administrative Requirements

The administrative structure under which art therapists function varies. In psychiatric settings, they are sometimes placed in occupational therapy departments or within recreational therapy programs. In some institutions, creative therapies (music, dance, drama, and the visual arts) constitute a separate department; in others, a broader spectrum of activity therapies makes up a department.

In its psychiatric applications, art therapy seems to function best in those programs in which the art therapists are directly responsible to the staff members who direct treatment or research. Not only does this arrangement place art therapy on an equal footing with other services, but it also makes it possible to develop fully the naturally intimate relationship between art therapy and strictly verbal forms of psychotherapeutic treatment.

In public school systems, the value of art therapy for handicapped students is gaining recognition gradually (Packard, 1976). It is to be hoped that more and more schools will become ready to employ qualified art therapists and to introduce such services without requiring that therapists also meet certification requirements as teachers. At present, art teachers who also have training as art therapists sometimes combine both functions.

THE SCOPE OF THE ART THERAPIST'S FUNCTIONS

Psychological Assessment

Paintings and sculptures, viewed as the result of many free choices, both conscious and unconscious, sometimes dramatically reveal facets of personality not easily accessible through either verbal interviews or the observation of less highly individual forms of activity. There is evidence that important diagnostic indications may be discovered through free art expression long before they can be identified by the more conventional projective procedures (Ulman, 1975b).

While the patient's manner of working, and any comments made are taken into account, the *symbolic content* and the *formal characteristics* of the work constitute a source of information uniquely available through the visual arts. Because staff members frequently find it difficult to focus on this kind of material, the art therapist must formulate his/her own impressions succinctly. The therapist thus becomes a preliminary interpreter, enabling colleagues from other disciplines to relate his/her findings to what they know about the patient from other sources.

No matter how informal the art therapy program is, the experienced art therapist dates all work and makes notes immediately after each session. This routine is connected primarily with treatment, but at the same time it enables the therapist to arrange works in sequence and select from them when called on to present an illustrated evaluative report. In addition, Kramer working with children, Ulman working with adults, and Kwiatkowska working with family groups developed procedures for collecting visual data in a single session (American Art Therapy Association, 1976). Analysis of such visual material, based on dynamic psychological concepts, illuminates not only pathology but also the resources of the whole personality and, in the case of families, basic patterns of interaction. What goes on between subject and therapist or within the family group constitutes an additional source of information (Kwiatkowska, 1967b, 1971; Kwiatkowska and Mosher, 1971; Ulman, 1975b).

As compared with standard psychological drawing procedures, subject matter is open to wider choice, and the art materials offered are richer. These techniques also differ essentially from the diagnostic use of art materials practiced by some occupational therapists. Probably because both Ulman and Kwiatkowska are artists, they introduced special procedures that tend to momentarily loosen defenses and circumvent stereotyped manners of response; these are derived in part from methods developed for similar reasons by an art educator (Cane, 1951). Kramer, too, uses her skills as an artist-teacher in evaluative as well as treatment sessions.

The very richness of this kind of material makes it difficult to standardize or classify. As a start toward this still distant goal, Levy and Ulman published experimental data confirming the preliminary hypothesis that psychopathology can indeed be recognized in paintings (Levy and Ulman, 1967; Ulman and Levy, 1968).

Training

In training hospitals, art therapists may offer courses for psychiatric residents and other interns. The general aim is to make students more sensitive to the communicative possibilities of art expression. They may thus be prepared to use some art therapy techniques themselves (Naumburg, 1966), to make the most of the collaborative services of an art therapist, or simply to respond constructively to art products spontaneously presented to them by patients. Both Ulman and Kwiatkowska have found effective the active use of art materials by staff trainees following directions similar to those given patients. In Ulman's practice with first year psychiatric residents, painting or clay modeling was followed by group discussion of what had been produced. At first, the art therapist also tried presenting patients' paintings and sculptures for didactic purposes, but it soon became apparent that the young physicians were much more interested in making and studying their own art productions. It seemed that the goal of these sessions— receptivity to the art work of patients—was approached most effectively by this indirect route.

Art therapists employed in schools sometimes introduce art teachers and classroom teachers to those art therapy methods that can be applied by members of other disciplines. Here, again, first hand experience with the expressive use of art materials seems to be the most effective method of instruction.

Treatment

The following discussion refers primarily to programs for adults. Art therapy with children is considered in a separate section.

Most art sessions with adults should last at least one-and-a-half hours, preferably two hours. Maximal flexibility, permitting even longer periods of uninterrupted work when interest warrants, is an ideal seldom met.

Referrals Whether the program's emphasis is on psychotherapy mediated by the use of art materials or on the therapeutic value of art itself, referrals should never be limited to those with previous artistic experience, demonstrated talent, or professed interest in art. Indeed, professional artists may find it particularly difficult to use art as therapy because of their enormous investment in art. It may even be impossible for them to work with art materials at all when their general functioning is badly impaired. On the other hand, some of the people who protest most heartily that they "can't draw a straight line" or "always hated art in school" can, if properly introduced to it, find this mode of expression at least congenial and even occasionally discover an unsuspected gift. Kwiatkowska has noted that families whose members lack any talent for art almost always respond well to its use as a medium of psychotherapeutic exchange.

The present state of knowledge scarcely allows a prediction about who will profit most from art therapy. It is worth trying when there is difficulty in verbal communication or when people are adept in the use of language to conceal thought and feeling.

It is sometimes said that freely expressive art work may delay an awareness of reality by encouraging people to dwell upon their fantasies. This belief seems to be based on the doubtful hypothesis that fantasy will be abandoned merely because its objectification is forbidden. In cases in which art may actually weaken fragile defenses that are in the course of construction or reconstruction, clients themselves will usually provide clues. The art therapist, sensitive to these clues, will not urge emotionally loaded expression upon people who are disturbed by it unless there is a treatment objective to be served. Fortunately, the materials of art therapy can, when indicated, be used for compulsive activity in the service of defense.

Therapeutic Procedures Art therapists have developed numerous modifications of method that are dictated by their own preferences and the particular needs of the institutions in which they work. Only the more widely tested art therapy procedures are outlined in the following paragraphs.

Individual Art Therapy In institutional practice, art therapy with clients who are seen individually usually is limited to situations in which intensive long term psychotherapy is possible and in which the ratio of staff to patients is high. Individual art therapy is generally interpretive, with art productions being encouraged primarily for their immediate communicative value. At times, drawings are made outside of the sessions while the sessions themselves are devoted entirely to verbal exchange. Whether individual art therapy constitutes the primary mode of treatment or whether it supplements conventional psychotherapy, the art therapist must either have the skills of a psychotherapist or be adequately supervised (Naumburg, 1950; Kwiatkowska and Perlin, 1960; Smith, Macht, and Refanes, 1967; Refanes and Gallagher, 1968). Private practice of art therapy with individual clients is increasing gradually.

Formal Group Art Therapy   Therapy groups in which each participant works on individual art productions that serve as a springboard for group discussion may function in hospitals, community mental health centers, and in private practice. Five to eight patients ordinarily constitute such a group.

This method, because of its strict time limits and the emphasis on verbal expression, is not apt to result in highly developed art work. It demands reasonably homogeneous groups that are likely to stay together for a predictable period of time. The skills of a group therapist are needed. Some art therapists may be able to conduct such sessions alone, while others may need to work with a suitable co-therapist. In any case, it is often very useful to have a participant-observer make notes during the entire session and share observations with the active group leader or leaders.

Formal group art therapy is subject to as many variations of emphasis and style as are other forms of group psychotherapy. Kwiatkowska's work in treating the intimate group presented by a patient, his/her parents, and siblings constitutes a highly advanced development of formal group art therapy which is discussed below.

In the course of her work in the psychiatric department of an urban general hospital, Ulman (1975c) observed that American working class adults do not readily make use of the conventional, organized discussion period. Furthermore, while modifications of art for use in group work are legitimate, such procedures are likely to interfere with the unique contribution that painting and sculpture can make for the very reason that they are essentially *solitary* pursuits, permitting *indirect* movement toward the outside world of things and persons. Kwiatkowska, however, remarks that this same circumstance makes it possible for the silent members of a formal art therapy group to participate through their pictorial or modeled productions when these provoke comment from others.

Collaborative Art Production   In some instances, clients are asked to collaborate, for example, in conducting a pictorial dialogue (Rhyne, 1973) or in producing a mural (Therapeutic art programs around the world, 1963;

Harris and Joseph, 1973). In such activities, emphasis is placed on the immediate experience and on the way in which it demonstrates or influences the relationships among group members. Both artistic development and the achievement of insight through the interpretation of symbolic content play a relatively minor part.

Informal Groups   In many art therapy programs, a number of patients work in the same room at the same time, each performing at his/ her own level, while the therapist strives to meet individual needs. Although the goals differ, this parallels the method of traditional art school classes in which students at many stages of development receive individual instruction. These classes are, therefore, referred to as *therapeutically oriented art classes*. Within them, there may be spontaneous group formation, and individuals are likely to do some interpretive work. On the whole, however, such informal groups are primarily adapted to *therapy through art* in Kramer's terminology, that is, art therapy in which each patient's ability to use art materials expressively is fostered and developed. The potentialities of a therapeutically oriented art class in relation to art therapy in community mental health services is discussed later.

Informal art therapy groups will vary in size according to circumstances, among them the kind and degree of the clients' disturbances. Larger groups can be handled when there is steady attendance rather than frequent turnover. Groups must be kept small enough so that the therapist does not become a mere dispenser of supplies and keeper of order. Twelve adults seen at a single time by one art therapist approaches the largest desirable number under most conditions.

Cultural Arbitration in the Therapeutic Milieu   When art is used primarily as a tool in psychotherapy, paintings and sculptures are apt to be regarded as private communications between client and therapist. When the completion of the artistic process is emphasized, however, as Kramer (1958) points out, the "communication is not meant for the therapist since . . . it is directed more generally to any individual or group . . . ready to receive the message." Thus, it becomes part of the art therapist's function not only to make art activity available to those who can use it but also to make the products of this activity available to the entire institutional population, staff as well as clients.

How will the therapist's handling of finished work best serve this purpose? To begin with, it is important that artistic communications be treated with respect, their value recognized but not inflated. The therapist discourages the destruction of any work and files all productions carefully, thus assuring clients that they and their art are taken seriously. If it is physically possible, there will be a casual, shifting display of pictures and sculptures in the art room itself. Serious efforts by both gifted and ordinary people may be given recognition by being hung on the walls of dining rooms, offices, and halls where there is usually a crying need for genuine, vital art work. Simple mountings, designed so that pictures may be changed easily, help works look their best and permit them to be replaced when their usually limited interest has worn thin. Questions about whether or not clients should be allowed to keep, give away, or sell their works should be answered flexibly, each case being judged on its merits.

But what of the pressure for institutional art shows open to the general public, featuring prizes, sales, and wide newspaper publicity? These stress talent (according to expert or popular standards) and competition. Doubts about the value of not only institutional exhibitions but also amateur art shows in the general community come into play here. An amateur, sick or well, is all too often encouraged to strive prematurely for superficial success. The disappointments bound to follow are particularly dangerous to the fragile ego structure of many psychiatric patients.

On the other hand, in some large institutions, notably prisons and prison hospitals, good emotional, social, economic, and vocational purposes have been served by public exhibitions open to all patients. In general, these are a segment of programs run with staff encouragement but little staff participation (Therapeutic art programs around the world, 1965). The art therapist's contribution to the public glory of his/her institution should ordinarily be confined to preparation of scientific or educational exhibits for professional audiences.

The artistically gifted mental patient poses a particular challenge. As mentioned previously, it may be especially difficult, perhaps even impossible, for the professional artist to use art as therapy. Naumburg (1966), however, has reported some successful work with neurotic patients whose presenting complaint was the blocking of their productivity as painters.

Young people whose outstanding talent is first discovered in a therapeutic setting must be given the utmost opportunity to develop it, yet should be shielded from the effect of unthinking adulation. The hospital or clinical staff must resist the temptation to exploit the talented patient's work for their vicarious satisfaction, and the patient, too, must be helped to resist the temptation to exploit his/her patienthood (Ulman, 1975c). If the patient's work, in Kramer's terms, "goes beyond the field of art therapy and belongs to the realms of pure art" (Kramer, 1958), then it should be allowed to stand in the community at large on its own merits; the artist's need for psychological help becomes irrelevant.

An art therapist should stand ready to serve as expert consultant for gifted patients in regard to vocational rehabilitation programs. The therapist needs, therefore, to be well acquainted with the demands and pitfalls peculiar to careers in both the commercial and fine arts. This special knowledge will tend to make him/her exceedingly cautious about encouraging patients to enter such trades or professions.

SPECIAL APPLICATIONS OF ART THERAPY

Art Therapy in a Research Center

Kwiatkowska introduced the use of art therapy at the National Institute of Mental Health in 1958. While each research setting presents its own special opportunities and problems, her account, which follows, of this particular program's development suggests the general adaptability of art therapy to the needs of psychiatric research. Furthermore, many of her experiences may be applied to art therapy in treatment facilities where the primary focus is not on research.

The setting was an open 12- to 14-bed ward. Most of the hospitalized patients were adolescents or young adults, and diagnoses varied from acute schizophrenia to psychoneurosis. The ratio of staff to patients was very high. All patients took part in intensive family therapy. Some also were treated individually, and some had parents receiving psychotherapy as couples. In addition, the large nursing staff was actively involved, not only in patient care but also in milieu therapy. An occupational therapist was assigned to the ward. Analytically oriented individual art therapy, as an adjunct to psychotherapy, seemed appropriate for this setting.

Patients referred were either those who had difficulty with verbal communication or those who communicated only on an intellectual level. Some psychiatrists were reluctant to collaborate with the art therapist, feeling that the patient's involvement with another person might result in a detrimental split of the transference. Others made referrals but preferred to have the art therapist carry on her work independently. Those physicians who were eager to collaborate more closely held regular weekly conferences during which the art therapist presented materials and obtained guidance in regard to therapeutic strategy. Experience with these patients also was presented and discussed at clinical conferences that included the entire staff. Thus, communication between the art therapist and members of other disciplines began to be established.

Some early activities were planned to familiarize both staff and patients with the expressive powers of art. The occupational therapist and some of the nurses were taken, along with small groups of patients, to visit art galleries. Discussion of pictures spontaneously selected by the group led to lively exchanges among the patients and between patients and staff members. Staff members became aware that even the viewing of art can stimulate the expression of one's own feelings and experiences. In keeping with the program's growing emphasis on the exploration of immediate personal relationships, formal group art therapy was tried with small groups of hospitalized patients for a time. The art therapy program finally found its focus, however, when sessions were instituted for a single hospitalized patient and his/her immediate family.

At first, each patient was seen alone by the art therapist before parents and siblings were invited to join the sessions. Experience showed, however, that a clearer view of family dynamics was obtained and that therapy proceeded with less difficulty when the art therapist's first contact was with the whole family group and took place as soon as possible after the patient's admission to the hospital.

As time went on, art sessions with family groups (patient, siblings, and parents) came to be used in three distinct ways: as an adjunct to family psychotherapy, as the sole mode of treatment, and as a means of evaluating family dynamics (Kwiatkowska, 1967a, 1967b).

It became routine for all new patients to be seen with their families for an *art evaluation session*. This session helped the staff decide whether or not the family should take part in family art therapy and whether or not it would be the sole mode of treatment or an auxiliary to conventional family psychotherapy. While family art evaluation was designed primarily for research purposes, it readily served as an introduction to therapy and sometimes even provided material for psychotherapy where no further use of art was made.

In the evaluation sessions, each family member was provided with a floor easel, a standard set of pastel colors, and white drawing paper, 18 × 24 inches in size. Procedures included free drawing in addition to definite assignments, such as family portraits, abstract representations of family members, and pictures started from a scribble and carried out both individually and by the family as a group. Pictorial, interactional, and verbal data all provided important diagnostic clues concerning individual family members and gave an unusually clear picture of family dynamics.

The way in which these observations became integrated with the research and treatment program as a whole dramatizes the striking development of staff communication that took place over the years. Interest grew, of course, mainly because the staff learned that material obtained in the art sessions made a substantial contribution to research (Day and Kwiatkowska, 1975). In addition, it became clear that many staff members who had never used art materials expressively found it difficult to respond to the graphic expressions of others. At the start of orientation sessions, pyschiatrists, members of the nursing staff, occupational therapists, and others were invited to use art materials with little instruction, just as individual patients and their families did. Later, theoretical discussions were held and illustrative case material was presented.

Interdisciplinary collaboration started with the handling of the family art evaluation sessions themselves. They were conducted by the art therapist and a participant-observer, usually a psychiatrist, social worker, or psychologist, who was working with the family. Psychologists, in particular, were interested in taking part to compare their own diagnostic material with that derived from family art evaluation.

The room in which the sessions took place was equipped with a recording system and a large one-way mirror. An audio-video machine was available. The family group was informed about the recordings and observers. Other members of the research team who were engaged in psychotherapy with the family observed from behind the mirror and, immediately after the session, discussed what had transpired.

At the staff conference, selected pictures were displayed on the wall to illustrate points relevant to the family's problem. Time was set aside for the art therapist to present her observations; to coordinate the reports, the family therapists (psychiatrists and social workers) had consulted with her before the conference.

Sometimes work with families that were not intact proved particularly revealing. For example, an offspring's unresolved feelings about a deceased or divorced parent were sometimes clearly indicated by family portraits in which such a parent would frequently be shown as important while emotional ties would be denied in verbal interviews.

A special project dealt with family art therapy as the sole treatment for families of adolescent schizophrenics and families of patients afflicted with other psychiatric illnesses. The staff was encouraged to try this new approach because with many patients, and particularly with families of schizophrenics, the usual psychoanalytic methods have not proved outstandingly effective. Such families find it hard to share the focus of attention (Wynne and Singer, 1967). Many utterances are so vague and amorphous that, after the words are said, not much is left to reflect upon, and there is little possibility of returning at a later session to something that needs clarification. The primitive level of functioning of some families presents seemingly insuperable difficulties. Unless the therapist can find a common mode of communication, a starting point accessible to both therapist and patients, he/she tends either to function at a level that family members cannot reach or to get lost in the fuzzy exchanges of the family group.

It appears that the graphic method may be useful for a number of reasons. It permits expression on a primitive level and is task-oriented. Because its products are tangible, durable, and can be reconsidered, they help the family focus on issues that would otherwise vanish before they could be explored. Everybody can take part at once; simultaneous expressive activity on the part of several family members does not result in chaos. The method is based on psychoanalytic concepts but allows one to rely to an unusual degree on observation rather than inference. The original objects of emotional investment, i.e., the art products, remain present and are part of the therapeutic process. Pictures and the transactions of the family while drawing them illustrate underlying dynamics and can be explored with the family group immediately or at a later time.

In *family art therapy* as the primary mode of treatment, all members of the immediate family were seen jointly by the art therapist and the collaborating psychiatrist. Art media were offered as a means of communication; aesthetic considerations were not emphasized. The art evaluation procedures were applied at the beginning of treatment and repeated every six months to gauge the course of therapy. Otherwise, the family was largely left to determine the character of the sessions; they were free to draw or paint whatever came to mind. Discussion of pictures usually took place spontaneously. When it did not, each participant was encouraged to talk about his/her own picture, and the others then discussed it. Remarks made by another were treated as his/her responses to the picture and his/her own use of the material, rather than as insights concerning the originator of the picture. Conclusions were tested and enriched by comparing recent pictures and performances with earlier ones.

> The Conants, one of the first families to be treated exclusively by means of family art therapy, had previously changed therapists many times and tried one kind of treatment after another. They worked on their problems by means of pictures for an unprecedented year and a half, during which it appeared that they learned to understand and deal with certain feelings better than they had previously been able to. For example, both George, the 19-year-old schizophrenic son, and his younger brother Edward made pictures concerned with their ambivalence about separating from the family. George represented himself abstractly by a shape outside of the family cluster but still attached at one point to a dominant mass symbolizing the mother (Figure 1). Edward portrayed himself in a more literal fashion, simultaneously inside and outside the family home (Figure 2). Thus, the schizophrenic patient suggested the pervasive character of his struggle against the forceful maternal figure, while his less severely disturbed brother presented a more circumscribed problem, his difficulty with moving out of his parent's home. These pictures helped the mother face her own reluctance to detach herself from the children.
>
> Near the close of the Conant family's association with the National Institute of Mental Health, George said, "We are not a close family, but this art therapy has brought us closer together than we ever were before. . . . We understand each other better. . . . The pictures helped my thinking. . . ."

Pictures have proved to be useful where words would be too definite a commitment in a tentative search for ways of relating to others. Further, the picture's enduring existence is especially important to schizophrenics who are often afflicted with the feeling that experience is evanescent. The pictures serve as a kind of scaffold to hold and arrange experience. They are used first as visual signs of feeling, and then are translated into verbal symbols that are more complex and more suitable for precise, rational thinking.

Devising art therapy techniques suitable for use in research demands flexibility and ingenuity. The history of the art therapy program at the

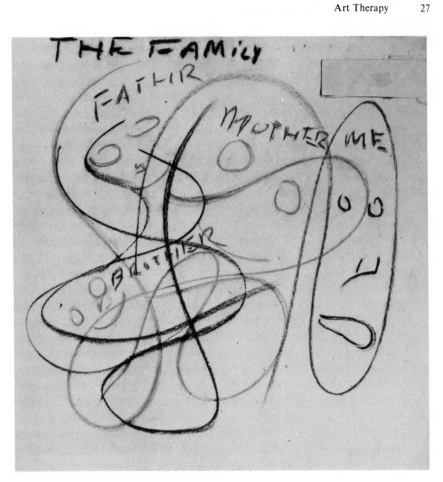

Figure 1.

National Institute of Mental Health shows how art therapy and psychiatric research can mutually contribute to each other's development.

Art Therapy with Children

Adults frequently feel lost or incompetent when faced with the idea of making pictures or sculptures. Children, on the other hand, usually like art from their first encounter with it. For many people, art is more accessible from the age of about four until the onset of puberty at 11, 12, or 13 than at any other time in their lives.

Provided that certain ego functions are intact, art seems to have unique powers to mobilize energies, not otherwise available, for a form of expression that makes considerable demands on a child's ego and fosters the

ON The Outside
Lookin' In

Figure 2.

development of structure and integration. Because art can be used when there is a high degree of pathology, it has particular value for the child whose disturbance restricts his/her capacity to participate in such activities as games and sports that make comparable demands and that children normally enjoy.

The Art Therapy Program in the Therapeutic Milieu In a milieu for children away from home, simple art materials such as paper, crayons, paint, plasticine, and construction paper should be available. Active occupations that help children under stress to grow should be fostered in preference to passive ways of spending time, such as watching television.

A scheduled art therapy program, conducted by specialists, and informal occasions for artistic expression elsewhere supplement each other. This principle was first expounded by Bender (1952). An art therapy program inspires children to do creative work during their leisure time, and the possibility of extending art activities beyond the confines of scheduled sessions gives more substance and reality to the idea of making pictures or sculptures.

As with adult programs, a room reserved *exclusively for art* is essential if the energies needed for artistic creation are not to be deflected into craft or play. It is also especially important for children to have a place where paint may be spilled, walls painted or spattered, and clay handled freely.

Groups should be small. The optimal size depends on the children's needs. A severely psychotic child may need one therapist's full attention, while less disturbed children may profit from working in groups of three or four. Nonpsychotic children usually work well in groups of eight to twelve.

Sessions should be long enough so that a child may become deeply engrossed in his/her work. A full hour is the minimal time, but it is better to allow one-and-a-half hours for older children. Scheduling should be flexible so that any child who becomes deeply involved in art can spend extra time in the studio.

Guidelines for Referrals   Art emerges from play with art materials when a child is about three to five years old. The making of objects that convey and express experience is preceded by a period when the child enjoys experimenting with art materials but does not yet use them to make symbolic objects. Retarded and otherwise handicapped children, of course, may arrive at symbolic expression much later or not at all.

Even at such a precursory stage, an art specialist is needed if this important preparation for symbol making is to fulfill its purpose. Here, the basic gestures of visual art have their beginning, and the foundation of hand-eye coordination is laid down. Only a person who understands and cares deeply about the natural evolution of expressive capacities in the visual arts can fully share the child's rejoicing in each new achievement, e.g., purposely making a line change its direction or making the ends of a curved line meet to produce a circular form. This shared rejoicing is the key to the adult's contribution to the early stages of children's development in art, as elsewhere.

Some psychotic and very retarded children seem to benefit more easily from music and dance therapy than from art therapy. Although these children seem to be stuck at the presymbolic stage, the attention of an art therapist may prove useful nevertheless. By offering materials that stimulate sensation and perception (finger paint, sandpaper, sheets of transparent colored acetate, etc.), the art therapist may help the retarded or autistic child to develop awareness of his/her own existence and power to act, leading toward a sense of self and the establishment of a body image.

Given crayons and paper, the very retarded start by making rhythmic movements just as normal children do, but, unlike their normal counterparts, they must be very gradually induced to realize that the marks they make are the results of their own movements. Eventually, they may learn to produce more organized configurations, usually circles, and these sometimes slowly achieve symbolic meaning.

Often, the usefulness of art to a disturbed child can only be determined by trying it out. There are children who are otherwise infantile who can function on a more mature level in art; in these cases, art therapy would be particularly valuable.

In art the child is given freedom while security is taken away, because art cannot be produced according to rules and regulations. Rigid defensive mechanisms that serve well in other situations, such as academic learning or crafts, are a hindrance in art. During the creative act itself, compulsive defenses must be partially suspended. This brings about an influx of repressed material and affect which are channeled into the creative act. Therefore, the art therapist must be prepared for a certain amount of emotional turmoil.

There are, however, children whose functioning depends on obsessive-compulsive mechanisms; they cannot sustain any activity that tends to put such defenses out of commission and thereby menaces their capacity to function at all. Children of another kind, those who are readily flooded by material from the unconscious, also may be endangered by an activity that tends to increase affect and fantasy. This does not mean that such children must be excluded from art therapy altogether, but rather that the art therapist must proceed with great caution, sometimes permitting the defensive use of art materials rather than trying to move such children into the possibly overpowering experience of the full artistic process.

Brain-damaged children, whose capacity to perceive and organize form is physically impaired, may find art hopelessly bewildering and frustrating when it is offered in usual ways. Methods have been developed that take the particular disabilities of the brain-damaged into account. The mechanics of handling art materials are introduced very slowly by means of carefully structured procedures before expressive use of the materials is undertaken (Gonick-Barris, 1976). These methods are very different from those more generally useful; therefore, brain-damaged children should be seen in art therapy separately from other kinds of handicapped children, particularly in the beginning, before they have demonstrated their readiness for freely expressive art work.

In none of these cases would handling art materials be absolutely contraindicated. Children who seem to become disorganized in their first encounter with art materials can sometimes learn to sustain the freedom and stimulation of art. If this can be achieved, it constitutes a gain. The therapist, however, must realize that art is not an infallible blessing and must learn to recognize a child's genuine distress which shows he/she is not ready for an emotional adventure. Two examples will illustrate the kind of decisions an art therapist may have to make:

> Seven-year-old Robert functioned at the borderline of psychosis. His obsessive defenses made it possible for him to perform well in those activities in which he could follow clearly defined rules. The freedom of art, on the other hand, often brought on wildly disorganized behavior. On the rare occasions when he was able to sustain the turmoil of the creative act, however, he expressed ideas and feelings which he could not have put into words. These moments were extremely precious to him, and he remembered each one of his successful creations with pride. Therefore, Robert was permitted to attend art therapy sessions in spite of the many times he became either unproductive or disruptive.

> Six-year-old David, a brain-damaged child who also maintained himself on the edge of florid psychosis, did very little in art. Even his occasional coherent drawings meant little to him. Therefore, art therapy was discontinued.
> If David ever became ready to profit from art work, he would probably clamor to be readmitted. Self-demand is valuable in many instances in which one tries to fulfill fluctuating needs. Final decisions about admission to art therapy rest with the adult, but it is advisable to be guided by children's responses.

Art and Play   The freedom of art links it to imaginative play. Both constitute islands wherein the reality principle is partly suspended. Forbidden wishes and impulses can be expressed symbolically. Painful and frightening experiences that had to be endured passively can be assimilated by reliving them more actively on a reduced scale. Affect can be safely discharged in play and also in art.

There are, however, essential differences. The rules of play are simple: it must remain distinct from real life and the child must be able to suspend it when necessary. Objects or people assume symbolic roles by a simple act of designation, by decree so to speak, e.g., two chairs become a boat, a boy turns into a lion. It is only necessary that the child and his/her playmate be able to maintain the fiction.

The goal of art, on the other hand, is the making of a symbolic object that contains and communicates an idea to the world at large. The idea depends largely on the child's wishes and fantasies, but the making of this object is a complex ego function that engages manual, intellectual, and emotional faculties in a supreme effort.

This distinction also applies to arts where no tangible object results. For instance, if a child *plays* at being an animal he/she may or may not sustain the fiction by appropriate noises and gestures; the play can go either way. If the child undertakes to *play the part* of the same animal in a dramatic performance, he/she must make every effort to imagine the animal and to convey the idea to the spectators; otherwise, he/she fails as an actor.

Young children often enjoy it when an adult participates in play, but as children grow older the role of the adult is reduced to that of the protector who interrupts imaginative play when it becomes dangerous to life, limb, and property and picks up the pieces after quarrels. Otherwise, the adult is supposed to stay out of the magic circle. In art it is different. Adult leadership and support are essential for art to grow and flourish. Art makes much greater demands on a child's faculties and moral courage than does play. Play is the prerogative of childhood. In adult life, art is one of the few areas of symbolic living that remains accessible (Kramer, 1971).

Art and Fantasy   When a child attempts to give his/her ideas more substance than is needed for play, the product of these efforts will show not only his/her ideas and fantasies, but also the capacity to give them shape. Strictly speaking, the finished product never represents simply the fantasy itself; it inevitably conveys the *child's relationship to the fantasy*. When art material is formed without adherence to prescribed patterns, it cannot help taking on the image of its maker.

Six-year-old Karl was much given to grandiose fantasies that consoled him in his actual isolation and helplessness. One day he wanted to paint a picture of a giant "as tall as the art room," using "all the colors," because the giant was to be very beautiful. On a long strip of brown wrapping paper he drew, with a black crayon, a life-sized head with faint features, and then two lines reaching from the head down to the bottom of the paper, representing legs and body at once. In the middle he placed a small rectangle, "the penis," above it a tiny circle, "the belly button" (Figure 3). That was all.

His picture remained as insubstantial as Karl really felt, and nobody could give him the power to paint the strong, colorful giant of his dreams.

Later, in the same session, Karl modeled a little dog and a dog-house. They were complete and well executed. The dog expressed Karl's real feeling about himself. Therefore he could make it well, within the limitations of his age and talent.

Of course one need not be a giant in order to paint good giants. Eight-year-old Billy was tuberculous, frail, and short, but his vitality was indestructible. He painted a strong man lifting a weight. The picture was simple but convincing. The man's biceps were clearly marked, and he stood firmly, a broad smile on his face (Figure 4).

Billy will not grow up to be a strong man, but his relationship to his fantasy of having bodily strength was straightforward and secure. Inasmuch as the strong man represents, in the symbolic language of an eight-year-old, the concept of an intact, potent male, the self-image had truth. Physical weakness had not destroyed Billy's feeling of intactness or interfered with his masculine identification. His inner strength enabled him to create a convincing hero.

The opposite can also occur. Husky bullies often produce particularly fragmented and feeble art, revealing the inner weakness for which no amount of physical strength can compensate.

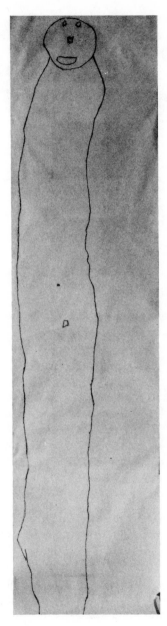

Figure 3.

Figure 4.

Confrontation in Art   Art has its own unalterable laws. Any act of creation implies a confrontation with some aspect of the artist's personality. Karl, drawing a giant, confronted his pathology. When he modeled a dog, he encountered the better integrated aspects of himself. Art always reveals truth, but not necessarily the whole truth. Different pictures may show different, sometimes contradictory, facets of personality.

Art invites the creation of a world that is egocentrically organized. The menace of confrontation with the self and its pathology is mitigated by the narcissistic gratification that the activity provides, by the creation in miniature of a universe that is made in the very image of its creator.

This narcissistic gratification is more important in art than wish-fulfillment. It makes possible the mobilization of great energy in the service of an activity that involves enormous risks of failure, disappointment, and conflict. This may occur even at times when the child is not ready to make similar efforts in other areas of life or to risk himself very far in psychotherapy (Kramer, 1971).

Herein lies the therapeutic power of art. Inasmuch as increased ego strength in one area leads to maturation in general, art therapy may bring about personality changes. *Art therapy that remains centered on artistic creation,* however, does not provide leverage for the resolution of deep conflict in the child's object relationships. This distinction becomes clearer as the function of the art therapist is described and illustrated below.

The Art Therapist's Function   The artist who conducts art session for disturbed children should be clinically trained. He/she becomes the ally of the child's ego by lending technical assistance and by helping him/her to be more accepting of repressed feelings and ideas. A therapist upholds the basic requirement that materials be used to produce works of art, thus counteracting the tendency toward dissipation into fantasy or play.

To perform this function well, an art therapist must recognize and respond to hidden as well as overt aspects of a child's production and behavior. He/she will not, as a rule, use his/her understanding for the spoken interpretation of deep, unconscious meaning. He/she will more often use it to help the child produce work that contains and expresses emotionally charged material. This mode of functioning is illustrated by the following examples:

> Eight-year-old Clyde, an inhibited, depressed child, had grave doubts about the size, permanence, and intactness of his sexual organs, even though they were normally developed. He was intelligent and a good sculptor. One day he modeled a gorilla about a foot high. He asked the art therapist how big he should make its penis. When she suggested that he show her what *he* thought, he shyly proffered a clay sausage the size of an adult man's penis. She made him hold the clay penis aganist his sculpture, pointed out that it was as big as the gorilla's legs, and asked him if he had ever seen a person with a penis as large as his leg? Clyde pondered. Then, without further hesitation, he sculptured a very life-like sexual organ whose proportion to the gorilla's body was reasonable (Figure 5).

Clyde was ready to begin to accept his status as a little boy whose penis was smaller than his father's but perfectly adequate for his own age and size. A response that made him ponder the problem of relative sizes, demonstrated to him the absurdity of his first idea and was, therefore, helpful on both the conscious and the unconscious level.

> On the other hand, when Bernard, six years old and mildly retarded, made a rudimentary clay figure and adorned it with an enormous penis, the art therapist accepted the figure wholeheartedly. Bernard was at a developmental stage during which realistic proportions are not yet conceived and size denotes only order of importance. He was a deeply insecure boy and making a penis at

Figure 5.

all was for him an act of supreme courage. The idea of realistic proportions would have had no meaning for him. He would have interpreted its introduction as a rejection.

In these instances, the art therapist responded to both the conscious and the unconscious elements in the child's behavior. The response was conditioned by a knowledge of child psychology, but the therapist purposely did not uncover or interpret unconscious meaning. Instead, the therapist supported the child in the creative work. Through artistic creation, the ego is helped to deal with heavily loaded material, not by repression or primitive mechanisms of defense, but through formed expression that is the fruit of the process of sublimation.

Art therapy can be used for the interpretation of individual functioning. For example, Clyde, who made the gorilla, was a child who always expected disaster. He never failed to predict that his sculptures would collapse in the making or blow up in the firing. His prophecies became something of a standing joke between him and the art therapist, and there was no doubt that this helped Clyde to gain insight into the way he functioned.

When another child messed up the background of 11-year-old Brian's picture, Brian declared that the whole painting was no good. He was about to destroy it, but the art therapist managed to wrest it away from him. Later she painted out all distracting spots in the background but did not touch the figure. When she presented Brian with the restored picture, he understood that there really had been nothing wrong with his work. He admitted that when the therapist assured him that his picture was salvageable she had not tried to console him with a lie. There was a moment of illumination when he saw how ready he was to believe that anyone who attempted to help him was a liar or a fool.

Interpretations such as these stop short of uncovering, but they lead to awareness of recurring patterns of behavior. This makes the child less a victim of his/her habitual ways of functioning, and, at times, it becomes possible for him/her to anticipate and control certain patterns or even to modify them (Kramer, 1971).

Art as Therapy   Throughout this discussion, the concept of *art as therapy* has been stressed in preference to that of *therapy using art as a tool*. The art therapist, who is also a trained child therapist or is supervised by one, may at times conduct psychotherapy through the medium of art (Gondor, 1954; Naumburg, 1973). Both approaches have their value in the therapeutic milieu, and the same therapist may employ either one according to the demands of the situation, provided that he/she is sufficiently trained or supervised. However, because the use of art materials in this second approach requires not an artist's training but the general skills of psychotherapy, detailed consideration of it belongs by rights under the heading of general child therapy.

Art as therapy is concerned in the main with strengthening the child's ego and fostering sublimation. It is focused on counteracting the chaotic discharge of affect and uncontrolled abandon to fantasy on the one hand and the formation of rigid mechanisms of defense on the other.

Its essence is the creative act itself, and its benefits depend on the power of art to transform a child's primitive modes of expression into creative work. Drive energy, which is otherwise dissipated in fantasy and play or locked into the vicious circle of repetitive symptomatic behavior, becomes available for making symbolic objects that serve as equivalents for life processes. In making them, the child builds a bridge between his/her inner world and the world around him/her. Such experiences contribute to the formation of a richer and more flexible personality.

Art Therapy in Community Mental Health Programs

It appears that long term hospitalization is on the wane and that candidates for sustained art therapy treatment will be outpatients who will attend voluntarily. While there is a place for all the treatment methods discussed above, it seems probable that the widest applications will be found for the informal groups previously referred to as therapeutically oriented art classes.

This form of art therapy meets numerous criteria set forth by those pioneers of psychiatric help for a broadened population who do not reject psychoanalytic theory but see the urgent need for radically new techniques. Such investigators have pointed to the appropriateness of methods that subordinate words and concepts to nonverbal and motor activities. They note the useful effect of deflecting pathology into endeavors that give social returns and satisfactions. They conclude that emphasis on insight, free association, and resistance analysis should be reduced in favor of catharsis and emotional reeducation and make the observation that involvement in problems and activities outside the self may bring about rather than follow internal change (Ulman, 1975c).

The therapeutically oriented art class is not a mere duplication of art classes already existing in the community. The art *therapist* uses knowledge and skills that even the best art *teacher* is unlikely to have. The therapist's understanding of sick people enlightens a myriad of split-second decisions in work with adults as with children.

In an informal art therapy group, painting and sculpture make a particular kind of contribution to the development of social relationships. Work in the visual arts is essentially solitary; therefore, the shy or withdrawn person can function fully in the art room without needing to make any direct approach to another human being. As he/she becomes ready for contact with others, he/she can move more easily by an indirect route, through shared interest in products so intimate that they are almost, but not quite, personifications.

Insights may be derived from the artistic process even when no verbal translation from symbolic imagery is attempted. What happens in the course of the art work is sometimes spontaneously appreciated as a sample of living.

An intellectual, alcoholic patient, Janet, was disappointed because, in spite of having studied the theory of perspective, she found herself unable to depict depth. Projecting imagery into a scribble and working more intuitively, she succeeded in conveying a vivid sense of the third dimension (Figure 6).

Her interest in the picture's symbolic content was subordinated to exhilaration over its formal success. "Now for the first time I really understand what my therapist means when he says I must learn to trust my feelings," she commented.

Margaret, an uneducated schizophrenic woman in remission, started in art therapy by repeating rigid, childish stereotypes. She progressed to the point at which her work had the attractive quality of folk art but retained hard outlines and tight organization in keeping with her obsessive-compulsive defense system. After some weeks, she produced a relatively free, loose composition (Figure 7). Ecstatically she declared, "It's the first thing I've done in my life that isn't *neat*." Gradually she became proud of the originality and effectiveness of her pictures; this seemed to be almost her first glimpse that she had worth and capability.

Figure 6.

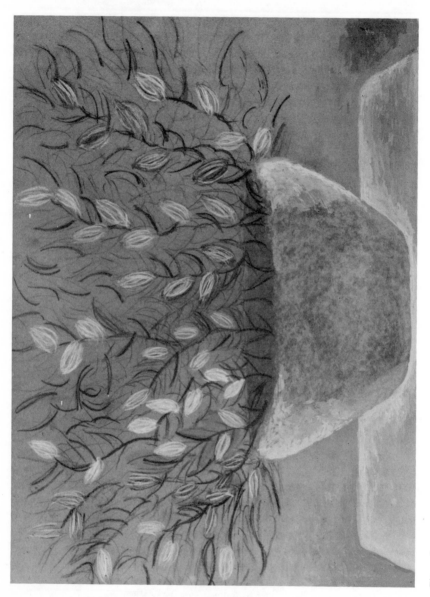

Figure 7.

Such insights do not depend on the analysis of imagery spontaneously projected from the unconscious, but both patients had been able to use energy that came from unconscious sources and had exercised more spontaneity than they were yet able to muster elsewhere in life. On a conscious level they were trying to make the best pictures they could, and the art therapist was supporting their efforts.

Another approach likely to prove suitable for application in community mental health services is family art therapy, which can help meet the needs of a wide population. Early involvement of the .patient's family, the linking of therapeutic with diagnostic procedures, and an informal, supportive atmosphere in initial contacts have been cited as important factors in making psychiatric treatment available to the masses.

CURRENT PROFESSIONAL ISSUES

Organized attempts to weld art therapists into a cohesive professional group began in 1969 with the formation of the American Art Therapy Association (AATA), which at present has its offices in Pittsburgh and receives mail at P.O. Box 11604, Pittsburgh, PA 15228. There are a number of state and regional art therapy associations that, as yet, are not affiliated with the national one. Procedures for affiliation are in the course of being developed.

Interest in the question of professional identity (touched on in the discussion of theory in the early pages of this chapter) has been gaining momentum. The development of art therapy literature devoted to theory-building and research, gradual until the 1960s, also has been proceeding more rapidly in the past decade. *The American Journal of Art Therapy,* founded by Ulman in 1961 and now affiliated with the AATA, was long the only professional journal in the field. It was joined in 1973 by *Art Psychotherapy,* also a quarterly publication.

Meanwhile, AATA is addressing itself to immediate, practical concerns which are briefly outlined below.

Training and Registration

The first two graduate programs leading to a master's degree in art therapy were announced in 1969. As of October 1976, there were 20 master's degree programs offering more or less concentrated training in art therapy. The AATA has designated the master's degree as constituting the professional entry level. However, nonacademic roads to clinical competence also are given recognition, and the organization is working to develop mechanisms for the endorsement of training programs offered by institutes and clinical facilities, as well as programs leading to academic degrees.

To obtain registration by the Association, practitioners also must have professional experience in the field that is not connected with training. As of early 1977, there were no programs of licensure for art therapists.

Payment for Art Therapy Services

The cost of art therapy services is, of course, subject to variation in population centers of different sizes and is likely to change more or less rapidly over time. As of early 1977, starting salaries for full-time art therapists with master's degrees or similar qualifications ranged from $9,000 to $12,000 per year. Private practice accounted for a much smaller percentage of the working time of art therapists than did salaried work in hospitals and other residential facilities, clinics, day centers, and schools. Charges for private individual art therapy sessions ranged from about $15 to $25 per hour, and sessions were commonly scheduled for from one to one-and-a-half hours, usually on a once-a-week basis. Charges to individual members of private art therapy groups were proportionately lower.

A major need of art therapy, as of other specialities in the broad field of therapeutic services, is assumption on the part of insurance companies of responsibility for payments directly to nonmedical practitioners. The position taken now and in the near future by private companies probably foreshadows, and may indeed influence, the policies that will eventually be established under national health insurance. At present, art therapy services offered by hospitals and other medically directed agencies are usually covered by insurance. Private art therapy is likely to be covered only if it is both prescribed and billed for by a physician.

Research Needs

Levy, Chairperson of AATA's Research Committee, defines the research needs of art therapy as follows:

Two avenues of research in art therapy urgently need to be pursued. First, ways must be devised to characterize the graphic and plastic works of clients in a way such that they can be compared with each other. The possibility of making such comparsions is prerequisite to understanding the relationship between changes in an individual's art and any therapeutic intervention that has taken place.

Equally urgent is the development of comparative studies calculated to demonstrate the relative effectiveness of various art therapy procedures in particular sets of circumstances.

Several other areas subject to research have long been of interest and will continue to be, but, in these, the need for systematic exploration is less urgent. The study of visual symbols and their meanings is one such potential research area. Assertions are often made that certain kinds of clients commonly use the same kind of imagery or assign similar meanings to particular symbolic forms. As yet, most of these assertions are actually hypotheses that remain to be tested. The belief that different levels of functioning are implicit in the content and structural character of art products is another assumption that is in need of more thorough investigation.

Relationship with Other Disciplines

Probably, the slowness of art therapy to develop a clear-cut definition of its range and functions is attributable in part to the complexity of its relationship with other disciplines, a complexity which, as suggested at the beginning of the chapter, stems from the nature of art itself.

In the performing arts, composer and virtuoso are not necessarily the same, but, in the visual arts, both roles are inevitably filled by one person. Therefore, the visual product bears the personal stamp of its creator; in a psychiatric context, it readily invites diagnostic inquiry and serves a more direct communicative purpose. Thus, the link binding psychiatric applications of painting and sculpture to both *psychological assessment* and *psychotherapy* is peculiarly intimate.

Child therapists often make use of rudimentary art activity in the course of play therapy. In recent years, a number of psychiatrists working with adults also have discovered the therapeutic advantages of expressive activity with art materials and have incorporated it into their own practice. Like art therapists, they point out that thinking in pictures develops earlier than does thinking in words and that, therefore, it is likely that psychological material may escape censorship and reach the light of day in the form of projected two- or three-dimensional symbols. They also note the value of the lasting record that is provided by work with the materials of the visual arts. This sets it apart from the other creative therapies and from verbal therapeutic procedures. Thus, the area of art therapy referred to as *psychotherapy using art as a tool* has been claimed by some psychiatrists to belong exclusively in their domain (Meares, 1960; Meijering, 1961; Vaessen, 1962).

In some psychiatric and other rehabilitation settings, *recreational* art programs further demonstrate the versatility of paint and clay and make for overlapping and possible conflict. Art classes stressing technique, skill, and, occasionally, commercial applications also may serve a good rehabilitative purpose, but such activities lie on the periphery of art therapy, if not outside of it altogether.

It is unfortunate that, in addition, the use of art materials sometimes is offered to distract the client from inner conflict. The art therapist must sometimes tolerate escapist performances in art, but active encouragement of such ways of using art material confuses the issue. A pack of cards provides more effective entertainment than a paint-by-numbers set, while card playing does not interfere with art.

The various programs in which art materials are used for divergent purposes in a single agency function best when there is sympathetic under-standing between the staff members responsible for their direction. It is highly desirable that one person coordinate all attempts to make the artistic activities of clients serve the common goal of rehabilitation. This coordina-tor needs to understand what distinguishes the various beneficial ways of using art materials from one another and to understand, as well, which ways of using art materials are ineffective at best and destructive at worst.

Art therapy and occupational therapy, each for its own purpose, use some of the same materials. Therefore, friction between these two dis-ciplines may easily occur. Clay can be used to make a sculpture or a dish, and paint serves the limited expressive function of decoration as well as purely artistic purposes. By and large, *crafts* are the province not of art therapy but of occupational therapy, and the occupational therapist's stand-ard training does not provide understanding of the *artistic* process. The basic distinction between art and craft has been succinctly stated by Kramer:

> . . . craft is the transformation of raw material . . . into useful and hand-some objects by a logical, comprehensible process. In art, amorphous, malle-able material is transformed not into a useful object but into a symbolic one, which conveys and expresses experience (Kramer, 1971, 1975a).

Patients are not ordinarily concerned with professional distinctions; thus, they will occasionally turn out sculptures in occupational therapy sessions and make ashtrays in the art room. Furthermore, some occupa-tional therapists may be equipped by experience and temperament to carry out an art program, and some art therapists may be equipped to branch into the applied arts in which original designs are carried out according to craft techniques (Gelber, 1962; Therapeutic art programs around the world, 1975).

The possibilities of collaboration between art and occupational therapy have scarcely been explored. For example, decorative motifs or ideas for designs originated in art therapy might be applied to craft products with the help of occupational therapists. The authors, however, know of only isolated instances when this has actually been done. At present, art therapists and occupational therapists need to strive for understanding of differences in methods and attitudes. Mutual respect and cooperation among staff members will make it more likely that patients will be reached by all programs that may serve their particular needs.

Even in psychiatrically supervised agencies, art therapy and art educa-tion begin to impinge upon each other. Especially in residential settings for handicapped children, special schools, or special classes, art is likely to be included in the program, and arts and crafts, are an accepted ingredient of organized free time. The importance of art for children in general is widely acknowledged and, for this very reason, the need for art as therapy for children laboring under mental and emotional handicaps tends to remain unrecognized. Much art therapy occurs unofficially when gifted teachers work with troubled children (Site, 1975), but their work must remain sporadic, hedged in by rules and regulations that are not geared to art therapy.

Recently, the tangled relationship between art therapy and art education has been receiving increased attention (Packard, 1976; Packard and Anderson, 1976). It appears that the attitude of art educators toward art therapy is changing.

In spite of Lowenfeld's long standing advocacy of a suitable "art education therapy" (1957), art educators have tended to guard jealously against any ulterior demand that might distract from their concentration on aesthetic education, which many of them view as their proper function. They may have been motivated in part by dismay over the tendency to dump into the art room the growing number of educational and behavioral misfits in the school population. This dismay probably helps to explain why Lowenfeld's long chapter, "Therapeutic Aspects of Art Education," has not appeared in any edition of *Creative and Mental Growth* since that of 1957, the last edition published during Lowenfeld's lifetime. In the 1970s, however, perhaps because jobs in art education have been scarce at a time when art therapy has been gaining ground, undergraduate and graduate schools of art education have been eager to introduce art therapy offerings.

Pine (1975), who has worked as a public school art teacher, as an art therapist, and as a psychotherapist to make the psychological benefits of art available to children, has delineated the common ground shared by these three disciplines as well as the subtle but important differences that distinguish them from each other. Further development of art therapy theory and delimitation of boundaries for art therapy practice should help to alleviate the tension between art therapists and members of related disciplines established for a longer time, but it seems unlikely that these tensions can be resolved once and for all. They have a real basis that cannot be wished away.

The arts, after all, exist to serve the psychological needs of mankind. Because of the intimate relationship between art and the needs of the developing personality, art education naturally contributes to personal well-being just as art therapy naturally opens the way to effective artistic expression. Psychotherapy seeks self-consciously the age-old goal of art, i.e., reconciliation of the individual's inner needs with the demands of the outside world.

Art educators, art therapists, occupational therapists, and psychotherapists who use art in their practice must live with the task of sharing their common ground as peacefully as possible and must learn to respect each other for the special knowledge and skills that are unique to each professional group.

REFERENCES

American Art Therapy Association. 1976. Art therapy: Beginnings and assessing clients for treatment, Pittsburgh, Pa. 45-minute color film.

Bender, L. 1952. Child Psychiatric Techniques. Charles C Thomas, Springfield, Il.

Cane, F. 1951. The Artist in Each of Us. Pantheon Books, New York.

Day, J., and Kwiatkowska, H. Y. 1975. The psychiatric patient and his "well" sibling: A comparison through their art productions. *In* E. Ulman and P. Dachinger (eds.), Art Therapy in Theory and Practice, pp. 345–360. Schocken Books, New York.

Gelber, B. L. 1962. Art and occupational therapies. Bull. Art Ther. 2:3–8.

Gondor, E. I. 1954. Art and Play Therapy. Doubleday, Garden City, New York.

Gonick-Barris, S. E. 1976. Art for children with minimal brain dysfunction. Am. J. Art Ther. 15:67–73.

Harris, J., and Joseph, C. 1973. Murals of the Mind. International Universities Press, New York.

Horowitz, M. J. 1965. Notes on art therapy media and techniques. Bull. Art Ther. 4:70–73.

Kramer, E. 1958. Art Therapy in a Children's Community. Charles C Thomas, Springfield, Ill.

Kramer, E. 1971. Art as Therapy with Children. Schocken Books, New York.

Kramer, E. 1975a. Art and craft. *In* E. Ulman and P. Dachinger (eds.), Art Therapy in Theory and Practice, pp. 106–109. Schocken Books, New York.

Kramer, E. 1975b. The problem of quality in art. *In* E. Ulman and P. Dachinger (eds.), Art Therapy in Theory and Practice, pp. 43–59. Schocken Books, New York.

Kwiatkowska, H. Y., and Perlin, S. 1960. A Schizophrenic Patient's Response in Art Therapy to Changes in the Life of the Psychotherapist. Public Health Service, U.S. Department of Health Education and Welfare, Washington, D.C.

Kwiatkowska, H. Y. 1967a. Family art therapy. Family Process 6:37–55.

Kwiatkowska, H. Y. 1967b. The use of families' art productions for psychiatric evaluation. Bull. Art Ther. 6:52–72.

Kwiatkowska, H. Y. 1971. Family art evaluation: Indication and contraindication. *In* I. Jakab (ed.), Conscious and Unconscious Expressive Art: Psychiatry and Art. Vol. 3, pp. 138–151. Karger, Basel.

Kwiatkowska, H. Y., and Mosher, L. 1971. Family art evaluation: Use in families with schizophrenic twins. J. Nerv. Ment. Dis. 153:165–179.

Levy, B. I., and Ulman, E. 1967. Judging psychopathology from paintings. J. Abnorm. Psychol. 72:182–187.

Lowenfeld, V. 1957. Creative and Mental Growth. 3rd Ed. Macmillan, New York.

Meares, A. 1960. Shapes of Sanity. Charles C Thomas, Springfield, Ill.

Meijering, W. L. 1961. La Thérapie Créative. Presented at the Third World Congress of Psychiatry, Montreal.

Naumburg, M. 1950. Schizophrenic Art. Grune and Stratton, New York.

Naumburg, M. 1958. Art therapy: Its scope and function. *In* E. F. Hammer (ed.), The Clinical Application of Projective Drawings, pp. 511–517. Charles C Thomas, Springfield, Ill.

Naumburg, M. 1966. Dynamically Oriented Art Therapy: Its Principles and Practice. Grune and Stratton, New York.

Naumburg, M. 1973. An Introduction to Art Therapy: Studies of the "Free" Art Expression of Behavior Problem Children and Adolescents as a Means of Diagnosis and Therapy. Revised Ed. Teachers College Press, New York.

Packard, S. P. 1976. Art for the exceptional child: Rapidly expanding job opportunities. Art Psychother. 3:81–85.

Packard, S. P., and Anderson, F. E. 1976. A shared identity crisis: Art education and art therapy. Am. J. Art Ther. 16:21–28.

Pine, S. 1975. Fostering growth through art education, art therapy, and art in psychotherapy. In E. Ulman and P. Dachinger (eds.), Art Therapy in Theory and Practice, pp. 60–94. Schocken Books, New York.

Refanes, C. C., and Gallagher, F. P. 1968. Art therapy as adjunct to long-term psychotherapy: Understanding psychodynamics through free drawings. Bull. Art Ther. 7:59–80.

Rhyne, J. 1973. The Gestalt Art Experience. Brooks/Cole Publishing Co., Monterey, Cal.

Site, M. 1975. Art and the slow learner. In E. Ulman and P. Dachinger (eds.), Art Therapy in Theory and Practice, pp. 191–207. Schocken Books, New York.

Smith, S. R., Macht, L. B., and Refanes, C. C. 1967. Recovery, repression, and art. Bull. Art Ther. 6:101–117.

Therapeutic art programs around the world: Albert Einstein Medical College, New York. 1963. Bull. Art Ther. 3:26–27.

Therapeutic art programs around the world: François-Michelle School, Montreal. 1975. In E. Ulman and P. Dachinger (eds.), Art Therapy in Theory and Practice, pp. 208–212. Schocken Books, New York.

Therapeutic art programs around the world: Medical Center for Federal Prisoners, Springfield, Missouri; California Medical Facility, Vacaville. 1965. Bull. Art Ther. 5:21–25.

Ulman, E. 1971. Art education for special groups: The emotionally disturbed. In L. C. Deighton (ed.), The Encyclopedia of Education. Vol. I, pp. 311–316. Macmillan, Riverside, N.J.

Ulman, E. 1975a. Art Therapy: Problems of definition. In E. Ulman and P. Dachinger (eds.), Art Therapy in Theory and Practice, pp. 3–13. Schocken Books, New York.

Ulman, E. 1975b. A new use of art in psychiatric diagnosis. In E. Ulman and P. Dachinger (eds.), Art Therapy in Theory and Practice, pp. 361–386. Schocken Books, New York.

Ulman, E. 1975c. Therapy is not enough. The contribution of art to general hospital psychiatry. In E. Ulman and P. Dachinger (eds.), Art Therapy in Theory and Practice, pp. 14–32. Schocken Books, New York.

Ulman, E., and Levy, B. I. 1968. An experimental approach to the judgment of psychopathology from paintings. Bull. Art Ther. 8:3–12.

Vaessen, M. L. J. 1962. Art or expression? A discussion of the creative activities of mental patients. Bull. Art Ther. 2:23–30.

Wynne, L. C., and Singer, M. T. 1967. Schizophrenic Impairment of Shared Focal Attention. Presented as the Tenth Annual Bertram Roberts Memorial Lecture, Yale University, New Haven, Conn.

DANCE THERAPY

Judith R. Bunney

While the recent surge of interest in dance therapy has been extensive, many misconceptions remain concerning this emerging profession and the requisite training prior to employment.

The purpose of this chapter is to clarify the nature and scope of services provided by dance therapists and the education and experience needed to develop the appropriate skills. Although this work is sometimes referred to as "movement therapy" or "dance/movement therapy," upon examination it becomes clear that the roots of this profession are planted firmly in modern dance and that skilled practitioners need to be well versed in the art of dance as well as in psychology and psychotherapy. Broad experience in dance is an essential background for the therapist to ensure that a wide range of movement is available to him/her. A thorough knowledge of the physiology of the body is also essential.

Dance therapy is a form of psychotherapy that makes use of movement and movement interaction as the bases for intervention. The work is done within a therapeutic context and is a powerful, direct medium because the instrument used is one's own body. Life and movement are inextricably interwoven: in looking at historical contexts of rhythm and movement, one finds their use as an expression of a person's most profound statements. Preverbal cultures used dance to mark ceremonies in the rites of life—birth, puberty, and death—and, to respond to the natural forces of the earth. These rituals served to unify people and are still recognized as powerful means of communication.

The connection between states of mind and bodily expressions of these states has long been studied, particularly in the research efforts of recent years. The interrelationship between the psyche and the body is easy to establish, because if one moves in a certain way, one begins to feel that certain way. Persons with emotional problems or those who are mentally and/or physically handicapped often communicate more through their movement patterns than through their verbalizations.

Thus, dance therapists are often the staff members who are able to initiate direct contact with clients who are thought to be inaccessible through other forms of therapy. In facilities where short term care is stressed, dance therapists are key members of treatment teams.

This newly recognized profession in the field of human services began developing in the 1940s, primarily in the United States. Two broad developments contributed to its evolution: the changing scope of mental health care during World War II and the increasing impact of modern dance. Psychoanalytic treatment became challenged by newer theories of treatment, including group therapy, activity therapy, and arts therapies. (The use of pharmacotherapy developed later, toward the late 1950s.) The 1930s and 1940s saw modern dancers explore new forms in the art of dance, moving away from the formalized structure of ballet and its classic tales and focusing on statements of the choreographer's own inner experiences.

A key person in the development of this new treatment modality was Marian Chace, pioneer in dance therapy at St. Elizabeths Hospital in Washington, D.C. She had been a concert dancer with the famed Denishawn troupe and, as a teacher of dance, noted that, although many of her students were not interested in professional training, they continued to study dance. In exploring their motivations and movement behavior, she began to develop her own theories about dance as a fundamental mode of communication and as a form of therapy for those having problems in communicating.

Her interest led her to study psychopathology and psychotherapy. As psychiatrists gave recognition to her work, they began sending patients to her. Eventually, she developed dance therapy as a treatment modality at St. Elizabeths and trained many young professionals. When the American Dance Therapy Association (ADTA) was formed in 1966, Marian Chace served as its first president.

GOALS OF DANCE THERAPY

Change is a basic goal for all forms of therapy, including dance/movement therapy. Changes in self-concept and awareness, in behavior, and in interaction are essential therapeutic goals, as are changes in the body itself that lead to the release of bodily tensions and blocks. Within the safety of the group, the patient can begin to take risks, express his/her feelings, make contact with others, and find new patterns of behavior to replace those that interfere with the ability to function. The therapist serves as facilitator or catalyst. What is brought into the sessions by the patients is assessed, and movement statements are clarified, developed, and processed. The opportunity for the release of tension and anxiety and for creative expression is offered.

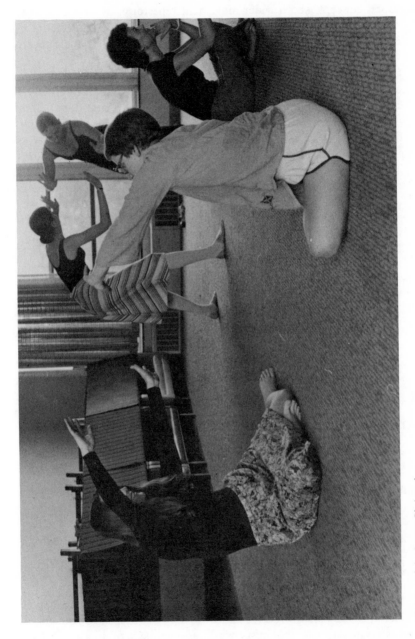

Photograph by Laura Christoplos.

51

Specific goals of dance therapy include: 1) the development of body image, self-concept, and a wider movement repertoire, 2) increased awareness of inner physiological states and their psychological counterparts, and 3) the exploration and integration of alternatives for verbal and nonverbal behavior.

Group sessions begin with patients assembling in a room with appropriate space, usually forming a circle for the warm-up. Exercises for stretching and limbering various parts of the body are done. Simple rhythmic movements flow through the group, aided by the therapist's clarification and development of movement statements. The therapist uses this period to assess the mood of the group, its needs and communications.

The middle section of a typical session sees the development of themes to be explored in movement. These flow from the movement interaction itself, rather than from preconceived plans brought in by the therapist. A group rhythm unfolds, and as the experience is shared, the group lends cohesion and support to individuals within it, lessening isolation.

The third identifiable portion of the sesssion focuses on closure, working toward resolution and restoration of centeredness for each individual member of the group.

There is a great deal of variety in dance therapy sessions, depending on the setting, the clients, and the particular training of the therapist. The various techniques of dance and movement vary, as do the uses of verbalization, interpretation, and directions.

Thus, spontaneity is a key factor in dance therapy sessions, with no established "right" way to move. It is important that the therapist not impose his/her own movements on the sessions; a clear knowledge of one's own movement repertoire and nonverbal messages is essential to the practicing dance therapist.

NATURE OF CLIENTS AND SETTINGS

Because dance therapy is used in the treatment of those persons having emotional, social, cognitive, and/or physical problems, dance therapists are employed primarily as clinicians in a wide range of facilities dealing in human services. Some of these facilities include: psychiatric hospitals, clinics, community mental health centers, developmental centers, correctional facilities, special schools, and agencies under the human resources umbrella.

Dance therapists work with children, adolescents, and adults, including the elderly. Some persons receive dance therapy in groups and some in individual sessions. Dance therapists work as members of treatment teams, often as co-therapists and, increasingly, as primary therapists. Some dance therapists are actively engaged in research, and many act as consultants.

Persons are employed as dance therapists in the United States, Canada, Europe, South America, the Middle East, and Africa. Registered dance therapists (Registry of the American Dance Therapy Association) are those considered qualified to teach in training programs, colleges, and universities, to supervise interns, and to engage in private practice.

EQUIPMENT

While music is not used all the time during the dance therapy sessions, the primary equipment requirements for such therapy sessions are a record-player and records of varying rhythms and moods. A space in which the group can comfortably move is essential. Some therapists use chairs or mats for various parts of the sessions, while others prefer bare, wooden floors. Space is a very important consideration. Cramped, poorly lit rooms do not facilitate movement experiences. On the other hand, space that is too large can be extremely threatening and disturbing to individuals who have body-boundary distortions.

Many dance/movement therapists utilize video-tape equipment to tape sessions, allowing direct and concrete feedback to the clients involved. The use of video is invaluable in teaching and research and in documenting movement behavior changes over a period of treatment. The therapist is thereby able to assess change and to clearly demonstrate the work in clinical case presentations and inservice training.

In addition to records, cassette recordings also are used, as well as a variety of musical instruments: drums, banjos, cymbals, gongs, beaters, and other rhythm instruments. The group often creates its own sound through clapping, stamping, and vocalizations.

Some therapists employ the use of props, especially to pull together a group that is having difficulties in coming together as a group or to aid in focusing a group statement. Props include scarves, balls, foam bats, or parachutes. Other therapists feel that props interfere with the naturally developing process within the group.

PROFESSIONAL TRAINING

Professional training in dance therapy occurs at the graduate level, and is conducted by Registered Dance Therapists (DTRs). There are currently several colleges and universities across the country offering graduate degrees in dance/movement therapy, and, while they differ in format, they produce well rounded practitioners who use movement as the process for therapeutic intervention. Core content of the curriculum in such programs includes courses in dance therapy, theory and practice, human development, observation and assessment of movement behavior, anatomy and kinesiology, psychological theories and psychotherapy, as well as a six-month clinical internship under the supervision of a DTR.

Undergraduate students who are interested in pursuing a career in dance therapy are encouraged to study the liberal arts with emphasis in psychology, dance, or a related field. In addition to anatomy and kinesiology, extensive training in a variety of dance forms is essential, including theory, improvisation, and choreography. Experience in teaching dance to normal children and adults is valuable background. Introductory or survey courses can aid in the evaluation of a student's interest and aptitude before entering a graduate training program.

ACCREDITATION OF TRAINING INSTITUTIONS

The national professional association is currently developing procedures for the approval of graduate training programs in dance therapy. After 1980, a master's degree from an ADTA-approved program, or its equivalent, will be a requirement for registry applicants. Because the dance therapist has direct contact with the public, it is expected that academic programs training dance therapists will eventually need to be accredited by an examining board. The peer-approval procedures are seen as a vital first step toward eventual accreditation.

REGISTRY

A registry exists under the auspices of the American Dance Therapy Association, the recognized professional association of dance therapists. Registration is a separate procedure and is based on specific professional standards to ensure the achievement of minimal training and experience. Some of the requirements include dance therapy training encompassing theory and practice, extensive dance training, and the study of human development, the body, psychopathology, and methods of observation and research. An internship in a supervised clinical setting is required, as is a period of paid experience as a dance therapist subsequent to training. After 1980, the requirements will include a master's degree from an ADTA-approved program in dance therapy or its equivalent. At this point, no state grants licenses or certificates to dance therapists.

RESEARCH NEEDS

As with any newly developing profession, the need for sound research studies is great. Dance therapists have evolved a theoretical framework and a body of knowledge, but attempts at validation are just beginning to emerge. Anecdotal reporting and case studies are being augmented by well designed and controlled studies. An increasing amount of research is being done in the field of nonverbal communication. The dance therapy profession needs to develop its own framework to study efficacy of various methods with specific populations.

While video and films have proved to be useful tools in recording movement behavior, the language and interpretation of the observer have been largely subjective. A more universally employed system for the observation of movement is greatly needed. Today, many dance therapists are being trained in a system known as "effort-shape," based on the work of Rudolf Laban, a dancer and choreographer. The effort-shape system describes the dynamics of movement. Although this system is not to be confused with a theory or technique of dance therapy, it is a research tool being used by that profession, as well as by psychology, anthropology, human development, dance education, or wherever assessments of movement behavior are codified.

DANCE THERAPY AND DANCE EDUCATION

There is often misunderstanding and confusion between dance therapy and a dance experience that may be recreational or educational in nature. There are basic differences in the roles and purposes of therapists and teachers even though certain aspects of training and technique are quite similar. Dance therapy is a form of psychotherapy and, as such, deals with material from the client/patient's unconscious and intrapsychic processes, within the context of a therapeutic contract.

Dance in education is designed for the student to learn specific techniques or choreography. A dance class can be therapeutic; the students grow by gaining competence and confidence. A recreational dance experience also can be therapeutic because it aids in socialization and is enjoyable. Dance teachers often teach dance to handicapped persons or persons in need of therapy. In this context, dance classes need not be transformed into therapy sessions.

The therapist encourages the patient to move in his/her unique way and avoids imposing a style and structure on the experience. The goal of dance education is the development of specific skills in movement, as presented by a teacher. The dance/movement therapist makes use of specialized training to focus on the emotional problems, movement limitations, body image disturbances, and fragmented communication patterns of the individual, with the goal of using movement as the process for intervention and treatment.

INTERDISCIPLINARY ASPECTS

Dance therapists working with an interdisciplinary treatment team participate in program planning for a group of patients or clients. Because he/she has special observational skills, the dance therapist is an important team member during intake and evaluation procedures. The assessment necessary for the appropriate placement of patients in dance therapy is one function performed by the therapeutic team. Another is assistance in diagnostic procedures and making acute observations that can be useful in differential diagnosis and discharge plans. Dance therapists are trained to note slight physical changes that may go unnoticed by other team members. (One dance therapist was able to diagnose a slight stroke in an older psychiatric patient by an accurate reporting of movement behavior and physical changes that had been missed by the ward personnel.) Thus a significant contribution to case presentations can be made by dance therapists, making these presentations more representative of the total human being. Expressive movement behavior is often a more direct statement about an individual than his/her verbalizations, especially when the client finds himself/herself in a new setting and is able to "cover" what he/she verbally communicates.

Dance therapists have unique skills to offer in the development of group interaction among team members, as discussed in the introductory chapter of this book. They can be called upon to conduct inservice workshops for team members, exploring movement interaction and developing understanding of the nonverbal level of communication that other professionals may need to enhance their skills. A great deal of this interaction occurs on the unconscious level, and bringing it into awareness facilitates the professional's knowledge of his/her nonverbal style and the messages he/she is giving to team members as well as clients. This vital aspect of personality and behavior style is often neglected in the training of individuals in many of the professions responsible for the delivery of human services. The development of verbal skills is often stressed to the point where overintellectualization is a potential hazard and nonverbal behavior is minimized. Basic understanding of interaction at the movement level and responsiveness to nonverbal messages can shorten the span of time it takes for a relationship to develop, whether it is with other staff members or with patients. Thus, it can be seen that dance therapists can function on interdisciplinary teams by directly providing services to clients, as well as by providing consultative services to an intermediary.

TIME AND COST OF SERVICES

Dance therapy sessions are flexibly structured to meet the needs of the individual client. Many children, particularly those who are autistic or who are severely emotionally disturbed, might begin their course of therapy with sessions of short duration, working on a one-to-one basis with a therapist. Sessions would increase to perhaps 30–50 minutes in duration, as the patient becomes further engaged in the process of therapy. Group sessions with an adolescent group might be 30–45 minutes in duration. Adult groups often have one-hour sessions, while individual adults are seen one to two hours per session.

The cost of the services of a dance therapist vary according to geographic regions. The range is $15–50 per session, based on qualifications and experience of the therapist, the length of the session, and the particular setting. Dance therapists who provide consultant services often charge $25–45 per hour or $200 per day for workshops. In institutional settings, dance therapists working full-time earn between $9,000 and $20,000 annually, according to the region in which they work and the individual qualifications and experience of the therapist. Many dance therapists are employed part-time or as consultants.

CONCLUSION

Dance therapy is a rapidly developing profession within the field of human services that can offer unique skills to interdisciplinary teams. This emerging profession uses movement as a psychotherapeutic process which furthers the emotional and physical integration of the individual. As a mode of therapy, it focuses on the whole person, using movement and movement interaction as the basis for intervention.

Currently, professional training takes place on the master's degree level. Procedures for approval of training programs are being developed, a first step toward their eventual accreditation. Registered dance therapists are those considered qualified to teach in training programs, colleges, and universities, to supervise interns, and to engage in private practice. Opportunities for research are manifold, with potentially wide-ranging implications.

Rhythmic dance action has long been recognized as a unifying force for human beings. Its use as a form of therapy is now seen as a powerful and direct means of establishing relationships and of communicating a person's most profound feelings.

PROFESSIONAL ORGANIZATION

The American Dance Therapy
   Association, Inc., Suite 230, 2000
   Century Plaza, Columbia, Maryland
   21044

SUGGESTED READINGS

Alperson, E. 1973–74. Movement therapy—A theoretical framework. Writings on Movement and Communication Monograph No. 3. American Dance Therapy Association, Columbia, Md.

Bartenieff, I. 1972–73. Dance therapy: A new profession or a rediscovery of an ancient role of the dance? Dance Scope 7:6–18.

Bender, L., and Boas, F. 1941. Creative dance in therapy. Am. J. Orthopsychiatry. 2:235–244.

Bernstein, P. L. 1972. Theory and Methods in Dance-Movement Therapy. Kendall-Hunt, Dubuque, Iowa.

Chace, M. 1953. Dance as an adjunctive therapy with hospitalized mental patients. Bull. Menninger Clinic 17:219–225.

Chace, M. 1958. Development of group interaction through dance. In J. H. Masserman and J. L. Moreno (eds.), Progress in Psychotherapy, Vol. 3. Techniques of Psychotherapy, pp. 143–153. Grune and Stratton, New York.

Chace, M. 1964. Dance alone is not enough. Dance Magazine 38:46–47, 58.

Chace, M. 1964. The power of movement with others. Dance Magazine 38:42–45, 68–69.

Chaiklin, S. 1969. Dance therapy. In Proceedings of the American Dance Therapy Association 4th Annual Conference, pp. 25–31. American Dance Therapy Association, Philadelphia, Pa.

Chaiklin, S. 1975. Dance therapy. In S. Arievi (ed.), American Handbook of Psychiatry. Basic Books, New York.

Clarke, F. R. 1967. A method of organizing treatment programs in large psychiatric hospitals. In Proceedings of the American Dance Therapy Association 2nd Annual Conference. Reprinted in Monograph No. 1. Writings on Body Movement and Communication. American Dance Therapy Association, Columbia, Md.

Dyrud, J., and Chace, M. 1968. Movement and personality. In Proceedings of the American Dance Therapy Association 3rd Annual Conference, pp. 16–20. American Dance Therapy Association, Madison, Wis.

Irwin, K. 1972. Dance as prevention of, therapy for, and recreation from the crisis of old age. In Monograph No. 2, pp. 151–190. American Dance Therapy Association, Columbia, Md.

Jones, M. S. 1953. The Therapeutic Community. Basic Books, New York.

Kalish, B. 1968. Body movement therapy for autistic children. In Proceedings of the American Dance Therapy Association 3rd Annual Conference, p. 49–59. American Dance Therapy Association, Madison, Wis.

Laban, R. 1960. The Mastery of Movement. MacDonald and Evans, London.

Laban, R., and Lawrence, F. C. 1947. Effort. MacDonald and Evans, London.

Mason, K. (ed.). 1974. Focus on Dance. 7: Dance Therapy. American Association of Health, Physical Education, and Recreation, Washington, D.C.

North, M. 1972. Personality Assessment through Movement. MacDonald and Evans, London.

Pesso, A. 1969. Movement in Psychotherapy: Psychomotor Techniques and Training. New York University Press, New York.

Rosen, E. 1957. Dance in Psychotherapy. Teachers College Press, Columbia University, New York.

Samuels, A. 1972. Movement change through dance therapy—A study. In

Monograph No. 2, pp. 50–70. American Dance Therapy Association, Columbia, Md.

Schmais, C., and White, E. 1968. Introduction to dance therapy, workshop in dance therapy: Its research potentials. *In* Proceedings of the Joint Conference of the American Dance Therapy Association, C.O.R.D., and the Post-graduate Center for Mental Health, New York.

Schmais, C., and White, E. 1969. Movement analysis: A must for dance therapists. *In* Proceedings of the American Dance Therapy Association 4th Annual Conference, pp. 52–59. American Dance Therapy Association, Philadelphia, Pa.

Schoop, T. 1974. Won't You Join the Dance? A Dancer's Essay into the Treatment of Psychosis. National Press Book, Palo Alto, Cal.

Smallwood, J. C. 1974. Dance-Movement therapy. *In* J. H. Masserman (ed.), Current Psychiatric Therapies. Vol. 14, pp. 115–121. Grune and Stratton New York.

DENTISTRY

Lawrence A. Fox

While being considered a limited health care specialty, dealing solely with the oral cavity and oro-facial structures, dentistry, at the same time, is one of the few professions that makes contact with a client throughout the client's lifetime. The extent to which this contact is needed, made available, or provided is dependent on a vast number of variables from without and within the profession. Nevertheless, the view of the dentist as merely the "caretaker of the mouth" is quite myopic.

Dentistry has evolved from a highly skilled profession, technically oriented toward reparation, into a new discipline comprised of health care providers who pursue dentistry from a new perspective. Still dexterously competent, but more holistic in their approach, contemporary dentists are being trained with a greater emphasis on the psychosocial interrelationships that exist between the professionals, the client, the family, and the community. No longer is the *raison d'etre* of the dentist simply reparative in nature. Clinicians have now become concerned with the delivery of better dental health care to the client and to the community, and it is through their community efforts that primary (i.e., health promotion and specific protection) and secondary (i.e., early diagnosis and early treatment) prevention are provided. It is with the recognition of these new emphases on prevention, total patient care, and a greater awareness of the behavior of the clients that the dental profession is now becoming a vital member of the interdisciplinary team.

FUNCTIONS OF DENTISTS AND DENTAL TEAMS

The introductory chapter of this book attests to the need to separate interdisciplinary teams according to their function: 1) those directly responsible for prescribing a client's treatment program and 2) those responsible for providing consultation services to an intermediary who, in turn, provides direct treatment to the client. Thus, within the context of interdisciplinary teamwork, certain disciplines are appropriately categorized into either the first or second group while others possess characteristics of both. Dentistry falls into this latter group.

Members of the first group undoubtedly see the role of dentistry in its more traditional role of providing consultation services to its clients, performing diagnostic examinations, and delivering a plan of treatment that strives toward the ideal while maintaining a constant of pragmatism. This reality considers not only the basic oral need of the client but also the physical, mental, emotional, and financial abilities of the client to deal with the specified treatment program. Dentists, operating within this framework, recommend to a client, the client's family, or social agency a plan of treatment that has often been referred to by the profession as "first-rate" dentistry. These utopian concepts were often created in professional schools that taught students to practice ideal dentistry on a captive population. The fee structures used were designed to maintain a patient population sufficient to continue the dental educational process. The humanistic side of the treatment plan was lacking in this system, however. As indicated earlier, with the changes in dental education, students are now better equipped to consider the real side of the client. For example, students formerly were sheltered from the special or exceptional patient, the common labels used in dentistry to refer to all types of handicapped clients. Now, through the efforts of some private foundations, in conjunction with the American Fund for Dental Health, the Academy of Dentistry for the Handicapped, the National Foundation of Dentistry for the Handicapped, and the American Academy of Pedodontics, dental graduates are exposed to handicapped persons during their formal training. In addition to learning how to perform dentistry with clients who have physical problems, students also are being sensitized to the gestalt that handicapped individuals bring into either the private or clinical setting.

The second type of team comes into play as dental professionals begin to move out of the confines of their own treatment areas and into a new forum. This is happening as the dentist, the dental hygienist, the dental assistant, and the preventive dental therapist, acting either individually or as part of a dental team, shift from being treatment-oriented professionals to their new role as advisors and educators. This movement started with the preventive dentistry surge that has swept through the profession during the past 10 years. Acting as educators, the dental person(s) or team educates and trains those individuals functioning out of the dental setting who can provide routine, day-to-day dental services for clients. This training may take the form of teaching parents how to clean their physically handicapped child's oral cavity on a routine basis. Similar training also may be necessary in daycare centers, residential facilities, or special education programs in schools and hospitals. The concept being promoted is that daily preventive oral care is an essential component of total health care for the client and should not be neglected. Through a series of health education strategies, persons who are responsible for a client's well-being are being taught that by practicing a good daily regimen of oral health care, their clients can avoid many of the problems that plague the majority of handicapped persons. For clients who are able to develop the dexterity required in certain self-help skills, appropriate training programs are being developed to prevent dental disease or minimize the incidence and severity of existing pathology.

Unfortunately, dentistry still must rely heavily on the human factor to control dental disease. This is in contrast with the field of medicine where, for many years, vaccinations have been available that afford protection from various diseases. While the dental profession has been trying, experimentally, to develop a vaccine that will alter the life span of oral flora, their efforts have been relatively impotent. Thus, prevention programs have been created for the handicapped to teach them, their parents, or aides to control

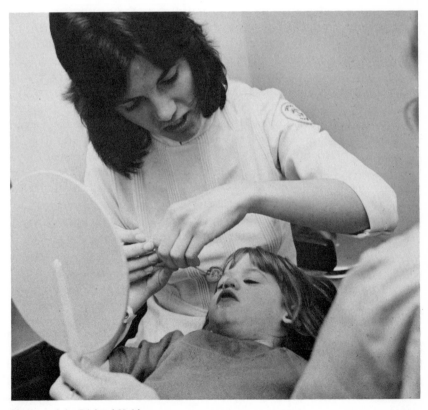

Photograph by Richard Holden.

dental disease. These programs have been detailed in other writings and are too elaborate to include in this discussion. One can, if interested in the particulars of such a program, refer to those references listed in the suggested readings at the end of this chapter. Suffice it to say here that preventive programs are usually divided into several phases, each of which deals with a specific component. First, the patient is positioned in a comfortable situation for cleaning to take place. The optimal position varies, depending on the specific handicapping condition. Next, the oral cavity is disclosed, using a food-coloring agent to identify where the bacterial plaque (film of bacteria on the teeth) is located. Now the actual cleansing can take place, using a toothbrush followed by dental flossing. The final phase of the program is the application of fluorides that alter the chemical structure of tooth enamel to make the tooth less penetrable by oral cavity acids. These acids are produced by the activity of certain oral bacteria with refined carbohydrates (sucrose, etc.) taken in as foodstuffs. Thus, it can be seen that, in addition to the phases of the preventive program briefly mentioned above, it is essential that the role of nutrition in the prevention of dental disease not be overlooked. (Consult the suggested readings and the nutrition chapter for further information.) It is important to note that the nutritional component of a preventive dentistry program involves more than telling persons to, "cut out eating sweets" and "eliminate in-between-meal snacks," to which the profession has given lip service for years. Today, a careful analysis of a person's complete food intake is performed. Specific recommendations then are made to alter the caries potential of the person.

There are a few other preventive devices such as water-irrigating devices, electric toothbrushes, and specially modified toothbrushes for disabled persons who are unable to utilize conventional ones. These devices should be considered only as adjunctive instruments and not as replacements for a sound preventive dentistry program. Thus, while a water-irrigating device may be considered a replacement for toothbrushing, it does not begin to substitute for the utilization of a brush.

NEED FOR DENTISTRY IN INTERDISCIPLINARY PROCESS

The potential scope of the dental team is vast. By virtue of their training, professionals functioning on a dental team are able to provide services to the entire array of handicapped clients who wish to make use of their services. The willingness and desire for services must be balanced by the understanding that, while dentistry often is represented on an interdisciplinary team, the amount of "interdisciplinaryness" is often a reflection of the hierarchy of the team members and the priorities established by those members. Thus, the utilization of dentistry within the framework of a team varies from one institution or bureaucracy to another.

Because few persons are free of at least some form of dental disease, every client should obtain a dental appraisal. In view of the nature and prevalence of dental disease, an ideal appraisal means that every client should receive a dental evaluation, a consultation to apprise the client or family of the client of the findings, a recommendation of a treatment plan, if necessary, and a preventive dentistry program to include proper oral hygiene and nutritional counseling.

Studies performed on populations of handicapped persons show that they suffer from a higher incidence of dental caries (decay) and periodontal (gum) disease than the nonhandicapped. This fact may lead one to believe that handicapping conditions, per se, cause greater amounts of dental disease. This does hold true for developmental defects such as cleft lip and palate and other dental anomalies of the enamel or other hard and soft tissues. These conditions, however, account only for a small percentage of defects. The defects referred to here, however, are the most common forms and are usually caused by neglect. Even neglect is a complex matter and not solely the responsibility of the client or family. It is this complexity that contributes significantly to the limitations of the dental team as it functions as part of the interdisciplinary team.

The most common reason for dental neglect is the clients' or clients' families' failure to consider the value of good oral health. Such neglect is evident in the fact that nearly one-half of the population in this country does not seek out dental care except for emergency purposes. The educational attempts that have been carried on for decades, which have promoted the idea of brushing three times a day and visiting the dentist twice a year, have not resulted in a significant increase in the percentage of persons seeking dental care. Nor has the incidence of dental disease changed appreciably. These facts provide graphic proof of the failure of the profession to educate the public.

The high per capita consumption of refined carbohydrates in the American diet, which is higher than ever before in history, also contributes significantly to the disease rate. The problem is compounded by additional factors including: the fear of going to the dentist, the lack of trained professionals in many areas (other than in major centers), the lack of adequate funding sources to provide dental care to a population whose families are already overburdened financially, and the lack of consideration by other professionals on the team of the true importance of dental care for handicapped or other populations. Many highly educated health care professionals also maintain the *laissez faire* dental attitudes that are deplored among the general public. Physicians, having been trained to care for every part of the body, unfortunately, often completely exclude the oral cavity. While it may be sensible to allow the dental professional to have exclusive domain over the oral areas, interdisciplinary teams, often under the purview of a physician, as a rule do not consider making dentistry a part of the team or, in those cases in which the dental team is made a component of the interdisciplinary team, usually insist that dentistry stay within its own territorial boundary with little or no other function. The dental professional is often poorly utilized as a member of the team, and the role that dental colleagues can play in striving for an improvement in the quality of services to handicapped clients is sorely neglected.

Certain disciplines are limited in the services they provide for their clients and deal only with those clients who display a specific need for their services, as determined by the prescription of the interdisciplinary team. Dentistry, on the other hand, while it has its limitations as discussed previously, does appropriately serve *all* clients.

Attention should be paid to interdisciplinary understanding and cooperation, not only because of the need to appreciate the intricacies of the other professions' approaches to the handicapped, but also to discover common ground for new areas of research. A prime example of this occurred when behavioral scientists, in developing a relationship with their dental colleagues, found that behavior modification programs, including operant conditioning, might have a notable place within the armamentarium of the dental professional who was faced with patients, on a daily basis, who were unmanageable in the dental setting. Before the behavioral approach, professionals in dental care had to rely on drug or anesthetic management of their clients. Today, behavior modification has become a tool for the dental professional to, in a more humane way, more effectively manage patients. It is not the intention here to expound the virtues of working with an interdisciplinary team or to applaud the opportunity for one profession to learn more about another profession and ultimately use the techniques and methods of that profession. The example used above is cited to demonstrate the benefits that accrued when two disciplines that had had nothing to do with each other discovered that there was common ground on which to work.

The more that each profession gains, even on an awareness level, the more professionals will be able to manage the person holistically. With certain exceptions, however, most interdisciplinary teams have not functioned in this fashion. Basically, teams have been composed of department or division directors who have established their priorities based on their own experiences and biases, and who have, from that vantage point, made a determination as to which disciplines should be represented. This, of course, defeats the entire concept of having an interdisciplinary team. While it certainly is appropriate that certain disciplines should have a greater involvement than others, this is no excuse for excluding any pertinent, recognized disciplines. The dental team has certain basic knowledge to gain from every division of an interdisciplinary facility. While dentistry is more closely allied with medicine, speech therapy, occupational therapy, and behavioral psychology, the dental team also must develop an awareness of what *all* the other disciplines are about and their *raisons d'etre*.

There are, however, many "ivory tower" professionals within certain disciplines who feel that they should decide what is important for their staff or students to know and who do not place disciplines such as dentistry on this priority list. While this is not intended to be a mass condemnation of the medical profession, in general it is felt that the physician has been the chief culprit. This omission is indeed unfortunate because the pediatrician is usually the professional who has, after the obstetrician, first and continued contact with the child. It would certainly seem appropriate that the pediatric colleagues of an interdisciplinary facility should have a knowledge and understanding of how to perform an examination of the oral cavity and its structures. This is not meant to imply that pediatricians should be trained in dentistry but, rather, that they should learn how to make early diagnoses of oral pathology for referral to the dental team. They also should have sufficient understanding of the nature of dental disease and its prevention so that, for example, they would not allow candy or other carbohydrates to be used as a form of reinforcement for good behavior with a young child. There are certainly other disciplines in which a similar problem exists, but because most teams historically have been under the leadership of medical colleagues, it is up to physicians to begin setting the standards for other professional disciplines to follow. If the physicians who direct teams believed that each person on their staff and all their trainees needed to gain basic knowledge of all disciplines, then other professionals would undoubtedly take this position as well. Because this has not been the case, the current state of affairs in interdisciplinary facilities is to be decried. Dentistry and other professions such as nutrition, audiology, and special education should exist not as luxuries or accessories to the team rather than essential components.

NATURE OF DENTAL PROGRAM
INTERVENTIONS FOR HANDICAPPED

As indicated above, there are few, if any, clients who cannot benefit from the services of the dental team. While some clients may need little or no dental reparative therapy, all can benefit from the education or reinforcement of proper oral health—the area in which most handicapped clients suffer. Indeed, those clients who have no problem with hand-motor coordination and are emotionally able to care for themselves, need only to be trained in the proper method of home care. Clients lacking either the cerebral and/or motor functions to care for themselves need to rely on others to provide this service for them. The client who is cared for by the family must have family support in order to learn how to perform daily hygiene tasks. There may be a natural reluctance on the part of the person(s) who has been delegated to take this responsibility. The reluctance may be caused, in part, by this person's discomfort in cleaning someone else's mouth, even if it is his/her own child. It also may be attributable to a reluctance on the part of the client to have anyone intrude into his/her oral cavity. If the client is physically handicapped, there may be the helper's fear that he/she may either hurt the client or get hurt himself/herself. While certain handicapped individuals may appear to be completely uncontrollable, the well trained professional should be able to identify the specific limitations of the client and work out a specialized program to be implemented by the person(s) responsible. For example, the client with the athetoid type of cerebral palsy is often one of the most difficult clients to manage because of the involuntary movements of the limbs. It becomes simply a matter of teaching the responsible person how to manipulate the necessary oral devices, in spite of these movements. Sometimes, it may be necessary to teach how to work in pairs, with one person utilizing some mild restraint on the limbs while the other performs the oral tasks.

The above comments are related specifically to the training or educational components of the dental services and do not refer to the therapeutic areas. Providing comprehensive service to all clients requires that the dental team members be well versed in the various techniques and methodologies essential to the provision of therapy. They also must be cognizant of the medical and psychosocial conditions of their clients before any therapeutic regimen can be instituted. A thorough understanding of complications that may arise as a result of the dental therapy is vital. This may be exemplified in the case of a client with Down's syndrome who becomes uncontrollable in the normal setting of the dental clinic, and the decision is made to utilize a general anesthetic in order to render the dental service. Without knowing the nature of Down's syndrome, the dental professional might be treading into dangerous territory. The fact that many children with Down's syndrome have cardiac problems and could be poor anesthetic risks is critical. While not all clients with Down's syndrome have concomitant cardiac problems, it is nevertheless essential to know this element of their condition and to consult a cardiologist before the initiation of dental therapy.

The appropriateness of recommending ideal dental therapy for the client who may have a terminal illness, perhaps with a shortened life span, becomes questionable, as does the same type of service for clients who are profoundly mentally and physically handicapped. The most appropriate service for these clients is usually palliative in nature, concerned with maintenance of good oral hygiene by those in attendance in order to keep the client comfortable. Clients who have become self-destructive by using their teeth for self-mutilation pose a serious dilemma to the dental professional. The treatment often recommended for these clients is extraction of those teeth creating the destruction to prevent the client from further self-imposed physical harm. This approach presents a conflict for dentists because of their training in preventive dentistry. The training emphasis has been to help patients keep their teeth for a lifetime. The decision to extract teeth that are usually healthy and vital is difficult. When the decision to extract is made, it does not come easily to the professional who is being forced to commit "dental euthanasia."

Often, when an examination of a handicapped client is performed and some forms of pathology are noted, the professional frequently makes light of the situation, avoiding any type of treatment at all. Typically, the problem is defined in the hope that it will disappear. Unfortunately, dental diseases are among the few diseases that do not heal through normal body defenses. Thus, the pathology will eventually exacerbate until the client sees the dentist on an emergency basis, perhaps with some form of abscess. Then the professional is faced with a more difficult task: the emergency patient usually is more difficult to manage, pain and discomfort are superimposed over the original problem, and the patient's threshold of pain probably has been lowered. The treatment of choice for this dentist often may be extraction of the offending tooth or teeth. Depending on the training and skill of the dental team, this procedure is going to be more difficult for the professional and, in turn, for the client. These comments are not meant to imply that all professionals practice in this fashion. It does, however, portray an almost universal, regrettable state of the art that exists in the profession.

While the mechanical and technical dental procedures performed on handicapped persons are essentially the same as those provided for any other client, the major differences in caring for these two groups fall into the areas of specialized apparatus, techniques, and a greater knowledge of medical conditions. The most important of these needs relates to an increased awareness of the total medical condition of the handicapped individual and its implication for dental treatment.

Consider the client who is being administered various medications to control seizures, hyperactivity, diabetes, or rheumatoid arthritis. The dental professional must not only be well versed in all these conditions but also in those pharmacological agents used to control or modify them. This knowledge is essential when one considers the implications of oral healing as well as the possible interaction effects of these drugs when combined with those administered by the dentist. As an example, phenobarbital, a drug often taken to control hyperactivity and/or seizures, is a respiratory depressant in some clients. The client taking phenobarbital prophylactically may be uncontrollable in the dental setting and may require some form of sedation in order to be managed. First, the dentist must be made aware that the person is taking this medication, and then he must make a decision on the best means of controlling the unfavorable behavior. If the dentist decides to use some of the more common medications that produce relaxation with the patient, care must be taken to select a drug that will not react adversely with phenobarbital and that, at the same time, will not depress respiration to a level at which it might become life-threatening. This situation occurs routinely because the drug management of medical problems is often the physician's treatment of choice.

As mentioned previously, many clients with both respiratory and cardiovascular conditions are poor anesthetic and surgical risks. Caution must always be exercised when a decision is made to treat these clients with almost *any* pharmacological agent. A thorough knowledge by the dental staff of the complete medical condition and all of its ramifications is essential. A prime example of this would be the patient with a history of rheumatic fever who runs a risk in the dental chair even when the dental hygienist is merely cleaning his/her teeth. The manipulation of dental instruments can set up a transient bacteremia and possibly produce SABE (subacute bacterial endocarditis), thus causing further injury to a previously damaged heart, possibly resulting in death. Although dental care is not often thought of as life-threatening, these examples point out the importance of the professionals being completely informed and knowledgeable about the medical history of clients. These cases are not an overdramatization of rare, isolated incidents. They are instead very common occurrences. Daily, dental staffs face clients with complicated medical conditions and must be prepared to deal with them.

There are numerous situations where, in addition to the previously mentioned reasons, drug therapy is contraindicated in the management of the antagonistic behavior of the patient. In these cases, the dentist should be accomplished in the use of behavior modification, i.e., operant conditioning in the dental setting. Behavioral psychologists have become key professionals in assisting the dental team in the development of programs to desensitize or recondition patients who are dental phobic and unable to cope even with routine care. Many of these patients are unable even to undergo a relatively innocuous procedure, such as polishing of the teeth, without suffering from extreme anxiety or even hysteria. The dentist, in using the simple token-reward systems developed by behaviorists, is now able to manage patients who previously were uncontrollable. By doing this, the dentist is not only able to control the behavior of the patient by a much safer mode than by drugs but is also able to shape the behavior of the patient so that, ultimately, dental therapy becomes a more pleasant experience for the patient. Needless to say, behavior modification, while being a notable tool in the area of patient management for the dentist, has its limitations. There are many clients who, because of their inability to comprehend the token-reward system, are ultimately nonresponsive to it. Others, because of the uncontrollable, frenzied nature of their behavior, are not amenable to this method of administering care.

Other clients may be classified as those who want to cooperate in the dental setting but, because of the nature of their medical condition, are unable to do so. Perhaps the best example of this group is the patient with the athetoid type of cerebral palsy who may often have the intelligence and desire to cooperate with the dentist but is unable to do so because of involuntary movements of some or all of his/her limbs. In these cases, restraining devices are used to protect the patient and doctor from injury and to maintain the body in a relatively immobile state to expedite therapy. These devices may be either commercially produced straps for the arms, legs, body, or head or homemade inventions using foam rubber, gauze, and adhesive tape. In either case, the device is carefully placed around the uncontrollable part or parts of the body and then fastened to some part of the dental chair to keep the area motionless. The patient is advised that this device is merely an aid and not a form of punishment. To the casual observer, these methods and devices for patient management may be viewed as punitive in nature; however, this is in no way the intent. Occasionally, some professionals may want to utilize restraining devices on belligerent patients; this philosophy should be condemned as inhumane practice.

Another device, although not used in the classical sense as a restraint, can be considered one under a more relaxed definition of that term. The mouth prop does not technically harness any part of the body; however, it does allow the professional to perform various oral manipulations and allows the family, teacher, or aide to manage diverse preventive dentistry apparatus. Mouth props are manufactured out of metal, metal and rubber, or rubber and are simply placed into the oral cavity and wedged between the maxillary (upper) and mandibular (lower) teeth on the opposite side of the mouth from which the operator is providing the service. Props also may be easily fabricated by placing five to six tongue depressors together, wrapping one end with cotton gauze and covering it with adhesive tape. This simple device can be used in the same fashion as the commercial ones and can be conveniently held on one side of the mouth with one hand. With the mouth propped open, a toothbrush or dental floss can be utilized on the side opposite to the prop. Another variation might be for one person to hold the prop while another person cleans the mouth. A custom-made mouth prop is an inexpensive device to be used at home to perform routine preventive dentistry tasks for patients who are unable to provide this care for themselves. In conjunction with this device, a simple, inexpensive aid (e.g., some form of dental floss holder) may be used to assist in cleaning the teeth. This holder eliminates the need to use two hands to run the dental floss between the teeth. Its use depends on whether the person performing the task has any help in the cleaning session and whether the client will allow manipulation in his/her oral cavity. In either case, a dental floss holder allows the person responsible for cleaning to hold a mouth prop with one hand and floss the teeth with the other. Developed within the past five years, these floss holders have been a boon to those preventive dentistry proponents who have been promoting the use of dental floss as an adjunct to the once-a-day routine cleansing of the mouth with a soft toothbrush.

DENTAL SERVICE SETTINGS

Dental services may be obtained from various types of institutions within a given community. The extent to which these services are rendered and the quality of these services are dependent on a number of factors, a prime one being the size of the community. Smaller communities may be mainly dependent on private care. The degree to which the private dental community is both willing and able to provide services for the multiplicity of handicapped persons is often dependent on the professional training of the dentist and his/her staff. The kinds of training that are necessary are discussed in a later section of this chapter. It is sufficient to note here that, for the most part, in spite of the efforts to train graduating dentists, the complexities of the handicapped population are often too great for most practitioners to handle in the private office. This is not to say that many clients who are quite manageable physically, emotionally, and who do not have medical complications cannot and are not treated in the private dental setting. As in many other professions, however, there is a general reluctance on the part of the dental profession to treat these clients in the private office. In the absence of professionals with specialized training, either in private or public facilities, neglect often becomes the treatment of choice.

If a community is privileged to have dental professionals who have received formal training in the management of the special patient, it is indeed fortunate. These persons often practice in a private setting and/or some private or public institution. In many cases, residential care centers may have their own facilities that can provide routine, ambulatory care for clients. Some of these offer a complete range of services and may even include inservice preventive dentistry programs for aides, attendants, and other auxiliary personnel who provide daily care for clients. In other cases, facilities provide little or no care, except perhaps for a screening examination on admission and/or emergency treatment to palliate discomfort or pain.

The UAF (University Affiliated Facility) concept, which was created out of legislation during President Kennedy's administration, might serve as a model for future interdisciplinary programming. The legislation created facilities to train professionals at all levels to serve on interdisciplinary teams established to provide treatment and education to the mentally and physically handicapped. Dental care offered in these facilities takes place under the supervision of highly trained professionals, assembled to teach dental professionals (graduate dental students, undergraduate students, dental hygienists, and dental assistants) the techniques and methodologies of managing the handicapped. In addition, the dental professional is, in the UAF setting, exposed to a team of professionals brought together to provide comprehensive service to their clients. The staff in the dental setting is thus no longer required to practice in professional isolation. Now, the dentist, when dealing with clients with complicated medical problems, can call upon medical colleagues to assist on the case. The family or client who is having difficulty in performing routine preventive dentistry tasks may work with the dental team and with specialists in disciplines such as occupational therapy and education to acquire self-help skills. Speech therapists also can cooperate with dental personnel when establishing appropriate therapeutic plans for clients who have speaking and swallowing difficulties. Behaviorists often work with the dentist in dealing with clients who evidence management problems in the dental setting. With few exceptions, the services provided in an interdisciplinary setting touch upon dentistry in some manner and to various degrees.

The UAF concept, created as an ideal, exists, in reality, as the exception to the rule when one evaluates the various types of institutions from which dental services may be obtained. There are between 30 and 40 UAFs. Within these facilities, dental services are often severely limited and, in some, nonexistent. The remaining facilities include: 1) the private dental community, which provides minimal services to a somewhat restricted population, 2) other clinical settings, operating under the aegis of the local or state health department, and 3) hospital dental departments.

Services provided in these latter three settings often are dependent on the expertise and interest of those individuals administering the programs. Health department dental clinics function autonomously, usually under the jurisdiction of medical directors. There is, for the most part, little interaction between clinical dentistry divisions and other divisions of health departments. In terms of the amount of involvement that exists between dental and other professions, the dental clinic can be considered little more than a private dental office.

On the other hand, many hospital dental departments, while not officially being set up in the UAF concept, over the years since their inception have managed to become more closely affiliated with other disciplines. The majority of hospitals providing services to handicapped populations evolved from children's or crippled children's hospitals established years ago, primarily to provide orthopaedic services to victims of polio epidemics.

Since that time, these hospitals have become broader in their base of services and often include dentistry. In many instances, these hospitals also have expanded to incorporate adult populations in their programs.

PROFESSIONAL PREPARATION

As indicated earlier, dental education is changing to include training in the area of the handicapped. With the aid of the Robert Wood Johnson Foundation, through the American Fund for Dental Health of the American Dental Association, 10 dental schools in the United States were funded to train the graduating dentist to work with the handicapped population. While somewhat limited in scope, these programs provide services to handicapped clients while preparing future dentists to work after graduation from dental school with the client.

Dental schools not only provide services to handicapped populations in the above programs but also in postgraduate education. Most of this education and, ultimately, service to the handicapped is confined to the specialty of pediatric dentistry. By definition, pediatric dentistry includes the evaluation, diagnosis, and treatment of children and adolescents and also includes those persons of adult age who are physically or mentally disabled. In this definition, the American Academy of Pedodontics, the official governing body of all graduate, postgraduate, and hospital programs in pediatric dentistry in the United States, has designated that a considerable portion of all specialty training be devoted to the management of the handicapped. The extent of training to work with the handicapped, however, varies from one academic institution to the next. While serving as institutions of learning, these facilities do provide a vital, and in some cases, a major commitment of service to the community.

Because any person with a license to practice dentistry or dental hygiene can, by law, provide care for any patient whom they feel they are qualified to treat, some form of specialty training is recommended. Specialty training can take place in the various settings described above, in addition to general dental practice residencies in hospitals in which some training with the handicapped may be included.

Up to this point, most of the discussion has been confined to the training of the general dentist and the specialist in dentistry. Other than the dentist, the only other dental professional who is presently trained and licensed to perform intraoral functions is the dental hygienist. Some states are now changing their statutes to allow dental assistants to perform limited oral functions and are also requiring formal training and licensure of these assistants. The dentist is required to attend eight years of dental school and is awarded a D.D.S. or D.M.D. degree. The dental hygienist in most states can be trained in either a two-year community college, receiving an A.A.

degree or certificate, or in a four-year program at the baccalaureate level, being awarded a B.S. in Dental Hygiene with the official designation of R.D.H. (Registered Dental Hygienist) coming after licensure. There are some states that do not yet require formal training, and a hygienist can be trained under a preceptorship after working for a number of years under the supervision of a dentist.

Specialized training for the hygienist, who, up to this time, has been performing routine preventive services for the general population, is now taking place in dental schools, hospitals, and UAFs. Currently, the hygienist in many institutions of learning is being trained to manage the physically and mentally handicapped in a private office setting in which he/she might be called upon to perform an oral prophylaxis (scaling, cleaning, and polishing of the teeth) and also to train the patient to perform certain preventive dentistry home-care procedures. In addition, the hygienist is being prepared to function in a clinical or institutional setting in which he/she would not only be responsible for the individual patients to whom he/she is assigned but also for those inservice educational programs designed to develop and maintain sound preventive dentistry practices. Training in the clinical area may take place within the regular dental hygiene curriculum for all students during the two- or four-year program or might be offered as an elective to only those students who express a special interest in this area.

The dentist, in order to develop specialized skills, must take two additional years of training beyond dental school. In these programs, training with the handicapped is a requirement. For those dentists and hygienists who do not desire to take the extra schooling, many continuing education courses are now being funded by private, state, and federal agencies to provide extra training to the professional who either was not previously afforded the opportunity or who had not seen the reason for it. Now, either because of the demands being placed on them by these populations and their advocates or because of a personal interest in learning more about the handicapped, they are seeking out additional knowledge.

The dental assistant, a vital component of the dental team, historically has been trained on the job. With increasing demands being placed upon the profession, many schools, both private-commercial or state-community operated, now offer various types of formal training in dental assistance. These programs range from several months to one-year certificate programs with the title of C.D.A. (Certified Dental Assistant) being awarded after successful completion of the certificate program and the certifying examination. With few exceptions, the dental assistant receives little or no training with the special patient and usually has to learn on the job or in special continuing education courses.

At present, there are no specific licensing requirements for dental professionals who perform routine care and prevention with handicapped populations. However, other certifying bodies that accredit organizations or institutions, do have rules and regulations. Unfortunately, these regulations are often written in vague terms and are thus open to a wide degree of interpretation. The Joint Commission on Accreditation of Hospitals has guidelines for what should be included in a hospital dental program, but, unless there are gross discrepancies, there are very few problems brought to the attention of the dental administration. The same would hold true for the Commission on Accreditation of Mental Retardation Facilities. Because most of these organizations are interested mainly in the overall medical care of the client population, it is seldom that the dental staff comes under severe scrutiny, except in cases of gross negligence. Thus, while there are accrediting bodies whose roles are to monitor institutions and programs relevant to the quality of care of the clients, they do not involve themselves in the intricacies of specific patient care. Monitoring usually consists of looking at other areas such as facility design, sanitation, and records review.

RESEARCH NEEDS

There are several areas of dental research that, if developed, could change the picture of the care that is presently delivered to handicapped populations. Some of the more notable areas are in the field of behavioral methods of managing patients, improved pharmacological agents that are safer and more effective, improved techniques and methodologies to manage the handicapped, creation of new equipment to make the dental experience more tolerable, more effective means of preventing dental disease (such as an oral vaccine for caries and periodontal disease), and improved experimentation on the use of the teeth as markers in the detection and diagnosis of various forms of intrauterine malformations (teeth can be used as markers for certain injuries that occur prenatally). While there are numerous other areas of research, the few detailed above are vital ones. Results of such research promise to make a significant improvement over present means of care.

COSTS AND INSURANCE

From a management standpoint, the time and the cost of providing dental care have been and continue to be problems, especially in light of the increasing use of third party payments. Much of this has historical significance because dentistry, from its inception, has been selling "nuts and bolts." It is not uncommon for the question to be asked, "How much do you charge for a filling?" Because there are so many variables that go into making up the answer, it is often difficult to predict, in advance, what a particular service will cost. This is especially true if service is performed on a patient who is difficult or unmanageable. While other professionals have been able to determine their fee structures according to the amount of time spent with a client, the dentist has not yet been able to do so. It is not uncommon to have a fee schedule for one-half or one hour of time of a physical therapist, a social worker, attorney, psychiatrist, etc. The dentist, however, often finds it difficult to defend the same approach with a client. To the client, "a filling is a filling," no matter how much time goes into providing this service. This, of course, is a reflection of the patient's or family's attitude toward the importance of dentistry in the overall health care of the client. Many families have a difficult time justifying to themselves why they should have to pay for time devoted to being educated about dental disease. Preventive dentistry programs may require two, three, or more sessions of counseling. If they were to receive counseling in other disciplines such as genetic counseling or family counseling, they would certainly expect to be charged a fee. People, however, have not been conditioned to going to a dental office or clinic and not having something tangible performed, such as a filling, a cleaning, or surgery. When families are faced with a visit or multiple visits to learn how to control disease, the dental staff is often faced with a natural resistance and reluctance because the clients frequently believe that no one needs to tell them about preventive dentistry; everybody knows how to brush their teeth and that candy causes cavities. Thus, it is thought that to charge a fee for this preventive dentistry program is absurd.

The attitude cited above is not a cynical view but a commonplace reaction in a dental setting. While there has been much improvement in the area of acceptance of preventive dentistry concepts, there is still a great deal of territory to be covered. These attitudes have been perpetuated by third party insurance carriers. Insurance companies view dentistry as expensive and a poor risk and, consequently, provide little, poor, or no coverage. It is difficult to explain that preventive dentistry is inexpensive and that, if people could be trained to prevent dental disease, reparative or surgical and prosthetic dentistry would not be necessary or, if they were, they would be less costly. Much of this has to do with the feeling of the inevitability of dental disease.

In addition to poor coverage, insurance companies still consider that a filling is a filling. If a client requires a filling, it is possible for that procedure to be completed in 15 minutes to one-half hour. If the patient is uncontrollable, however, and requires sedation, the dentist may need one hour or maybe even two hours to treat that same tooth. Under these circumstances, the dentist is not given any additional money for that extra time and effort. In some cases, the only fee received might be six to 10 dollars for several hours of difficult work. This is an inequitable system. Also, third party insurance companies do not usually pay for preventive dentistry services, thereby providing little or no incentive for the professional wishing to provide this service. Thus, the dental professional is faced with either providing an important service and not getting reimbursed or not delivering the service at all. Other professionals faced with the same dilemma have submitted claims for services not performed in order to receive equitable financial rewards for their services. This is not meant to justify such behavior but is presented to spotlight the shallowness of the system.

To further complicate the system, because third party insurance does not recognize the importance of preventive dentistry, the dentist often receives more money to remove a tooth than to repair it by means of a filling. There is a greater incentive for the surgical removal of teeth rather than the repair. To demonstrate further how inane this system is, the insurance company will, in addition to paying the dentist to remove teeth, also pay hundreds of dollars to replace them.

It is estimated that nearly one-third of our country today is covered by some form of third party dental insurance, whether it is governmental, individual-private, or through union benefits. With this trend, it will not be long before all Americans have some type of coverage for dental care whether it is a comprehensive plan or a limited one. The problem, however, remains the same: dental care, while being considered a luxury and an expensive one, has yet to come to terms with the time and costs necessary to provide quality dental care for handicapped populations. Most of the fee schedules that have been created for private offices or third party coverage do not take into account the problems dental professionals face in caring for handicapped patients. A mechanism for equitable reimbursement does not presently exist.

The purpose of this discourse has been to capture the essence of the rationale of the dental team functioning within an interdisciplinary framework. It is also intended to demonstrate the polarization of professional philosophies that exists within the dental profession and between dentists and colleagues from other professions. While the concepts and information within this chapter are familiar to many in the dental profession, they, to this date, have not been isolated and presented in a written format to other human service professions. Thus, the intent is to reveal some of the problems typical of professional teams and to present pertinent information for use by team members. By doing this, it is hoped that an increased awareness on the part of other professionals may be realized and an appropriate forum created so that dentistry may exist more harmoniously with the other disciplines as they function cooperatively on interdisciplinary teams.

PROFESSIONAL ORGANIZATIONS

Several organizations have been most instrumental in improving the quality of dental care to the handicapped population. These are given here as a means of reference for further information:

Academy of Dentistry for the Handicapped, 1240 East Main Street, Springfield, Ohio 45503

American Academy of Pedodontics, 211 East Chicago Avenue, Suite 1235, Chicago, Illinois 60611

The American Dental Association, 211 East Chicago Avenue, Chicago, Illinois 60611

The American Society of Dentistry for Children, 211 East Chicago Avenue, Chicago, Illinois 60611

National Foundation of Dentistry for the Handicapped, 1121 Broadway, Suite 5, Boulder, Colorado 80302

SUGGESTED READINGS

Dental management of the handicapped child (A Symposium). 1974. The University of Iowa, Iowa City, Iowa.

Fox, L. A. 1973. Preventive dentistry for the handicapped child. Pediatr. Clin. North Am. 20:245–258.

Fox, L. A. 1974. Dentistry for the handicapped child. Dent. Clin. North Am. 18:533–735.

Fox, L. A., and O'Brien, E. M. 1976. Dentistry. *In* R. B. Johnston and P. R. Magrab (eds.), Developmental Disorders, Assessment, Treatment, Education, pp. 341–362. University Park Press, Baltimore.

Nizel, A. E. 1972. Nutrition in Preventive Dentistry: Science and Practice. W. B. Saunders, Company, Philadelphia.

Nowak, A. J. (ed.). 1976. Dentistry for the Handicapped Patient. The C.V. Mosby Company, St. Louis, Mo.

EDUCATION

Florence Christoplos
and Peter J. Valletutti

EDUCATION: NATURE AND GOALS

An understanding of potential educational contributions to interdisciplinary efforts is dependent on an awareness of the unique nature of educational goals. In a rapidly changing society, *all* institutional goals should be frequently reexamined. Educational goals are especially subject to societal values, however, and should thus be more sensitively and more widely reexamined by all the citizens of a society and not just by professional educators. "What should the young be taught?" is a question for which there is no final answer. Periodic reconsideration by succeeding generations ensures a balance between stability and flexiblity needed for societal growth and institutional relevance.

Neglect or refusal to consider educational goals and their priorities is nevertheless widespread. Horizontal and nonprioritied listings of multifarious goals are grossly inflexible and ineffective. Such listings, however, are the frequent consequence of neglecting periodic goal examination. When everything is supposed to be taught to everyone, education becomes lost in a morass of superficial training; students either learn in spite of educational floundering or join the legions of educationally handicapped.

Answers to the problems of ranking educational goals cannot be found in educational or social research and technology. The values and beliefs, including myths, of the society determine such priorities. Determining priorities is particularly difficult in societies that are complex and profess a pluralistic philosophy of development. The difficulty is evidenced by the bypassing in much of the professional literature of discussions of educational goals in favor of methodological discussions. This neglect occurs despite the obvious futility of arguing how best to accomplish something without clearly understanding what is to be accomplished.

Nor does the neglect of goal identification clarify the interfering and possibly handicapping interaction effects that exist among various goals. Consider, for example, generally desirable goals such as positive attitudes toward continued learning, valuing of human rights and differences, and compassion for others. Whether or not such goals are assigned to the domain of educational responsibilities is irrelevant because the methods used to achieve more narrowly stated educational skill and knowledge objectives affect these broader attitudinal goals. *How* more narrowly stated objectives are taught has a powerful impact on the broader goals of attitude and value development. The high risk of social disparagement resulting from school failure, the competitive striving for grades, and the emphasis on comparative scores inherent in standardized testing cannot help but adversely affect goals of compassion and respect for the dignity of others. Laurels for achievement are won because of the *lesser* achievement of others as assessed by society. Achievement is primarily an individual experience rather than a group experience in our society, and failure results in a keenly felt sense of individual inadequacy.

The problem of goal conflicts is not raised here to resolve it but rather to stress the difficulty of describing the role of education and the educator within the interdisciplinary team. With handicapped persons even more than with the nonhandicapped, the question of goal priorities is crucial and is a primary concern for the educator. For example, the best way to teach beginning math to a 16-year-old, illiterate, cerebral-palsied youth cannot be determined without considering such elements as:

1. The possible long range effects of group or individualized instruction on social development
2. The wisdom of using traditional curricula that stress the development of math concepts rather than curricula that stress functional math applications such as money, map reading, chart reading, time estimation, and time mechanics skills
3. The advisability of delaying all efforts to teach math until specified social and physical competencies are more proficiently managed (priorities!)

Teachers work with students who are expected to progress toward the achievement of at least the seven main objectives of education as developed by the 1937 Commission on Reorganization of Secondary Education (1937): health, command of fundamental processes, worthy home membership, vocation, citizenship, worthy use of leisure, and ethical character. Educators usually assume that a number, if not most, of the above objectives will be learned incidentally rather than intentionally throughout the formal school years. Nevertheless, students are expected to exhibit progress toward all the objectives in their informally demonstrated behavior, in and out of school.

From time to time, teachers may change their priorities for an individual student, small groups, or an entire class. The obvious neglect or retardation of one area of development or another in a particular student, however, is dramatic and difficult to ignore when the student is attending classes with peers for many hours, many days, over many years. However, justifying the exclusion of specific traditional skills from a student's curriculum in order to stress nontraditional skills requires clarifying values and expectations. This task is not easy for professional *or* lay persons who maintain traditional views based on personal experience with traditional education. The problem is caustically described by satiric example in *The Saber-Tooth Curriculum* (Benjamin, 1939): killing saber-toothed tigers continues to be part of the educational curriculum after the animal is extinct. Indeed, educators today spend as much, if not more, time justifying outdated curricula than examining current values and needs.

In education, the problem of setting goal priorities is more difficult than, for example, it is in medicine. Few would question the need to sacrifice a limb to save a life. No such clarity exists concerning the need to sacrifice one educational goal for another. Changing traditional school curricula is akin to heresy. We may discuss *how* to teach the naming of rectangles, squares, and triangles to preschoolers or to severely handicapped students, but we ignore or disparage those who question *if* we should teach these skills. As with many other professions, the technology of "how" has far outdistanced the ability to answer value questions of "why" or "to what end."

A potent argument for reexamining curriculum content for mentally handicapped people is found in Edgerton's survey (1967) of the self-expressed needs of independently functioning retarded adults. He raised serious questions about the appropriateness of what is taught to the mentally handicapped. Those persons interviewed considered number skills, time, and direction skills of far greater practical value than reading skills. Nevertheless, if any one skill holds priority in education today, it is reading. If the content of the school curriculum were to be changed based upon estimations of present and future needs for specific segments of the school population, then mastery of specific skills would be much affected. How much and how well one learns are undeniably related to what one is required to learn.

Intraprofessional problems in goal identification are further complicated by interprofessional differences in goal orientation (Christoplos, 1970). For example, medically oriented professionals generally tend to focus on goals of eliminating or minimizing biologically or physically based problems, most often by searching for causes to treat. Psychologically oriented professionals generally tend to focus on goals of changing, eliminating, or developing present behaviors, most often by manipulating the present environment. Educationally oriented professionals generally tend to focus on broad, long range goals of adjustment and achievement by developing skills, knowledge, and attitudes that may be useful in a largely unpredictable future. Thus, educational goals must be dynamic and fluid enough to be sensitive to the uniquely developed and expressed student indicators (measurable and intuitive) that suggest a proper curriculum has been implemented or still needs to be identified.

Defining specific achievement objectives is, therefore, only part of the educational concern. Measuring unique indications of advancement toward long range goals that cannot reliably be researched is an elusive, but equally essential, aspect of education. Unfortunately, this task often defies definition and mastery criteria. Such objectives remain in the realm of tacit knowledge (Polanyi, 1966) in that those areas of knowledge at the frontiers of our understanding are intuitively acknowledged but as yet unarticulated. Broadly stated goals, to be achieved at some distant point in time, in an unpredictable future, are not easily subjected to rigorous evaluation. The result is diminished accountability and lack of precision in goal identification, a factor to be faced rather than changed.

A further difficulty in goal identification in education rests with education's extraordinary sensitivity to and control by the public. More educational change has, in fact, been precipitated by pressures from noneducational sources than by educators themselves. And why not? Haven't all of us experienced years of educational treatments? Therefore we "know" from first hand experience. Aren't the schools public institutions that have an obligation to be responsive to the public in establishing policy? Therefore, as citizens, are we not fulfilling a civic responsibility by expressing our opinions? To withhold advice may be regarded as an indication of public apathy toward the improvement of education.

In conclusion, therefore, when educators are participants on interdisciplinary teams, the initial problem of educational goal identification for a client must first be resolved by the education team member and clarified to the noneducational team members. Unless this resolution is achieved early in the team process, educational concerns are likely to be lost or blurred by the team focus on psychological and/or medical problems and goals. A vigilant and articulate educational team member is critical.

THE ROLE OF THE EDUCATOR

The nature of educational goals suggest, in part, the unique characteristics of the educator's role. Above all, the educator is a generalist; a gestaltist looking at the student's broad individual life-style and goals. Educators tend to be more holistically than analytically oriented (Witkin, 1976). Although day-to-day classroom activities may be more analytical in nature, the primary focus of attention in education should be long range. This long range focus logically must influence the evaluation of day-to-day classroom activities as much as immediate achievement records. An educator must keep in the foreground of attention the ultimate goals that are implicit in the individual student's curriculum.

Certainly, long range goals are not the exclusive interest of educators. All service professionals are interested in what happens to a client beyond the immediate habilitation or rehabilitation goals. The difference is one of emphasis. Educators must focus attention on the acquisition of strategies of learning and problem solving, attitudes and values related to continued learning, intelligent and active citizenship, vocational and social competency, aesthetic and humanistic awareness, health, and recreational habits. Day-to-day curricula should have a clear relationship to these broad goals. Furthermore, beyond each separate goal, the educator needs to be aware of the interaction effects of any single intervention or treatment on any or all of the other long range goals.

In addition to a special awareness of long range goals and their interrelatedness, the educator also must be conversant with how learning is shaped by the constraints arising from the nature of the disciplines from which the curriculum is derived. For example, the nature of aesthetics requires the learner to explore and work with various media and to develop a heightened sensual sensitivity in order to express his/her personal ideas, affect, or emotions through the art media. Unlike aesthetics, however, the nature of mathematics requires an understanding of the principles and theorems that control a completely objective system of knowledge. The nature of these and other specific disciplines determines the methods of teaching in each area of knowledge, with greater or lesser degrees of reference to authoritative sources being one of several factors to consider in teaching techniques. Thus the educator, whose specialty may superficially be viewed as how to teach, should be guided by what and who to teach as well. The educator is thus the supreme generalist, deeply dependent on information from other disciplines for greater understanding of the nature of clients and of subject matter, but independently responsible for applying information from other disciplines to the total learning environment.

For the handicapped, much in the way of treatment intervention is realized through education. The educator is expected to incorporate specialized treatments from other disciplines into the larger educational plan. For example, in addition to the usual educational elements and their interactions (e.g., student, subject, teacher, learning environment), with the handicapped, the teacher also may consider such elements as motivating a student to wear a prosthetic device, reducing frustration for a volatile personality, providing practice for needed motor skills, unusual sleep or rest patterns, specialized nutritional needs, provision of Braille or enlarged print texts, and innumerable other special needs. In addition, overriding learning needs may have to influence all other considerations, as, for example, when teaching functional living skills to severely handicapped persons. The teacher must, at all times, explicitly teach the safety hazards involved at all points, a knowledge that may be assumed to be incidentally learned by nonhandicapped students but not so with this particular group (Bender and Valletutti, 1976).

Another aspect of the educational process that requires a more holistic than analytical approach is the prolonged association of the handicapped with educators and education. Next to parents and family members, only educators have the opportunity for observations of clients over such long periods of time and under such varied conditions and times of day. Insight into broad developmental patterns would be difficult, if not impossible, without this unique opportunity for comprehensive observation. The effects and intereffects of treatments are a daily reality to the observant teacher who spends approximately six hours daily with a student in different situations for months at a time. Thus, in working with the handicapped, observation skills of teachers and family members may be of tremendous value to other service disciplines as well as to themselves in assessing both client needs and effectiveness of interventions.

Training of observation skills must not be limited to techniques in observing and recording measurable behaviors. General inferences about behavior that are intuitively understood also must be given serious consideration and weight, particularly in arriving at educational decisions. In fact, that which is tacitly understood (in Polanyi's sense of critical but unarticulated knowledge) is often more comprehensive and important than more narrow and measurable behaviors. Focusing on discrete behaviors will often serve to destroy the understanding of overall purposive actions that encompass and yet go beyond the immediate behavior. For example, whether a student pronounces words smoothly and correctly is not as important as whether the student's thoughts, needs, and feelings are intelligently and appropriately expressed. Whether a student throws a ball correctly is not as important as the student's confidence and enjoyment in participating in a game of catch with peers. In both these cases, an excessive attention to a more narrowly stated problem can actually interfere with the broadly stated need.

Because of the prolonged relationship of the teacher and student, the effects of the teacher's personality and teaching style on the student and of the student's learning style on the teacher become important considerations (Thelen, 1967). The research efforts of Thomas, Chess, and Birch (1968) and Thomas and Chess (1977) are particularly pertinent to an understanding of the interpersonal and emotional problems that arise from interaction conflicts between personality patterns and under particular situational demands. The combination of the personality characteristics of irregularity, nonadaptability, negative mood, high intensity, and high persistence were identified as most frequently associated with behavior disorders. The more common identification of these same characteristics as indications of a disturbed personality has led to extensive and unnecessary, as well as punitive, referrals and labeling. The researchers found that, through understanding the personalities of two interacting individuals (e.g., parent and child or teacher and student), an accommodation in situational expectations often occurs. When characteristics are understood as differences in personality and not as disturbed personalities, more severe problems of adjustment may be averted by considerate accommodation to these differences.

Clearly, then, teachers should be especially aware of their own personality as well as those of their students. With such awareness, three benefits accrue: 1) requirements, expectancies, and organization of time and classroom activities and furniture are modified to accommodate personality interactions; 2) respect for variations in personality reduces labeling of students as deviant; 3) consequent overreferrals for psychiatric help are reduced. Instead of lip service to individual differences, educators should focus on the nature of unique differences and the required environmental and personal accommodations that can be made.

Another essential feature of the teacher's role is the need to obtain the cooperation and participation of the parent or parent surrogate in the student's educational program. The importance of parent-teacher cooperation has become so obvious, at least in early childhood programming (Bronfenbrenner, 1974), that no educational demonstration grants are being awarded in that area unless multilevel parent involvement is incorporated into the program plan. In those cases where parents are participating at all levels, including policy making advisement, a full compatability with and an understanding of school goals must exist. Under such circumstances, parents become the most vocal advocates of school needs and policies. In those cases where parents have not yet assumed a full partnership role, teachers must assume the critical responsibility of clarifying, justifying, and educating parents to school needs and policies. Schools are thus responsible for being extremely sensitive to the values, life-styles, and expectations of the families who entrust their children to them. Bronfenbrenner's review of research clearly shows that as family participation increases, child achievement increases. Furthermore, it is indisputable that public education is a service institution in which sensitivity to public pressure is considered an essential aspect of responsive and effective policy making.

The final characteristic of the teacher's role to be discussed is the group nature of schooling. With current trends toward the greatest possible normalization of experience for all handicapped students and with increasing student heterogeneity, teachers are provided with a constant framework of reference to normality. Although individualization of school programs is constantly being advocated, group goals are and will remain a part of the educational system. At times, group goals will take precedence over individualized goals. The teacher must be aware of the intereffects of goals not just for one student but for all students. Socialization skills that are learned at school are as essential an educational component as academic ones. These socialization skills are intricately meshed with the group goals set for students and classes. Heterogeneous socialization experiences are, perhaps, that developmental component which the school is uniquely equipped to provide, encourage, and facilitate. This component serves as an equalizer among students, at best imbuing them with a vital sense of responsibility to others and society. An exclusive emphasis on individualized goals fails to consider this important need for developing a social and civic consciousness.

School-based interdisciplinary interventions have not had a notably successful history. A large portion of school funds has been allocated to obtain the services of noneducational professionals. Little funding support, however, has been given either to teach consulting professionals what educational concerns are or to teach educators about the limits and nature of the advice they receive from noneducators. Educators have often found themselves frustrated and confused because the interdisciplinary information provided them revolved around causes of problems or around a limited set of immediate behaviors and objectives. This information invariably did not treat the problem of how this focus on causes and limited behaviors is related to important educational goals or expectations.

The teacher is generally recognized as the central recipient of interdisciplinary attentions in school settings, a recipient who, in addition to the more educationally specific task of preparing educational goals and programs for all students, is expected to:

1. Identify the most propitious time for remediation of problems
2. Seek appropriate resources for assistance in both understanding and remediating the problem
3. Provide needed information to the professional resources being asked for assistance
4. Interpret information and suggestions coming from professional resources
5. Infer programmatic implications from suggestions and information coming from professional resources
6. Implement suggestions from professional resources in the classroom
7. Involve parents in the implementation process
8. Evaluate the intervention effects so that helpful feedback and modification of programming may occur

PROBLEMS AND ISSUES IN INTERDISCIPLINARY COOPERATION

As a result of unsuccessful interdisciplinary procedures, teachers have resented interventions as interferences, have misunderstood and sabotaged prescribed interventions, and have felt imposed upon and looked down upon by noneducational service professionals who prescribe from afar, who promise inflated results if suggestions are followed, and who have no idea of the realities of spending six hours a day, five days a week, in close contact with large numbers of students.

In offering advice to teachers, another aspect of the school situation that must be considered is that social adjustment to school experiences is necessary for achievement of other educational goals. Flexibility in curriculum and classroom management may not be available to all teachers. They may have no control over scheduling or materials that are administratively prescribed. Community boards of education may impose further policy constraints that a teacher is obliged to follow. All children and youth (and increasingly the all is taken more and more literally) are expected to be served by public educational institutions. Students are expected to live with one another and with school authorities in a productive and cooperative manner for from 12 to 21 years. Students and their mentors learn that they must spend a certain number of prescribed hours, for a certain number of prescribed days, in a prescribed number of rooms, in a prescribed building, participating in prescribed activities, often in a prescribed manner. These organizational and plant requirements become another element to be considered. Individual problems of students can be realistically considered only when the above constraints are viewed along with the nature of educational goals, the nature of teacher values, skills, personality and teaching style, and the nature of the student's unique learning profile.

In interdisciplinary efforts to consider this vast array of variables that inevitably affect decisions, team members should have learned from experience what *not* to do:

1. They should not write reports that are incomprehensible to those reading them.
2. They should not make recommendations that are far removed from any possibility of implementation.
3. They should not advise others to use skills and materials that are not available to them.
4. They should not ignore the goals and problems of people directly involved in the problem situation.
5. They should not ignore the goals for other students in the classroom.
6. They should not initiate actions and programs for others without staying around to face the consequences.
7. They should not analyze problems by examining only one component

of the problem, e.g., psychological assessments, and ignoring broad institutional analyses and interventions.

8. They should not rely solely on indirect communications, e.g., reports and letters, to obtain knowledge of a problem but should make site visits.
9. They should not show such disrespect for teacher planning and management as to take students out for testing and examination without sufficient prior consultation and notification.
10. They should not assume that teachers are merely recipients of advice and information.
11. They should not ignore teaching styles, teacher observations, teacher inferences, teacher expectations of students (individual and group), and the pressures on teachers from outside the classroom.

How then may interdisciplinary teams successfully contribute to the teacher's effectiveness in the classroom? And what educational information may the team effectively utilize in its deliberations? These two questions are interdependent because education and noneducation team members profit equally from discussions and exchanges of information on the following:

1. How the handicapped student is affected by the physical environment of the classroom, learning areas, and the school building
2. The appropriate or expected length of time the student is likely to concentrate on a single task, quiet or active tasks, and easy or difficult tasks
3. How the student reacts to independent and group activities
4. The nature of specific recreational and leisure time skills and activities that should be included within the student's educational program
5. The various activity pacing possibilities, i.e., does the student need to complete the task in one sitting, or does he/she need to return to the task periodically before the task can be expected to be completed? Should there be a gradual or rapid change of activity? Must there be a slow or rapid instructional pace?
6. The nature of student interaction styles with peers and authorities
7. The levels of cognitive, perceptual, motor, social and aesthetic development
8. The student's reinforcement preferences
9. The effects of personality influences on curriculum, i.e., is the student slow to warm up to new places and tasks, what is the intensity of his/ her reactions, and what is the regularity of his/her habits?
10. How is the student affected by specific medication regimens and what are the possible effects on teaching and learning that teachers must attend to?

11. The nature of the student's nutritional needs, restrictions, regimens, and preferences
12. The nature of the student's learning style, i.e., is it visual or auditory, discovery or directed, impulsive or reflective, holistic or analytical, and is instruction better received from peers or adults?
13. The student's physical, emotional, and mental limitations vis-à-vis specific tasks and curricula areas
14. The nature of the values and goals of the student, of his/her family, and of the community
15. The rights of teacher and student and their responsibility in decision making
16. The care, use, and desirable practice regimens for use of prosthetic and orthotic devices

In cooperative efforts to determine the effects and intereffects of the intervention efforts, all team members are required to clarify and refine their observation techniques, their understanding of disciplinary similarities and differences, and their language. The team must become as one in their efforts to avoid parochialism and partitioning of responsibilities. Good will and openness to one another are fundamental. Within this cooperative effort, the educator may best contribute in the way of informal observation conclusions about client values and life-styles. The teacher, as a result of longer daily and yearly time periods spent with the student and his/her peers in a variety of situations, can be a most valuable informal observer. In addition, the teacher's long range observations are extremely valuable as a confirmation of the observations made by other disciplines, observations that frequently occur under more artificial conditions. The sharing of observational data may perhaps serve as a means of sharpening the observational skills of all participating team members. Such sharing should take place under conditions of mutual respect, good will, and open mindedness, with understanding of interdisciplinary differences in goals and perspectives. Proceeding from these conditions, a beginning toward effective and productive, continuing interdisciplinary teamwork may take place.

SELECTED PROFESSIONAL AND ADVOCACY ORGANIZATIONS

American Association on Mental Deficiency, 5201 Connecticut Avenue, N.W., Washington, D.C. 20015

Association for Children with Learning Disabilities, 2200 Brownsville Road, Pittsburgh, Pennsylvania 15210

National Association for Retarded Citizens, Inc., 2709 Avenue E East, Arlington, Texas 76011

The Council for Exceptional Children, 1920 Association Drive, Reston, Virginia 22091

REFERENCES

Bender, M., and Valletutti, P. J. 1976. Teaching the Moderately and Severely Handicapped. Vol. II. University Park Press, Baltimore.

Benjamin, H. 1939. The Saber-Tooth Curriculum. McGraw-Hill Book Company, New York.

Bronfenbrenner, U. 1974. A Report on Longitudinal Evaluations of Preschool Programs: Is Early Intervention Effective? Vol. II. DHEW Publication No. OHD 74-25, Government Printing Office, Washington, D.C.

Christoplos, F. 1970. A multi-disciplinary paradigm. J. Learn. Dis. 3:47–48.

Commission on Reorganization of Secondary Education. 1937. Cardinal Principles of Secondary Education. Bulletin 1918, No. 35, Government Printing Office, Washington, D.C.

Edgerton, R. B. 1967. The Cloak of Competence. University of California Press, Berkeley, Cal.

Polanyi, M. 1966. The Tacit Dimension. Doubleday, New York.

Thelen, H. A. 1967. Classroom Grouping for Teachability. John Wiley and Sons, Inc., New York.

Thomas, A., and Chess, S. 1977. Temperament and Development. Brunner/Mazel, New York.

Thomas, A., Chess, S., and Birch, H. 1968. Temperament and Behavior Disorders in Children. New York University Press, New York.

Witkin, H. A. 1976. Cognitive style in academic performance and in teacher-student relations. In S. Hessick (ed.), Individuality in Learning, pp. 38–73. Jossey-Bass, San Francisco.

GERONTOLOGY

Elise Michael
and Nancy Wilkey

Gerontology, derived from the Greek *geros,* means the study of the aged and the aging process of the later years. As an academic field of study and research, gerontology has been in existence since at least the 1920s. As a field of human service, it is little more than 10 years old and, as such, has been called the fastest growing field in academe (Watkins, 1977).

It is appropriate that a volume focusing on interdisciplinary approaches to human services includes a chapter on gerontology because gerontology, as a field of basic study, is multidisciplinary and, as a field of human service, is interdisciplinary. The human individual ages as a physical being whose organ systems and basic cellular structure are changed with the passage of time, a concern of physiologists. In addition, there may be changes in personality, perceptions, learning, and memory, all aspects of aging which interest psychologists. People are social beings whose roles in later years are markedly different from those of young adulthood. Sociologists are interested in these aspects of aging. Biochemists and economists study aging from the perspective of their disciplines. Gerontology, therefore, is a field of study that embraces the contributions made by multiple disciplines to the study of aging.

Human service professionals use the knowledge provided by these disciplines as a theoretical base in the solution of problems faced by the aged and the aging. No one professional group has all the knowledge and skill needed. Many professionals, including counselors, educators, social workers, nurses, doctors, recreational, occupational, and physical therapists, nutritionists, dentists, and architects, must use their specialized knowledge to meet the needs of the elderly. If the results are to be effective and efficient, these professionals must work, not alone, but as a team.

Ten years ago, there were five university gerontological centers, plus a few academic programs. Today, there are at least 15 centers. According to a national directory published by the Association for Gerontology in Higher Education, there are 1,257 different educational programs (Watkins, 1977). Many of these programs have received support through the passage of the

Older Americans Act of 1965 which created an Administration on Aging. This legislation was a response to the increasing numbers of elderly in the population whose needs are pressing.

This phenomenal growth has occasioned some concern about service quality. In the haste to implement programs, there has not always been sufficient planning. In addition, adequately prepared personnel are not available to develop and teach in rapidly proliferating programs.

DEFINITION OF AGING

When does a person become old? Kalish (1975) has suggested five ways of defining the word: 1) in terms of chronological age, 2) in terms of physical change, 3) in terms of behavioral change, 4) in terms of social roles, and 5) in terms of self-report. Since the passage of Social Security legislation in 1935, the chronological focus has, perhaps, provided the most salient definition. This legislation provided that the individual who had paid Social Security taxes for a certain number of years could retire at age 65 and receive Social Security benefits. Since 1935, employers have increasingly linked the age at which benefits may begin with mandatory retirement. Thus, age 65, the age of retirement, has come to be defined as the chronological age at which one becomes old.

Retirement at age 65 implies loss of a social role—that of worker or wage earner. This frequently means that the person becomes less active. Lack of activity may lead to physical deficits. When society defines one as old, one may come to view onself as old. Thus, Kalish's definitions can be seen as overlapping because the definition of old in terms of chronological age may be related to the other definitions.

INCREASING NUMBERS

In 1970, approximately 10% of the United States population was 65 or older. This segment of the population is growing and will continue to grow into the next century. At the turn of the 20th century, life expectancy at birth was 48.2 years. In 1974, it was 71.9 (Brotman, 1977). This increase in life expectancy has largely resulted from medical advances in the field of maternal and child health. Fewer mothers die because of childbirth-related factors. Better maternal care also results in more infant survivors. In addition, better control and better treatment of childhood diseases mean more children live to become adults.

Some gains have been made in the mortality rates of older age groups. The control of infections through the use of antibiotics and chemotherapeutic agents and technological advances in diagnosis and treatment of other diseases have led to these improvements. Advances in the field of

Photograph by Laura Christoplos.

geriatrics (medical treatment of the elderly) have, as yet, not produced striking results. In 1900, those who reached the age of 65 could expect to live 11.9 more years; in 1974, that age group could expect to live 15.6 more years. In approximately 70 years, therefore, the increase in life expectancy at age 65 has amounted to only 3.7 years.

Comparison of absolute numbers shows that, in 1900, those between 65 and 75 years of age totaled three million; by 1940, the number of people in this age group was nine million, and, by 1970, it had reached 20 million (Bouvier, 1974). Part of the increase can be attributed to the increase in life expectancy that occurred during the period. Most of the gain in numbers, however, can be attributed to the extensive immigration that occurred around the turn of the century. It is projected that the over-65 age group in the United States will number 29 million in the year 2000. Effects of the post-World War II baby boom will be felt in the year 2020 when the over 65 population will reach 40 million (Bouvier, 1974).

CHARACTERISTICS OF THE ELDERLY

Today, those who fall in the age category of 65 and above number approximately 20 million. The median age of the elderly is 73 years (Brotman, 1974). This means that about 10 million are 65–73 and 10 million are over 73, with the older members of this second group increasing in numbers more quickly (Brotman, 1974). Included among the present elderly population are those who came to the United States in the great wave of immigration that swept the country in the latter part of the 1800s and the early 1900s. Characteristics of this immigrant group are quite different from those of the elderly group born in the United States. While the educational level of both groups is below the current standards of today's formal learning, there are also differences that reflect the culture into which each was socialized as a child. Chief among these is language. English became a second language for the immigrant, and many continued to speak the native tongue in the home. Many settled in ethnic enclaves where they continue to live. The effect of ethnicity on the aging process is largely unknown because this characteristic has been neglected in gerontological research (Ward, 1977).

In the upper age groups, women are likely to outnumber men two-to-one (Randall, 1977). Although more males than females are born, males tend to die sooner than females, this statistic being observable even in utero. In the twenties, the ratio of men to women tends to equalize, but, beyond that age, females predominate. By the time old age is reached, two-thirds of elderly women are widows (Butler and Lewis, 1977). Women tend to marry men older than themselves and to outlive their husbands. At the time of widowhood, women find a limited number of similarly aged men for remarriage. Compounding this situation is the fact that those relatively few men who outlive their wives are likely to remarry younger women. This leaves a large number of females without companionship and without male partners for sexual gratification. The effects of widowhood on the aging process is another area in gerontology in which little is known (Kent, 1972). It is known that females are likely to be more isolated in old age and that they have higher rates of illness than do males (Ward, 1977).

In considering changes that occur in the individual as a result of aging, differentiating between the changes that occur because of the process of aging and changes that occur because of disease is difficult. Four out of five elderly persons have some known pathological condition. At the present time, it is known that a decrease in acuity of hearing, especially in the upper sound frequencies, is one change that does occur. Also, there is a decrease in near vision and in the ability to see at night. Changes in the nervous system slow reaction time. A general decrease in energy level comes with aging. Normal aging brings diminished renal function and alteration in sleep patterns. The decrease in energy that accompanies aging is associated with a diminished level of activity. Therefore, the number of calories needed is reduced.

Caloric intake, however, is frequently governed more by cultural patterns than by physiological need; the result is often an intake of excess calories.

In contrast to the common societal stereotype of the elderly person as a bedridden invalid, the elderly tend to rate their health as good (Maddox and Douglass, 1974). They also tend to remain in their homes in the community.

Almost all of the elderly are, to some extent, victims of negative attitudes toward old people. In a society oriented toward youth and achievement, old age is dreaded and feared. Even those who study old age are not immune. It has been said that using the term aging rather than old is one reflection of societal attitude; aging implies that no one actually reaches old age, only moves toward it (Slater, 1964).

Cross-cultural studies have indicated that the esteem in which the elderly are held is dependent on the characteristics of the society in which they live (Slater, 1964). In general, societies that are authoritarian and static and in which important life decisions are made by the society or the extended family tend to allot higher prestige to the elderly than do societies characterized by democratic governmental systems and high regard for individualism. These latter societies hold old people in low esteem (Slater, 1964).

The United States, in general, is of the latter type. There are commu-

nities in some areas, such as rural pockets in Appalachia and ethnic enclaves within urbanized settings, whose characteristics tend to approximate
those of traditional societies. These subcultures may hold positive attitudes
toward the old. A recent study of the attitudes of rural adolescents toward
the elderly gives some evidence in support of this notion (Ivestor and King,
1977). Most studies of attitudes of the young toward the old, however, show
that the feeling is negative (Kastenbaum and Durkee, 1964b).

Negative attitudes toward the old are not the exclusive domain of the
young. Many elderly persons hold the same attitudes toward themselves
and, consequently, do not want to be defined as old. These negative feelings
result in low self-esteem which can lead to depression, a common
manifestation in this age group (Kastenbaum and Durkee, 1964a).

Retirement, or loss of occupational role, marks a point at which one
becomes a consumer rather than a producer of goods and/or services. This
role loss is accompanied by prestige loss, in the eyes of both the young and
the old themselves. Retirement may be forced, or it may be voluntary.
Recently, it has been estimated that two-thirds of wage and salary workers
retire voluntarily (Atchley, 1972). It is important to note, however, that the
majority of those who retire voluntarily do so for reasons of health
(Atchley, 1972). Thus, the definition of voluntary must be qualified.

Whether retirement is forced or voluntary, it usually means a drop in
income. In 1973, there were 3.4 million individuals aged 65 or older and
800,000 heads of families in the same age group with incomes below the
poverty level. The median per capita income was $2,400 for older women
and $4,500 for older men. In addition, there were 1.5 million elderly heads
of families who were classified as near-poor (Transportation for the Elderly,
1975). Many of these individuals and families had existed at or near the
poverty level most of their lives.

Currently, others at or near the poverty level are those who formerly
had an adequate, if not abundant, income and have become "new poor."
The problems that this latter group must face and adjust to are quite different from problems of the former group. This group lacks homogeneity, a
consideration often not taken into account by those who try to help in
retirement adjustment.

Another consequence of retirement is the shift from time spent in
productive activity to free time. In order to receive full Social Security
benefits, part-time employment, even if obtainable, must be limited
severely. It is difficult for those who value work to find meaning in time not
spent in gainful employment (Pfeiffer and Davis, 1974).

There are other correlates of retirement. There is the loss of interaction
with colleagues in the work situation as well as loss of work-related
activities, such as union and sports participation. Many workers have

looked to their work as a means of structuring time, and upon retirement, this structure is lost (Freidmann and Havighurst, 1954). Many of those who fall in the 65 and older age group were socialized into work roles before the 40-hour work week and, consequently, did not have large amounts of leisure time during much of their work life. They have not learned how to use leisure time, and the cessation of work and work-related activities represents major losses. There is some feeling that the meaning of work and leisure is changing. Those who retire in future years may have less difficulty in dealing with the transition from producer to consumer.

Contrary to commonly held beliefs, approximately 95% of the elderly live in the community rather than in institutions. Many of these elderly are faced with housing problems. Examination of the data on the housing situation shows that 70% own their homes, 27% rent, and 3% do not own homes and do not pay cash rent (Struyk, 1977). Fifty-five percent of elderly households are located in metropolitan areas, 16% are outside metropolitan areas (nonrural), and approximately 29% are located in rural areas (Struyk, 1977). Rural housing tends to be lower in quality than urban, but neighborhood conditions tend to be better. Regardless of location, it has been estimated that as many as 30% of the elderly live in substandard housing. Factors contributing to the deterioration of their housing include a fixed, limited income, limited physical abilities needed to maintain their properties, and escalating inflation.

Efforts, to date, to improve substandard housing have not been effective in providing decent housing for the elderly. Responsibility for this failure lies with the elderly themselves and with the communities. For example, some elderly are reluctant to live in public housing. Several reasons have been suggested for this reluctance including: unwillingness to be associated with the stigma of public housing, aversion to leaving their familiar surroundings and neighborhoods, lack of resources necessary to avail themselves of the opportunity, and emotional attachment to their own homes. For the elderly who are hesitant because of this latter reason, these houses may represent their life savings, even though they may be of limited value on the current market. Some communities have not provided a range of housing options for the elderly. As a result, the elderly in these communities, may have neither the option to live in public housing nor the resources to remain in their own homes. Community resistance has been a deterrent to the provision of adequate housing programs. Members of the community voice opposition to such programs on the basis of limitations to the tax base, creation of transportation problems, and disruption of residential ambience. The decrease in tax base and transportation problems are reality-based, while the disruption of ambience reflects a stereotypic prejudice.

In both rural and urban areas, transportation is difficult. With increasing age, it becomes increasingly difficult to get to such necessary places as health centers, banks, shopping centers, food stamp centers, and recreational centers. Declining physical abilities and income may limit private transportation as a solution to the problem. For some, public transportation represents a means of remaining mobile, but this means often is contingent upon learning a new set of transportation skills. Some elderly are unwilling or unable to learn the necessary skills, thus rendering this option inaccessible. For others, especially those in rural areas, public transportation may not be available. The urban elderly, however, with their greater opportunities for public transportation, may not use it. Availability of public transportation does not ensure its utilization. Some of the reasons offered for not using public transportation are reduction of services during nonpeak hours, lack of safety, lack of convenience imposed by needing exact fares, and lack of vehicle design to accommodate the physical changes accompanying aging (Transportation for the Elderly, 1975).

The elderly, in particular, and society, in general, have become concerned for their safety. Persons and possessions are no longer safe. As the elderly become more alone, as their physical and perceptual abilities decline, and as their schedules become more predictable, they become more vulnerable to physical assault. As a result, many elderly limit their activities outside the home to daylight hours. They are also unwilling to leave their homes on days Social Security checks are to be delivered, meeting the mail carriers at the door to prevent theft. Many of the elderly, especially those living in the high crime, center city areas, have become virtual prisoners in their own homes. It is interesting to note, however, that the crime rate against older people is no higher than against younger people (Hicks, 1977).

In spite of the fact that most elderly are not invalids, health becomes poorer in old age regardless of the methods used in its assessment (Lawton, 1974). Research on the normal aging processes has not clarified the relationship between these processes and disease processes. Despite confusion about this relationship, advancing age brings with it higher risk as evidenced by the fact that four out of five elderly persons suffer from some chronic condition (Brody, 1974). Many conditions are included in the classification of chronic conditions, such as visual or hearing impairments and disabling arthritis or heart disease. However, many elderly, classified as having chronic conditions, are neither disabled nor infirm. More specifically, about 25% have major problems resulting from a chronic condition, and only 5% require institutionalization (Butler and Lewis, 1977).

Regardless of the impact of chronic conditions on the elderly, they are a major utilizer of health services. They have more physician visits, more days with some degree of disability, more and longer hospital stays, and they spend more on drugs than younger age groups (Brotman, 1974). It has been estimated that elderly persons occupy 25% of all acute hospital beds and consume over 90% of the nation's resources spent on nursing homes. Surprisingly, they are not using outpatient psychiatric clinics; only 2% of the users of these facilities are elderly.

Another source of variation between older and younger populations is in expenditures for health services. Approximately 68% of the senior citizen's health bill is paid for by public funds (Hammerman, 1974). The remaining 32% may cause a financial burden or may be completely prohibitive for many elderly. The services provided by public funds place higher priority on treatment than prevention and rehabilitation. For example, 86.1% of all the elderly's hospital bill is paid, 71.3% of the doctor's bill, 60% of nursing home costs, but only 23% of the combined services of home care, dentistry, eyeglasses, and drugs (Hammerman, 1974). Such uneven distribution of payments helps to account for unfilled drug prescriptions and reluctance to take drugs because the prescriptions will have to be refilled. Many elderly only can afford to *be* sick because this is cheaper than assuming the costs involved with prevention.

HUMAN SERVICES NEEDED

From this analysis, certain needs become evident. These include: improvement in housing, transportation, safety, income, and health care facilities; opportunities to work; opportunities for meaningful activities and social interaction; assistance with adjusting to the loss of spouse; help in changing community attitudes toward the elderly. If the quality of life of this increasing minority is to improve, services must be provided to meet these needs.

For purposes of planning, Lowy (1972) has classified these needed services in five categories: 1) medically oriented, 2) oriented toward enhancing a person's ability to participate in the activities of daily living, 3) oriented toward maintaining social contact and participation, 4) problem solving and socially supportive, and 5) financial assistance. The medically oriented services include preventive, treatment, and rehabilitative services in a variety of settings. One of the more recent trends is for these services to be provided in the home. Even though the elderly prefer this setting, home services have evolved slowly.

Regardless of the setting, the elderly need adequate, efficient, appropriate, and convenient health services. Among the criteria for evaluating such services are the time it takes to be seen in the service, the convenience of transportation to the agency, the number of different personnel the elderly person must see, the amount of time the personnel in the agency allow for the person with declining physical abilities, and the complexity of the payment procedures. Reluctance to use these services indicate that these criteria are frequently not met.

For many senior citizens, services to enhance their ability to carry out the activities of daily living are necessary to enable them to maintain a level of independence. The elderly, themselves, rate these services higher than many other services (Keith, 1976). Assistance with homemaking, chores, grocery shopping, home repairs, and meal provision are some of the activities that are needed and are being provided in many communities.

Many programs have been developed to help the elderly remain active and involved in their environment. Currently, much attention is being paid to assisting the elderly in finding employment. Educational and recreational opportunities are increasing in number. The elderly are being offered many volunteer types of activities such as acting as foster grandparents, visiting the elderly, and providing transportation for the immobilized. For still others, there is contact with the environment through telephone visits. These are just a few of the approaches to helping the elderly maintain social contact and participation.

Counseling services are also essential. As noted previously, the elderly go through many disruptive changes such as loss of job, spouse, and health. Counselors can help the elderly to live with the consequent effects of these changes. Additional support can also be provided through legal, informational, and referral services, because the elderly are faced with many legal and emergency problems that are beyond their limited resources.

The elderly, because of reductions in their income, need financial assistance, which is available from a number of government programs. These include Social Security benefits, nutritional programs, Medicare, Medicaid, and food stamps. In order to use these services, the elderly must be aware of their existence and be able to overcome the bureaucratic complexities necessary to receive them.

Analysis of individual characteristics of elderly clients also suggests other variables that must be considered in the delivery of human services to this population. The wide variations within the aging process, the individualization of aging, and the heterogeneity of the group, indicate the need for a wide range of services for each category of service, allowing for a selection of alternatives. For example, in the area of housing, the elderly need to be able to select and live in a type of housing that is best suited to their needs. For some, this will be independent housing in houses, apartments, and mobile homes. For others, congregate living such as retirement residences, hotels, and apartments with common dining and service facilities will be preferable. Still others will need supervised housing in nursing and personal care homes (Levine, 1976). Government sponsored low rent housing is one means of providing living facilities. An alternative to furnishing housing facilities is providing the assistance necessary for the elderly to remain in their own homes, such as property tax relief measures, subsidized utilities and maintenance, and repair and chore services. Additional help could be given to the elderly to alter the design of their homes to be more compatible with their physical changes, thus allowing them to remain in their own homes.

Funding, interest, and creativity also influence the services that are being provided. For example, in the field of education, educators are realizing that education is a life experience, not just an experience for the young. Educational opportunities are being made available in a number of settings, including formal educational settings. Classes are being offered in nontraditional settings such as multipurpose centers, apartment complexes for the elderly, and in retirement homes for the aged. During the summer, the elderly are being provided with opportunities to live on college campuses in "Elderhostels," a concept that is growing across the country. A number of colleges provide offerings for which the elderly students move from campus to campus, taking a variety of courses throughout the experience. Not only is there wide variation in setting but also in offerings. Course offerings vary from regular courses, to current affairs, to special concerns of the elderly such as retirement, leisure time, and health.

Because many services are being supported by governmental or voluntary resources, these programs have limitations. For example, they are primarily designed for the low income elderly; therefore, those of modest means frequently are not eligible for these services. As stated previously, costs that have been reduced may still be a financial burden as may occur in the use of public transportation and health care services. The use of Medicare is compounded by the complexity of the reimbursement procedure. Many elderly are overwhelmed by the number of forms to be completed. In addition, these services are threatened by termination if funding is not continued or if contributions decline.

Finally, if services are to be used at their maximal capabilities, the services must be available, appropriate, effective, and efficient. Those services that require traveling, that have limited hours of operation, and that require long hours of waiting are not extensively supported by the elderly.

Currently, policy planners and decision makers lack the needed gerontological research on which to base the development of appropriate services. Some questions that remain unanswered are: When is institutional living preferable to community living? Do some elderly prefer institutional living to community living? What kinds of services are necessary to meet the needs of such a heterogeneous group? What services are needed by all older persons? What services do some older persons need on a temporary basis to help them through some unusual or critical experience such as loss of job, loss of a spouse, or an acute illness? What is the nature of the services needed during such periods? What services are needed by some elderly over a long period of time? Why do only some elderly avail themselves of services? How can community resistance to needed services be overcome? Answers to these questions will usher in an expansion of gerontological knowledge.

HEALTH SERVICE PERSONNEL

For the senior citizens who need large amounts of care by human service professionals, whether community-based or institutional, problems are presented by the lack of sufficient personnel. Negative attitudes toward the aging are again implicated. Frequently, professionals do not wish to work with this age group. Service personnel have been conditioned to consider success in treatment synonymous with cure and/or alleviation of the problem. Such an association is frequently not possible; this service area often does not provide personnel with a clear measure of success. Workers with the elderly need to develop new criteria for measuring success. Personnel are lacking also because of the fact that the rate of compensation, both monetary and with regard to status, for these services is often so low that competent, caring professionals cannot be attracted. Budgets do not allow for adequate numbers of positions; consequently, some clients are neglected, and professionals become frustrated and depressed by the less than optimal care that they can provide. Research is needed to determine the characteristics of people who prefer working with the elderly. The development of programs of recruiting and retaining personnel is dependent upon greater knowledge of career choices. Another approach is to find means of improving the status of human service providers for the elderly.

Adequate care for the elderly requires an interdisciplinary effort. Client condition dictates the members of the team. For the institutionalized client, organizational imperative and/or client need will dictate the leader of the human services team. For the community-based elder who needs large inputs from community resources, the team frequently must be client-formed and client-led. Unfortunately, the client is usually removed from the decision-making process, and this factor invariably affects the utilization of services. Unless the client is exceedingly competent, knowledgeable, and persistent, the results may, at best, be fragmented and, at worst, be tragic.

A variety of human service personnel is needed to provide services for the elderly. Each discipline has its own requirements for its preparation. Each discipline has its own means of certification of qualified practitioners. For the purposes of this chapter, only, the unique preparations related to working with the elderly are considered.

Because gerontology is a relatively new field, human service disciplines are only beginning to include this expanding body of knowledge into their curricula. Factors stimulating this inclusion are an increasing number of aged persons, an interest in their problems, and government funding of such programs. Before this recent trend, the providers of human services to the elderly prepared themselves on-the-job or, at most, attended a workshop or summer institute. Even after the need for educational programs was recognized, additions to curricula did not emerge immediately. Reasons offered for the delay were lack of qualified teachers, lack of student interest in gerontology as a field of study, a limited body of gerontological knowledge, and curricula that were already overcrowded (Lawton, 1976). For example, the disciplines of medicine, dentistry, and nursing have been very slow in affecting such changes (Gordon, 1972; Libow, 1977; Sargent, 1976).

With the increasing demand for people prepared to work with this age group, educational programs are now beginning to appear. The Administration on Aging under the Older American Act of 1965 has been supporting programs both to prepare and to utilize personnel. These programs include the skills of the human service disciplines, gerontological and/or geriatric knowledge, and functional skills such as administration, teaching, and research. There is little agreement as to the knowledge and skills needed by all human service providers in contrast to those that are only needed by specific disciplines.

A number of other variations exists in the nature of current educational offerings. One variation is focus. Some offerings are single discipline focused while others are multiple. Closely related to this variation is the number of educational institutions involved. Some educational programs are offered by a single institution while others are offered by a gerontology center comprised of a number of educational institutions. The latter are multidiscipline focused as well. Still another variation is level of offering; undergraduate, graduate, and/or continuing education levels. Undergraduate courses are designed to influence career decisions, alter attitudes toward aging, and provide students with knowledge that can help with living and planning for old age. In addition, some programs offer a concentration in gerontology to prepare graduates for functioning in direct service positions or lower level administrative ones (Sargent, 1976). Gerontological offerings at the graduate level are designed to prepare graduates for leadership positions in teaching, administration, and research. With this as a goal, these offerings must be more comprehensive in depth and breadth than those on the undergraduate level.

In addition to the other human service personnel, there are three categories of personnel specific to the field of gerontology: senior center directors, housing managers, and nursing home administrators (Kahl, 1976b).

Nursing home administrators have the responsibility of managing the personnel and services of a nursing home. This human service provider needs not only managerial skills but also knowledge of the legal constraints of operating a nursing home, of the health care delivery system, and of the aging process. Because of the emerging nature of this field, the preparation of this provider has not been well defined; however, licensing is required in all states and the District of Columbia. In all states, applicants must be 21 years of age, of good character, and suitable for such a job. The last two criteria lack specific guidelines for selection. Other requirements for licensing, in relation to educational requirements and renewal of licenses, vary from state to state. All states require that the applicant pass a written examination covering principles of administration, management of a long term care facility, the role of government in long term care, environmental health and safety, and the medical, psychological, and social aspects of care (Kahl, 1976a). Some states require additional preparation, such as an internship before the examination. As with other human service disciplines, educational institutions are offering programs for nursing home administrators. Short term and formal academic programs are evolving at the associate, bachelor's, and master's degree levels.

Housing management is another relatively new field that includes managing finances, personnel, policies, tenant selection, and rent collection, maintenance of the physical plant, tenant-management relations, and leasing and occupancy procedures. Managers need to be able to deal with housing problems as well as the social, psychological, and health problems of the aged.

The recent emergence of this human service provider has prevented the precise delineation of required professional preparation. Today, most training is on-the-job or in the form of continuing education. Currently, attempts are being made to upgrade the preparation of housing managers. The National Center for Housing Management has developed training programs for housing managers, and educational institutions are developing such programs. Two graduate programs have become available in retirement housing administration. The U.S. Department of Housing and Urban Development (HUD) is encouraging, through grants, the development of additional programs in housing management (Levine, 1976). HUD also is encouraging the professionalization of this field by requiring certification of those persons working in federally supported housing projects (Levine, 1976). By January 1978, all of these housing managers must be certified.

Similarly, the senior center director has emerged as another human service provider. Again, the director is an administrator managing an agency. The size of the agency influences the size of the staff and the range of programs for which the administrator is responsible. Fund raising, preparation of budgets, and the preparation of grant proposals are additional skills needed by this administrator. Preparation of the senior center director has not been delineated nor are educational programs available. The University of Oregon (Eugene) and the University of Michigan (Ann Arbor) offer courses in Senior Center Administration, while several state agencies on aging provide inservice courses for center administrators (Rones, 1976).

From this examination of the educational preparation of human service providers working with older persons, it is evident that many questions remain unanswered regarding the nature of offerings and the level of offerings required.

SUMMARY

Gerontology is a relatively new field for human service disciplines. Personnel in this field are provided with the opportunity to work with an increasingly large minority who are faced with multiple problems. As society has become more aware of the problems of the elderly, there has been an increased demand for services to alleviate their problems. Research is needed to provide policy makers with the knowledge upon which to base social policy and services.

PROFESSIONAL ORGANIZATIONS

Because many professions provide human services for the elderly, the following professional organizations and their addresses are included.

American Association of Homes for the Aging, 529 14 St., N.W., Washington, D.C. 20004

American College of Nursing Home Administrators, 8641 Colesville Road, Silver Spring, Maryland 20901

The American Geriatrics Society, 10 Columbus Circle, New York, New York 10019

American Health Care Association, 1200 15th St., N.W., Washington, D.C. 20005

American Nurses' Association, Inc., Division on Gerontological Nursing, 2420 Pershing Road, Kansas City, Missouri 64108

American Occupational Therapy Association, 251 Park Avenue South, New York, New York 10010

American Physical Therapy Association, 1740 Broadway, New York, New York 10019

American Public Health Association, 1015 Elizabeth Street, N.W., Washington, D.C. 20036

American Psychological Association, Division of Adult Development and Aging, 1200 17th St., N.W., Washington, D.C. 20036

American Sociological Association, 1722 N Street, N.W., Washington, D.C. 20036

American Speech and Hearing Association, 9030 Old Georgetown Road, Bethesda, Maryland 20014

Association for Gerontology in Higher Education, 1 Dupont Circle, Washington, D.C. 20036

The Gerontological Society, 1 Dupont Circle, Washington, D.C. 20036 (This organization consists of four components: Biological Sciences, Clinical Medicine, Psychological and Social Sciences, and Social Research, Planning, and Practice.)

The International Federation on Aging, 1909 K St., N.W., Washington, D.C. 20006

National Association of Social Workers, 1425 H St., N.W., Washington, D.C., 20005

National Association of Housing and Redevelopment Officials, The Watergate Building, 2600 Virginia Avenue, N.W., Washington, D.C. 20037

The National Association of State Units on Aging (Address shifts as presidency shifts)

The National Center on Black Aged, 1730 M Street, N.W., Suite 811, Washington, D.C. 20036

National Council for Homemaker-Home Health Aide Services, Inc., 67 Irving Place, New York, New York 22209

National Federation of Licensed Pratical Nurses, Inc., 250 West 57th St., New York, New York 10019

National Interfaith Coalition on Aging, 298 South Hill St., Athens, Georgia 30301

National Recreation and Park Association, 1601 North Kent, Arlington, Virginia 22209

REFERENCES

Atchley, R. C. 1972. Social Forces in Later Life. Wadsworth Publishing Company, Belmont, Cal.

Bouvier, L. F. 1974. Demograph of aging. In S. J. W. Bier (ed.), Aging: Its Challenge to the Individual and to Society, pp. 37–46. Fordham University Press, New York.

Brody, S. 1974. Evolving health delivery systems. Am. J. Public Health 64:245–248.

Brotman, H. B. 1974. The fastest growing minority: The aging. Am. J. Public Health 64:249–252.

Brotman, H. B. 1977. Life expectancy. Gerontologist 17:12–22

Butler, R. N., and Lewis, M. I. 1977. Aging and Mental Health. The C.V. Mosby Company, St. Louis, Mo.

Freidman, E., and Havighurst, R. 1954. The Meaning of Work and Retirement. The University of Chicago Press, Chicago.

Gordon, R. H. 1972. Meeting the dental needs of the aged. Am. J. Public Health 62:385–388.

Hammerman, J. 1974. Health services: Their success and failure in reaching older adults. Am. J. Public Health 64:253–256.

Hicks, N. 1977. Life after 65. Black Enterprise 7:18–22.

Ivestor, C., and King, K. 1977. Attitudes of adolescents toward the aged. Gerontologist 17:85–89.

Kahl, A. 1976a. Nursing home administrator. Occup. Outlook Q. 20:35–37.

Kahl, A. 1976b. Special jobs for special needs: An overview. Occup. Outlook Q. 20:2–5.

Kalish, R. 1975. Late Adulthood: Perspectives on Human Development. Brooks/Cole Publishing Company, Monterey, Cal.

Kastenbaum, R., and Durkee, N. 1964a. Elderly people view old age. In R. Kastenbaum (ed.), New Thoughts on Old Age, pp. 250–262. Springer Publishing Company, New York.

Kastenbaum, R., and Durkee, N. 1964b. Young people view old age. In R. Kastenbaum (ed.), New Thoughts on Old age, pp. 237–249. Springer Publishing Company, New York.

Keith, P. M. 1976. A preliminary investigation of the role of the public health nurse in evaluation of services for the aged. Am. J. Public Health 66:379–380.

Kent, D. P. 1972. Social policy and program considerations in planning for the aging. *In* D. P. Kent, R. Kastenbaum, and S. Sherwood (eds.), The Power and Potential of Social Science, pp. 3–19. Behavioral Publications, Inc., New York.

Lawton, A. H. 1976. The training of medical manpower in geriatrics. Geriatrics 31:111–113.

Lawton, M. P. 1974. Social ecology and the health of older people. Am. J. Public Health 64:257–260.

Levine, C. C. 1976. Housing manager. Occup. Outlook Q. 20:37–41.

Libow, L. 1977. The issues in geriatric medical education and postgraduate training: Old problems in a new field. Geriatrics 32:99–102.

Lowy, L. 1972. The role of social gerontology in the development of social services for older people. *In* D. P. Kent, R. Kastenbaum, and S. Sherwood (eds.), The Power and Potential of Social Science, pp. 20–36. Behavioral Publications, Inc., New York.

Maddox, G. L., and Douglass, E. B. 1974. Self assessment of health. *In* E. Palmore (ed.), Normal Aging II, pp. 55–63. Duke University Press, Durham, N.C.

Pfeiffer, E., and Davis, G. C. 1974. The use of leisure time in middle life. *In* E. Palmore (ed.), Normal Aging II, pp. 232–243. Duke University Press, Durham, N.C.

Randall, O. 1977. Aging in America today. Gerontologist 17:6–11.

Rones, P. L. 1976. Senior citizen director. Occup. Outlook Q. 20:41–43.

Sargent, J. Q. 1976. Career preparation. Occup. Outlook Q. 20:7–11.

Slater, P. 1964. Cross cultural views of the aged. *In* R. Kastenbaum (ed.), New Thoughts on Old Age, pp. 229–236. Springer Publishing Company, New York.

Struyk, R. 1977. The housing situation of elderly Americans. Gerontologist 17:130–139.

Transportation for the Elderly: The State of the Art. 1975. DHEW Publication 75-20081. U.S. Government Printing Office, Washington, D.C.

Ward, R. 1977. The impact of subjective age and stigma on older persons. J. Gerontology 32:227–232.

Watkins, B. 1977. Gerontology comes of age as an academic field. Chronicle Higher Ed. 14:10.

LAW

Marcia Pearce Burgdorf and Robert L. Burgdorf, Jr.

LEGAL RIGHTS AND THE LAW

In recent years, the tenor of efforts by and on behalf of handicapped persons and other human service clients has shifted from requests for charity from potential benefactors to demands for recognition and implementation of legal rights. Judicial decrees may sometimes be employed to facilitate social change when all manner of appeals to abstract justice and humanitarian impulses proves futile. The term legal rights does not refer to the wide range of services or opportunities that would be *helpful* to a person, nor even those to which there may be a *moral* right, but rather it refers to those things to which a person is entitled by *legal* requirements, matters that may be enforced in a court of law.

In general, legal rights are drawn from one of two basic sources. Certain principles and fundamental rights are held to be so important and inalienable that they are spelled out in the solemn documents that are the foundation of government in this country: the Constitution of the United States and the constitutions of the various states. The remaining legal rights are the result of specific provisions of statutes enacted either by Congress or by the state legislatures.

It is obviously impossible to discuss all the legal rights possessed by individuals in America. The aim here is to briefly outline some of the constitutional and statutory rights that are of special importance to human service clients and to the professionals who serve them.

It is important to recognize that simply because a right exists does not guarantee that it has been recognized in fact or that it has been enforced by court action. Frequently, people are unaware of their rights and afraid or unable to fight for their rights. For these reasons, some of the legal rights listed in this chapter have not yet been universally recognized and some have not yet been the subject of definitive judicial rulings. It is submitted, however, that all of these rights are sound and substantial and will be protected by courts.

The advocacy movement on behalf of human service clients and other consumers has become increasingly litigative in recent years. As a result, judicial precedents have been established that recognize the rights of such individuals in a number of areas. It is only a matter of time until the courts are given an opportunity to declare that legal guarantees with regard to other issues as well shall not be infringed upon.

The Right to Equal Educational Opportunity

Put succinctly, the right to equal educational opportunity is the right of every child of school age to be allowed access to an appropriate program of free public education suited to his/her needs. The application of this principle condemns as unconstitutional any attempt to exclude any group of children from the public education system.

Until recently, however, it was a common practice for public education agencies to refuse admission to children with certain handicapping conditions. In the past few years, the educational rights of such children have been secured by legal actions and by new federal and state legislation.

> In these days, it is doubtful that any child may reasonably be expected to succeed in life if he is denied the opportunity of an education. Such an opportunity, where the state has undertaken to provide it, is a right which must be made available to all on equal terms.

These words of the United States Supreme Court in *Brown* v. *Board of Education,* 347 U.S. 438, 493 (1954), are the cornerstone of the concept of the right to equal educational opportunity. In recent years, courts across the land have made it clear that this right to equal education belongs to handicapped persons as well as to racial minorities. In other words, with regard to handicapped children, "zero reject" public education is mandated.

Education lawsuits on behalf of handicapped children began in 1969 with the case of *Wolf* v. *Legislature of the State of Utah,* Civil No. 182646 (3rd Jud. Dist. Ct. Utah, Jan. 8, 1969), in which the exclusion from the public school system of two so-called trainable mentally retarded children was held to be unconstitutional. In 1972, a similar decision was handed down with regard to all mentally retarded children in the state of Pennsylvania (*Pennsylvania Association for Retarded Children* v. *Commonwealth of Pennsylvania,* 343 F. Supp. 279 (E.D. Pa. 1972)). Later in the same year, the principle that denial of a public education program to handicapped children is violative of the United States Constitution was applied to children with all types of handicaps in the District of Columbia (*Mills* v. *Board of Education of District of Columbia,* 348 F. Supp. 866 (D.D.C. 1972)).

These cases unleashed a veritable avalanche of equal educational opportunity lawsuits around the country. Few states have not had at least one major lawsuit dealing with the educational rights of handicapped citizens. The early cases were concerned primarily with instances of outright exclusion: situations in which handicapped children were refused admission to the public school system and not provided any public education program whatsoever. Subsequent cases have addressed more peripheral issues such as appropriateness of programs, placement and review procedures, funding mechanisms, and access to records.

As litigative activity has continued, the concept of equal educational opportunity has come to include the following component rights:

1. Zero reject education, i.e., requiring that there be no handicapped children excluded from a free public education
2. Due process protection, i.e., requiring that every special educational placement, denial of placement, and transfer must be preceded by constitutionally adequate notice and hearing procedures
3. Centralized responsibility, i.e., allocating to a single agency the duty to ensure that educational programs are provided to all children
4. Individualized program, i.e., requiring an individualized program suited to the needs and designed to maximize the capabilities of each particular child
5. Periodic review, i.e., mandating that placement in every special educational program must be reviewed periodically to determine whether or not the program has accomplished the specific objectives that were outlined in the individualized program plan
6. Least restrictive program and setting, i.e., requiring that special education programs must be provided in the least restrictive and most normalizing environment possible so that each child is educated in a setting as close to the normal classroom as possible
7. Access to and confidentiality of records, i.e., mandating that students and their parents be allowed access to school files and records relating to the student, while restricting unauthorized persons from having access to such files and records

The constitutional basis for such rights has recently been supplemented by federal legislation that makes their recognition and implementation a prerequisite for the receipt of federal funding (Education for All Handicapped Children Act of 1973, P.L. 94-142). Moreover, the past few years have witnessed the enactment of many state special education statutes that seek the recognition and implementation of similar principles.

Residential and Community Services:
The Right to Freedom and to the Least Restrictive Alternative

The United States Supreme Court has declared that Americans possess a constitutional right to freedom or liberty (*O'Connor* v. *Donaldson,* 422 U.S.

563, 573, 576 (1975)). This right to be free cannot ordinarily be restricted by the states or federal government, except in very limited circumstances when the governmental authority can show compelling reasons for such intrusion upon individual liberty. As one court has declared:

> The power of the state to deprive a person of the fundamental liberty to go unimpeded about his or her affairs must rest on a consideration that society has a compelling interest in such deprivation (*Lessard* v. *Schmidt,* 349 F. Supp. 1078, 1084 (E.D. Wis. 1972)).

When the state decides to provide a service for its citizens, it is required to do so under conditions that are as minimally restrictive to personal liberty as possible. In legal terminology, that is the concept of the least restrictive alternative. It is obvious that governmental agencies are not permitted to choose to provide services in ways that are inhumane or dangerous to the citizens being served, but the least restrictive alternative mandate goes further and requires that the state and its officials must examine all the alternatives for providing a service and choose the one that is as unrestrictive as possible. The Supreme Court has declared:

> In a series of decisions this Court has held that, even though the governmental purpose be legitimate and substantial, that purpose cannot be pursued by means that broadly stifle fundamental personal liberties when the end can be more narrowly achieved. The breadth of the legislative abridgement must be viewed in the light of less drastic means for achieving the same basic purpose (*Shelton* v. *Tucker,* 364 U.S. 479, 483 (1960)).

This requirement of the least restrictive alternative has been applied by the courts to residential mental health and mental retardation facilities, to juvenile institutions, and in many other contexts. This has engendered a general tendency away from large residential institutions and toward smaller community-based alternatives.

To ensure that freedom is encroached upon as little as possible, the U.S. legal system mandates that procedural protections be applied whenever a public agency or official seeks to restrain the liberty of an individual. The Fifth and Fourteenth Amendments specify that "liberty" shall not be deprived except in accordance with "due process of law."

Therefore, the confinement of an individual for any reason must be justified by compelling governmental interests established in an appropriate proceeding accompanied by relatively stringent procedural safeguards. Moreover, any such confinement must cease as soon as the reasons for it no longer exist.

In general, the only situation in which the state has compelling interests sufficient to justify the confinement of a person occurs when that person has committed a crime or can be proved to be dangerous to self/others. In the past, many states have restricted the liberty of individuals for the alleged purpose of helping them by providing them with treatment or other services. The continuing legal validity of such supposedly altruistic rationales for confinement is highly doubtful in the absence of a demonstration of danger to self or others.

At the very least, the courts have made clear that when the state restricts a person's liberty for the declared purpose of providing a service, then the state is constitutionally required to actually provide that service. With regard to juvenile institutions, mental hospitals, mental retardation facilities, and other residential programs, the courts have ruled that when a citizen is deprived of some right (liberty), supposedly in return for the benefit of receiving a service (treatment), then the state is mandated by the due process clause to make sure that the service is actually provided. This tit-for-tat, *quid pro quo* requirement has been labeled the right to treatment. Some courts have indicated that financial difficulties are no excuse for failure to provide such a necessary service: "inadequate resources can never be an adequate justification for the state depriving any person of his constitutional rights" (*Welsch* v. *Likins,* 373 F. Supp. 487, 499 (D. Minn., 1974)).

The above mentioned principles can be summarized very simply. First, the state can never restrict an individual's liberty except upon an illustration of compellling state interests demonstrated in a constitutionally adequate due process proceeding. Second, a person ought to be required to give up as little freedom as possible in order to obtain a service from the state. Third, when a person does bargain away some of his liberty to obtain a service, he/she is certainly entitled to receive that service. The federal and state constitutions ensure that these three principles, which amount merely to elementary fairness, must be followed.

The Right to Equal Employment Opportunity

There is no constitutional right that guarantees any person a job. There is, however, a federal constitutional right to be considered for public service without the burden of invidiously discriminatory disqualifications (*Turner* v. *Fouche,* 396 U.S. 346, 362 (1970)). Thus, while a person may not be absolutely entitled to employment, he/she cannot be arbitrarily and unfairly discriminated against. Therefore, the total elimination of black, poor, female, or handicapped persons from consideration for a job would be constitutionally prohibited.

As early as 1915, the United States Supreme Court declared that:

the right to work for a living in the common occupations of the community is of the very essence of the personal freedom and opportunity that it was the purpose of (the fourteenth) Amendment to secure (*Truax* v. *Raich*, 239 U.S. 33, 41 (1915)).

This declaration of the fundamental nature of equal opportunities in employment provides a sound basis for challenging as unconstitutional any employment practices that unfairly discriminate against any group of persons. This constitutional foundation plus various civil rights measures have provided a basis for legal actions that have successfully challenged employment discrimination against racial and ethnic minorities and women.

Handicapped people are the most recent group to join the battle against employment discrimination. Statistics from the President's Committee on Employment of the Handicapped and from other sources demonstrate that handicapped persons are very dependable workers. In fact, some handicapped persons have specialties in certain tasks and perform better than average members of the general public. For these reasons, handicapped individuals are entitled to equal opportunities to qualify for, and to be promoted in, employment. Denial of this right to equal employment opportunities may violate state and federal constitutional guarantees of equal treatment: "Equal Protection of the Laws." Moreover, the Rehabilitation Act of 1973 (Section 504) prohibits discrimination on the basis of handicap in any program or activity receiving federal financial assistance. Armed with these legal weapons for attacking job discrimination, several blind persons have successfully brought suits challenging their exclusion from teaching opportunities in the public schools, a qualified laboratory technician with epilepsy has obtained a favorable order in her suit challenging her exclusion from a hospital job, and a number of similar lawsuits are presently underway. Such litigative efforts can be expected to continue until handicapped people are permitted to have an equal chance to compete for employment opportunities in our society.

The Right to Vote

A long line of United States Supreme Court cases makes it clear that the right to cast one's ballot is a constitutionally protected right. Increasingly, it is becoming apparent that persons with physical or mental handicaps may not constitutionally be deprived of their rightful vote. It may be legitimate to limit the franchise to those who understand its meaning and effect, but there can be no blanket presumption that persons with any particular handicap are incapable of such understanding. Recently, Attorney General Opinions in several states have stated that residents of institutions for the mentally ill and mentally retarded, provided they meet other requirements for voting, cannot be denied the right to vote in local or national elections simply by virtue of their residence in the facilities. In 1975, the Supreme Judicial Court of Massachusetts ruled that residents of Belchertown State School, a state-operated facility for mentally retarded persons, were eligible to vote (*Boyd* v. *Board of Reg. of Voters of Belchertown,* 334 N.E. 2nd 629 (Mass. 1975)). Similar attempts to secure the right to vote have been undertaken in other jurisdictions.

Physically handicapped persons have begun to resort to legal actions to attack the presence of architectural barriers which render many polling places inaccessible to them. One of the primary ingredients of citizenship in our society is the right to vote and express one's preference upon issues and political representatives. This fundamental right may not be taken arbitrarily from any group of individuals.

The Right To Meaningful Access to the Courts

Due process of law is one of the most basic guarantees of the American governmental system. Most people take for granted that they have the right to sue or be sued, to invoke ordinary legal processes. Sometimes, however, certain groups of persons have been denied this right. Persons who have been labeled mentally incompetent are often not permitted to sue or be sued. For physically handicapped persons, especially those in wheelchairs, the lack of proper entranceways, ramps, and elevators may make it impossible for them to enter the courtrooms. Persons in residential institutions may be prevented from corresponding with an attorney or the courts and thereby blocked from pursuing any judicial action.

The constitutional mandate and the more modern trend, however, are toward increasing protection for the right of access to the judicial system. This right must be most carefully safeguarded because without it there are no means for enforcing any of a person's other constitutional and statutory rights. Courts have frequently made it clear that one's right to communicate with the courts and with one's lawyer is to be guarded with the utmost care.

Mere access to the courts is, however, of little value unless one can be sure that any such judicial proceeding will be both meaningful and fair. For example, the presence in court of a deaf person or a person who does not speak English will not have much effect unless such a person is provided an interpreter. Mere physical presence is not enough; understanding participation is what is needed. When there is a question as to whether or not a mental handicap or other condition interferes with an understanding involvement in the proceedings, a guardian *ad litem* may be appointed to champion the interests of the individual.

The Right to Marry, Procreate, and Raise Children

The rights to enter into marriage and to bear and raise children have all been declared by the United States Supreme Court to be fundamental rights protected under the U.S. Constitution. Unfortunately, in the past, these rights have frequently been denied to many persons. Marriages have been prohibited or declared invalid, involuntary sterilizations have been performed, and children have been removed from the home, simply because the person involved happened to have a handicapping condition such as epilepsy or mental retardation. Moreover, welfare recipients and persons on probation and parole have sometimes been pressured to undergo sterilization procedures that they would not freely have chosen.

Restrictions upon the marital, parental, and sexual activities of such individuals may violate constitutional guarantees of equal protection and due process as well as other constitutionally protected rights such as privacy and family integrity (*Alsager* v. *District Court of Polk Cty., Iowa,* 406 F. Supp. 10, 15 (S.D. Ia. 1975)). The blanket denial to any category of people of the right to marry, to procreate, or to raise children is a permanent, irrebuttable presumption of the type that has been condemned in other contexts by the United States Supreme Court.

In Ohio, a judge who had ordered a sterilization operation performed upon a mentally retarded girl, the doctor who performed the operation, the hospital where it was performed, and social and welfare workers who suggested the surgery were sued for three million dollars on the basis that their action had deprived the girl of her constitutional rights (*Wade* v. *Bethesda,* 237 F. Supp. 671 (S.D. Ohio, 1971)). The United States District Court for the Southern District of Ohio found that the judge was totally without authority to order the operation. Shortly thereafter, the defendants agreed to settle the case voluntarily for a substantial sum of money. A United States Court of Appeals has recently reached a similar conclusion in an action arising in the state of Indiana (*Sparkman* v. *McFarlin,* 45 L.W. 2462 (7th Cir., Mar. 23, 1977)).

A federal court has ruled that an Iowa proceeding, wherein five children had been removed from the home of their parents, who were "of below average intelligence" and had allegedly neglected the children, was unconstitutional in violation of due process and the "fundamental right of family integrity" (*Alsager* v. *District Court of Polk Cty., Iowa,* 406 F. Supp. 10, 15 (S.D. Ia. 1975)).

Several courts have condemned the use of pressure tactics by probation and parole officers, welfare workers, and personnel of residential institutions to induce their clients to undergo sexual sterilization procedures.

It is apparent that the rights of marriage, procreation, and parental nurture of children may no longer be denied with impunity.

Self-Determination:
Freedom of Choice, Guardianship, and the Necessity for Informed Consent

Freedom of Choice   The only freedom which deserves the name is that of pursuing our own good in our own way, so long as we do not attempt to deprive others of theirs, or impede their efforts to obtain it. Each is the proper guardian of his own health, whether bodily, or mental and spiritual. Mankind are greater gainers by suffering each other to live as seems good to themselves than by compelling each to live as seems good to the rest (John Stuart Mill, in Castell, 1947, pp. 12–13).

Whether this freedom is called "self-determination," "liberty," the right to "pursuit of happiness," or "freedom of choice," it has long occupied an honored place in American law. Citizens of the United States have come to take for granted that they may chart their individual courses, make their own decisions, and put their ideas into action. The right to make choices and exercise personal preferences is close to the heart of the traditions of individual liberty upon which the American system of government is founded.

Guardianship   Elderly persons, individuals with mental handicaps, and those having severe physical handicaps have frequently been denied their opportunity to exercise their freedom of choice. Through guardianship proceedings authorized by state laws, the decision-making ability of older persons is divested from them and assigned to persons appointed to be their guardians. Thereafter, decisions are made by the guardian on behalf of the ward. The legally appointed guardian is placed in the same relation to the ward as a parent is to a minor child. The ward is viewed as being incompetent to manage his/her own affairs, and therefore the law grants the guardian the responsibility and authority of taking care of the ward.

There are two conflicting policy considerations at work here. On the one hand, a handicapped or elderly person should be allowed to exercise the ability to make free choices like any other person. On the other hand, one would not like to see truly incompetent individuals taken advantage of by unscrupulous individuals, waste or misuse their property or money, or harm themselves or others through their inability to deal with their affairs. It is readily apparent that a person can be competent in some matters while simultaneously being incompetent in others. Thus, a person might be fully capable of managing his/her daily life but not have the requisite competence to manage a large estate or securities investments. An elderly individual may exhibit an ability to lead an otherwise normal life in the community but be unable to take care of nutritional, medical, or other personal needs.

Unfortunately, until recently, guardianship laws have tended to be an all-or-nothing proposition; they have required that a person be declared either totally competent or totally incompetent. A person who exhibited an inability to cope in any particular area and was, therefore, judicially determined to be incompetent, lost all authority to make decisions or to exercise rights in all other areas as well. Unless and until there was a subsequent judicial determination that the person had regained competence, only the guardian could make economic, legal, and personal choices for the ward. Under the guise of protecting the ward, the guardianship proceeding actually deprived such persons of all their rights, their opportunity to exercise their unimpaired faculties, and almost every semblance of human dignity. Guardianship practices in this country have borne out the often quoted warning of former Supreme Court Justice Brandeis:

> Experience should teach us to be most on our guard to protect liberty when the government's purposes are beneficient. . . . The greatest dangers to liberty lurk in insidious encroachment by men of zeal, well-meaning but without understanding (*Olmstead* v. *United States*, 277 U.S. 438, 479 (1928); Brandeis dissenting).

The modern trend, and one that appears more in line with constitutional guarantees, is toward a system known as limited guardianship. The concept of limited guardianship permits a court to declare a particular person to be incompetent for a specific purpose and to appoint a guardian to act to protect that person's interests. The individual is only incompetent with regard to the particular matters involved in the determination of incompetence. He/she retains the right to make decisions and exercise authority in all other areas.

Even more progressive are attempts to sidestep guardianship almost altogether by setting up systems of supportive services for elderly and handicapped individuals that would provide special assistance to these people in the areas in which their competence is lacking (see Cohen, Oosterhout, and Leviton, 1976.) For example, instead of appointing a guardian for a person who is unable to manage financial matters, a contractual arrangement might be worked out wherein some person or agency would assist in financial management on a temporary basis, while simultaneously providing training on monetary matters so that the client might eventually learn to manage his/her own finances. Likewise, instead of having an elderly person declared incompetent and placed in a nursing home, sufficient supportive services, such as food preparation, medical attention, and housekeeping, might be arranged so that the person could continue to live at home in the community.

Necessity for Informed Consent   Professionals in the fields of human services have no authority to do anything to or for a client except with that individual's consent or, in the case of minors or legally incompetent persons, with the consent of the client's parents or legal guardian. This principle is a logical corollary to the client's right to freedom of choice and self-determination. A member of a human services field who engages in coercive or nonconsensual activities upon clients risks legal liability. The only generally accepted exception to the rule that consent is required is that physicians may provide medical treatment in an emergency without consent, if such consent is impossible or impracticable to obtain. In all other circumstances, the client has a right to be left alone (*Olmstead* v. *United States,* 277 U.S. 438, 479 (1928); Brandeis dissenting), which makes consent indispensable.

The right of consent is dependent upon the right to be informed:

True consent to what happens to one's self is the informed exercise of a choice, and that entails an opportunity to evaluate knowledgeably the options available and the risks attendant upon each (*Canterbury* v. *Spence,* 464 F. 2nd 772, 780 (D.C. Cir. 1972)).

The law, therefore, has placed upon professionals a duty to inform their clients of the meaning and implications of services that are available.

How much is required to be revealed? Courts have answered by saying that the professional's duty to disclose information is measured by the client's right of self-decision, that is, the professional must reveal any information that is material to the client's choice of options. Thus, the test for determining whether a potential peril must be divulged is its materiality to the client's decision. A professional person does not have to give a client a minicourse on the scientific bases of the techniques employed in the profession, but the client is entitled to a full and complete disclosure of all information relevant to a meaningful decisional process.

The combination of the right to make one's own decisions and the right to be provided the appropriate information relevant to such decisions constitute the legal requirement that is termed informed consent. Such informed consent is an absolute prerequisite for the rendering of all types of human services.

When an individual is a minor or under legal guardianship, the right of informed consent is ordinarily exercised by the individual's parent or guardian. This authority, called substitute consent, is not, however, unlimited; parents and guardians are not empowered to give consent to things that are harmful to the welfare of the child or ward. Courts have held that parents may not consent to the refusal of life-saving medical treatment for their children, nor may they consent to involuntary sterilization of their children. Some courts have held that parents may not compel a minor daughter to have an abortion, and other judicial decisions have decreed that parents or guardians do not have the untrammeled authority to consent to the long term incarceration of their children or wards in residential facilities. These matters are of such import and so inherently dangerous to the welfare of the child or ward that parents and guardians are not permitted to give legally valid informed consent.

The Right to Privacy, Confidentiality, and Access to Records

The United States Supreme Court has recognized that the U.S. Constitution creates a fundamental right to privacy. This right prevents the encroachment of government agencies and officials into matters that are the personal or private concern of individual citizens. The protected areas, where state intervention is prohibited, are called zones of privacy. Like state agencies, private agencies and professionals are not permitted to invade the privacy of their clientele but must obtain the client's approval before treading upon personal and sensitive matters. In some states, intrusion upon an individual's privacy may give rise to a legal course of action called invasion of privacy against the intruder.

One aspect of privacy is the concept of confidentiality. The ethical principles and codes of many professions specify that information learned about and communications from a client are to be held in strict confidence and may not be shared with others except with the client's consent. The inviolate nature of such professional/client confidentiality has in many instances been recognized by law. Thus, the confidentiality of communications with one's lawyer, often referred to as the attorney/client privilege, is widely accepted in both statutory and case law, so that not even a court can compel an attorney to disclose the confidences of a client. Likewise, the confidential nature of communications to physicians, priest-confessors, psychiatrists, and psychologists has received general recognition. On the other hand, the confidential status of information received by members of other professions, such as social workers, journalists, counselors, and welfare workers, has not yet been universally recognized by the law. Some members of such professions have, however, felt strongly enough about the ethical standards of their professions regarding confidentiality that they have been willing to risk contempt of court proceedings and possible jail terms rather than reveal confidential communications.

It is important to note that the privilege of confidentiality is a right of the client and not the professional. If a client engages in confidential communications with a professional, the professional may not reveal those communications without the permission of the client. Conversely, if the client chooses to allow privileged communications to be revealed, the professional has no right to refuse to do so. The right of confidentiality can be waived by and only by the client.

A serious danger to the right of privacy and the confidentiality of information is presented by the records that are kept by public and private agencies and professionals. Such records frequently contain personally identifiable information of a highly confidential nature. In the wrong hands, these records could be tremendously damaging to a person's reputation, finances, employment opportunities, or mental health. Abuses of credit reports and other financial records are well known, and records of a more personal nature are susceptible to even greater misuse. For these reasons, both federal laws and some state statutes have begun to address problems of restricting access to records. For example, the federal Family Educational Rights and Privacy Act, 20 U.S.C. § 1232g. (commonly known as the Buckley Amendment), provides detailed guidelines for access to educational records. Many state laws have been passed to ensure the confidentiality of medical and psychological records.

The obverse side of the coin from restricting access to confidential records is permitting the individual who is the subject of such records to have access to them. To protect one's privacy rights and to verify the accuracy of information recorded, an individual may need to see what the records say about him/herself. Moreover, in addition to acting as a monitor to the contents of records, there may be other, more substantive reasons for wishing to examine confidential records. Thus, parents may need to see school records regarding their child in order to properly evaluate the child's educational needs, status, and progress and to make an informed judgment of the appropriateness of a proposed educational program for the child. A person may need to view his/her medical records to obtain an accurate understanding of his/her medical condition or to assess the propriety of treatment rendered. Access to mental health records may be necessary to allow preparation of a defense to commitment or guardianship proceedings.

Therefore, efforts have been made to expand the rights of the interested party to include access to otherwise confidential records containing personally relevant information. The Buckley Amendment, for example, gives parents of school children (or the children themselves if of the age of majority) the right to inspect, challenge, and correct school records regarding their children. The federal Fair Credit Reporting Act, 15 U.S.C. §1681, requires credit bureaus to initiate procedures for ensuring accuracy of credit records and to clearly and accurately disclose the information in their files. Medical and hospital records have been the subjects of similar efforts. In the case of *Gaertner* v. *State,* 385 Mich. 49, 187 N.W. 2nd 429 (1971), the Supreme Court of Michigan held that confidentiality of records was a right of the patient and not the hospital and that the concept of confidentiality could not be used to bar a patient or the patient's legal representative from examining hospital records. In one unusual Maryland case, *Tenenhaus* v. *Schmeltzer,* Case No. 9780-75 (District Court No. 6, Rockville, Md., Feb. 11, 1976), a dental patient successfully sued to obtain an x-ray of her teeth from her dentist on the ground that, having paid for the x-ray, she, not he, owned it.

It is true that the release of some records, particularly mental health records, might be harmful to the patient's well being. The modern trend appears to be, therefore, to except from the patient's right of access to medical records those particular records or portions of records that the doctor or hospital believes would cause serious harm to the patient. However, the validity of the reasons for suppressing such information might thereafter be subject to challenge by the patient in court. Otherwise the patient should have access to all the patient's medical or hospital records.

The development of the law regarding access to records can be seen from the above discussion to have two prongs. On the one hand, the confidentiality of such records is receiving increasing protection, and access to them is becoming increasingly limited. At the same time, however, the right of a person to see his/her own records is being greatly expanded.

The Right of Access to Buildings and Transportation Facilities

While the right to freedom of movement, the opportunity to come and go when and where one pleases, is a laudable facet of the American way of life, people confined to wheelchairs, some elderly persons, blind people, deaf people, and other persons having physical disabilities affecting mobility find themselves blocked from access to many buildings and systems of transportation. Narrow doorways, flights of stairs, revolving doors, lack of markings apprehendable by blind people, inaccessible bathrooms, and other architectural barriers have made it difficult or impossible for such persons to enter and move around many buildings. Likewise, many airports, train stations, and bus terminals are not fully accessible nor are the transportation vehicles themselves, and there are related problems, such as public address systems at transportation terminals, the use of which frequently illustrates a disregard of the needs of deaf and hearing-impaired persons.

This reality is, however, in sharp contrast with existing legislation. As one lawyer has noted:

> The right of handicapped people to move freely in the community and have equal access to public buildings and transportation is explicitly recognized in a myriad of state statutes. White cane laws protect blind and visually handicapped persons in each state. These laws have been supplemented in about half the states by comprehensive civil rights acts which protect blind and other handicapped persons against discrimination in public accommodations, housing, and other areas. Architectural barriers legislation also exists in some form in every state. The state legal structure is reinforced at the national level. Various acts have set forth congressional policy on equal access to transportation for handicapped and elderly persons. Creation of the Architectural and Transportation Barriers Compliance Board (P.L. 93-112) has strengthened enforcement of the federal Architectural Barriers Act (Laski, 1976, p. 13).

In recent years, handicapped persons have begun to resort to court actions to ensure that the legislative mandates become reality. Lawsuits against bus lines, rapid transit systems, airlines, public accomodations, urban subways, and state and local government agencies have been undertaken to secure access to public facilities and to attack architectural barriers to buildings and transportation systems.

The Right to Specific Statutory Benefits

There are a multitude of state and federal statutes providing various types of benefits for eligible classes of citizens. Examples include welfare and unemployment benefits, vocational rehabilitation services, veterans' benefits, social security benefits, programs to aid handicapped persons, elderly persons, indigents, and other groups. It is obviously impossible to list all such programs here or to discuss the criteria for eligibility for each. The most important principle that should be noted about such benefits is that, if a state or federal statute specifies that a particular benefit shall be available to a certain class of people, a member of that class who meets the eligibility requirements has a legally enforceable right to receive the benefit. The wording of the statute and any rules or regulations promulgated under it determine who is eligible and under what conditions; a person who meets the criteria obtains a legal right to have the benefit. Clients seeking services mandated by statute are not merely charity seekers subject to the mercy or beneficence of the service provider; rather, they are the possessors of a legal right that justifies their actions in demanding the benefit to which they are entitled.

The Right to Fair and Equal Treatment
by Public Agencies and Other Rights

A generalization that can be drawn from the several rights listed above is that human service clients are entitled to be treated in a fair and equal manner by the agencies and officials who serve them. Indeed, a simplistic summary of the Fourteenth Amendment guarantees of "equal protection" and "due process of law" would require that public agencies must treat all people with equality and fairness. Stated conversely, invidious discriminations or unfair actions by public bodies or officials are forbidden by the Fourteenth Amendment to the United States Constitution.

This right to fair and equal treatment is a rough touchstone against which the legal propriety of almost any type of program can be measured. It is an umbrella type of right that encompasses all of the rights previously listed and many additional ones. It is impossible to discuss in a few short pages all of the constitutional and statutory rights about which the courts have ruled or are in the process of considering. A brief sampling of some of the additional rights possessed by individuals might include: 1) the right to send and receive mail, 2) the right to equal access to medical services, 3) the right to choose and practice a religion, 4) the right to have relationships with one's peers, including members of the opposite sex, 5) the right to equal access to welfare, social security, and other social service programs, 6) the right to freely express oneself, whether it be through the choice of one's hair length, clothing styles, music, or otherwise, 7) the right to be free from culturally biased and other improper testing and classification procedures, 8) the right to equal opportunities for housing and freedom from discriminatory zoning ordinances, 9) the right to enter into contracts, 10) the right to nondiscriminatory treatment by policemen and firemen, 11) the right to be free from medical experimentation, 12) the right to travel, and 13) the right to be free from governmental encroachment upon a normal life-style and life cycle. This list could go on and on, but all such rights may be capsulized under the concept of fair and equal treatment by professionals, service agencies, and public officials. Such are the requirements of the law.

REVIEW OF PRESENT LEGAL CONSTRAINTS

Requirements for Professionals

The key word that describes the type of constraints currently facing all professionals is accountability. The decisions made by doctors to treat or not to treat a patient, by a teacher as to how to teach a pupil, by an employment counselor to place or not to place a person in a job, and by a social worker as to how to counsel a client are all under increasing scrutiny. This is a relatively recent development. For many years, professionals were placed on a pedestal as the "experts;" whatever their decision, it would prevail unquestioned. Times have changed, however, and one of the changes has been an erosion of the uncritical deference afforded the decisions of professional persons.

In general, professionals have become increasingly able to provide more creative and appropriate services to human services clients. Many more options have become available because of developments in educational, medical, and other techniques and because of society's recognition that handicapped individuals have a right to appropriate services. This expanding ability to use very potent instruments and techniques to serve human services clients has, however, been tempered by an increasingly wary societal attitude toward unfettered professional discretions. Any significant change can engender concern, and the idea of accountability has raised fear in most professionals. A consideration of the requirements that the legal system is imposing on professionals will clarify what this word accountability really means.

Accountability At the most basic level, accountability requires that a professional must be able to explain in reasonable terms what he/she is doing for a client and why the method of treatment, education, counseling, etc. was chosen over other options. This first step is simply verbalizing a process that most professionals presently follow, i.e., assessing the client's problem and developing a strategy of how to solve or ameliorate the problem. Accountability then asks professionals to go, perhaps, one step further and to explain the whats and whys of their actions. The explanation should not just be expressed in the jargon of the profession but should be easily understood by the client, the client's family, and other persons who are involved in helping the client.

At no time is the law requiring the professional to provide the ultimate or perfection in quality services. While this ideal is both admirable and the one that should be strived for, it is neither achievable nor required. What is required is that the professional render competent services designed to meet the individual's needs. This is clearly a general principle that must be tested and measured by the circumstances in each situation. An examination of other requirements discussed below helps to clarify professional responsibility.

Written Plans   In both the areas of education and treatment, the courts and subsequently federal law have required written documentation by professionals of educational program plans and individual treatment (habilitation) plans (*Wyatt* v. *Stickney,* 325 F. Supp. 781; 334 F. Supp. 1341 (1971)). This means that, in addition to the requirement of a reasonable explanation for a particular type of program or treatment, the professional(s) involved in a case must document why this specific program was chosen, what the program is, and what progress the client makes. The written plan, then, is the record of evaluation or diagnosis of the client, the professionals' prescribed program to meet the client's needs, and a periodic review of the program to determine the client's progress.

Public Law 94-142, Education for All Handicapped Children Act (P.L. 94-142, 20 U.S.C. 1401 et seq.), is very specific about the types of written plans educational professionals must have for all handicapped children to ensure that each child is receiving an appropriate educational program. Likewise, P.O. 94-103, the Developmental Disabilities and Rights Act (P.L. 94-103, 42 U.S.C. 6001–6008), speaks to the requirements for developing program plans for institutional populations and for those disabled individuals in community programs receiving federal funds. For further information, a careful reading of these laws would be beneficial.

The efforts necessary from professionals to comply with these requirements for written plans will be helpful not only to the individual client in receiving and monitoring services but also in helping other professionals assist in the provision of continuity of appropriate quality services.

Client Involvement   One of the other factors that relates to the accountability of professionals is the involvement of the client himself/herself in the decision-making process, a factor which is often overlooked. The law now mandates that in almost every setting the participation and consent of the handicapped person is required (P.L. 94-103, 42 U.S.C. 6001–6008). When the client is a minor or an incompetent individual, there must be someone representing him/her in any decision-making role. Parents, guardians, and advocates can fill this role, but it is important to remember that almost all human services clients are able to express their own feelings and desires and should be allowed to participate themselves.

Least Restrictive Alternative   The next requirement is that whatever the outcome of the decision-making process is, the decision must conform to the concept of the least restrictive program or setting with regard to the individual's rights. The program, treatment, etc. must be provided in the least restrictive and most normalizing environment possible. This concept means that when, for example, an appropriate educational program can be provided in the community, the child should not be sent to a residential school simply because he/she is handicapped. The sensibility of this is clear: it is unfair to force a handicapped child to leave home and family when the services can be provided in the community. Similarly, the concept of least restrictive alternative relates to other human services professionals as well.

The requisite application of the principle of the least restrictive alternative to the provision of services by professionals is a basic underlying tenet of American law. It is extremely important that professionals dealing with human services clients recognize that these individuals have the same legal and human rights as everyone else, and that they must be treated in as normal a manner as possible.

Challenges to Professional Decisions   The last requirement of human services programs may seem a bit strange or ominous to professionals, that is, that their decisions are open to challenge. This phenomenon is extremely hard to understand because professionals, until recently, have had total authority for decision making. The fact, however, that a professional's advice or decision might be challenged does not mean that he/she no longer has the power to make decisions. It simply means that professionals must be able to explain and justify their reasons and must be open to questions. Many areas of decision making in the human services area are now open to formalized scrutiny through the administrative hearing process. In education, there are due process hearings to review educational placement decisions. In health and social welfare, there are social security, disability, and welfare hearings to challenge eligibility, awards, etc. In the medical area, there are administrative-type hearings, and the recent increase in malpractice lawsuits further demonstrates a willingness to challenge professionals.

In both of these areas of challenge, administrative and litigative, the best response is that a professional must have rational reasons for his/her actions and must be able to explain them to the satisfaction of others. As consumers become more aware of their rights and as society begins to question the decisions of all authority figures (e.g., politicians, doctors, lawyers, school principals) there will be more challenges to professional decisions. Many professionals who did not previously carry liability insurance are beginning to do so. Professionals must now do a good job of explaining the value of their services—what they can and cannot do for the client—in order to obviate, in almost every instance, the client's challenge to professional decisions.

Service Agencies

Service agencies are obviously those agencies that provide the direct care services of education, treatment, etc. to the human services client. Their basic function is to serve. In many instances, these are the agencies and the staff that have rendered excellent services to the human services clients over the years. These agencies have developed an expertise and have been able to provide many quality programs for clients.

There do seem to be some problems, however, and one of the most common difficulties expressed by service providers is the lack of funds to provide proper programs. In addition, although they may like to offer a certain type of service, they are not responsible for doing so. The courts have spoken to these two basic problems, lack of funds and lack of responsibility, in numerous cases. The courts have been very clear that where the responsibility of service provider agencies is established, they must *serve*. In a case dealing with the first issue, lack of funds, *Mills* v. *Board of Education of the District of Columbia,* 348 F. Supp. 866 (D.D.C. 1972), the school district was named as a party and appeared before the court. The school district's basic argument was that, while they wished to provide education programs for all handicapped, they simply did not have the money to do so. This was a case in which many handicapped children (e.g., emotionally disturbed, mentally retarded, physically handicapped, learning disabled, etc.) were either inappropriately provided with programs or were out of school. The court said that it was a violation of these children's constitutional rights to exclude them from the public school system and, therefore, lack of funds was not a sufficient excuse. Some people call this Judge Waddly's "no third grade rule," that is, if the school system had gotten rid of all third grades in the District of Columbia, they would have had enough money to provide programs for the handicapped. This inference is clearly carrying the decision further than the court intended to go. However, the judge did mean that the school system could not provide special programs and extracurricular programs, such as band, football, and advanced science programs at the same time that it was excluding handicapped children from school. The court gave the school district two choices: either raise more money so that programs could be provided for *all* children, or divide the available money more equitably among all children so that the burden of lack of funds would not fall more heavily on the disabled than it did on the normal. This decision is a good example of the fact that lack of funds will not absolve a service agency of its responsibility to provide programs.

Another key problem that many human services clients face when they approach service agencies is the determination of which particular agency is responsible for providing the needed service. One of the most important suits on this issue is the case called *In Re G.H.,* 218 N.W. 2nd 441 (N.D. 1974). This case, concerning a handicapped child who was born severely disabled, can be referred to as the "no buck-passing case" because the child was in need of services and none of the agencies were willing to provide her with them. Gail was born with only one eye which was misplaced on her face, a cleft palate, and no hands and no feet; she was diagnosed as mentally retarded with a variety of other complications. She became a ward of the state early in her life and was provided with a variety of services, especially medical care, that significantly improved her condition. Her cleft palate was repaired. She had plastic surgery on her face and was given an artificial eye so that her face looked reasonably normal, and she had an operation on her arms so that she had use of the stumps. In fact, she learned to play the piano and became an artist. As Gail grew and progressed, it was clear that she was not mentally retarded and was a very capable young woman. However, because of her disability, she clearly needed some remedial education in order to catch up with her peer group. She was placed in a private school program that was appropriate for her. However, the state agency that had guardianship over her said, "It is not our responsibility to provide her with education. We will provide food, clothing, and shelter, but not education." The local school districts said, "It is not our responsibility to provide education for Gail because her parents do not live in the district. Nobody pays taxes for her. We think it should be the responsibility of the state Department of Education." The state Department of Education said, "It is not our responsibility to provide the program for Gail. Gail has lived in the school district all her life, and it is a local school district's responsibility." Instead of determining among themselves who should pay the $3,000, the three agencies fought among themselves and took the case all the way to the state's Supreme Court, which probably cost the state at least $250,000, in order to determine which of the agencies should pay the $3,000. The Supreme Court of the state was, needless to say, unhappy with the three agencies' inability to resolve the issue of responsibility of providing for Gail's education; it pointed the finger very clearly at the local school district and said that the buck stops there. The local school district may request assistance from one of the other agencies to provide an appropriate program for a handicapped child. But even when it is unable to gain assistance from other agencies, it must assume the responsibility alone and cannot deny a service to a client. This principle of "no buck-passing" is applicable not only in the area of education, but in the area of treatment, welfare, and social security. The courts are being very clear that where agencies have the responsibility to provide programs, they must serve their populations.

The final requirement placed on service agencies is that these agencies not only must not discriminate or deny services to their clients, but must also provide quality services. In *Welsh* v. *Likens,* 373 F. Supp. (D. Minn. 1974), the court found that the state Department of Mental Retardation, which was responsible under state law for running institutions, had the legal mandate to provide programs for mentally retarded citizens in the least restrictive environment. However, this agency did not have many community placements or alternatives to their institutions. The court held that it was this agency's responsibility to develop and set up less restrictive alternatives and that, where they had the legal mandate to provide services to mentally retarded individuals, the lack of services or alternative community placements could not be used as an excuse to deny the client the right to the least restrictive alternative. Probably the most noteworthy portion of the decision was in holding that the service agency had the *affirmative duty* to provide these services and to develop them where they did not presently exist.

It is clear from the examples above that a service agency has very definite legal constraints placed on it that are designed to assist and to clarify the service agency's role in actually providing service to its clients.

THE ROLE OF THE LAWYER ON THE INTERDISCIPLINARY TEAM

Although there are probably numerous roles a lawyer could play on an interdisciplinary team, there are two basic roles that this professional should undertake. The first of these roles would be the traditional role that lawyers play, that is, advocating the rights of a particular client or group of clients. This direct representation of an individual's interests would often bring the lawyer into an adversarial relationship with other professionals. While serving on an interdisciplinary team, a lawyer following this role would serve as an advocate to challenge and to question what the other professionals prescribe for the client. Obviously, this role could cause a great deal of tension in the group and is probably the very reason why interdisciplinary teams do not often include lawyers! This role is certainly a valid role for a lawyer, especially when professionals, who are not attuned to the rights of individuals, are making important life decisions for a human services client. Even though this can be a valid role, this is probably not the optimum use of a lawyer on an interdisciplinary team. As noted in Chapter 1, the current trend in the purpose of interdisciplinary teams is to encourage cooperation among the various professionals in order to enhance the quality and quantity of services provided to clients. The traditional role of lawyers runs contrary to this purpose.

The second role a lawyer might play on an interdisciplinary team is that of an advisor to the other team members on the rights of human services clients. The lawyer would not be representing an individual client *per se,* but the more general group of human services clients. This role is clearly more in line with the underlying concept of an interdisciplinary team. A lawyer in this role could not only alert the team members to the rights of the client but also could be invaluable in assisting the team in securing services for the client. For example, an interdisciplinary team may evaluate a client and determine that its client is ready to enter the employment market. Efforts, however, to place the client are thwarted because of the client's past history of illness or disability. The lawyer, in this situation, can take an affirmative role in apprising potential employers that their actions are illegally discriminatory and that they have an affirmative action responsibility that could be satisfied by employing the client.

The lawyer in this second role would be an integral member of the interdisciplinary team and a real boon to the efforts of the group. This type of role is a new one for lawyers. Many professionals are unaware of the potential value that a lawyer can contribute to an interdisciplinary team. The stereotype of lawyers as those persons who bring suit against other professionals and hotly cross-examine them dies hard. That is not to say there will be no problems when a lawyer functions in a cooperative, consulting role to other members of the team. There could be unusual situations that could create some ethical conflicts for the lawyer (and the other professionals). In a situation where an interdisciplinary team recommends, over the protest of the lawyer member, a sterilization for a handicapped client, the lawyer may be obliged to refer the individual to private counsel in order to protect that individual's civil rights. For the most part, the presence of a lawyer on the interdisciplinary team will ensure that decisions that would clearly violate the individual's rights and that would create liability for team members will be avoided.

There have been several successful attempts to integrate lawyers into interdisciplinary teams. Perhaps one of the most successful examples is the Georgetown Adolescent Intervention Team (GAIT) at the Georgetown University Affiliated Facility for Developmentally Disabled Persons. This team evaluates children who are referred by the District of Columbia Juvenile Court because of a suspected disability. The team not only evaluates the child but also proposes a treatment program when it is warranted. The lawyer is a very important team member who has sensitized the other members to the legal issues and who has learned a great deal of relevant information from the other professionals. This team has been able to serve many clients who formerly were not identified as handicapped and has succeeded in suggesting to the court community alternatives to institutionalization.

As the role of the lawyers changes from the adversarial role to include more role options, interdisciplinary teams will have a larger group of trained lawyers from which to draw. Clearly, the lawyer has much to offer a client as a viable member of an interdisciplinary team.

THE GROWTH OF PUBLIC INTEREST LAW ACTIVITIES

Lawyers have traditionally represented the wealthy and powerful interests in our society. The legal professional has often been skeptically viewed as protecting the rich against the poor, the politically well connected against the common man. By and large, this is true. During the history of the United States, the law has more often been a method of maintaining the status quo than a method of bringing about social change. There have always been lawyers who have represented human and civil rights, but the majority of work in which lawyers have involved themselves is money-making, business law.

In the last 20 years, there has been a tremendous growth in public interest law. From the famous 1954 *Brown* v. *Board of Education* (373 F. Supp. 489 (D. Minn. 1974)) public school desegregation case of the Warren Court, has come a challenge to lawyers to use the legal system as a very effective method of law reform. Even when the litigants are poor members of minority groups, the courts have been very responsive to the arguments of these public interest lawyers. Public services attorneys have successfully attacked some of the most difficult problems in our society from pollution, the wasting of natural resources, the rights of mental patients, the power of large corporate conglomerates, to the manufacture of dangerous products. One of the most successful law reform groups is the Center for Law and Social Policy in Washington, D.C. Another extremely successful and more famous D.C. group is Nader's Raiders.

Ralph Nader is a hero and an example to thousands of lawyers who have chosen to make public interest law their lifetime career. Contrary to old patterns and expectations, public interest lawyers on behalf of a particular interest group, or on behalf of consumers in general, are striking at the very interests of money and power that the legal professions so long protected.

In addition, the government has contributed significantly to this trend by funding a system of legal services, on the state and local level, to protect the rights of poor people, senior citizens, and other groups who have not had ready access to the legal system. The Legal Services Corporation Act of 1974 (P.L. 93-355, 42 U.S.C. 2996 et seq.) passed by Congress has established a national agency to assist these local programs with both technical assistance and funding. There are thousands of legal services lawyers working with indigent and needy clients throughout this country.

As for the legal profession's role in the civil rights movement, lawyers have had a real leadership position in establishing that handicapped individuals have the same human and legal rights as everyone else. Out of the experience of representation of various other minorities came the skill and expertise that contributed to the success of the civil rights movement for handicapped persons. Since the filing of the first class action lawsuit in 1971, there have been approximately 200 successful court cases affecting all of the states. From a handful of attorneys in 1971, the handicapped-rights bar has grown to a group of several hundred lawyers. Numerous law schools have established courses on the rights of disabled citizens and the number is on the rise.

The responsibility of the legal profession to advocate for the rights of disabled citizens goes much further than the efforts already initiated. With the passage of the antidiscrimination law (Voc. Rehabilitation Act, 29 U.S.C. 794), there will be a need for an even greater number of lawyers to advocate for and to implement these rights. Members of the private bar need to become more involved. Publicly funded lawyers can do a great deal of the work but the cooperation of private lawyers is needed if there is going to be enough access to legal services for all who need it.

The bar also must bear a large responsibility in educating handicapped individuals, society in general, and especially other professions to the rights of these citizens. Public awareness of rights is one of the best possible methods of enforcement. The legal profession has just begun its efforts in this area and has a great deal of work to do.

Public Law 94-103, 42 U.S.C. 6001–6008, requires that, in order for a state to be eligible to receive federal funds for handicapped individuals, each state must establish an independent system of advocacy for handicapped persons. An integral part of this system is the requirement of access to legal advocacy. The system is to be designed to let each disabled person have an opportunity to reach outside of the service delivery system to challenge the care and services he/she is receiving. This is a unique concept and probably will go a long way toward enforcing these rights to services of disabled individuals.

The role of the lawyer will sometimes be an adversarial one. This is necessary to ensure the rights of disabled citizens. The role also can encompass legal consultative services provided in a cooperative manner to assist in the implementation of these rights. The civil rights movement still has much progress to make before its goals are attained. Joseph Califano, commenting in his news release to the press on April 5, 1977 on the sit-in of handicapped persons in offices of the Department of Health, Education and Welfare throughout the country, said:

> They (handicapped Americans) seek redress for discrimination they have suffered. They seek to end years of neglect and to be free from unjust practices that are demeaning and offensive, imposing unconscionable restraints on their ability to dramatize their plight in our society and before our government.

The legal profession has a major responsibility to see that this terrible suffering comes to an end.

REFERENCES

Cohen, B., Oosterhout, B., and Leviton, S. 1976. Tailoring guardianship to the needs of mentally handicapped citizens. 6 Maryland Law Forum 91.

Laski, F. 1976. Legal advocacy, positive factor in rights for disabled people. Am. Rehabilitation 1:12–17.

MUSIC THERAPY

Alice Jeanne Ludwig

Music exalts each Joy, allays each Grief,
Expels Diseases, softens every Pain,
Subdues the rage of Poison, and the Plague;
And hence the wise of ancient days ador'd;
One power of Physic, Melody and Song.
                                John Armstrong,
              The Art of Preserving Health (1744)

DEVELOPMENT OF MUSIC THERAPY AS A DISCIPLINE

The societal beliefs listed in this poem were accepted in 1744 A.D. and are rarely challenged today. They are based on commonly observed effects of music on man's social, emotional, and physical behavior and stress the inherent, curative potential of music. This concept of the "power of music" is repeated throughout recorded literature from the Egyptians and the Greeks to present times. Music as a mystical, magical, curative process, beyond man's understanding, impeded the establishment of music as an objective and scientific therapy.

The profession of music therapy as an organized specialty is relatively young. For many years it struggled to demystify its public image and to define itself in terms of a behavioral science. As a consequence of two World Wars, advances in physical and psychiatric treatment, notably the development of psychotropic drugs, led to the development of many new disciplines in mental health, including music therapy. In the post-World War I era, music was employed successfully in military hospitals for diversion and control. The response to patriotic songs, military marches, and hymns is often automatic and stereotyped, and thus music is used to affect and control the behavior of large groups. Background music may be used to achieve specific effects; sedative music is slow and muted, while stimulative music creates an atmosphere of gaiety and excitement. Recorded music is useful in the field of anesthesia. It has been used in childbirth and in general

135

and dental surgery. Research indicates apprehension is lessened, the pain threshold is increased, and the amount of anesthesia needed is reduced. In electric shock treatment, music has been utilized both in the waiting period before shock, during treatment, and in the recovery room. The selection and the quality of the recordings are extremely important.

The "control" aspects of music have been recognized from ancient times. These effects were examined and explained in part by a number of physiological studies done in the 1920s in which the effects of music upon respiration, heart beat, blood pressure, etc. were measured. In that same period, some references to the effective use of music in the treatment of nervous disorders such as hysterias and phobias were published. By the 1930s, the use of music in psychiatric hospitals was well established, although it was generally unspecific in nature and lacked rationale.

At that time, the work of the Menninger Clinic in Topeka, Kansas blazed a new pathway with the introduction of the concept of milieu therapy. There, for the first time, the activities of sports, music, and arts and crafts were prescribed for controlled therapeutic effects, and the therapeutic effects of these activities were evaluated as part of the total structured environment. Personnel supervising the activities were guided by means of frequent staff consultation with concerned psychiatrists and psychologists.

This use of prescribed activities within the framework of a guided interpersonal relationship between therapist and patient formed the new concept of activity therapy that burgeoned after World War II, particularly sparked by the demand from veterans' hospitals for activities to absorb the interest and energy of long term patients. The early hospital musicians, recruited from music education and performance backgrounds, had developed a body of empirical knowledge through clinical experiences. In cooperation with other activity therapists, a small group began to continuously examine the nature of clinical demands, to assume therapeutic responsibilities, and to seek inclusion on the treatment team. Techniques were refined and information exchanged in meetings, and by the late 1940s formal training for music therapists was available in several colleges and universities, although there was little agreement as to course content or training requirements. With the development of chemotherapy, focus changed from the control of destructive physical behavior to attempts at active treatment. This trend was reflected in the virtual disappearance of locked wards, hydrotherapy rooms, and insulin therapy. While the concept of milieu therapy was rarely completely adopted in the tradition-bound state hospitals, the need for treatment above the custodial level gave new impetus to the development of adjunctive therapy. Nonmedical therapists were necessary members of the therapeutic team and were overwhelmed by demands for services.

Most early music therapy was done in psychiatric settings and evolved from the work of the hospital musician, who provided music for chapel services, often conducted a patient choir or chorus, and encouraged patients to begin or resume the study of an instrument. The program orientation reflected the musician's training as either educator or performer. In contrast, the college-trained music therapist had an increased potential for therapeutic contributions, and, as a consequence, the demand for trained music therapists increased rapidly. Hospital programs varied greatly in the demands placed upon these workers. By the mid-1950s there were hospitals where well staffed music therapy departments functioned as a part of a large scale therapeutic program; in other places, a lone music therapist worked with a hospital population of 6,000 persons. Perforce, in such situations the emphasis was on group activities as the therapist moved from ward to ward involving patients and ward attendants in group sings, rhythm sessions, and simplified square dances.

Traditionally, the mental hospital dealt with a stable long term situation, and both patient and staff functioned in a sheltered, sealed-off environment. This environment was formally organized, hierarchical in nature, with roles clearly defined. The patient was at the base of the power pyramid and usually regarded as one to be acted upon. He/she was assigned to occupational therapy or music therapy in the same way he/she was assigned to hydrotherapy or insulin shock treatment—by the decision of the physician in charge. Hospitalized for months and even years, musically illiterate patients learned to read music and play instruments and participated in performing major choral works and entire musicals. The patients' participation in these events often proved of major therapeutic value in establishing social relationships and in providing increased self-esteem, although the original motive for participating may have been to relieve the awful tedium characteristic of the "other 23 hours." While the musical skills of the therapist provided the tools for accomplishing these goals, the understanding of psychodynamic principles was at least as important. Beyond the valuable contributions made by providing diversion, education, and useful occupation, the music activity proved to possess other dimensions that seemed to cut more directly to the heart of the malfunctioning. Because music is a symbolic language and is nonverbal, there is the possibility of using it communicatively when direct communication has become impossible. It can provide social involvement and still permit a nonthreatening degree of distance, thus relieving the painful isolation of mental illness. As a creative art form, it can elicit emotion and channel its expression into acceptable pathways. It can be used to encourage aggression or to control regression.

The concept of milieu therapy with its emphasis on prescribed, therapeutic activity gave new status to the field as music therapists, along with other activity therapists, became members of the therapeutic team, although described by terms like "adjunctive," "ancillary," or "supportive" (supportive, of course, to the team leader or prime therapists: the medical representative). "Prescribed activities therapy" is still to be found in some hospitals, but, generally, the notion of the psychiatric team has been replaced by the broader concept of the interdisciplinary approach to clinical services. The role of the music therapist, among others, has broadened from the "ancillary" or "adjunctive" function and, today, he/she may be the therapist of choice in a particular case and function as the prime therapist with all the attendant decision-making responsibility.

After the development of the psychotropic drugs, the most important development in the field of mental health was the change of treatment locale from the large psychiatric hospital to the community where the patient's problems had their origin. This procedure developed from the new philosophy of community mental health. A premium was placed on keeping the psychiatric patient close to his home and two major changes in treatment were involved: short term hospitalization for the acutely ill and the corollary of continuing care within the community.

As the field of mental health altered, as the parameters expanded into the community, and as the enormous hospital-cities were dispersed, new facilities and new approaches had to be developed. In addition to the rather traditional outpatient clinics and general hospital psychiatric wards, alternative treatment facilities multiplied. These included partial hospitals (night or day), social groups and clubs, self-help groups (Synanon, AA, etc.), community health centers, and even more innovative treatment approaches. Trends departing from the traditional medical model often depended on new staffing patterns. Physicians and nurses were supported or replaced by nonmedical mental health workers, as suggested in the recommendations of the Joint Commission on Mental Illness and Health (1961). Today, technicians, usually activity therapists or teachers, function in many settings as prime therapists, responsible for all aspects of patient care except for prescribing medication and admitting or discharging from the hospital. These remain the legal responsibility of the psychiatrist.

FUNCTIONS OF THE MUSIC THERAPIST

Music is an enormously versatile tool, and in the hands of a skilled person, it can contribute to the treatment of almost every disability. Despite its potent qualities, however, music, of itself, is not the therapeutic agent, nor is it a universal Band-Aid. Barnard (1953) addressed this issue: ". . . it is he (the music therapist) who molds the music to the therapeutic goals . . . it is the atmosphere he creates, the relationship he establishes with the patient and the direction in which he turns their attention that makes music therapy out of musical activities" (p. 48). The understanding of how music can influence man's behavior and the utilization of this knowledge in helping the mentally and physically disabled to achieve change are the goals of the music therapist. Implicit in these goals is reliance on training and research.

The music therapist uses music as the basic tool in his/her efforts to attain prescribed behavioral changes, primarily in nonmusical areas of functioning. As used by the music therapist, music refers to a variety of activities including passive listening (background music), active listening, dancing, singing, playing instruments, and song writing.

Psychologically, variables of interest and motivation, as well as the potent force of familiarity, must be considered in selecting a particular piece of music as a stimulus. Music from one culture may have little or no meaning to members of another group, and the choice of inappropriate or unfamiliar music may reduce the therapeutic value of the experience. Classical music may prove wildly irrelevant to an inner city ghetto child, and hard rock may be disruptive and overwhelming in a nursing home or geriatric facility. Occasionally, there is danger of developing overdependence on music when it is employed as an escape from reality or encourages nontherapeutic fantasy. It is the constant responsibility of the music therapist to be aware of negative responses and to monitor the physical and psychological reactions of the patient.

In addition, the music therapist must understand how the patient relates to music. The question is often raised: Must the patient be musical in order to benefit from music therapy? To answer, one would have to examine the concept of musicality. It has been suggested that, like intelligence, music is a theoretical construct; that is, there is no specific locus in the brain nor any specific organ of the body that determines musicality. Instead, a number of discrete abilities can be identified that are found in musical persons. In parallel to several psycholinguistic models, music may be viewed as having expressive, receptive, and associative channels, and each of these can be viewed as having many levels of response ranging from primitive to high cortical levels. The motor or encoding (expressive) aspect would be involved in playing an instrument, singing, or dancing. The integrative (associative) functions probably would be best represented by composition or musicology, while decoding (receptive) musically would involve enjoyment and critical appreciation. Weakness or disability in the receptive level is possible in persons with a highly developed encoding ability; a good singer or performer may have critically "bad taste" or poor musical memory. Professional critics with superior knowledge and keen aesthetic sensibilities may be incapable of singing on pitch and may not even have the ability to play an instrument.

Little or no correlation has been found between intelligence and musicality. In the retarded, as in the general population, these aptitudes exist on a wide continuum with the possibility of intraindividual differences of ability in each area. Thus, the person who responds to hearing music with great interest and who responds to musical stimuli with intense pleasure may be considered musical equally with the person who sings on pitch, possesses a beautiful voice, and a good sense of rhythm. Either may also be categorized as intellectually retarded or gifted depending upon adaptive behavior and IQ. For the music therapist, the patient's interest or responsiveness to the modality is sufficient.

Notwithstanding its proven benefits, music is not effective with all individuals. Any powerful intervention has a potential for both positive and negative effects, and the trained music therapist is alert to the possibility of overexcitation on both a physiological and a psychological level. Arousal may lead to increased attention or to disorganization, depending on intensity of physical reaction to pitch, volume, or rhythm. Occasionally, the frequency range of some instruments, e.g., violins or large church organs, proves noxious to persons with neurological damage. Extreme discomfort and even epileptic seizures may result. Clearly, for such persons music functions as an aversive rather than positive stimulus. Overexposure to highly stimulating music may break down fragile defenses in some psychotics. Performance before an audience may be useful as a therapeutic activity, but, unless judgment is exercised, it can prove harmful to the patient. While self-comparison with the group may be a reality experience, if the comparison is ego-shattering, it may be destructive and antitherapeutic. At other times, performance may encourage narcissistic feelings and exhibitionism.

Sears (1968) identifies the core process by which music therapy effects change: it provides experiences in structure, in self-organization, and in relating to others. Music offers structure because it exists only in time, and the demand for time-ordered response is based in objective reality. In addition, the experience may be structured to any level of ability and can be adapted to psychological levels based on either mood, motivation, intellect, or level of musical knowledge. Thus, realistic time-ordered musical response can range from primitive to highly sophisticated levels of singing, dancing, instrument playing, and listening at every developmental level. Experience in self-organization and self-actualization through music is attained by communication of attitudes and feelings on a nonverbal level and by gratification provided by success-oriented musical experience. Social interaction can be promoted nonverbally through musical experience, e.g., ensemble music demands that the individual subordinate his/her own interests to the group effort if music is to result. The experience of being needed and of being responsible for the group's success can enhance feelings of affiliation. Normalizing participation in community activities can range from attending concerts to membership in church choirs or community choruses and bands.

The music therapist working in a psychiatric hospital rarely works with the stereotypic ideal patient, i.e., the chronic ambulatory, responsive and reliable. Instead, the therapist is confronted by an acutely ill person who will probably be hospitalized for less than 90 days. The rapid turnover of patients makes it difficult to organize and maintain traditional performing groups such as glee clubs, choirs, and dance bands. Rather, there is a need for musical techniques and activities designed to accomplish therapeutic goals such as catharsis, gratification, and relaxation, as well as to reduce the trauma of hospitalization. The music therapist concentrates on providing experiences with immediate gratification: patients play by ear rather than learning to read music; the preferred instruments are the harmonica, the autoharp, the ukelele, and the guitar. He/she may function as co-therapist in group psychotherapy sessions. Interventions are offered at an intense level and are designed to make full use of the patient's adaptive abilities. While individual psychotherapy is rarely available, various therapies are used intensively to reach the patient. For example, music therapy sessions may be employed as an anxiety-reducing prelude to group psychotherapy when the patient has proved unable to communicate verbally.

Music therapy is currently in use in many clinical and educational settings and is applicable in almost every age range. It is as appropriate in a preschool setting as in a geriatric facility. The main area of service remains the psychiatric treatment facility, closely seconded by the special education schools and classrooms, particularly in programs for the moderately and severely mentally and emotionally handicapped. In addition, many nursing homes, daycare centers, rehabilitation centers, community health agencies, and treatment centers for physical disabilities employ music therapists. Music as a nonverbal modality has been found useful in the rehabilitation of socially maladjusted and delinquent youth, and a number of therapists are working in detention centers and prisons throughout the country. The subspecialty of pediatric music therapy developed shortly after music therapy began in psychiatric settings, and, of all areas of application, the use of music with the mentally retarded has grown most rapidly. This, of course, has coincided with the rapid growth of all services for the mentally retarded.

In the 1930s and 1940s, the large training schools and hospitals for children had impressive fife and drum corps, marching bands, and choirs as part of the musical activities under the direction of professional musicians or music educators. The therapeutic goals of such programs were limited, but, given the harsh reality of institutional life and the attendant cultural deprivation, the music experience often provided ego gratification, meaningful interpersonal contact, and increased sensory stimulation, which proved beneficial, and even therapeutic, for the children involved. Occasionally a child might exhibit dramatic improvement in functioning as a result of such participation and might then further profit from the resultant increased attention. This individualized attention moved from an educational to a therapeutic level of interaction. Increasingly, as the goal of the institution changed from maintenance to rehabilitation, there was increasing concern with process, and, as the balance shifted, music therapists were hired to replace music teachers.

An example of a large scale institutional program to which music therapy contributes is Sunland Center in Florida. It serves 650 clients ranging from severely and profoundly retarded children and adults in beds or wheelchairs to young adults working in the Vocational Rehabilitation Unit. As described by the superintendent and the director of music therapy, this comprehensive program seems to provide every client with musical experiences chosen to implement rehabilitative goals. The music therapy department includes a director, four music therapists, and two interns.

Music therapy programs at Sunland include the In Reach Program serving the profoundly retarded in their cottages, the School Program that "cores" with educational objectives to teach primary concepts through music, the Deaf Program, the Autistic Program, and the Choir and Band Programs in which individual tutoring is used to teach instruments. Among the activities at Sunland to which music therapy contributes are:

1. Folk and square dancing
2. Creative and ballet dance
3. Art and music
4. Guitar and piano class
5. Music appreciation class
6. Choir
7. Band
8. Talent shows

Goals include increasing attending behaviors, verbal interaction, socialization skills, self-esteem, movement of handicapped limbs, and improving recall and retention. Similar programs exist in many parts of the United States, although few are as comprehensive.

MUSIC THERAPY AS PART OF COMMUNITY INTERVENTION

Transition from the artificial environment of the hospital or treatment center to the "real world" is made as soon as possible. Ideally, the return is supported by the continuing relationship of therapist and patient, and often music therapy is continued on an outpatient basis or by referral to a music therapy center.

Community therapy demands increased flexibility and responsibility from the music therapist. The patient is subject to greater stress, because he/she deals daily with the reality of social isolation, rejection, and financial need, as well as the anxiety symptomatic of the illness. Environmental stress directly affects the quality of the relationship between therapist and patient, and the need for relevance is apparent. There is a necessity to personalize the therapeutic relationship and to understand the significant relationships and the patient's environment. Because the patient is no longer captive, he/she can terminate therapy if it is not perceived as helpful. This, too, affects the quality of the therapeutic relationship.

The concept of community treatment includes the goal of adjustment within the community, and research indicates a major predictor of adjustment is the degree of social isolation. Without treatment and support, life in an inner city welfare hotel may not differ significantly from life on the ward of a state facility and may result in a high rate of recidivism. Musical interests can be used as normalizing factors by which the therapist can guide the former patient into participation in the musical life of the community. Presenting musical performances in the treatment center, attending public concerts, and/or joining church choirs or community choruses are important tools in rehabilitation and can be important reentry points into the social fabric of the community.

Creative answers to the need for community centers, in which supervised music therapy can be obtained, exist in New York City and in Cleveland, Ohio. A pioneer, community-based service was developed in New York in 1963 by the nonprofit Creative Arts Rehabilitation Center (a/k/a/ Music Therapy Center). There, individualized and small group music therapy for outpatients evolved as a logical response to the movement toward community psychiatry. Today, it has developed into the first psychiatric social rehabilitation program to be based on creative arts therapies. This highly effective agency emphasizes the importance of environmental and relationship factors as well as the role of the arts in promoting emotional and social growth. Referrals are accepted from treatment centers and private psychiatrists, and close contact is maintained throughout treatment by means of reports and consultations. The emphasis on individual therapy is unique.

The educational aspects of the Creative Arts Rehabilitation Center (CARC) reflect its orientation to the community. It is a National Association for Music Therapy (NAMT)-approved graduate clinical training facility in the specialization of community music therapy. Many papers on the subject of community music therapy have been written by the director, Florence Tyson, and published in various journals including the *Journal of*

Music Therapy. CARC has produced three stimulating training films that demonstrate music, dance, and combined therapy techniques in the treatment of cases of severe organicity and chronic schizophrenia. These films are used in over 500 universities and clinical training facilities. An alternate model of the community music therapy center has developed at the Cleveland Music School Settlement under the direction of Anita Louise Steele. A variety of programs and services for children and adults are offered by the music therapy department both in the school itself and throughout the community. Other community agencies are offered the possibility of contracting for music therapy services by the hour, day, or week. Supervision and staffing are provided by the school. The usual contract period is for one year. In this way, agencies that would like to explore the possibilities of a music therapy component are able to begin without assuming full financial and supervisory responsibility. The program has expanded rapidly since its inception and serves a variety of public and private agencies. This facility is also an NAMT-approved training facility for community specialization. Articles by the director have been published in the *Journal of Music Therapy*.

MUSIC THERAPY IN EDUCATION

The expansion of community-based special education programs increased the demand for special music. Generally, the administrative assumption is that the music specialist in the public school should provide music for all students, but in many cases it has happened that the music specialist does not adapt to the needs of handicapped students and clings to educational goals that are inappropriate and even destructive. As a result, the specialty of pediatric music therapy has developed to fill a recognized gap in services. As the field of special education has moved toward the goal of individualized and prescriptive teaching, music therapy has followed. With specialized training, the possibilities of effectiveness have increased. The affective component of music is being utilized in clinical and educational settings to effect behavioral change, both cognitive and psychological. The goal of utilizing music so discriminatively as to control the stimulus in amplitude, direction, and even degree of affective involvement lies within reach. It is clear that the degree of cognitive development is not predictive of affective sensibility. The severely retarded individual feels joy and pain, suffers from rejection and loss, and responds to love. Musical experiences provide opportunities for significant participation at any ability level, provide for meaningful group experiences, and, as nonverbal language, facilitate communication.

When the learning experience can be made gratifying and successful, the student's appetite for new knowledge can be increased. Children tend to regard music activities as play, and even those who have become failure-oriented and avoid involvement are often open and trusting in music. The music therapist who can simplify, rearrange, or match the demands of music activities to the ability level of the student can provide rapid success in skills that are valued in our culture. It is not necessary to read music to play well; music can be learned by rote and played by ear. Above this level, memory can be stimulated by other than traditional notation: pictures, colors, or verbal mediation can be used. The music and the instruments used are matched to the value system of the child and his/her environment; soul, rock, and blues played on harmonicas and guitars can be relevant music in some settings. In other communities, the emphasis may be on folk music. The normalizing potential of music is utilized. Emphasis is on the needs of the client, not on the value system of the therapist.

For the behaviorally disturbed, the order and structure of music have proved valuable. The predictability of the beat and the orderliness of song structure satisfy the need for security. Trust is established. The response of the autistic child to music has been noted by almost every writer on the subject.

One of the most promising new directions in which music therapy is developing is in the use of music in contingency contracting. The fact that children almost universally regard music as a highly reinforcing activity makes it useful.

Both background music and participation in musical activities have been used in the treatment of the physically handicapped. Because all aspects of sensing are ultimately affected by psychological factors, involvement in music may increase the range of function dramatically. Almost every possible degree of physiological involvement can be evoked through musical performance. Music therapists have adapted music instruction to improve muscular strength, joint motion, and coordination. The structure of music can provide an acceptable medium for repeated rehearsal. Participation in a "dance" may enable a child to reach a new level of performance in learning to walk rhythmically and confidently. A client with a limited range of arm motion may find strumming the autoharp so enticing that he/she makes longer and stronger strokes. Feedback is immediate and gratifying.

THE MUSIC THERAPIST ON THE INTERDISCIPLINARY TEAM

The possibility of effective treatment is enhanced by close cooperation among the members of the treatment team, and the efforts of any member can be supported and enhanced by the special knowledge and techniques of another discipline. Often, when the physical or occupational therapist has specified the movement to be achieved, the music therapist may provide the means. Each therapist however, understands the treatment from the standpoint of his/her own discipline and must learn how to communicate these understandings. For example, relaxation is an important objective in the treatment of cerebral palsy, and background music is usually helpful in achieving this goal. However, sedative music reduces tension in persons with athetosis, while stimulative music relaxes those with spasticity. Alternatively, in rare cases, the reaction to music may be increased irritability and loss of coordination. There is no substitute for observation and consultation with other members of the team.

The affinity between speech and music has led to coordinated efforts between speech and music therapists in many treatment centers. Common areas include interest in communication and self-expression, as well as concern with pitch and rhythm. Music is effective in the treatment of delayed speech, aphasia, voice problems, and articulation disorders. It may be used to focus attention on the relevant dimension of sound when basic problems of arousal or lack of attending behavior exist. Songs and musical games increase the value of auditory cues, and attention can be engineered through manipulation of the basic elements of the stimulus, e.g., speed, rhythm, and melody. Paired associate experiments using music and language have been successful in increasing vocabulary. Other interdisciplinary studies indicate the value of music in the treatment of cleft palate. Interesting work has been done through which patients are taught to control nasal emission by playing preband instruments or even brass. Because both overblowing and insufficient force are immediately reflected in the tone produced, the patient gains in autonomy by using self-evaluation. Instruments used include kazoos, harmonicas, and tonettes.

Application with the hearing-impaired chiefly involves vibration and rhythm. Music is a highly motivating diagnostic aid because there is a wide range of frequencies used in orchestral instruments. The person with a partial hearing loss can receive meaningful sound input in the intact frequency range, and relevance and pleasure naturally increase attention and motivation. Music contributes to the development of more adequate speech patterns both through improved rhythmic patterning and by stimulating pitch variation. Vibration can be used to improve attending behavior, while percussion groups and dancing provide important social stimulation, among other benefits. As the music therapist joins educational teams for diagnosis and remediation, he/she is able to contribute special techniques and materials of surprising potency. For example, the modality is useful in establishing basic learning skills in the developmentally disabled. Short term auditory memory, the most intractible of psycholinguistic abilities, can be affected by musical mediators. Other experimental studies have established the value of music as a mnemonic organizer as may readily be observed in the obsessive humming of advertising jingles. Paired associate experiments suggest application with the learning-disabled as well as the mildly retarded. The music therapist, functioning as a resource person by consultation and by demonstration, can apply unique skills to group problems. Such cross-modal activity is often the most stimulating and fruitful aspect of working on a rehabilitation team.

EDUCATION AND TRAINING OF THE MUSIC THERAPIST

For the music therapist, education and training involve learning to use music to accomplish the goal of all professional health workers: the relief of physical and emotional distress. As medical health workers, music therapists must understand the interrelationship of man and society and the origins of physical, social, and emotional illnesses. They must learn how to function as professionals and must appreciate the ethics, the obligations, and the limitations of the professional role. A research orientation is essential.

As described in previous sections dealing with applications for children and adults, music therapy activities are numerous and diversified, demanding many specific skills of the therapists. In addition to performing ability on the major instrument, music therapists must have basic proficiency in voice and piano, a working knowledge of orchestral instruments, and skill in arranging and conducting. They must know the informal, social instruments such as the harmonica, guitar, ukelele, and autoharp. They must be ready improvisers and play many different styles of music, including popular, rock, soul, folk, and religious, as well as classical. These skills are not acquired in a two-year professional entry-level sequence at college but are based on the intensive study of one or more instruments for years before entering college. They are later refined and augmented during the four years of undergraduate study. The apprentice musician also must have developed aesthetic sensitivity and should have personally experienced the healing and expressive power of the art.

As the field of music therapy increased in importance and the practice became more complex, the need for formalizing training and educational procedures became pressing. Students were asking for training, and colleges were devising programs. In 1949, the National Association for Music Therapy (NAMT) was formed by a small group of interested professionals, including music therapists, occupational therapists, physicians and psychiatrists, and clinical psychologists. Government was represented by officials from the veterans' hospitals, who were pioneer employers of music therapists. A primary concern of the new organization was to improve professional qualifications and standards, and the first step taken was to establish training procedures for persons wishing to enter the field. After four years of negotiation among the NAMT members, the clinicians, and

the half-dozen colleges and universities involved in establishing degree curricula, the NAMT, in 1953, published minimal educational and clinical
training requirements for persons wishing to enter the field. This involved a
four-year degree course plus an internship in a psychiatric hospital. The
curriculum was approved by the National Association of Schools of Music
(NASM), the principal accrediting agency for higher education music programs. Over 40 colleges and universities currently offer the NAMT-
approved course leading to certification. As stated in *A Career in Music
Therapy* (NAMT, 1975), the NAMT-approved college curriculum includes
the following components:

Music Therapy	minimum of 10 semester hours
Psychology or Educational Psychology	10–12 semester hours
Sociology and Anthropology	6–8 semester hours
Music	60 semester hours
General Education	30 semester hours
General Electives	6 semester hours

A six-month period of clinical training in an approved music
therapy program under the direction of a Registered Music
Therapist is required in addition to the 128 hours of on-campus
training. This clinical training follows the four years of academic
work and generally precedes the granting of the degree.

Generally, training is on the undergraduate level, but eight universities
now offer advanced degrees, and doctorates in music therapy are granted at
the University of Kansas and the University of Georgia.

The professional music therapy core includes courses on the psychology of music, the influence of music on behavior, music in therapy, and
hospital orientation. It is the least standardized aspect of the requirements,
most clearly reflecting the differing psychological and philosophical orientations of the various universities, although all stress research.

The NAMT has, over the years, favored the presentation of student
research at its national conferences and in its journal, and close connection
between academic and clinical settings has encouraged the maintenance of
interest in research even after the baccalaureate is completed.

Overall, the 60-hour music requirement was adapted from programs
preparing music educators, although emphasis within the preparation is
increasingly on breadth of exposure rather than narrow specialization.
Theory and performance are no longer emphasized.

The provision of a lengthy clinical component, originally consisting of
a six-month continuous residential placement in an approved psychiatric
setting, echoed the medical model. Originally, it was felt that the large hospital psychiatric setting provided the broadest possible base of preparation,
because many psychiatric hospitals treated both children and adults and

often included a population of retarded persons. Professional supervision was available, and similar settings provided the major source of employment, so the experience was vocationally relevant.

Modifications have been made over the years. A report on the state of clinical training (Graham, 1971) indicated the existence of at least three current models for music therapy, including the traditional (analytical) model, the behavior modification model, and the social competence model. By 1976, the list of Approved Clinical Training Centers had grown to more than 100, and the placements were considerably more varied in nature. While most placements were still in either psychiatric hospitals or state-training schools, the movement toward community-based services is reflected in placements in settings with names such as Psychoeducational Center, Mental Health Institute, Children's Center, Public School, Developmental Center, Music School Settlement, Mental Retardation Center, United Cerebral Palsy Center, Sheltered Workshop, Music Therapy Center, Human Resource Institute, and Behavioral Analysis Research Associates.

Within the approved model, some latitude is permitted the colleges. For example, a few universities give academic credit for the internship; others continue to regard internship as a professional entry requirement separated from the academic component. Thus, they avoid the inherent problems of quality control and responsibility in the nonacademic environment.

As the role of the music therapist alters and new competencies are identified, the nature of academic preparation is necessarily affected. Pressure is constantly exerted on every aspect of training. There are moves to liberalize entry requirements and to alter the internship to expand preparation. There is little or no consensus, however, even among the clinicians who represent the here and now. Some feel the behavioral science component must be increased and that the practicing music therapist needs increased training in group therapy techniques. Others cite the need for more knowledge of learning theory and behavior modification. A minority call for a more humanistic approach. Within the core, the demand for earlier field experience is reflected in an additional short term or summer practicum in a clinical setting. A few schools are experimenting with competency-based models within the 60-hour music requirement. With so many competing directions available, some question the emphasis on performance ability. Even the traditional placement of music therapy programs within the college music departments is challenged by those who state emphasis in the title is not on music but on therapy.

To ensure that the approved minimal requirements continue to reflect contemporary practice, committees within the NAMT are delegated the responsibility to review and evaluate curriculum and standards and to make recommendations to the membership at the yearly national convention.

Following completion of the approved sequence, the graduate is eligible for NAMT registration and certification as a Registered Music Therapist (R.M.T.). In a number of state and federal civil service positions, the R.M.T. or eligibility for such registration is specified as a qualification. While this is not true of all positions for music therapists, the R.M.T. is a desirable identification which helps to establish a basis for evaluating a candidate's preparation for the position of music therapist.

Since 1957, the NAMT has had formal registration and certification. Only persons meeting the academic and clinical training requirement, *or its equivalent,* are able to qualify for certification as an R.M.T. Annual regional and national conventions are held. NAMT-sponsored publications include the *Music Therapy Yearbook* (NAMT, 1951–1962), the *Journal of Music Therapy* (NAMT, 1963–present), *Music in Therapy* (Gaston, 1968), and the latest contribution, *The Music Therapy Index* (Eagle, 1976). Information, including film listings, career information, as well as applications for membership, is available from the national headquarters in Kansas:

National Office
National Association for Music Therapy, Inc.
Post Office Box 610
Lawrence, Kansas 66044
Telephone: (913) 842-1909

A second professional organization was formed in 1971, the American Association of Music Therapists (AAMT). It received NASM accreditation in 1975. A prime purpose of AAMT, as stated in the membership application, is to include the many who are enthusiastic about and supportive of the field of music therapy. This tolerance is also expressed in the avowed belief in upgrading the skills of practicing professionals through continuing education to make full registration possible. A number of practicing music therapists have qualified for AAMT registration by demonstrating equivalent proficiency and experience, rather than by graduation from an approved program.

In developing music therapy training programs, AAMT provides guidelines to participating colleges but seems to permit some autonomy, because it does not mandate methods of academic and field training or curricular course requirements. The approved curriculum is competency based rather than tied to semester hours, and responsibility for internship and supervision is the province of the certifying college. At present, three universities have become affiliated with AAMT and have initiated approved music therapy sequences. Graduates of these programs qualify for provisional registration with AAMT. After completion of two years of full-time professional work as music therapists, they are awarded full certification as Certified Music Therapists (C.M.T.).

For further information or membership application write:

Executive Secretary, American Association for Music Therapy
c/o Division of Music Education, New York University
777 Education Building
35 West Fourth Street
Washington Square, New York 10003

MUSIC THERAPY RESEARCH TRENDS AND ISSUES

In any discipline, theory is characterized by a main current and many conflicting currents. Presently, the major currents in psychiatric thought are represented by four theoretical models: the biophysical, the psychodynamic, the behavioral, and the socioecological positions. Most research in music therapy is based on the latter three, but interesting and possibly productive counter-currents reflect popular interest in psychophysiological and psychic phenomena. Some music research explores these areas in relation to the effects of music on both the autonomic and the central nervous systems. Studies of music therapy in relation to biofeedback, psychedelic peak psychotherapy, and altered states of consciousness have been published recently. With more sophisticated instrumentation, aesthetic and emotional responses to music may be quantified reliably, producing valuable information for the music therapist.

Wagner (1975), in discussing biofeedback, suggested that future electroencephalographic (EEG) research should include investigation of the relation between music and that neurophysiological area variously termed "vigilance," "arousal," or "activation." A provocative finding cited is that musicians produce almost one-third more alpha waves (generally associated with meditative states or day dreaming) than do nonmusicians during music listening experiences.

The psychedelic experience is pursued through meditation and/or drug experiences. Music is used at the few clinical research centers in the United States permitted to experiment with high doses of hallucinatory drugs in the psychotherapeutic treatment of alcoholics, narcotic addicts, and terminal cancer patients. The aim is to produce a peak experience or altered state of consciousness (ASC). Bonny and Savary (1973) report on a technique to achieve the ASC by using music alone. It is stated that much of the phenomena experienced under the influence of a psychedelic drug also evolves through the process of eliciting ASC with appropriate programmed music. As a supportive therapy used with other treatment systems, music is used to facilitate release of intense emotionality and to affect a narrowing of attention and heightening of concentration. Music reportedly contributes to the cosmic or transcendental experience that can occur during these sessions. The *Journal of Music Therapy* has published reports on these efforts through the past few years, as well as articles on music and transactional analysis, music and relaxation, and other group therapy techniques.

It is more than possible that future developments in the field of music therapy may be based on all or some of these pioneer efforts. It is already clear that, as a "firing-line professional," i.e., as the person actually working with the patient, the music therapist needs the information supplied by research to determine the validity of present techniques and to discover more effective treatment procedures. As the music therapist leaves the security of the therapeutic team and advances further into the community setting, he/she is forced by the demands of the new roles of clinician, educator, and consultant into assuming ever greater responsibilities. Eventually, the music therapist must do battle with the problem looming in the background, i.e., prevention rather than treatment. This is true of all mental health workers.

The activity therapists inherited the position on the firing line because the traditional medical model was clearly unable to deal with the large number of potential clients. The increased availability of treatment within the community, the reduction of stigma, increased sophistication, and lessening of formality have all contributed to the greater demand for treatment. At the same time, the ratio of psychiatrists to patients is declining steadily, estimated five years ago to be at the unworkable ratio of one psychiatrist per 13,000 population. Even this ratio is not reflective of the reality because most psychiatrists tend to cluster in a few large cities, leaving the bulk of the population without any possibility of service. A similar situation of shortage exists for all mental health workers, including music therapists. As a consequence, a trend has developed in some large facilities for music therapy activities to be conducted by music specialists, supervised and directed by experienced music therapists.

The old sibling rivalries between available services have become increasingly irrelevant in the clear light of pressing and insatiable need for mental health manpower. They should be abandoned along with other relics of our past history. We are all justified, we are all needed, and we are all overwhelmed by the demand for our skills.

REFERENCES

Barnard, R. 1953. Music therapy as an adjunct therapy. *In* E. Gilliland (ed.), Music Therapy 1952, Second Book of Proceedings of the National Association for Music Therapy, pp. 45–49. National Association for Music Therapy, Lawrence, Kan.

Bonny, I., and Savary, L. M. 1973. Music and Your Mind. Harper and Row, New York.

Eagle, C. (ed.). 1976. Music Therapy Index, Vol. 1. National Association for Music Therapy, Lawrence, Kan.

Gaston, E. (ed.). 1968. Music in Therapy. Macmillan, New York.

Graham, R. M. 1971. A new approach to student affiliations in music therapy. J. Music Ther. 8:43–52.

Joint Commission on Mental Illness and Health. 1961. Action for Mental Health: Final Report of the Joint Commission on Mental Illness and Health. Basic Books, New York.

National Association for Music Therapy. 1951–1962. Music Therapy Yearbook. Articles and Proceedings of National Conferences. Allen Press, Lawrence, Kan.

National Association for Music Therapy. 1963 to present. Journal of Music Therapy. National Association for Music Therapy, Lawrence, Kan.

National Association for Music Therapy. 1975. A Career in Music Therapy. National Association for Music Therapy, Lawrence, Kan.

Sears, W. W. 1968. Processes in music therapy. In E. T. Gaston (ed.), Music in Therapy. Macmillan, New York.

Wagner, M. 1975. Brainwaves and biofeedback. Implications for music research. J. Music Ther. 12:46–58.

SUGGESTED READINGS

Alvin, J. 1975. Music for the Handicapped Child. 2nd Ed. Oxford University Press, London.

Alvin, J. 1975. Music Therapy. Hutchinson, London.

Bright, R. 1974. Music in Geriatric Care. St. Martin's Press, New York.

British Society for Music Therapy. British Journal of Music Therapy. 48 Lancaster Road, London.

Dobbs, D. B. 1966. The Slow Learner and Music: A Handbook for Teachers. Oxford University Press, London.

Eagle, C. (ed.). 1976. Music Therapy Index, Vol. 1. National Association for Music Therapy, Lawrence, Kan.

Edwards, E. 1976. Music Education for the Deaf. 2nd Ed. Merrian Eddy, New York.

Farnsworth, P. R. 1969. The Social Psychology of Music. 2nd Ed. Iowa State University Press, Ames, Iowa.

Gaston, E. (ed.). 1968. Music in Therapy. Macmillan, New York.

Gordon, E. 1971. The Psychology of Music Teaching. Prentice-Hall, Englewood Cliffs, N.J.

Herbert, W. K. 1974. Opening Doors Through Music. Charles C Thomas, Springfield, Ill.

Knight, D., Pope, L., Ludwig, A., and Strazulla, M. 1957. The role of varied therapies in the rehabilitation of the retarded child. Am. J. Ment. Defic. 61:508–515.

Levine, H., and Levine, G. 1975. Teaching Music in Special Education. Teaching Resources, Boston.

Ludwig, A. J., and Tyson, F. 1969. A song for Michael: Case history and analysis. J. Music Ther. 6:82–86.

Lundin, R. W. 1953. An Objective Psychology of Music. Ronald Press, New York.

Madsen, C. K., Greer, R. D., and Madsen, C. H. 1975. Research in Music Behavior: Modifying Music Behavior in the Classroom. Teachers College Press, Columbia University, New York.

Madsen, C. K., and Madsen, C. H. 1970. Experimental Research in Music. Prentice-Hall, Englewood Cliffs, N.J.

Michel, D. E. 1976. Music Therapy. Charles C Thomas, Springfield, Ill.

National Association for Music Therapy. 1976. What You as a Career Counselor Need to Know about Music Therapy. National Association for Music Therapy, Lawrence, Kan.

Nordoff, P., and Robbins, C. 1971. Music for Handicapped Children. St. Martin's Press, New York.

Nordoff, P., and Robbins, C. 1971. Music Therapy in Special Education. John Day, New York.

Schullian, D., and Schoen, M. 1948. Music and Medicine (Facsimile ed.) Essay Index Reprint Service, New York.

University of the State of New York. 1971. Improving Music Experiences for Emotionally Handicapped Children: Proceedings of the Institute. University of the State of New York, State Education Department, Division for Handicapped Children, Division of the Humanities and the Arts, Albany, N.Y.

University of the State of New York. 1971. The Role of Music in the Special Education of Handicapped Children. University of the State of New York, State Education Department, Division for Handicapped Children, Division of the Humanities and the Arts, Albany, N.Y.

Unkefer, R. F. 1957. Music Therapy in the Rehabilitation of the Adult Blind. State Department of Social Welfare of Kansas, Topeka, Kan.

Wolfe, D. E., Burns, S., and Wichmann, K. 1975. Analysis of Music Therapy Group Procedures. Golden Valley Health Center, Minneapolis, Minn.

Wolpow, R., Vorrill, G., and Bremer, D. 1975. Recreational Music Therapy for the Profoundly and Severely Mentally Retarded. New York State Department of Mental Hygiene, Albany, N.Y.

NURSING

Karen Gordon-Davis
and Judith Strasser

The nursing profession is in a stage of rapid growth. Nursing functions are changing, and the transition is altering the form of nursing. Nurses are in a unique position because of their broad educational preparation in the physical and behavioral sciences and the liberal arts. Holistic approaches to issues, individuals, and group situations make nurses valuable assets to interdisciplinary planning and the provision of health care services. Moreover, nurses are prepared to function in a variety of ways.

To provide the reader with an awareness of these various services, the authors have chosen a historical approach to the nursing profession, followed by a description of the profession itself and the people served and then a review of some of the pertinent issues.

HISTORICAL PERSPECTIVE

Human history is divided into three epochs of social evolution. Each epoch can be characterized by advances in economic activity. Savagery, the most rudimentary, was based on hunting and food gathering. Barbarism began with food production and advanced to agriculture and stock raising. Civilization brought the ancient world to the point of commodity production and exchange.

In the beginning of the process of evolution, society was nurtured and healed within the structure of the matriarchal clan. Women were the food gatherers, the farmers, the child rearers, and the *carers*. Women preserved society through taboos surrounding procreation and cannibalism. Through gathering and administering herbs and roots, women eventually became the *curers* as well.

Some anthropologists contend that the use of mechanical weapons by men (and women's refusal to wield weapons) led to the origin of patriarchy and the resulting family and social structure known today. Somewhere during this transition from matriarchal clan to patriarchal family and society a distancing phenomenon evolved which caused women to be either penalized or pedestaled. Nursing, comprised for the most part of women, also was penalized or pedestaled.

During the 18th and much of the 19th centuries, women in the United States enjoyed the majority status in the medical arena. Women practiced the healing arts both within and outside the home. Penalization occurred when science and reform were pitted against art and tradition. The male physician entered into battle against the female healer. This contention was most visible in the realm of childbirth, which had previously been an area reserved to women.

In spite of a 1912 Johns Hopkins' study which indicated that nurse midwives were more competent in the delivery of babies than most American physicians, midwives were depicted as callous, unclean, and illiterate.

The medical profession set out to, and effectively did, eliminate female health practitioners. Male physicians became dominant, and medicine was for the most part eliminated as an occupational choice for women. State health practice acts forbade women to function as midwives or independent practitioners, the doors to medical schools were closed to women, and nursing remained their only avenue for employment in the United States' health care system.

Most nurses were basic helpers who cared for relatives or neighbors. It was only with the advent of Florence Nightingale in the mid-19th century that trained nurses appeared and that some notion of nursing theory evolved.

Following the Crimean War and the involvement of many upper class women in nursing, ideals of graciousness, femininity, and obedience were extolled for the practicing nurse. Penalizing nurses diminished, and pedestals were erected.

With the end of the 1800s, suffragettes were proclaiming equal rights for women. World War I created needs for women in the service and in other occupations, and soon after the war the vote was awarded to women. During this period, nursing theory was virtually nonexistent. Most nursing books were basic procedural manuals originating from hospitals. Emphasis was on making the patient comfortable through physical alteration of the environment. People who required the services of a nurse were presumed to be sick and therefore dependent.

World War II called forth a greater involvement of women in occupations formerly believed to be "men's work." Nurses in the armed services, Red Cross, and at home proved that women were neither frail nor unintelligent. Nursing theory progressed to the point where nursing was considered both an art and a science imbued with a spirit of dedication to service. Nursing education became grounded in biological sciences such as chemistry, anatomy, physiology, and microbiology, and the art of observing medical signs and symptoms was stressed.

Following World War II, nursing began to utilize the behavioral and social sciences. The evaluation of conceptual models in nursing was given impetus by the civil rights movement, the feminist movement, the advance of knowledge in the physical, social, and behavioral sciences, the existence of a national health care system which required governmental intervention, and a national proclamation that health care services were the right of all individuals.

Today, nursing is, like other professions, in a process of definition both to itself and to the public. Despite misrepresentation by the news media for almost half a century, and despite patriarchy, penalization, and pedestaliza-tion, nursing has advanced rapidly in the development of conceptual constructs and theory, in the beginnings of nursing research, and in a deeper understanding of technological advances.

PROFESSIONAL NURSING

Before describing the purposes and goals of the nursing profession, it is necessary to clarify what a profession is, who professional and technical or paraprofessional nurses are, and what nurses do and for whom, with what tools and skills.

To be a professional implies a lengthy period of intellectual study and training. Lengthy, as it applies to nursing, has been defined recently as that period of time needed to obtain a baccalaureate degree in nursing. Accord-ing to this definition, large numbers of people who are providing nursing services are not in fact professional nurses.

Groups providing nursing services include hospital nursing assistants, home health aides, licensed practical nurses, and registered nurses who are diploma school graduates and graduates of associate degree programs. Both diploma (two- and three-year hospital-based programs) and associate degree (two-year college programs) graduates, by virtue of their graduation from such programs, are eligible to take a state licensing examination. After achieving a passing grade on the examination, these nurses are registered in the state in which they took the examination and may write R.N. (Registered Nurse) after their names. Graduates of baccalaureate programs (four-year college programs) are eligible to take the same examination, which, if passed, affords the baccalaureate graduates the same privilege. Graduates of practical nurse programs (often a one-year program affiliated with a hospital) take a separate state examination and upon satisfactory completion of that examination are entitled to write L.P.N. (Licensed Practical/Vocational Nurse) after their names. Nursing assistants function in hospitals and private homes under the direction of a professional or technical nurse, have varied lengths of training time, and require no licensure or certification.

In short, as defined by the nursing profession, a professional nurse in the United States is a graduate of a four-year college program who is licensed/registered in at least one state. Technical nurses are graduates of two-year college programs or diploma programs. Practical nurses are graduates of one-year training programs, and assistants/aides are unlicensed with varied training periods usually conducted at a health care institution.

Nursing programs also provide for advanced preparation at both the master's and doctoral levels. However, of the 586,842 registered nurses employed in 1966, only 2.7% had one or more graduate degrees (ANA, 1970–1971).

Many nurses with doctoral degrees have advanced preparation in fields other than nursing. This situation leads to confusion; it is only on an individual basis that primary affiliation can be determined. For instance, a nurse-sociologist may prefer to be considered a sociologist-nurse.

NURSING FORM AND FUNCTION

Further clouding the issue of who is or is not a professional nurse is the notion of the *expanded role*.

For years nurses have used the language and tools of medicine. Nurses have spoken in medical terms, have used physical curative tools, and have branched into medicine as *nurse-midwives* and *nurse-anesthetists*. Registered nurses at various levels of preparation have been accepted into training programs for these specialized expansions of role and have aided physicians in performing technical tasks with the added caring dimension of nursing. Moreover, nurses have provided and are providing medical-curative services in medically isolated rural and inner city locales. Nurses also have provided medical services during times of catastrophe.

Today nurse-practitioners are trained to perform physical examinations and to order diagnostic tests and specified medications for clients. Nurse-practitioners act as primary health care providers for individuals and groups. Nurses, in their expanded role, demonstrate curative (medical) skills in addition to caring (nursing) skills.

Training periods for nurse-midwives, anesthetists, and practitioners vary considerably in length of time: from four to six months to two or more years. It is perhaps worthy of note that some nurses functioning in expanded roles may not be considered professional nurses by their peers, because by definition the professional nurse has a baccalaureate degree.

Much questioning and debate in nursing circles has centered around the idea of professionalism and the requirement of a specific body of knowledge. Nurse educators contend that nursing knowledge, although grounded in the physical and behavioral sciences, is unique. Other factions request clarification and greater specificity as to what, in fact, is unique to nursing.

The purpose of nursing is to provide nuturing care and health services to individual persons and to groups of people. The ultimate goal is the promotion of as high a level of wellness as possible in individuals, families, and society at large.

Nursing services are rendered both directly and indirectly. Direct service implies a caring relationship, a holistic approach to the unit of care (individual, family, or community), the ability to integrate and arrange in priority the approaches of other disciplines to that unit of care, education of the care unit for health promotion and illness/accident prevention, and use of technical/mechanical skills. Direct nursing services can be administered either institutionally or extrainstitutionally and require only a nurse and a unit of care.

Indirect nursing services include nursing research, nursing administration, and the education of nurses in generic programs and through continuing education. Indirect nursing services originate from institutions of higher learning.

The scope of professional nursing varies with the individuals practicing nursing. Licensed practical nurses, associate degree registered nurses, and diploma school registered nurses are prepared to function in a technically skilled way with relatively less skilled assessment and strategic abilities than registered nurses. Registered nurses, on the other hand, who are prepared for nursing at a baccalaureate level should be able to acquire technical skills rapidly and should possess more assessment abilities, a wider range of intervention strategies, and greater skill in forming and monitoring relationships to achieve specific ends. Registered nurses with master's degrees and doctoral degrees may function as nursing service administrators, nurse educators, consultants, or clinical nurse specialists. These nurses possess a wide range of skills. Registered nurses in expanded roles perform some medical functions as well as nursing functions.

The following three tables present a concise description of kinds of nurses, types of functions, and requirements for practice.

Limitations of nursing services are at present difficult to determine. Finances, public expectations, law, and the absorption of many nursing functions by other disciplines make this area cloudy but pave the way for the present process of internally defining what it is in fact that professional nursing has to offer the public.

Clients for whom nursing services are appropriate include all people. Every individual, group, or society exists somewhere along a health-illness continuum. Everybody is either *well, worried and well, early sick,* or *sick.*

Table 1. Qualifications and functions of nurses

Title	Abbreviation	Educational qualifications	Certification or licensure	Performed function
Nursing assistant/ nursing aide	N.A.	Inservice education at health care institution. Testing and performance evaluation as provided by institution.	Institutional sanction— no licensure or certification	Varies with type of institution. May provide some direct patient/client services under supervision.
Licensed practical/ vocational nurse	L.P.N. L.V.N.	Completion of accredited practical nursing program. Passing score in state licensing exam.	State licensure	Administration of treatments and medication as prescribed within limits. Under authority of physician or registered nurse.
Registered nurse	R.N.	Completion of accredited nursing program: 1. diploma 2. associate degree 3. baccalaureate Passing score in state licensing exam.	State licensure	Administration of treatments and medication as prescribed within limits. Performs technical functions. Accountable to nursing service supervisor/ director. Professional responsibilities: Teaching (individual/group); health promotion; illness prevention; supervision.

Table 2. Functional tracts of nurses

Title	General medical/ functional tracts		Nursing functional tracts
Registered Nurse (R.N.)	1.	Medicine (general)	Direct service
	2.	Medicine (special—coronary or pulmonary care subspecialty)	1. Clinical service/client teaching
	3.	Surgery (general)	
	4.	Surgery (special—surgical intensive care, operating room, subspecialty)	Indirect service 2. Administration (additional education beneficial)
	5.	Obstetrics (includes well baby, premature infant, mother in labor, and ante- and postpartum, family planning, etc.)	3. Nursing Education (additional education beneficial) 4. Research (additional education beneficial)
	6.	Gynecology	
	7.	Pediatrics	
	8.	Geriatrics	
	9.	Psychiatry	
	10.	Emergency Service (includes all of the above tracts)	
	11.	Community Health (includes all of the above tracts except special medicine and surgery)	

Primary, secondary, and tertiary prevention can be offered by professional nurses to those situated in the first three health states, and care of the sick has always been considered a nursing function. Caring for the sick requires various skills and levels of preparation according to the type and degree of illness.

Nurses, functioning as members of interdisciplinary teams, can perform a myriad of tasks. These tasks should evolve progressively within some shared framework and should pertain to clearly delineated goals. The roles of nurses in interdisciplinary action teams would be determined by the situation at hand. Nurses could function in any or all phases of planning, performing, and evaluating as *advocates, clarifiers,* and/or *implementers* of the *triage.*

Nurses have long functioned as *advocates,* helping to protect clients from often confusing and sometimes depersonalizing systems of service. This role is shared, of course, with other disciplines such as social work but is an area of expertise for nurses. One such example is the current move-

Table 3. Nursing role expanded, extended

(R.N.) Title	Classification/Degree	Preparation	Expanded role	Extended role
Clinical specialist	Master's degree with clinical specialization	Accredited master's program in nursing		Highest order of professional nursing practice. Provides nursing care drawing on wide knowledge base. Collaborates with health team members. Provides leadership to other nurses as a role model. May function independently.
Nurse-midwife[c]	Certification and ongoing education required (many have master's degree)	Satisfactory completion of approved nurse midwifery program	Provides prenatal monitoring and family teaching, assists mother with labor, delivers uncomplicated cases, conducts postpartum evaluations and gynecological checkups, acts as primary provider of family planning services.	Follows medical specialty.

	Certification	Education	Function
Nurse-anesthetist[c]	Certification	Completion of approved school of anesthesia	Administers anesthesia. Responsible to physician.
Nurse[a] Practitioner[b] 1. Pediatric[c] 2. Geriatric 3. Primary Care 4. Family	Certification pending	Satisfactory completion of nurse-practitioner program and internship, if required	Secures health/illness history, performs comprehensive physical examinations, teaches family/client, orders specified laboratory procedures, recommends medical regimen, follows health progress, acts as primary provider.

[a] Nurse Practitioners/Associates/Clinicians are not physicians' assistants because of their nursing background, although in actual practice it may be difficult, if not impossible, to distinguish between the functioning of the two.

[b] All nurses are practitioners, but all are not nurse-practitioners.

[c] Nurses who function in expanded roles may also have preparation for the extended role of clinical specialist. They are, however, two clearly separate roles: the expanded role being medical/curative and the extended role being nursing/caring.

ment toward a patients' bill of rights in which nursing has played a large part.

Because of a broad behavioral and scientific knowledge base, nurses, as *clarifiers*, could function in the clarification of both process and product. Clarification of who we are, where we are going, and how we will get there are major tasks as anyone who has worked in a small group can testify.

Triage is the process of determining priorities of need and fitting those needs with appropriate services. As interdisciplinary team members and, again, because of a broad base of knowledge, nurses could prove to be assets for effecting appropriate services that are cost effective. For instance, nurses could be utilized in areas dealing with simple medical, social, educational, or behavioral problems, and could determine when greater depth of expertise (higher cost) is required to achieve specific goals.

RESEARCH NEEDS

In order to keep pace with technology, the social sciences, and the identification of the function and effects of nursing interventions, nursing leaders acknowledge a fundamental need for research. In 1952, *Nursing Research,* a journal containing various research studies, was first circulated. Despite a small circulation, the movement underlining the importance of research in nursing had begun. Today, major universities hold research symposia in nursing, and nursing research is treated with greater emphasis at graduate and undergraduate levels.

Some conflicts concerning the value of pure versus applied research have surfaced, but in general it is thought that *nursing* research is what is greatly needed. Both pure and applied research would be beneficial for a profession with such a dearth of hard data.

One item of prime importance will be success in determining differences in quality as well as in quantity of nursing care. Many tasks in nursing are functional and easily quantified. Functional tasks also are performed by nonprofessional personnel. Therefore, it rests with nursing researchers to identify qualitative differences inherent in professional nursing performance. Without validation that professionalism in nursing is cost efficient and effective, nursing functions may well be allocated to nonprofessional personnel.

Funding for research in nursing is a major problem. Money for such purposes is generally not available through health care institutions, in part because costs have soared during the present inflationary cycle. Although nursing research would benefit patients in hospitals and residents of nursing homes at the direct care level, the public has not been made aware of such a possibility.

Nursing research is conducted by students fulfilling requirements for degrees and is supported by some nursing administrators. Large university hospitals may budget small sums for nursing research. By and large, most nursing research is clinical and uses an interdisciplinary approach. Because of the state of the art of research, studies of communities as entities are limited to groups of researchers. Studies of individuals or small groups are quite feasible.

Many leaders in professional nursing contend that the future of the profession lies in researching the effects of professional nursing functions, in describing what professional nurses do, in delineating how nursing functions differ from what nonprofessionals or paraprofessionals do, and in specifying how much professional nursing costs.

TIME AND COST OF SERVICES

In 1974, there were 407 registered nurses per 100,000 population in the United States. Statistics from the year 1972 indicate that educational status was as follows (ANA, 1974–1975):

Diploma school graduates	801,780
Baccalaureate graduates	133,085
Master's-prepared graduates	21,527
Nurses with doctoral degrees	1,539

In 1972 and 1973, 529,667 registered nurses were employed in hospitals, 58,241 in public health facilities, 33,116 in mental health facilities, 5,587 in osteopathic hospitals, and an estimated 55,617 in physicians' offices. Licensed practical nurses numbered 427,000 with 260,000 employed by hospitals, 73,000 in nursing homes, and 4,000 in public health facilities. Ninety thousand were functioning as private duty nurses, industrial nurses, or in various other areas (ANA, 1974–1975).

Programs for registered nurses numbered 889 (National League for Nursing) accredited and 530 nonaccredited. The cost of preparation varied, with the highest yearly expenditures per student made by diploma schools. Baccalaureate and associate degree programs cost the student as much as any college student, depending on the type of institution attended. Costs to the college, however, are higher per student because of needed laboratory space, equipment, and clinical supervision. Recommended faculty/student clinical supervision ratio ranges from one to two faculty members per 10 students. The clinical supervisor/student ratio is decided upon by evaluating client care needs and the type of clinical setting. For instance, a student nurse in an intensive care unit would require closer supervision than would a student in many ambulatory units.

The estimated numbers of budgeted nurse-faculty positions for 1974 were as follows (ANA, 1974–1975):

Diploma schools	8,092
Associate degree programs	5,899
Baccalaureate and doctoral programs	8,322
Practical nurse programs	5,504

The median annual salaries for baccalaureate faculty in 1973 were: instructor, $10,526; assistant professor, $12,400; associate professor, $15,061; and professor, $19,998.

Few registered nurses in service positions are remunerated on a fee-for-service basis. Most nurses are paid by institutions. Cost to the consumer is reflected in his/her total bill. Private duty nurses are paid according to a specified time frame, and, in 1974, these nurses earned $32-45 per eight-hour shift.

Nurses' salaries are generally higher in community hospitals than in medical centers, particularly those associated with universities. Presumably, this is because of other benefits such as higher status, educational benefits, and social rewards linked with institutions of higher learning. The average starting monthly wages for registered nurses in 1973 were as follows:

	Medical Center	Hospital
Nurse-anesthetist	$940-1,158	$1,005-1,231
Nurse-practitioner	880-1,036	817-1,006
Head nurse	855-1,040	810-986
Staff nurse	717-898	706-869

Median annual salary in 1974 for licensed practical/vocational nurses was $7,210. Median annual salaries for community health nurses from 1970-1974 were as follows (ANA, 1974-1975):

	Official Agency	Nonofficial Agency	Board of Education
Staff nurse	$10,835	$ 9,503	$10,616
Supervisor	13,425	12,160	14,800
Director	16,240	15,225	

It is thought provoking to observe that nurses employed by institutions are at times paid for their presence or availability rather than for services rendered. Nurses who are on call or who staff the night shift may perform no direct client service. These nurses often perform administrative, clerical, or no functions and have minimal client contact.

CURRENT ISSUES

Nurses, as professionals, function from within the existing health care delivery system where they greatly outnumber all other medical and paraprofessional health care deliverers. Because of their preparation, nurses possess a holistic understanding of their clients' needs and a broad knowledge base concerning the disciplines that provide service to these clients. Issues that affect nurses, their interdisciplinary functioning, and their delivery of health care services are both external and internal. Because of the varied levels of preparation, membership in professional organizations, and varying professional activities of nurses, their responses to issues may differ considerably. Therefore, only the issues will be described with little attempt to define consensus of response.

The health care system itself is an external issue affecting nursing. The present focus on *distributive health care* as well as the trend of third party payers to advocate *health promotion* and *illness prevention* are causing role shifts in nursing. Nurses involved in episodic services provide direct care for the sick or injured in hospitals. Nurses involved in distributive services also provide direct care, but the main focus is on health teaching. *Funding* within the health care system is presently directed toward institutions providing *primary care services*. The notion of primary care includes the first contact and/or a continuity of contacts. Because form follows function which follows funding, nurses are performing primary care skills, acting as primary providers (primary care nurse-practitioners), and functioning as primary care nurses in inpatient primary care nursing units. These nurses frequently do not wear caps or white uniforms (presently devalued as symbols).

Primary care fosters *allegiance to the client* (whether individual or group). Traditionally, nurses have been loyal to institutions that were usually controlled by the medical profession. Individual nonmedical health service administrators were generally authoritatively weak (and low salaried) so that control was exerted easily by those with the most economic power, i.e., physicians. Today, administrators are better prepared and medical staffs are more and more controlled by government, law, the public, and insurance companies. In this transition, nurses are pulling away from allegiance to institutions or medicine, and are increasingly becoming client advocates. This position creates considerable tension because institutions, not clients, usually pay nurses' salaries. Exceptions to this include extrainstitutionally hired private duty nurses and a few nurses who are paid on a fee-for-service basis.

The autonomy of professional nursing is a pertinent issue today, partly because of the diminishing control of physicians, and partly because of the *usurpation of past nursing functions* by new divisions of labor such as pharmacy technicians, inhalation therapists, dental hygienists, unit clerks, unit managers, and laboratory technicians.

Internally, nurses are searching for *clarity in articulation* of what nursing is and *autonomy* over the domain of what nursing does. Emphasis is on theory building, research, and upgrading educational preparation. Areas of internal strife include the fairly recent "war" between nursing education and nursing service. Twenty or more years ago, directors of nursing service also functioned as directors of schools of nursing. The promotion of college versus diploma education led to the demise of this dual role and the latent anger of those who stayed (nursing service) and those who went (nursing educators). This dilemma of loyalty, though oversimplified, has exerted a great and negative influence on the nursing profession's growth in both service and education. Present steps toward the mutual acknowledgment of the complementary value of nursing education and nursing service in some areas of the country may be reversing this trend.

Identity, status, and the *"isms" of sex and race* are additional internal issues affecting the nursing profession and practice. Developing a clear identity for both a profession and individuals within a profession, whose background and functioning are eclectic and diverse, poses many questions. The role and status of nurses are diverse. Status may be identified at almost any place along a continuum ranging from menial labor to middle management.

Sexism and racism exert a profound effect upon nursing. The nursing professional is most often female. This can most likely be attributed to the fact that the stereotype of the nurse was that of a mother (nurturer and carer of patients) and a wife (helper of physicians). Today, such stereotypes are gradually disappearing, and more men have the courage to become nurses. Furthermore, more blacks and other minorities are now enrolled in nursing programs from which they were previously excluded. Only a few exemplary black schools of nursing education existed in this country, but their graduates are present today at the highest levels of professional nursing.

It is worthy of note that nurses in general are only recently becoming active with regard to the feminist and civil rights movements.

Internal issues of educational preparation are still unanswered and the questions posed are somewhat unsettling. How should nurses be prepared for what kind of a world tomorrow? Which health issues are priorities? Will nursing control its destiny through state Nurse Practice Acts and state licensing examinations or will institutional licensure allow each hiring institution to specify educational preparation and service performance?

Internal questions concerning the small numbers of nurses committed to their own professional organizations are of prime importance as are the external questions of nursing's role in regional health planning, kinds and evaluation of services, and the provision of services where needed.

Internally, major tasks are those involving nursing research and theory building. This task will be pursued following attention to the priorities of functioning. These priorities are not easily identified because of the diversity of levels and the types of work in which nurses are involved. Interdisciplinary functioning with a clear appreciation and understanding of what nursing is and can offer can help both the public and nursing itself. With continuing practice, education, and theory development, new forms will gestate and new life will permeate the present systemless system of health care provisions.

PROFESSIONAL ORGANIZATIONS

The two most prominent nursing organizations are the American Nurses' Association (ANA) and the National League for Nursing (NLN).

The ANA was comprised of 196,024 members in 1974. Membership is limited to nurses and nursing students and, in the light of the total number of nurses, appears rather small. Purposes of the ANA include the fostering of high standards of nursing practice, the promotion of the professional and educational advancement of nurses, and the promotion of the welfare of nurses toward the objective that all people receive better nursing care. The ANA is comprised of four Commissions (Nursing Education, Nursing Services, Economics and General Welfare, and Nursing Research), five Divisions on Practice (Community Health, Geriatrics, Maternal and Child Health, Medicine and Surgery, and Psychiatry and Mental Health), the Congress for Nursing Practice, Affirmative Action, Council of State Boards of Nursing, Coordinating Council, American Academy of Nursing, and Programs and Services.

In 1974, the National League for Nursing (NLN) consisted of 15,219 individual members and 1,793 agency members. The chief functions of the NLN include licensure of nurses and accreditation of schools of nursing.

Nurses belong to other professional organizations that may be linked to one or both of the larger nursing organizations, medical groups, government, or education. These organizations may be based on the individual's place of work, type of work, or medical, governmental, or educational association. Some of these organizations are:

American Association of Critical Care Nurses
American Association of Industrial Nurses
American Association of Nephrology Nurses and Technicians
American Association of Neurosurgical Nurses
American Association of Nurse Anesthetists
American College of Nurse Midwives
American Public Health Association
American Urological Association
Association of Operating Room Nurses
Emergency Department Nurses Association
Nurses' Association of the American College of Obstetricians and Gynecologists
United States Nurse Corps (Military Divisions)
United States Public Health Service
United States Veterans Administration Nursing Services

The following list provides the titles, addresses, and primary publications of major nursing organizations.

American Nurses' Association, Inc. (ANA), 2420 Pershing Road, Kansas City, Missiouri 64108

Washington Office: 1030 15th Street, N.W., Washington, D.C. 20005, Publication: *The American Journal of Nursing*

American Nurses' Foundation, Inc. (ANF), 2420 Pershing Road, Kansas City, Missouri 64108, Publication: *Nursing Research Report*

National Commission for the Study of Nursing and Nursing Education (NCSNNE), 208 Westfall Road, Rochester, New York 14620, Publication: *The Lysaught Report*

National Federation of Licensed Practical Nurses (NFLPN), 250 W. 57th Street, New York, New York 10010, Publication: *Nursing Care*

National League for Nursing (NLN), 10 Columbus Circle, New York, New York 10019, Publication: *Nursing Outlook*

SUGGESTED READINGS

American Nurses' Association. 1970-1971, 1974-1975. Facts About Nursing. American Nurses' Association, New York.

American Nurses' Association. 1976. Analysis of a Proposal for Credentialing Health Manpower. American Nurses' Association, New York.

American Nurses' Association Committee on Education. 1965. First position on education for nursing. Am. J. Nurs. 165:106-111.

Booth, R. Z. 1972. Primary care: The role of the nurse. Newsletter. Ambulatory Services. University of Maryland, Baltimore.

Brown, E. L. 1970. Nursing Reconsidered: A Study of Change. J. B. Lippincott, Philadelphia.

Committee for Economic Development. 1973. Building a National Health Care System. Research and Policy Committee, Washington, D.C.

Dunn, H. L. 1961. High Level Wellness. R. W. Beatty, Ltd., Arlington, Va.

Eulers, R. 1971. National health insurance: What kind and how much? N. Engl. J. Med. 284:881-885.

Freeman, R. B. 1970. Community Health Nursing Practice. W. B. Saunders Company, Philadelphia.

Health Maintenance Organization Act of 1973. Public Law 93-222, 93rd Congress, S.14. 1973.

Illich, I. 1976. The expanding medical industry, the money and the myths. America 134:373-376.

Leininger, M. 1970. Nursing and Anthropology: Two Worlds to Blend. John Wiley and Sons, Inc., New York.

Leininger, M. 1973. An open health care system model. Nurs. Outlook 21:171-175.

Leone, L. 1967. Statewide Planning for Nursing Education. Southern Regional Education Board, Atlanta.

Lysaught, J. P. 1973. From Abstract into Action. (The National Commission for the Study of Nursing and Nursing Education). McGraw-Hill Book Company, New York.

McMullan, D. 1975. Accountability and nursing education. Nurs. Outlook. 23:501-503.

Mead, M. 1949. Male and Female. Dell Publishing Co., New York.

Reed, E. 1975. Woman's Evolution. Pathfinder Press, New York.

Reil, J. P., and Roy, Sr. C. 1974. Conceptual Models for Nursing Practice. Appleton-Century-Crofts, New York.

Rogers, M. E. 1970. Theoretical Basis of Nursing. F. A. Davis Company, Philadelphia.

Terris, M. 1973. Crises and change in America's health system. Am. J. Public Health 27:313–317.

University of Maryland School of Nursing, Graduate Department. n.d. Philosophy. University of Maryland, Baltimore.

Walsh, M. E. 1972. On nursing's role in health care delivery. Nurs. Outlook. 20:592–593.

NUTRITION AND FOODS

Mary T. Goodwin
and Bonnie Liebman

Nutrition encompasses one's relationship to food biologically, psychologically, socially, and culturally. It is an essential factor in the promotion of health and the prevention of disease, as well as in the recovery and rehabilitation from illness and injury. The experiences of eating and being fed are integrally associated with one's deepest feelings about self. Good food served with care can evoke feelings of love, acceptance, and security, while poor quality food presented begrudgingly, or in a dehumanizing style, engenders feelings of rejection, fear, and insecurity. This is a particularly serious matter for the handicapped person, who is often dependent on others for food preparation and feeding. Food experiences offer opportunities for developing self-reliance, leading to an improved self-image and a feeling of competence. Food shared with others can break down class and status barriers; persons become equals and communication is enhanced. Individual uniqueness, ethnicity, and culture are expressed through food experiences. For the handicapped, sensory development through food can be enticing, exciting, and enjoyable. Sights, sounds, smells, feel, and taste appeal of real food become a fascinating adventure. Food activities provide powerful learning situations because of sensory appeal and emotional connotations.

This chapter explores the potential for using nutrition and food experiences to enrich self-image, to stimulate and reinforce developmental skills, and to nurture the body, mind, and spirit of the handicapped person.

The most important single factor in achieving and maintaining good health is proper nutrition. The quality and quantity of food eaten has a major influence on one's state of health and social well-being. For the handicapped person, optimal nutrition can maximize growth, development, productivity, and sense of well-being, as well as increase resistance to disease. Each person has different nutritional needs depending upon age, size, heredity, physical activity, and state of health. Roughly 50 nutrients have been identified as essential for human nutrition. The National Academy of Sciences–National Research Council has established Recommended Dietary Allowances (RDA) to provide a standard for good nutrition. To obtain a supply of all 50 nutrients in proper proportion, a varied diet of natural foods is best (See Table 1).

Nutrition problems that cause or exacerbate the conditions of the handicapped today include under- and overnutrition, the quality and safety of the available food supply, and the development of disease. Chronic undernutrition, resulting from restricted intake of one or more nutrients, is more common in the United States than severe life-threatening malnutrition. A reduced growth rate, higher morbidity, and increased susceptibility to childhood diseases accompany the problem. Undernutrition can contribute to a variety of developmental disorders ranging from mental retardation to suboptimal physical and mental performance. Current research indicates that chronic undernutrition may delay mental development by limiting the individual's interest in environmental stimuli rather than by irreversibly impairing mental ability. The effects of undernutrition depend on its severity, the age of the individual at its onset, and the duration of the nutritional insult.

Overnutrition complicates mobility of the handicapped while increasing the risk of diet-related diseases such as heart disease, cancer, diabetes, and stroke.

Availability of food implies access to a variety of wholesome foods in the home, at the marketplace, and in institutions. Handicapped persons need high quality nutritious foods, carefully prepared and attractively served in an accessible manner. The changing nature of the food supply—from foods natural and fresh from the farm to those fashioned in factories—has resulted in the prevalence of numerous food additives, some of questionable safety. Little is known about the synergistic additive and the accumulative effects of these additives. Research is currently being conducted to determine whether artificial colorings and flavorings contribute to the development of hyperkinesis in some persons.

In addition to food additives, excessive processing reduces nutritional quality. Meats and vegetables are "extended" by synthetic food products; fruit juices are diluted to "drinks," and natural foods are replaced by formulated ones, such as artificial blueberries. Adding vitamins; and minerals to synthetic or overly processed and refined foods does not supply or restore integrity. Synthetic foods should be used only when whole foods cannot be tolerated. For example, persons with phenylketonuria (PKU), an inborn error of metabolism, require a special formula to replace protein foods in their diet.

Table 1. Food and Nutrition Board, National Academy of Sciences–National Research Council recommended daily dietary allowances[a] (revised 1974)—*Designed for the maintenance of good nutrition of practically all healthy people in the U.S.A.*

	Age (years)	Weight (kg)	Weight (lbs)	Height (cm)	Height (in)	Energy (kcal)[b]	Protein (g)	Fat-soluble vitamins				Water-soluble vitamins							Minerals					
								Vitamin A activity (RE)[c]	(IU)	Vitamin D (IU)	Vitamin E Activity[e] (IU)	Ascorbic Acid (mg)	Folacin[f] (μg)	Niacin[g] (mg)	Riboflavin (mg)	Thiamin (mg)	Vitamin B6 (mg)	Vitamin B12 (μg)	Calcium (mg)	Phosphorus (mg)	Iodine (μg)	Iron (mg)	Magnesium (mg)	Zinc (mg)
Infants	0.0–0.5	6	14	60	24	kg × 117	kg × 2.2	420[d]	1,400	400	4	35	50	5	0.4	0.3	0.3	0.3	360	240	35	10	60	3
	0.5–1.0	9	20	71	28	kg × 108	kg × 2.0	400	2,000	400	5	35	50	8	0.6	0.5	0.4	0.3	540	400	45	15	70	5
Children	1–3	13	28	86	34	1,300	23	400	2,000	400	7	40	100	9	0.8	0.7	0.6	1.0	800	800	60	15	150	10
	4–6	20	44	110	44	1,800	30	500	2,500	400	9	40	200	12	1.1	0.9	0.9	1.5	800	800	80	10	200	10
	7–10	30	66	135	54	2,400	36	700	3,300	400	10	40	300	16	1.2	1.2	1.2	2.0	800	800	110	10	250	10
Males	11–14	44	97	158	63	2,800	44	1,000	5,000	400	12	45	400	18	1.5	1.4	1.6	3.0	1,200	1,200	130	18	350	15
	15–18	61	134	172	69	3,000	54	1,000	5,000	400	15	45	400	20	1.8	1.5	2.0	3.0	1,200	1,200	150	18	400	15
	19–22	67	147	172	69	3,000	54	1,000	5,000	400	15	45	400	20	1.8	1.5	2.0	3.0	800	800	140	10	350	15
	23–50	70	154	172	69	2,700	56	1,000	5,000		15	45	400	18	1.6	1.4	2.0	3.0	800	800	130	10	350	15
	51+	70	154	172	69	2,400	56	1,000	5,000		15	45	400	16	1.5	1.2	2.0	3.0	800	800	110	10	350	15
Females	11–14	44	97	155	62	2,400	44	800	4,000	400	12	45	400	16	1.3	1.2	1.6	3.0	1,200	1,200	115	18	300	15
	15–18	54	119	162	65	2,100	48	800	4,000	400	12	45	400	14	1.4	1.1	2.0	3.0	1,200	1,200	115	18	300	15
	19–22	58	128	162	65	2,100	46	800	4,000	400	12	45	400	14	1.4	1.1	2.0	3.0	800	800	100	18	300	15
	23–50	58	128	162	65	2,000	46	800	4,000		12	45	400	13	1.2	1.0	2.0	3.0	800	800	100	18	300	15
	51+	58	128	162	65	1,800	46	800	4,000		12	45	400	12	1.1	1.0	2.0	3.0	800	800	80	10	300	15
Pregnant						+300	+30	1,000	5,000	400	15	60	800	+2	+0.3	+0.3	2.5	4.0	1,200	1,200	125	18+[h]	450	20
Lactating						+500	+20	1,200	6,000	400	15	80	600	+4	+0.5	+0.3	2.5	4.0	1,200	1,200	150	18	450	25

[a] The allowances are intended to provide for individual variations among most normal persons as they live in the United States under usual environmental stresses. Diets should be based on a variety of common foods in order to provide other nutrients for which human requirements have been less well defined.

[b] Kilojoules (kJ) = 4.2 × kcal.

[c] Retinol equivalents.

[d] Assumed to be all as retinol in milk during the first six months of life. All subsequent intakes are assumed to be half as retinol and half as β-carotene when calculated from international units. As retinol equivalents, three fourths are as retinol and one fourth as β-carotene.

[e] Total vitamin E activity, estimated to be 80% as α-tocopherol and 20% other tocopherols.

[f] The folacin allowances refer to dietary sources as determined by *Lactobacillus casei* assay. Pure forms of folacin may be effective in doses less than one fourth of the recommended dietary allowance.

[g] Although allowances are expressed as niacin, it is recognized that on the average 1 mg of niacin is derived from each 60 mg of dietary tryptophan.

[h] This increased requirement cannot be met by ordinary diets; therefore, the use of supplemental iron is recommended.

For most individuals, a wide variety of whole food is best. The choice of foods and the form in which it is served can benefit or cause distress to the handicapped. Some complications plaguing many handicapped persons can be reduced or avoided by changing their diet. Constipation can be eliminated by increasing consumption of full fiber foods, especially whole grain products. Obesity may be controlled by increasing intake of low calorie foods with high nutrient and bulk density, such as fresh fruits and vegetables, while decreasing intake of fat and refined carbohydrate foods, such as fried foods, foods high in animal fat, and refined breads, cereals, sweets, and pastries. Dental health problems can be diminished by reducing intake of sugars and refined carbohydrates and increasing raw fruits and vegetables that clean the teeth and stimulate the gums. Heart disease, artery disease, cancer, diabetes, stroke, and cirrhosis of the liver are six of the 10 major causes of death and disability in this country. These diseases are directly linked to the food we eat. Highly refined foods and foods with excessive fat, sugar, and salt contents are implicated.

In January 1977, the U.S. Senate Select Committee on Nutrition published Dietary Goals for the United States. These goals provide a useful guide for individuals and institutions:

1. Increase carbohydrate consumption to account for 55–60% of the energy (caloric) intake.
2. Reduce overall fat consumption from approximately 40–30% of energy intake.
3. Reduce saturated fat consumption to account for about 10% of total energy intake, and balance with poly-unsaturated and mono-unsaturated fats, which should account for about 10% of energy intake each.
4. Reduce cholesterol consumption to about 300 mg per day.
5. Reduce sugar consumption by almost 40% to account for about 15% of total energy intake.
6. Reduce salt consumption by about 50–85% to approximately 3 g per day.

(The goals are expressed graphically in Figure 1.)

These goals suggest the following changes in food selection and preparation:

1. Increase consumption of fruits and vegetables and whole grains.
2. Decrease consumption of meat and increase consumption of poultry and fish.
3. Decrease consumption of foods high in fat and partially substitute poly-unsaturated fat for saturated fat.
4. Substitute nonfat milk for whole milk.
5. Decrease consumption of butter fat, eggs, and other high cholesterol sources.

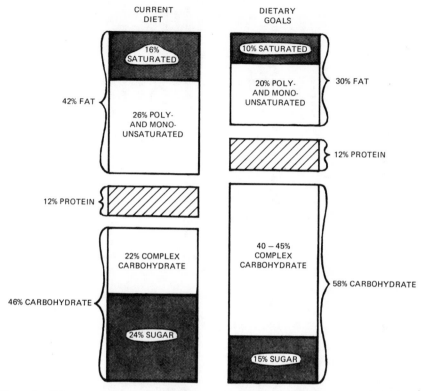

Figure 1. Dietary goals for the United States as set forth by the U.S. Senate Select Committee on Nutrition. (Current diet information taken from: Friend, B. 1974. Changes in Nutrients in the U.S. Diet Caused by Alterations in Food Intake Patterns. Agricultural Research Service. Department of Agriculture. Proportions of saturated versus unsaturated fats based on unpublished Agricultural Research Service data.)

6. Decrease consumption of sugar and foods high in sugar content.
7. Decrease consumption of salt and foods high in salt content.

Basic nutritional information is essential for intelligent guidance and education of the handicapped and their families. Interdisciplinary teams should be attuned to the need of incorporating nutritional education and guidance into their planning. Tables 2 and 3 provide the basic educational information upon which the planning may be based.

NUTRITION PROBLEMS

The role of diet as a vital component in the treatment of a number of disorders is well recognized. Cystic fibrosis of the pancreas and certain inborn errors of metabolism, e.g., phenylketonuria, homocystinuria, and

Table 2. A brief guide to basic nutritional information

Key nutrient	Function	Consequences of deficiency	Sources	Comments
Energy Carbohydrates (CHO) Simple (sugar) Complex (grains) (Should supply 55–60% of energy (calories).)	Provides energy.	Weight loss, fatigue, lowered resistance to infection.	Grains, cereals, breads, potatoes, corn, legumes, fruits, small amounts in vegetables.	Percentage of calories from CHO in the American diet should be increased. Minimally processed foods contain a higher nutrient density along with energy—whole grains and fresh fruits and vegetables are best.
Fiber Cellulose Hemicellulose Lignin Pectin	Promotes healthy bowel function; may help prevent colon cancer and control obesity, diabetes, and heart disease.	Diverticulosis, constipation, hemorrhoids.	Whole grain products (wheat berries, yellow cornmeal, whole barley, rye, oats) wheat bran, legumes, vegetables and fruits.	Whole grains with their full fiber content are best. Fiber is low in the U.S. diet.
Lipids (Should supply 25–30% or less of energy.)	Supplies large amounts of energy in a small amount of food. Promotes healthy skin by supplying essential fatty acids, carries vitamins A, D, E, K.	Dry, rough, itching skin; poor growth.	Vegetable oils, meats, butter, cheese, egg yolk, nuts.	Calories from fat should be decreased. Excess dietary fat from animal sources may be a factor in heart disease and some forms of cancer.
Protein (Should supply 10–15% energy.)	Builds and repairs all tissue in the body. Helps form antibodies. Supplies energy.	Growth failure, lowered resistance to infection.	Meat, fish, poultry, eggs, cheese, milk, yogurt, dried beans and peas, peanut butter, nuts.	Plant proteins may be eaten in combination for cheaper and lower fat protein sources.

Fat Soluble Vitamins			
Vitamin A	Helps keep skin smooth. Helps keep mucous membranes firm and resistant to infection.	Night blindness; lowered resistance to infection; dry, rough, itching skin.	Liver, egg yolk, deep yellow fruits, dark fruits, dark green vegetables, whole milk, vitamin A fortified skim milk, margarine, butter.	Laxatives decrease absorption. Substances made from vitamin A, called retinoids, are being tested as cancer preventing agents. These chemicals are different from vitamin A. Excessive amounts of the vitamin can be toxic and should not be taken without a doctor's supervision.
Vitamin D	Helps the body absorb calcium and phosphorus. Helps incorporate calcium and phosphorus into bones.	Rickets, osteomalacia, faulty bone growth.	Fish liver oil, fortified milk, sunshine converts substances in the body to vitamin D.	Excessive amounts may be toxic, possibly causing kidney damage and abnormal calcium metabolism.
Vitamin E	Acts as an antioxidant, protecting fats and vitamins A and D from rapid destruction. Maintains integrity of red blood cells.	Drastic deficiency not apt to occur, except in severe illnesses (malabsorption).	Green, leafy vegetables, wheat germ, oils (except coconut oil), nuts, liver.	Freezer storage lowers vitamin E content of fried food. Health claims for large supplements as yet unsubstantiated. More than 200 IU (20 times the RDA) reported to cause nausea and intestinal distress.

continued

Table 2. (Continued)

Key nutrient	Function	Consequences of deficiency	Sources	Comments
Vitamin K	Maintains blood-clotting factors.	Tendency to bleed excessively.	Dark, leafy vegetables, soybean oil, egg yolk, liver.	Prolonged antibiotic and anticoagulant therapy can cause deficiencies. Can be synthesized in the intestine so body not dependent on a dietary source.
Water soluble vitamins				
Vitamin B_1 (Thiamin)	Helps release energy from food. Helps promote normal appetite and digestion. Helps keep the central nervous system healthy. Helps prevent irritability.	Beri-beri (characterized by numbness or tingling of toes and feet, paralysis of legs, atrophy of leg muscles), sensitivity to noise and pain, fatigue and poor appetite.	Wheat germ, nuts, pork, peas, whole grain and enriched breads and cereals, dried beans, meat fish.	
Vitamin B_2 (Riboflavin)	Helps the cells use oxygen. Helps keep eyes, skin, hair healthy. Helps prevent scaly, greasy skin around the mouth and nose.	Cracks at corners of mouth (cheilosis), eye irritation, dermatitis.	Milk, cheese, liver, chicken legumes, whole wheat and enriched breads and cereals, dark green leafy vegetables.	Easily destroyed by light if in solution (as in milk).
Vitamin B_3 (Niacin)	Helps keep the nervous system healthy. Helps keep skin, mouth, tongue, digestive tract healthy. Enables the cells to use other nutrients.	Pellagra, weakness, poor appetite, scaly dermatitis, mental confusion.	Peanut butter, fish, meat, poultry, greens, breads and cereals, sesame seeds, soybeans.	
Vitamin B_6 (Pyridoxine)	Helps the body use and make protein.	Anemia, hyperirritability, dermatitis.	Wheat germ, whole wheat breads and cereals, eggs, bananas, legumes, fish, meat, greens.	Pregnancy, oral contraceptives, and excessive use of alcohol substantially increase need.

	Function	Deficiency Symptoms	Food Sources	Remarks
Pantothenic acid	Helps release energy from food. Helps detoxify certain drugs.	Irritability, restlessness, mental depression, impaired muscle coordination, decreased antibody formation.	Eggs, milk, legumes, liver, wheat bran, wheat germ, peanuts, peas, poultry, corn, asparagus, broccoli, sweet potatoes, kale, fish.	
Vitamin B_{12} (Cobalamin)	Assists in manufacturing blood. Maintains healthy nervous system.	Pernicious anemia, irreversible neurological damage.	Liver, kidney, meat, milk, cheese, oysters, fish, yogurt (not in plant foods).	Vegetarians eating no eggs or milk should take vitamin supplement.
Folacin (Folic Acid)	Involved in many biological functions including blood formation.	Macrocytic anemia.	Yeast, whole grains, legumes, cowpeas, lentils, navy and kidney beans, liver, asparagus, corn, broccoli, greens.	Pregnancy, oral contraceptives and excessive use of alcohol increase need.
Vitamin C	Needed for synthesis of collagen, the cementing material that holds body cells together. Helps body resist infection. Strengthens blood vessels. Helps prevent fatigue. Helps heal wounds and broken bones. Keeps gums healthy.	Scurvy characterized by listlessness, lack of endurance, fleeting pain in legs and joints, small hemorrhages under the skin, bleeding gums; lowered resistance to disease.	Kale, brussel sprouts, strawberries, broccoli, collards, mustard greens, green pepper, cantaloupe, citrus fruits.	Easily destroyed by heat, exposure to air and by addition of baking soda when cooking vegetables. Health claims for large supplements as yet unsubstantiated. 2–4 g (50 times the RDA) reported to cause physiological disturbances.
Biotin	Needed for synthesis of fatty acids. Produces energy from glucose.	Deficiency unlikely.	Egg, liver, pork, chicken, salmon, sardines, cauliflower, cowpeas, green peas.	Deficiencies produced by eating large amounts of raw egg whites (cooking destroys the anti-biotin factor).

continued

Table 2. (Continued)

Key nutrient	Function	Consequences of deficiency	Sources	Comments
Minerals				
Calcium	Assists in bone and tooth formation. Assists in blood clotting. Assists in muscle contraction and relaxation.	Rickets, poor growth.	Milk, cheese, sesame seeds, egg yolk, meat, legumes, whole grains, nuts, green leafy vegetables, mustard greens and collards.	May be excessive in U.S. diet. Best absorption thought to be in 1:1 ratio with calcium—current ratio is 2–3(P):1(C).
Phosphorus	Assists in bone formation. Helps body use energy.	Poor growth (dietary deficiency not likely to exist).	Milk, cheese, meat, egg yolk, whole grains, legumes, nuts.	
Iron	Serves as a constituent of heme, a part of hemoglobin molecule.	Anemia, fatigue, listlessness.	Liver, meat, eggs, soybeans, molasses, green leafy vegetables, dried fruits.	Anemia is the most common deficiency disease.
Iodine	Component of thyroxin, a hormone which regulates the rate that the body uses energy.	Simple goiter.	Sea food, iodized salt.	
Magnesium	Regulates cardiac, skeletal muscle, and nervous tissue function. Plays an intricate role in most cell functions.	Tetany, convulsions, muscle dysfunction.	Whole grains, pumpkin seeds, nuts, eggs, fish, green vegetables.	Alcoholics have increased need. Deficiency symptoms rarely occur—only in malabsorption or alcoholism.
Sodium	Maintains fluid balance in body (osmotic pressure).	Weakness, fainting.	Table salt, processed food, monosodium glutamate.	U.S. diet may be too high in sodium. May contribute to the development of hypertension.

	Function	Deficiency Symptoms	Sources	Comments
Potassium	Necessary for muscle contraction and regular heart rhythm. Maintains fluid balance in body (osmotic pressure).	Muscular weakness and paralysis.	Fresh fish, green beans, red beans, milk, grapefruit, oranges, bananas, tomatoes, spinach.	Widely available in adequate amounts in most diets.
Chromium	Helps in metabolism of glucose. Protects against toxic effects of lead.	Abnormal glucose tolerance.	Meats, whole grain breads and cereals.	Growing concern that U.S. diet may be deficient in chromium.
Zinc	Promotes growth and wound healing.	Abnormal hair and nail formation, deformed bone formation, defective healing, impaired sense of taste.	Oysters, peas, whole grain cereals, liver, oatmeal, beef clams, corn, peanut butter, milk.	Growing concern that U.S. diet may be deficient in zinc.

Nutrient requirements are dependent upon the body's need for 1) energy, 2) growth and development, 3) regulation and maintenance of bodily functions, and 4) the ability of the body to use nutrients. The body needs: 1) water, 2) energy (from carbohydrate, fat, or protein), 3) protein, 4) essential fatty acids and fat soluble vitamins, 5) water soluble vitamins, and 6) mineral elements.

Table 3. A daily food guide

Servings recommended	What counts as a serving	Some ways to use in meals
Vegetable-fruit group 4 or more, including:	½ cup of vegetable or fruit; for example, 1 medium apple, banana, or potato, half a medium grapefruit or cantaloupe.	Vegetables or fruit are part of most meals. Serve some raw and some cooked, some with crisp textures and some with soft; contrast strong flavor with milk, and sweet with sour for variety in meals. Brighten meals with color—a slice of red tomato or orange, a sprig of dark greens, or other colorful vegetables or fruit. Both vegetables and fruit are used in salads and as side dishes; some vegetables in casseroles, stews, and soups; and some fruits raw, as juices, and in desserts, such as cobblers, pies, or shortcakes. Many people include their vitamin C food as a citrus fruit or as juice such as melon or strawberries (when in season) at breakfast, in hot or cold cereals, in breakfast drinks, or alone.
1 good or 2 fair sources of vitamin C	Good sources: Grapefruit or grapefruit juice, orange or orange juice, cantaloupe, guava, mango, papaya, raw strawberries, broccoli, brussels sprouts, green pepper, sweet red pepper. Fair sources: Honeydew melon, lemon, tangerine or tangerine juice, watermelon, asparagus, cabbage, cauliflower, collards, garden cress, kale, kohlrabi, mustard greens, potatoes and sweet potatoes cooked in the jacket, rutabagas, spinach, tomatoes or tomato juice, turnip greens.	
1 good source of vitamin A at least every other day	Good sources: Dark-green and deep-yellow vegetables and a few fruits, namely, apricots, broccoli, cantaloupe, carrots, chard, pumpkin, spinach, sweet potatoes, turnip greens and other dark green leaves, winter squash.	
Bread-cereal group 4 or more	Count only if whole grain or enriched: whole grain (full fiber) breads or cereals are best. One-half cup cooked wheat berries, rice, millet, grits, bulgur (cracked wheat), spaghetti, macaroni, noodles, cornmeal, rolled oats, oatmeal, buckwheat. One slice of bread or similar serving of baked goods made with whole grain or enriched flour. One ounce ready-to-eat cereal.	Foods from this group are served at breakfast as toast, muffins, pancakes, or grits or cereals, cooked or ready-to-eat; at lunch and dinner in a main dish with beans and vegetables as in a casserole or as a side dish. Because breads and cereals are well liked and usually inexpensive, they are used more than four times a day in most households.

Milk group

Child, under 9—2-3
Child, 9 to 12—3 or more
Teenager—4 or more
Adult—2 or more
Pregnant woman—3 or more
Nursing woman—4 or more

One eight-ounce cup of fluid skim, low fat, or whole milk, buttermilk, evaporated or dry milk (reconstituted). As alternate, 1-inch cube cheddar-type cheese, or ¾ cup cottage cheese; 1 cup plain yogurt. Skim milk has the butter fat removed, reducing the calories by one-half.

Milk may be served as a beverage, at meals or for snacks. Milk products may be included on cereals and in preparation of other foods—soups, bean, meat or grain main dishes, custards, puddings, baked goods.

Protein foods

3 or more

One cup dried beans or peas, 3 tablespoons peanut butter, 2 ounces of lean cooked meat, poultry or fish, or 1 serving from the milk group. An egg makes ½ a serving of protein.

A full serving of protein is made when these foods are served in these combinations:

⅔ cup rice and ¼ cup beans

¾ cup rice and 1 cup milk product

1 cup whole wheat and ⅔ cup milk

½ cup beans and 1 cup milk

2 slices whole wheat bread, 2 tablespoons peanut butter, ¼ cup milk product

Foods from the protein group usually appear as an ingredient in the main dish of a meal—soup, stew, salad, casserole, or sandwich. Small amounts of two or more foods from the group used during the day can add up to a serving. Egg used in custards and peanuts of sunflowers seeds count, too.

Rice and bean casserole

Pudding made with powdered skim milk and rice

Milk in cereal, bread

Bean chowder or beans with cheese and tomato sauce

Peanut butter sandwich and glass of milk

To translate nutrients listed in the Recommended Daily Dietary Allowances into food, the food groups, serving sizes, and cooking suggestions are listed above. The guide includes whole foods only. Their fake counterparts do not have the same physical characters or nutrient content. Because many handicapped persons have decreased energy expenditures and high nutrient needs, there is little room in their diets for low nutrient foods high in salt, fat, and sugar. In the long run, these foods may bring further distress to handicapped individuals.

maple sugar urine disease, are examples of such disorders encountered in dealing with the handicapped.

Diet is gaining increasing recognition as a significant etiological factor in the development of a number of diseases. Six of the 10 leading killer diseases in the U.S. have been designated as diet related, and other relationships have been postulated. Feingold (1975) ascribes hyperactivity in children to the prevalence of artificial colorings and flavorings in the diet. Evidence obtained thus far is equivocal, but studies are currently being conducted to assess the validity of his hypothesis. In view of these developments, physicians are becoming aware of the wisdom of including a nutritional assessment in the regular physical check-up. For a discussion of the procedures to be used in evaluating nutritional status see the section, Interdisciplinary Role of the Nutritionist, below.

Obesity

Excessive weight gain may be a problem of particular significance for many handicapped individuals because immobility may limit caloric expenditure. When exercise cannot be recommended as an aid to weight loss, dietary control gains added importance. Caregivers have a tendency to feel that because the handicapped are deprived of other pleasures in life, they deserve to overindulge in food.

Overeating, however, does not give rise to a happier individual. The self-image of the handicapped person is threatened enough without the added burden of social ostracism as a result of obesity. More importantly, obesity may be aptly termed a life-threatening condition, increasing the likelihood of the development of cardiovascular disease, high blood pressure, atherosclerosis, hernia, gallbladder disease, diabetes, and cirrhosis of the liver. Obesity furthermore aggravates osteoarthritis and other bone and joint disorders and increases the hazard of surgery. In addition to the cost in human suffering, such complications add to the financial drain on the handicapped person's family. Obesity constitutes an additional practical problem for those handicapped persons who must be lifted or carried by others.

Good nutrition need not be viewed as a restrictive regimen. Handicapped and nonhandicapped persons alike can enjoy an enormous variety of low calorie, whole, healthful foods. Consider the assortment of fresh fruits and vegetables that are high in vitamins, minerals, and fiber (adding bulk for satiety) and lower in cost than refined, energy-intensive, processed foods. An activity such as "Come to Your Senses," (described in detail below under Selected Programs and Activities) illustrates how handicapped persons can take pleasure in experiences with food in a healthful and enriching manner. Emphasizing the cultural and educational aspects of food may shift the focus of mealtime away from eating while keeping it an event anticipated with enthusiasm.

Weight Reduction

A sound weight reduction plan should be based on a reduction in calories with a maintenance of adequate nutrient intake. The composition of the diet, whether high protein, low carbohydrate, or high fat, makes no difference in terms of weight loss as long as calories are reduced. (Low carbohydrate diets will cause an initial rapid weight loss, but this is caused by water loss and will be reversed as soon as carbohydrates are eaten in normal amounts.) Radical changes in the composition of the diet, however, may have other ill effects. High fat diets can lead to atherosclerosis, heart disease, cancer of the colon or breast, gallbladder disease, and other serious problems. Furthermore, these diets are ineffective because they do not limit calorie intake. Amino acid formula diets have not been thoroughly tested to determine their safety. They are extremely expensive, and some nutritionists believe a vitamin pill and lean chicken or nonfat milk would supply the same nutrient value. Under no circumstances should these diets be maintained for long periods of time because they are totally synthetic and do not contain essential trace minerals found in natural foods.

High protein, moderate fat, and low carbohydrate diets are not dangerous provided that some carbohydrate is eaten and that kidney function is normal. They do have the disadvantages of being relatively expensive and difficult to maintain because of the restriction on many foods. The safest and least expensive diet is one that reduces calories by 1) eliminating all foods low in nutrient density such as high sugar, high fat foods and 2) increasing low calorie, high nutrient density, high fiber foods, such as fresh fruits and vegetables. High fiber foods, such as whole grains, have satiety value by adding bulk to the diet. Intake of protein, vitamins, and minerals should be watched carefully as these nutrients may be of particular importance to the handicapped individual.

Undernutrition

Undernutrition in the handicapped is most commonly the result of insufficient food intake. A muscular or neurological disorder or a surgically induced disability may cause difficulty in swallowing, chewing, mouth closure, or tongue movements. Anorexia may be a feature of certain chronic disease states (e.g., kidney disease and cancer) or may be a result of treatment (e.g., drugs and radiation therapy). On the other hand, eating may be a demoralizing experience for people with limb dysfunction attempting to feed themselves. Failure to eat also might be a symptom of general psychological depression.

Caregivers of undernourished individuals are tempted to encourage eating regardless of the food ingested. It should be kept in mind that food is needed to build or rebuild body tissue and should, therefore, be wholesome and nutritious. It is frequently assumed that sweet foods are a good source of supplemental calories. However, other foods, such as nuts, peanut butter, cheese, dried fruit, and whole grains are high in other nutrients as well as calories and are less likely to lead to other diet-related illness such as tooth decay. Furthermore, sweets might have an appetite-depressing effect if eaten before or between meals. The emphasis should be on providing nutritious, enticing, exciting foods in a way that stimulates both the mind and the senses. Mealtime should be many great adventures, into many lands with regional foods, into history with favorite foods from the past, and into art with a variety of colors, forms, and shapes. It should be a tactile treat with an abundance of textures, aromas to titillate the appetite, and tastes that would make an ascetic drool. A magnificent food adventure like this may be the answer to eating problems. *Creative Food Experiences for Children* (Goodwin and Pollen, 1977) contains suggestions for activities with food for people of all ages.

Drug-Nutrient Interactions

The interaction of nutrition and drugs is an important consideration for the handicapped person who may be under long term treatment. Drugs may affect nutritional status in a nonspecific way be depressing appetite or by increasing fat deposition. Or they may alter the malabsorption, utilization, or metabolism of certain nutrients. Laxatives containing mineral oil prevent absorption of carotene and the fat soluble vitamins A, D, E, and K. Neomycin, an antibacterial agent, may cause malabsorption of vitamin B_{12}, iron, calcium, fat, and fat soluble vitamins, especially vitamin K. Long term treatment with diphenylhydantoin and phenobarbitol (anticonvulsant drugs) can lead to rickets or osteomalacia by inducing vitamin D and/or calcium deficiency. Prolonged use of aluminum hydroxide antacids may cause phosphate depletion leading to bone demineralization. Vitamin C and folic acid serum levels are lowered in patients taking large doses of aspirin for rheumatoid arthritis. Prolonged and high dosage salicylate therapy also might lead to anemia caused by blood loss.

Medications also may interact with certain foods to produce dangerous reactions. Monamine oxidase inhibitors, used to treat both psychological depression and high blood pressure, can precipitate headaches, palpitation, and hypertensive crises when foods high in the amino acid, tyramine, are eaten. Such foods include aged cheese, wine, broad bean pods, beer, and ripe bananas.

Surgery, Trauma, and Wound Healing

Major surgery, infection, burn, and skeletal or other injury can increase caloric requirements up to 40% above normal. An accelerated breakdown of body protein accompanies these conditions and may persist for as long as six weeks following the injury. Tissue breakdown occurs during this catabolic phase, even when high protein supplements are fed. Therefore, efforts to build up protein stores are concentrated during the presurgical and the postcatabolic periods when appetite returns to normal. Protein should comprise 20–25% of caloric intake during the recovery period. Losses of water soluble vitamins, especially riboflavin, thiamine, and folate, may be substantial during trauma, and these vitamins should be given in amounts greater than Recommended Daily Allowances. Supplements of folic acid and iron may be recommended if major blood loss has taken place.

Proper wound repair may be important to the handicapped persons for healing of bedsores as well as surgical or other injury. Nutritional status affects healing capacity in several respects. Proper nutrition and an adequate supply of protein and the B vitamins, in particular, are thought to increase resistance to infection. Several nutrients are involved in regeneration of skin and other tissues. These include protein, folacin, zinc, niacin, and riboflavin. Vitamin C is essential in the formation of connective tissue (scab) needed to protect the healing wound.

THE PSYCHOSOCIAL DIMENSION OF FOOD

The social, cultural, and psychological significance of food in the lives of the handicapped can scarcely be overstated. Sharing of food is one of the prime social contacts; provision of food is one of the prime signs of caring. Food is intimately wound up with deep feelings of love or hate, security or fear of abandonment, and acceptance or rejection. The quality of nourishment and the manner in which it is presented has had profound effects on self-image and self-esteem.

Bettelheim (1970) believes food plays a major psychological role in human life.

> Eating and being fed are intimately connected with our deepest feelings. They are the basic interactions between human beings on which rest all later evulations of oneself, of the world, and of our relationship to it. Eating experiences condition our entire attitude to the world, not so much because of how nutritious is the food we are given, but because of the feelings and attitudes with which it is given (p. 15).

In the institutional setting, the psychological environment has an effect on the acceptance of food, and the quality of the food has an impact on the psychological environment.

In May 1976, the *Washington Post* reported on the overhaul of food service practices at the Montgomery County Detention Center in Maryland. Inmates had been fed for five or six years on frozen TV-type meals served in aluminum foil pans. While fed this way, groups of inmates, on a regular weekly basis, threw their trays against the wall in anger. When a switch was made to fresh foods, prepared on the premises by an inmate chef, complaints about the food dropped to "almost nothing."

It is plausible to speculate that feelings about taste and nutrition were not the sole motivators of the inmates' disgust over the way they were being fed. The original form of food service had been dehumanized and was therefore dehumanizing. The switch not only improved nutrition (more fresh fruits, vegetables, and salads, the option of whole wheat bread, less added sugar) and saved money ($0.20–0.30 per day per capita), but, perhaps, even more important, "picked up morale immediately."

Institutional food service programs frequently serve food in a dehumanizing fashion, and the food itself is often unpalatable. The U.S. Department of Justice has expressed concern over these effects on the mentally ill and mentally retarded. Is a poor food program abusing the body, mind, and spirit of the recipient? If the health of the persons in these institutions is undermined or not protected, is this a violation of human rights? Are there grounds for litigation on behalf of the residents?

The food served the handicapped should resemble a normal diet as much as possible, unless contraindications exist. For other family members or staff at institutions to eat from a different menu, in a separate place, may suggest the food was not good enough for them.

> The social climate of a mental institution changes immediately if the entire staff, up to the top of the hierarchy, takes its meals with the patients. The fact that patients, staff, and doctors eat together, and eat the same fare, immediately reduces the tension, the potentiality of violent outbreaks. And this not just at mealtime but all during the day and throughout the institution. Nothing is more divisive than when people eat a different fare, in different rooms (Bettelheim, 1970, p. 20).

Food can be an expression of personal uniqueness, portraying ethnicity, individuality, and regionality; or, food can reflect homogenization, dehumanization, and feelings of being faceless and forgotten. Children and adults with handicaps need to feel they belong to a loving society that will take care of them. What better way to do this than by having special celebrations for days of meaning to them? Involving parents or grandparents or others from the community can be an indication of their relatedness to the past and of regional or ethnic roots. Appropriate foods can serve as a thread to knit the traditions of the past and present; tasting parties, stories, ceremonies, and music associated with the food will add flair and color to the lives of not only the handicapped but of all who participate.

One important area for developing self-reliance with the handicapped is through food experiences. Learning how to choose foods to best take care of one's body, simple food preparation, or feeding oneself can be great triumphs for some handicapped persons. The artist in everyone can emerge by using food creatively. When one uses imagination and creativity, the experience becomes a wonderfully humanizing event. The activity, "Your Personal Food Shield" (described below under Selected Programs and

Activities), brings exciting involvement and instant rapport between the handicapped person or family and the professional.

FOOD AND THE DEVELOPMENTAL PROCESS

Optimal nutrition is essential for all children to maximize their growth, development, learning, and behavior potential. In the plan for managing the handicapped, the nutritional needs of the whole child must be considered, not merely the treatment of the disorder or disease. Food and feeding play a special role in the developmental process. Through feeding the child discovers how to use various parts of his/her body, i.e., eyes, hands, and muscles in the mouth. Children put objects in their mouth to feel them. They are attracted to a bright red strawberry or a deep green pea. Sensory experiences with food can be used to develop a taste for nutritious food as well as to promote development of skills. Motor skills may be improved with feeding and, for older children and adults, with food preparation. Examples of motor skills include grasping a spoon or a shiny red apple, kneading dough, mixing muffins, tossing a salad, squeezing a lemon, spreading peanut butter on whole wheat bread, stirring a milkshake, beating eggs, rolling out oatmeal cakes, and chopping celery. Fine muscle development is promoted in the feeding process; picking up a blueberry, a cube of carrot, apple, potato, or peach, sprinkling wheatgerm on top of yogurt, garnishing a casserole with tiny sprigs of parsley, separating egg yolk from egg white, shelling peas, measuring ingredients for salad dressing, slicing crusty rye bread, and sorting nuts. Hand-eye coordination also is improved in food preparation.

Learning the feeding process is an essential adaptive skill. Mastering the skills for food preparation and feeding can give the handicapped a feeling of self-esteem, self-sufficiency, and self-respect. The nutritionist and occupational therapist can work together on a sequence of food activities to build these developmental survival skills.

Food is a rich vehicle for communicating nonverbal messages of love or rejection through the giving and receiving of food. Language development can be facilitated using food illustrations: freezing or boiling water, melting butter, shaking orange juice, peeling an apple, popping popcorn, dissolving gelatin, and beating eggs. Social skills come alive with good food and good friends; a warm smile at the sight of a favorite food and friend, sharing food and sharing self, and appreciating differences and similarities. Planning, preparing, and creating parties, picnics, and other social events are pleasant ways to promote skill development. Because food is wrapped in so much meaning and interfaces with so many facets of life, it can be effectively used to open up new worlds for the developmentally disabled.

INTERDISCIPLINARY ROLE OF THE NUTRITIONIST

Qualified nutritionists are those who hold a master's degree in nutrition, including or supplemented by 1) public health courses from an accredited college or university, 2) an approved hospital dietetic internship or equivalent training and experience in a health care program that meets requirements for registered dietitian, and 3) two years of full-time, progressively responsible experience in nutrition, one year of which must have been in a public health agency. Experience in health services for adults, mothers and children, and chronically ill patients is also desirable.

Qualified nutritionists contribute experience and valuable information and skills to the interdisciplinary health care team. The assessment of a client's nutritional status involves the services of several disciplines on the health care team. The screening process should include nutritional questions (the food shield described below under Selected Programs and Activities, is an excellent device for identifying personal food history and feelings and attitudes toward food), physical examination, anthropometry, hemoglobin or hematocrit, serum cholesterol, and other laboratory studies when feasible. The nutritionist should review the findings with the physician. If there is no evidence of nutritional disorder or of physical problems that interfere with the eating process, the person should be reevaluated in one or two years. If signs of abnormality are found (e.g., suggestions of monotonous or bizarre diets, malabsorption, specific nutrient deficiencies, obesity, or undernutrition, anemia, hypercholesterolemia, difficulty in chewing or swallowing, or self-feeding), follow-up with further dietetic, laboratory, or roentgenographic evaluations should be done to verify initial screening results.

The nutritionist should then work with the entire health care team, and with the client or caregiver to draw up a nutritional care plan. Prenatal to present history and physical, psychological, socioeconomic, dietary, and laboratory information should be considered, and a specific recommendation and its expected outcome should be formulated. A time frame for weight loss and reduction in skin-fold thickness could be constructed for an obese individual, for example. A schedule for obtaining appropriate dental appliances for a person unable to chew food could be established. A dietary plan should be based on: 1) body needs, 2) personal food preferences, 3) socioeconomic situation, 4) cultural or ethnic customs, 5) food purchasing, preparation, and storage facilities and abilities, 6) eating skills, and 7) ability to utilize available resources (homemakers, food assistance, etc.).

In addition to dietary counseling, anticipatory guidance should be given, appropriate referrals should be made (food assistance, dentist, etc.), and the future appointment for follow-up should be scheduled. The nutritionist should make periodic checks on food intake and weight gain or loss to monitor nutritional adequacy. The person involved in food preparation should be counseled to make sure the diet consists of a variety of whole foods and is in keeping with the family patterns. When necessary, the nutritionist should provide assistance in obtaining tools and techniques to facilitate self-feeding. The patient's record should contain 1) Subjective data—diet history, 2) Objective data—physical findings, growth patterns, 3) Assessment—diagnosis and severity, and 4) Plan for recommended action and follow-up (SOAP).

The nutritionist may set up a class for the handicapped or their caregivers on specific nutrition and feeding problems, nutrition education, and consumer issues such as "supermarket survival," best buys and rip-offs, food safety, food additives (both intentional and accidental), food quality, whole foods versus convenience foods, alternative systems, co-ops, buying clubs, community gardens, and the community's responsibility to provide easy access to food and fair prices. The class could involve other members of the health care team, such as the occupational therapist. Bringing the handicapped and their caregivers together would help establish a community support system. Focusing on food initially provides creative involvement that can be expanded to other areas.

Collaboration between the occupational therapist and the nutritionist is needed to identify and obtain the equipment, appliances, tools, and accessories involved in the eating process that are required by the handicapped to ensure consumption of an adequate diet. Difficulties with self-feeding, chewing, swallowing, or holding food in the mouth may be reduced by changing the form of the offered food or by introducing exercises that the caregiver can use to help the handicapped to suck, swallow, control the tongue, or chew. Utensils can be obtained for special problems, e.g., spoons may be high arched for those unable to extend the elbow, or finger rings may be attached for those who need help holding the spoon (see Figure 2).

The nutritionist is able to provide guidance to achieve the dietary goals, and to find the food form easiest for the handicapped to handle. For example, when self-feeding is begun, foods that stick to the spoon should be used, thick applesauce, peanut butter, mashed potatoes, and cooked oatmeal. The occupational therapist determines whether a special chair or table is necessary, whether dental appliances might improve eating, and which table utensils and equipment are most suitable, i.e., special spoons, rubber spoons (as a starter), plastic dishes, plate guards, rubber mats to prevent sliding of dishes, or a clump of clay for an anchor. The occupational therapist may be involved in working out the physical arrangement for the feeding process as well as any special requirements for purchasing, preparation, and storage. The nutritionist provides assistance in planning for nutritional needs and working out a diet, adjusting size, shape, texture, consistency, color, and form to conform with the handicap. For example,

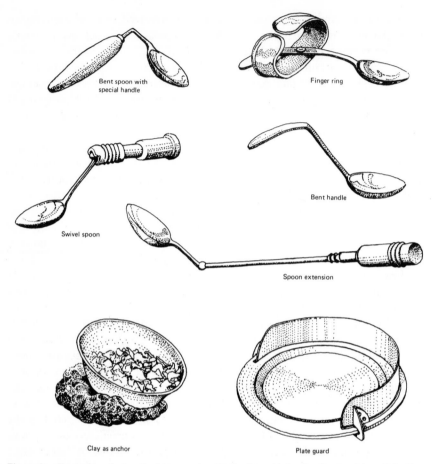

Figure 2.   Examples of utensils that may be obtained to aid the handicapped in self-feeding. (Reproduced from *Feeding the Child with a Handicap,* DHEW Publication No. (HSA) 75-5609.)

soft, low calorie, high nutrient foods, such as fine chopped greens or mashed sweet potatoes, may be served, using herbs, lemon, or orange juice for seasoning rather than butter. For the handicapped in a family setting, a plan with sequential steps should be developed, beginning with practice in holding a spoon and eating alone and gradually phasing into family meals. Handicapped persons who have mastered certain food skills should have opportunities to teach others in a similar situation. Handicapped persons want to be needed and want to share their accomplishments with others.

Tools and equipment to meet special needs may be adapted from everyday ones. For a long handle spoon, an iced tea spoon is fine; for dishes that are not easily knocked off tables, a dish with a suction cup on the bottom used for feeding toddlers works well. Rubber bath and shower strips may be placed on the bottom of dishes to prevent sliding. Department stores may have cooking utensils easily adapted for the handicapped. A local carpenter or cabinet maker may be able to design necessary furniture. A local potter may make appropriately designed dishes. Hardware, stationery, and speciality shops may have tools and equipment easily modified to meet a specific need.

The following sources may be helpful for kitchen equipment and tools:

Aluminum Housewares, Inc., 411 North 7th Street, St. Louis, Missouri, 63101

Bancroft's, 251 East Fifth Street, St. Paul, Minnesota 55101 (General mail-order firm)

Bausch & Lomb Safety Products, 655 St. Paul Street, Rochester, New York 14605

Bazar Francais, 666 6th Avenue, New York, N.Y. 10010

L. L. Bean, Inc., 248 Main Street, Freeport, Maine 04032

J. A. Preston Corporation, 71 5th Avenue, New York, N.Y. 10003

Fred Sammons, Inc., Box 32, Brookfield, Illinois 60513

Whole Earth Catalogue, Portola Institute, 558 Santa Cruz, Menlo Park, California 94025

The nutritionist and social worker should work with the handicapped to determine access to shopping, cooking, eating, and storage facilities, and to assess economic capabilities. Maximal use of community resources through a food management plan should be drawn up, implemented and evaluated for food assistance and information. The Women's, Infants', and Children's Supplemental Food Program (WIC), food stamps, Meals on Wheels, Title VII group feeding programs, free or reduced priced lunch and breakfast programs in schools, special food services for daycare and group homes, and summer feeding programs are some of the federally funded food programs. The nutritionist should provide assistance on where to shop for quality food, should find volunteers to shop if necessary (schools or youth clubs may offer this service), and/or should encourage group preparation of meals at a church or community center. Other members of the family may need food or nutrition assistance. The social worker should bring this to the nutritionist's attention. The social worker also should help with referral mechanisms and counseling services.

The nutritionist may contribute to dental care by assisting in the identification of oral problems interfering with eating a balanced diet and the prevention of dental problems. The nutritionist should make sure dental appliances function properly. In planning food intake, the nutritionist should be concerned with the nature of food and the frequency of eating, keeping in mind the total nutrition of the handicapped. Foods high in refined carbohydrates (sugars and refined starches and sticky sweets) should be reduced or avoided. Raw fruit and vegetable intake should be increased, and a variety of sensory experiences should be used to make foods conducive to good dental health, total nourishment, and pleasure.

Nutrition is of the utmost importance in geriatrics to maintain a high level of health, to maximize productive life, and to prevent premature aging, disease, and disability. For the disabled elderly, a carefully worked out nutrition assessment and personalized nutrition plan is essential. In addition to other problems related to the handicap, malnutrition secondary to disease or drug intake and poor emotional attitude are critical issues with the elderly. Moreover, the elderly are frequently victimized by food quackery and deceptive advertising. The nutrition plan should be based not only on individual dietary needs, psychosocial factors, and economics, but also on reducing isolation and encouraging socialization through planned parties, picnics, group gatherings, etc. Involving the elderly in programs for children in daycare or schools promotes healthy cross-generational relationships. Elderly persons can share the history of their food experience with the children. The activity "To Grandmother's House We Go," described below in detail under Selected Programs and Activities, is appropriate for involving the elderly.

Education for the handicapped should include a strong food and nutrition component. The emphasis should be placed on nutritional needs for personal health, self-reliance in management of one's food needs, food selection, preparation, and storage, and eating capabilities. Sensory pleasures should be used as a tool in awakening and maintaining interest in good eating. Consider a few ways in which food fits into an educational program: studying 1) food history—where foods originated, how they came to this country, ways food was raised in the past and is raised today, 2) the changing nature of the food supply, 3) food in different cultures, 4) food politics, 5) consumer rights to quality, choice, availability, fair prices, and safe food free of potentially harmful additives or environmental contaminants, and 6) creative and imaginative ways to prepare food.

For the mentally handicapped, food is a fascinating teaching tool because all learning is through the senses and food appeals to all the senses. Fractions can be demonstrated by cutting an apple into sections or measuring ingredients for oatmeal cookies. Children may not know how to count but can tell if there are enough cookies on a plate to go around. Food, in addition, has strong emotional connotations. Bettelheim (1970) tells a story illustrating the "intimate (connection between) learning to read—that is, feeding knowledge to the child—with feeding him food: A nonreader finally learned to read after he had been hand fed by his teacher when he asked her, 'Feed me,' when he meant 'Read to me.' Without recognizing it, he knew that (she had) not only to teach but to feed the whole child, feed food to his body as she fed food to his mind." (For additional suggestions on uses of food in education of the handicapped, see Figure 3).

All learning is through the senses. Food appeals to all senses making it a powerful learning tool.

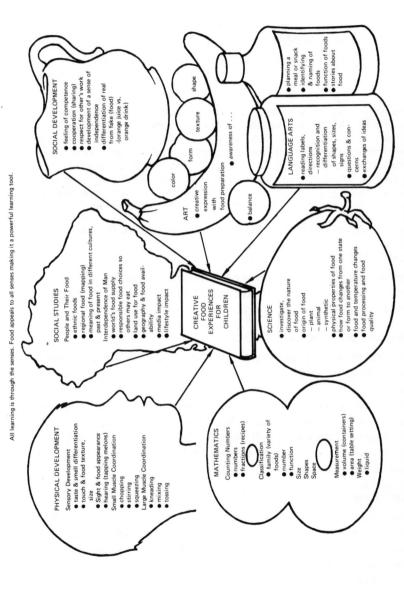

PHYSICAL DEVELOPMENT

Sensory Development
- taste & smell differentiation
- touch & food texture, size
- Sight & food appearance
- hearing (tapping melons)

Small Muscle Coordination
- chopping
- stirring
- squeezing

Large Muscle Coordination
- kneading
- mixing
- tossing

SOCIAL STUDIES

People and Their Food
- ethnic foods
- regional food (mapping)
- meaning of food in different cultures, past & present

Interdependence of Man
- world's food supply
- responsible food choices so others may eat
- land use for food
- geography & food availability
- media impact
- lifestyle impact

SOCIAL DEVELOPMENT
- feeling of competence
- cooperation (sharing)
- respect for other's work.
- development of a sense of independence
- differentiation of real from fake (food)
  -(orange juice vs. orange drink)

ART
- creative expression with food preparation
- awareness of . . .
  color   form   texture   shape
- balance

LANGUAGE ARTS
- reading labels, directions
  — recognition and differentiation of shapes, sizes, signs
- questions & concerns
- exchanges of ideas

- planning a meal or snack
- identifying & naming of foods
- function of foods
- stories about food

CREATIVE FOOD EXPERIENCES FOR CHILDREN

SCIENCE
- investigate, discover the nature of food
- origin of food
  — plant
  — animal
  — synthetic
- physical properties of food
- how food changes from one state or form to another
- food and temperature changes
- food processing and food quality

MATHEMATICS

Counting Numbers
- numbers
- fractions (recipes)

Classification
- family (variety of foods)
- number
- function

Size
Shapes
Space

Measurement
- volume (containers)
- area (table setting)

Weight
- liquid

Figure 3. Potential contribution of food experiences in curriculum for the handicapped.

197

FOOD ASSISTANCE

School Feeding Program

Lunches and breakfast are provided for school children by school feeding programs. Low income children can receive meals at free or reduced prices. Funds are made available to the states for purchase of food, maintenance, operation, and expansion of nonprofit school lunch programs.

Part 210-10(F) of the National School Lunch Program regulations states:

> Substitutions may be made in foods listed in paragraph (a)(1) if individual participating children are unable because of medical or other specific dietary needs, to consume such foods. Such substitutions should be made only when supported by a statement from a recognized medical authority which includes recommended alternate foods. (The type "A" lunch requirements are 1) one half pint of milk, 2) two ounces edible portion as served of a lean protein food, meat, fish, eggs, cheese, etc., 3) three-fourths cup serving of two or more vegetables or fruits or both, and 4) one slice whole grain or enriched bread.)

Contact the principal in the neighborhood school for further information.

Special Milk Program

A special milk program allows any school or nonprofit child care institution to provide needy children with free milk. Contact the principal in the neighborhood school for further information.

Child Care Food Programs

Nutritious meals for preschool and school-age children in child care facilities are provided by child care food programs. Through grants and/or other means, states can initiate, maintain, or expand nonprofit food service programs for children in institutions providing child care, e.g., daycare centers, family daycare program, Head Start centers, and institutions providing daycare service for handicapped children. Contact the director of the center or institution or the Food Service Director for the state Board of Education for further information.

Summer Food Programs

Summer food programs help get nutritious meals to needy preschool and school-age children in recreation centers and summer camps, or during vacations in areas operating under a continuous school calendar. Any nonresidential public or private nonprofit institution or any residential public or private nonprofit summer camp is eligible if it develops a summer food program for children from low income areas. Federal funds are given to eligible institutions for the costs involved in obtaining, preparing, and serving food under this program (including administrative costs and rental of office space and equipment). Church organizations, recreation departments, and community action committees frequently offer the summer food programs along with recreation and crafts. Contact the director of the center or institution or the Food Service Director for the state Board of Education for further information.

Supplemental Food Program for Women, Infants, and Children (WIC)

This program is operated on a project basis and administered through the state health agency. Selected foods are provided free to infants, to children up to the age five, and to pregnant and lactating women who are eligible on a health/nutritional and economic need basis. Contact the local health department for further information.

Food Stamps

The food stamp program enables eligible low income households to buy more food of greater variety to improve their diets. The program is usually administered by the local welfare department. To qualify for food stamps, households must meet certain nationwide eligibility standards. Food stamps are free to persons with very low income. Cost is based on a sliding scale according to income. Contact the local welfare agencies for further information.

Nutrition Programs for the Elderly

Nutrition programs for the elderly, administered by the state Agency on Aging unless another agency is designated, provide meals for older Americans, primarily from low income groups, within the county or project area. In addition to serving nutritionally sound meals, the program provides supportive services such as nutrition education, shopping assistance, recreational activities, transportation to the center site, health services, and information referral. Contact the local office or Commission on Aging for further information.

Community Food and Nutrition Programs

In some communities, community food and nutrition programs, administered by the Community Services Administration (formerly OEO Emergency Food and Medical Services Programs), may be available. These programs are usually directed by local community action agencies. Transportation and legal aid or assistance with "fair" hearing also may be available through local community action agencies.

Meals on Wheels

Home-delivered meals, or Meals on Wheels, a nonprofit program of home-delivered meals, is a community service administered by an official volunteer, or welfare agency. The service is provided to ill, disabled, and elderly persons whose physical, emotional, mental, or social conditions handicap their ability to obtain or prepare meals for themselves. Such services often make it possible for individuals to remain in their own homes, rather than entering institutional care, or to obtain special diets which they are unable to prepare. Support is usually from local sponsorship and income generated from the meals. Contact the local health department or office on aging for further information.

Church Missions and Community Organizations

Many church missions and community organizations maintain an emergency food pantry that is an excellent resource for individuals and families in need of food on a short term basis.

The following organizations will provide free assistance in getting food programs into your community or in making the existing programs work in the public interest:

Food Research and Action Center (FRAC), 2011 I Street, N.W., Washington, D.C. 20006 (food stamps, school and summer school feeding programs, food programs for the elderly)
The Children's Foundation, 1028 Connecticut Avenue, N.W., Suite 1112, Washington, D.C. 20036

(Women's, Infants' and Children's Supplemental Food Program, school feeding, and institutional feeding)
Community Nutrition Institute, 1910 K Street, N.W., Washington, D.C. 20006
(*Weekly Report* on food programs, update on food and nutrition information; cost: $14–25 per year)

EVALUATING NUTRITIONAL RESOURCES DEVELOPED BY SPECIAL INTEREST GROUPS, FOOD ASSOCIATIONS, AND FOOD INDUSTRIES

The handicapped are frequently victimized by deceptive advertising, promising to cure many ills and problems. There is no magic food. A well balanced diet containing a wide variety of natural foods is best. A wide range of materials providing nutritional information is developed with funds from vested interest groups. These materials should be carefully scrutinized to protect the well-being of the handicapped. A food association may heavily emphasize use of those foods that are products of companies who fund them, such as cereal or dairy industries. The promotion material may not give the full scope of information about a product, even if certain limitations are considered. For example, the dairy industry may equate the nutritional value of ice cream, one of its products, with that of milk, although it does not have the same nutrient density as milk. However, ice cream is high in sugar and saturated fat, and, even though most people enjoy it, it should be eaten as a treat on special occasions rather than as a part of the daily food pattern.

Powdered skim milk or fluid skim milk makes a contribution to our daily food needs. Nevertheless, one may have difficulty in finding references to these foods in information prepared by certain dairy concerns. Information developed by industries whose products are high in cholesterol or saturated fat may not give a balanced presentation of the role of these as risk factors in heart disease or cancer. Information disseminated by cereal companies may not give the facts on sugar and tooth decay.

The following guidelines may be of some assistance in using resources:

1. What interest groups have produced the materials?
2. Does the health and well-being of the recipient of the materials have priority over a particular product?
3. Is the information consistent with the promotion of good eating habits?
4. Is there acceptable evidence for the statements made?
5. Is the information presented complete?

SELECTED PROGRAMS AND ACTIVITIES[1]

Your Personal Food Shield

Objective   To discover one's relationship to food through the creation of a food shield. This activity is a powerful tool for actively involving individuals or groups in evaluating attitudes and feelings about food. Individuals are able to identify the strengths and weaknesses of their own food history. They increase their self-esteem by recognizing their own uniqueness and by examining factors with negative influences, which become targets for change. Only one item focuses on nutritional awareness; the others are designed to examine the meaning of food in their lives. Items in the food shield may be changed to suit personal needs. For example, if the person is trying to control weight, one component may be, "Under what conditions do you eat more than your body needs?" Expect some to have blanks on certain items. Encourage each person to write or draw in the first food that comes to mind for each category. The leader also should create and share a shield. This technique may be used effectively with individuals in the health care setting as the basis for developing a nutrition plan with the patient (getting away from the "dependence syndrome" associated with health care), or with groups of all ages, from young children to senior citizens, and professional groups. In the atmosphere of trust and friendship that develops, people come alive and share deep feelings about themselves. Individuals also

---

[1] The activities, "Your Personal Food Shield," "Come to Your Senses," and "To Grandmother's House We Go," by M. T. Goodwin, were adapted and reproduced with permission from JCPenney FORUM, Fall/Winter 1977, pp. 9 and 20–22.

become aware that they can have more control over their bodies and lives and receive support from the group

Activity A shield protects; the food you eat should protect your health and social well-being. A shield usually has a family "coat of arms." A food shield should reflect the unique personal food history of the individual or family. Instructions for creating a food shield are as follows:

1. Draw on a sheet of paper "Your Favorite Food," (make as large as possible).
2. Divide the food into 9–12 parts, depending on how many items you wish to discuss.
3. Draw or write the following items using a section for each:
    a. Favorite food as a child, prepared by your mother.
    b. Foods you have hunted, fished, or gathered (wild foods, foods from your garden, etc.).
    c. Favorite food as a teen-ager.
    d. Favorite ethnic foods (from your own ethnic background).
    e. Favorite regional foods.
    f. Foods you have for celebrations.
    g. Foods you eat for comfort when sad.
    h. Foods you eat to rejoice when you are feeling good.
    i. Foods you eat when you are sick, or foods that make you sick.
    j. Foods you enjoy preparing and sharing.
    k. Foods your body needs, because of age, size, sex, activity, or special situation (handicapped, special diets).
    l. The most magnificent food experience you have ever had.
4. If the group is larger than 10 or 12, ask for volunteers to present their shields. Encourage discussion about himself/herself, and attitudes toward food and self.
    a. Favorite food as a child prepared by your mother—discuss early memories about food. Why was the food special? Was it the taste, texture, or amount? Was it rarely available or associated with a special occasion? Was it your mother's specialty, etc.
    b. Foods hunted, fished, gathered—may give some idea of self-reliance. Talk about picking berries, gardening, etc.
    c. Favorite foods as a teen-ager—if it is a "junk" food, how do you feel about it now? Why did you like it? Was it a good buy or a "rip-off?" If individuals have lived in other cultures, compare cultural likenesses and differences.
    d. Ethnic food—emphasize the importance of having roots or being a unique person. Discuss how ethnic food can be an affirmation of belonging. Ask about the family history of the food.
    e. Regional foods—may tell where people have lived, show awareness

of foods common to a particular region, and recall enjoyment of regional festivals or events where food was an important part of the festivities.

f. Celebrations—may have important personal meaning, indicate family, traditions, and occasions (e.g., anniversaries and religious events). These contribute to a sense of family security, support, and care. Suggest establishing a family calendar of celebrations.

g. Food for comfort—may be childhood foods that give a feeling of security or junk foods eaten to satisfy a self-destructive impulse or whim of indulgence.

h. Feeling-good foods—are usually foods that promote a higher quality of health. Get at the psychological meaning of food.

i. Food for sickness—may provide fascinating insights into cultural or family attitudes toward food and health. Foods that make people sick may indicate a sensitivity to body needs.

j. Foods you enjoy preparing and sharing—may show cooking skills or lack of them.

k. Food for your body—indicates awareness of nutrition and personal body awareness. Persons may express desire to improve diet by increasing or decreasing certain food categories.

l. Most magnificent food experience—provides insight into how much dash, color, and excitement food has for individuals.

The leader should identify the positive factors and use them to formulate a strategy for change.

Come To Your Senses!

Objective To improve health and increase pleasure for all ages by encouraging the eating of more fruits, vegetables, and grains through heightened sensory awareness.

Through the senses, the handicapped are in touch with themselves and the world around them. The quality and depth of involvement depends on sensory development. All learning is through one's senses. Food has the potential to be one of the richest learning experiences because it appeals to all the senses. People can expand or limit and enjoy or deprive themselves through the quality of sensory experiences. Today, all too many are culturally depriving themselves or are being culturally deprived by limiting their food experiences to taste for sugar, fat, and salt.

Activity The challenge is to liberate the senses in the marvelous world of food and to savor the subtle sights, sounds, smells, touch, and tastes of foods. Time should be allowed for sensory absorption.

Sights: The Food Rainbow Fill a farm basket with as many colorful fresh fruits and vegetables as are available. Some ideas:

Primary colors: *Red*—apples, tomatoes, strawberries, watermelons
                   Yellow-bananas, lemons, yellow string beans, squash
                   Blue—blueberries, blue plums, blue grapes
Secondary colors: *Purple*—eggplant, bermuda onions, red cabbage
                   Orange—oranges, tangerines, persimmons, pumpkin
                   Green—peas in a pod, avocados, celery, broccoli

Encourage participants to examine the various shades and tints of color within each fruit and vegetable. Some fruits, such as apples, come in a variety of colors. Compare the interior and exterior colors of foods. Suggest that participants note how colors change with cooking. Emphasize the visual delight of color.

Sizes and Shapes: The Minute to the Monumental   Take a trip to a supermarket or a fruit and vegetable stand. Identify the many shapes and sizes, from tiny red currants to huge watermelons, from stalks of rhubarb to egg-shaped mangoes, from soft curly endive to crisp flowerets of broccoli. Consider the seemingly endless variety.

Compare the insides of fruits and vegetables, whether layered (artichokes, brussel sprouts, cabbages, and onions), hollow (peppers and tomatoes), firm (eggplant, potatoes, and apples), juicy (strawberries, oranges, and melons), or seeded (pea pods, pomegranates, and tomatoes). Collect samples of dried beans and peas, green and yellow split peas, red and brown lentils, garbanzo, fava, adzuki, kidney, pinto, soy, mung, and black turtle beans. Note the subtle differences in shapes and sizes.

Sounds: Listen and Hear   Ask participants to describe food sounds or tape these sounds and ask participants to identify them from the tape.

Gathering	apples dropped into a basket, slosh of milk in a coconut preparation
Preparation	popping of corn or cranberries, sizzling of fish under a broiler, bubbling of soup, simmering of stew, chopping of celery, slicing of bread, spreading of peanut butter, squishing of garlic through a press, beating batter for bread, grating of orange rind, kneading of dough, cracking of eggs, squeezing of a lemon, shucking of corn, crushing of nuts, crackling of crusty bread.
Eating	crunching nuts, chewing raisins, biting into an apple, swallowing orange juice, chomping on a raw carrot, squishing a cherry tomato

Smells   Put a variety of herbs and spices in separate small containers. Some suggestions:

Herbs	parsley (fresh or dried), sage, rosemary, thyme, basil, oregano, dill, tarragon, spearmint, anise
Spices	cinnamon, cloves, ginger, nutmeg, cardamon, coriander, chili powder, paprika, turmeric

Place a number on each for identification. Ask participants to sniff and write the name on a piece of paper.

Obtain whole roots, seeds, barks, or leaves from which herbs and spices are made. See whether they can be identified whole, and, if not, what must be done to elicit their aroma.

Discuss favorable food smells: freshly baked bread, stuffed chicken roasting in the oven, tomato sauce simmering on the stove, peeling of an orange, chestnuts roasting on an open fire, apples baking, and granola browning.

Discuss or visit places that smell of foods (open markets, ethnic restaurants, community festivals, neighborhood bakeries, and herb and spice or tea shops). Have participants sniff their way through a supermarket and identify the smells, or drive or walk by a fast food restaurant and sniff. Or, suggest they sniff their way around a farm.

Keep In Touch!

Objective: To discover new foods and heighten the awareness of foods' differing qualities through the tactile sense and taste.

Activity

"Finger Food Feel and Mouth Food Feel"

1. Put fruits or vegetables into a paper bag one at a time. Have participants put one hand in the bag and feel the food carefully, discovering its textures and shapes. Ask them to identify the food. Some suggestions follow:

fuzzy—peach	sleek—eggplant
waxy—apple	prickly—pineapple
firm—carrot	seedy—raspberries
soft—persimmon	light—bell pepper
hard—winter squash	heavy—pomegranate
hairy—kiwi	sticky—dates
bumpy—cauliflower	moist—strawberries

2. Wash the fruits and vegetables and cut them in pieces the size of finger goods. Have each participant eat a piece slowly and describe the mouth feel.

   "Taste of Life—A Time to Feast"

1. Collect a wide range of raw fruits and vegetables. Here are some suggestions:

   sweet—strawberries, pineapple, mango
   sour—cherries, lime, rhubarb
   sweet and sour—kiwi, kumquat (massage before
   eating to blend flavors)
   bitter—radish
   strong—turnip, brussel sprouts

bland—mushrooms, cucumbers
creamy—persimmon
tart—plum
snippy—watercress
pungent—onion, garlic
sharp—mustard greens
mellow—cantaloupe
spicy—apple
tangy—raspberries

2. Have participants take a sample of as many as desired and eat each slowly, savoring the flavor. Discuss familiar tastes, new tastes, and favorite tastes.

Note: These are great classroom activities for young and old. If budget is limited, select a few characteristic foods. Learning to enjoy new food is a little like learning a new language. Some learn quickly and others slowly. Activities may be repeated using different forms of the same basic foods to increase sensory awareness and pleasure.

To Grandmother's House We Go!

Objective To promote cross-generational relationships and a sense of family history and belonging, by finding out your family foods, fasts, and feasts, and to examine the impact of changing from foods fresh from the farm to "fake from the factory."

Sociologists tell us that among the causes of alienation today is a lack of a sense of roots or belonging. This is attributable in part to our age-segregated society (children in daycare centers and senior citizens in retirement communities). Food offers much opportunity to return to the roots, open up new avenues of communication, bridge generations, deepen one's sense of belonging, and foster feelings of love and security. This activity is for all ages. Family interviews may be taped and cherished for generations to come. If participants do not have grandparents living in the community, other persons from their generation may be interviewed. Senior citizens and parents may be invited to the classroom to tell their food history. Pictures, utensils, cookbooks, dishes, and typical foods of the time would enhance the presentation. Ideally, each student would interview grandparents, parents, and self to look at change and what it has wrought in his/her own family.

Activity

1. Have each student conduct an interview with grandparents, parents, and self, based on the following list:
   a. Describe your earliest food memories.
   b. What foods were "everyday foods?"

   c. Where did the food come from (farm, wild or domesticated plants or animals, local general store, supermarket, neighbors)?

   d. Who obtained the food? How much was produced at home and how much was purchased?

   e. What foods were produced on the farm by the family or in the local community?

   f. From what part of the country or world did the purchased foods come?

   g. In what form were foods purchased: bulk, whole, fresh, processed, individually wrapped, frozen, canned, or dried?

   h. What fruits and vegetables were available throughout the year? Which ones were seasonal?

   i. Estimate what percentage of calories came from sugar, complex carbohydrates, fat, and protein. How much salt was added to food?

   j. Are the common causes of death the same now as then?

   k. Who prepared the food? Was the responsibility shared? How much time was involved?

   l. How and by whom were cooking skills taught?

   m. Did the family usually eat together? What was the serving protocol?

   n. What events were celebrated by the family or community feasts and festivals?

   o. What foods were served, and what ceremonies or rites accompanied them?

   p. Did fasting precede the feast or were food restrictions part of the ritual?

   q. Describe the differences and similarities of foods then and now with reference to taste, appearance, and smell.

   r. In your opinion, have food ways improved or declined over the years? What influence has the change had on the quality of life?

   s. Do you have a food wish or experience you would like to pass on to future generations?

2. Have each individual or small group of individuals present their findings to the class.

3. Compare similarities and differences in food behavior of persons of the same generation and across generations.

4. Identify changes brought about by technology and describe their influences on family health and quality of life.

Based on the information collected and analyzed, have each student project his/her future food behavior, building on the best of the past and considering the realities of the present.

RESOURCES FOR NUTRITION INFORMATION

Local and State Resources

Public health nutritionists in state and local health departments
Nutritionists in volunteer agencies, such as visiting nurse associations, heart associations, diet counseling services, diabetes associations, and those agencies in local hospitals
Nutritionists and dietitians in clinics, health centers, and hospitals, particularly dietetic departments in teaching hospitals
State and local cooperative extension services
Professional organizations concerned with nutrition, such as American Dietetic Association, American Home Economics Association, and American Public Health Association, with their state or local affiliate chapters
University and college nutrition and medical faculty members
State and local welfare agencies
Local community action agencies

National Resources

American Academy of Pediatrics, 1801 Hinman Avenue, Evanston, Illinois 60204

American Association of Retired Persons, 1225 Connecticut Avenue, N.W., Washington, D.C. 20036

The American College of Obstetricians and Gynecologists, One East Wacker Drive, Chicago, Illinois 60601

American Dental Association, Bureau of Dental Health Education, 211 East Chicago Avenue, Chicago, Illinois 60611

The American Dietetic Association, 430 North Michigan Avenue, Chicago, Illinois 60611

American Foundation for the Blind, 15 West 16th Street, New York, New York 10011

The American Home Economics Association, 2010 Massachusetts Avenue, N.W., Washington, D.C. 20036

American Institute of Nutrition, 9639 Rockville Pike, Bethesda, Maryland 20014

The American Medical Association, 535 North Dearborn Street, Chicago, Illinois 60610

American Public Health Association, Food and Nutrition Section, 1015 18th Street, N.W., Washington, D.C. 20036

Center for Science in the Public Interest, 1757 S Street, N.W., Washington, D.C. 20036

Community Nutrition Institute, 1910 K Street, N.W., Washington, D.C. 20006

Institute of Rehabilitation Medicine, New York University Medical Center, 400 East 34th Street, New York, New York 10016

National Council of Senior Citizens (National Senior Citizens Education Research Center, Inc.), 1627 K Street, N.W., Washington, D.C. 20006

National Council on the Aging, 1828 L Street, N.W., Suite 504, Washington, D.C. 20036

National Foundation/March of Dimes—Health Information Department, P.O. Box 2000, White Plains, New York 10602

National Society for Crippled Children and Adults, 2023 West Ogden Avenue, Chicago, Illinois 60612

National Research Council, National Academy of Sciences, 2101 Constitution Avenue, Washington, D.C. 20418

Society for Nutrition Education, 2140 Shatluck Avenue, Suite 1110, Berkeley, California 94704

Superintendent of Documents, U.S. Government Printing Office, Washington, D.C. 20402 (Request to be put on mailing list for publications related to food, nutrition, and health)

U.S. Department of Agriculture, Washington, D.C. 20250
Agricultural Research Service, Consumer and Food Economics Research Division
Federal Extension Service
Food and Nutrition Service

U.S. Department of Health, Education, and Welfare, 5600 Fisher's Lane, Rockville, Maryland 20852
Health Services Administration/ Bureau of Community Health Services
Food and Drug Administration

ACKNOWLEDGMENT

We would like to express our thanks to Peg McConnell for her assistance in gathering resource materials.

REFERENCES

Bettelheim, B. 1970. Food to Nurture the Mind. The Children's Foundation, Washington, D.C.

Feingold, B. F. 1975. Why Your Child is Hyperactive. Random House, New York.

Goodhart, R. S., and Shils, M. E. 1974. Modern Nutrition in Health and Disease. Lea and Febiger, Philadelphia.

Goodwin, M. T., and Pollen, J. 1977. Creative Food Experiences for Children. Center for Science in the Public Interest, Washington, D.C.

Johnston, R. B., and Magrab, P. R. (eds.). 1976. Developmental Disorders: Assessment, Treatment, and Education. University Park Press, Baltimore.

Roe, D. A. 1976. Drug-Induced Nutritional Deficiencies. The AVI Publishing Company, Inc., Westport, Conn.

Senate Select Committee on Nutrition and Human Needs, U.S. Senate. 1977. Diet Related to Killer Diseases 11. Part 2. Obesity. Washington, D.C.

Senate Select Committee on Nutrition and Human Needs, U.S. Senate. 1977. Dietary Goals for the United States. Washington, D.C.

U.S. Department of Health, Education and Welfare. 1975. Feeding the Child with a Handicap. Bureau of Community Health, Rockville, Md.

U.S. Department of Health, Education and Welfare. n.d. Preliminary Guide for Developing Nutrition Services in Health Care Programs. Bureau of Community Health, Rockville, Md.

SUGGESTED READINGS

The American Dietetic Association. 1971. The nutrition component of health delivery systems (ADA position paper). J. Am. Diet. Assoc. 58:537–546.

Christakis, G. 1973. Nutritional assessment in health programs. Am. J. Public Health. 63 (Suppl. 1).

Dahl, T. 1972. The Nutritional Functional Area in Comprehensive Health Care Delivery—Performance and Cost. Minnesota Systems Research, Inc., Minneapolis.

Egan, M. C., and Hallstrom, B. J. 1972. Building nutrition services in comprehensive health care. J. Am. Diet. Assoc. 71:491.

Fomon, S. J. 1976. Nutritional Disorders of Children—Screening, Follow-up, Prevention. U.S. Department of Health, Education and Welfare, Bureau of Community Health Services, Rockville, Md.

Goodwin, M. T. 1977. Better Living through Better Eating. Montgomery County Health Department, Rockville, Md.

Institute for Rehabilitation Medicine. 1970. Mealtime Manual for the Aged and Handicapped. Expandless Special Editions: Division of Simon and Schuster, Inc., New York.

Katz, D., and Goodwin, M. T. 1976. Food: Where Nutrition, Politics, and Culture Meet. Center for Science in the Public Interest, Washington, D.C.

Moyer, A. 1977. Better Food in Public Places: A Guide for Improving Institutional Food. Randall Press, Emmons, Pa.

OCCUPATIONAL THERAPY

Stella Gore Lansing
and Pat Nuse Carlsen

PROFESSIONAL PURPOSES AND GOALS

Occupational therapy may be viewed as an applied health service concerned with the quality of daily living from birth to death. The scope and delivery of occupational therapy is as complex and varied as human activity. The ability to direct and lead one's own purpose in life may be seen as the most unique and primary indicator of general well-being or health. Health is maintained through a balance of daily occupation in work, education, play, self-care, and home management, all of which develop and change throughout the life span. (The terms play, work, and self-maintenance will be substituted hereafter in reference to this broad variety of occupying activities or major categories of occupational roles.)

The heritage and concern of occupational therapy demand that both purpose and balance in living be applied to health service delivery. It is the belief of this discipline that "Man, through the use of his hands, as they are energized by mind and will, can influence the state of his own health" (Reilly, 1962, p.1). The scientific basis of the profession has developed through integrative study in the biological, behavioral, social, and medical sciences.

This brief introduction to the philosophy of occupational therapy may be helpful to students and professionals, both in observation of its practitioners and in further study of this chapter. Any definition or discussion of occupational therapy is bound by the concept that services are provided that facilitate a client's achievement of health through occupation in purposeful activities. Occupational therapy may be described as a bio-psycho-social approach to health care that concentrates on an individual's abilities to perform, maintain, and balance daily occupational roles. Performance of these roles requires mastery of tasks and relationships necessary to actively engage in play, work, and self-maintenance activities. The premise of the

211

profession is that occupation is a major health determinant: the goal-directed use of a person's potential, capacities, resources, time, energy, interest, and attention will influence the quality of human development and life adaptation. A person's ability to perform or cope with occupational roles may be threatened or impaired by physical, psychological, or social problems. The occupational therapist can assist the client with the adaptation processes necessary to promote a balanced, satisfying, and productive life style. This intervention process will require attention to the enhancement and integration of common behavioral components: the sensory-integrative, motor, cognitive, psychological, and social functions as these relate to performance of daily activities. The occupational therapist works with consumers in all age and diagnostic groups. Services provided include performing assessments, analyzing and interpreting assessment findings, and designing client-specific activity programs in a broad variety of health care, educational, and social settings (Carlsen, in preparation).

The goals of occupational therapy intervention with individual clients or groups are always related to:

1. The *development* and *maintenance* of functions and skills necessary for performance of age-appropriate activities
2. *Prevention* of deterioration and/or loss of those functions necessary to engage in play, work, and the various self-maintenance activities
3. *Remediation* or *rehabilitation* of functional deficits that impair performance of daily activities
4. *Facilitation* of a consumer's ability to influence and change his/her own health status through each successive stage of life
5. *Collaboration,* communication, and cooperation with the client, his/her family, and other service providers in planning and achieving goals.

SCOPE AND DELIVERY OF OCCUPATIONAL THERAPY SERVICES

Although no profession can be all things to all people, occupational therapists must take a global approach because their fundamental concern is with the development, integration, and maintenance of function. This integration of function in skill and role performance is of prime importance in a balanced life style throughout each individual's life span. Practice must be related to each client's overall mastery and achievement of goals and balance in the broad scope of work, play, and self-maintenance roles. The performance requirements of these roles are constantly changing and adapting through the growth and development of the individual.

Therefore, the occupational therapist must be familiar with the overall human development process, must be aware of its components and sequence, and must relate these to the needs of an individual functioning within a continuum of health and illness (Figure 1). Inherent in this concept

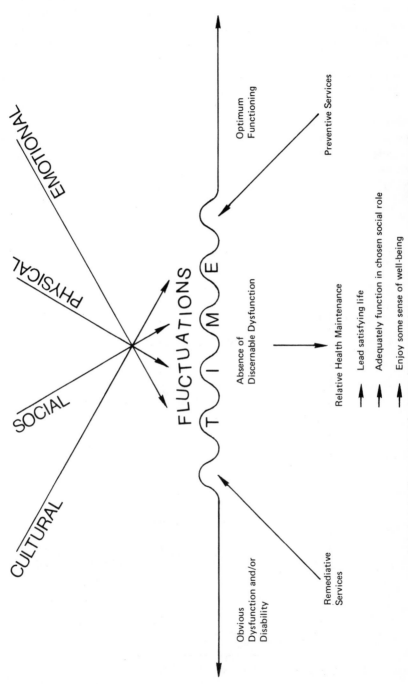

Figure 1.   Interaction of developmental processes and health (adapted from Pelligrino, 1973).

is a second: occupational therapy services must be relevant and responsive to the rapidly changing cultural and environmental demands in the life styles and health needs of today's consumer.

Figure 2 is a schematic representation of the process through which a consumer might encounter and receive occupational therapy services. In a healthy state, the individual is able to adapt and achieve a satisfying life, function adequately in chosen personal, social, and occupational roles, and enjoy some sense of well-being (Pelligrino, 1973). (See also Figure 1.) The normal performance of these roles is determined by four factors. First, the person's basic *biological endowment,* which includes the various body systems, functions, and innate capacities, provides that individual with the potential to develop and learn a variety of skills. Second, there is a hierarchical *maturation* of these skills as the person grows and accomodates to

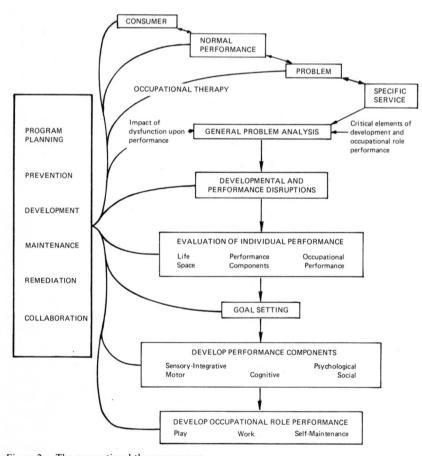

Figure 2.   The occupational therapy process.

his/her environments, assimilating new experiences and learning. The interaction between the individual and cultures, physical space, and other environmental elements becomes increasingly complex throughout a lifetime. Normal performance, therefore, must change and adapt because it is influenced by the third factor group of *cultural, spatial, and temporal requirements*. The individual must learn to effect a satisfying balance between meeting internal needs and external requirements. The emergent *personal requirements* change in response to the other three factors and are the fourth determinant of one's normal performance.

PROBLEMS IN PERFORMANCE

Throughout the course of life, a person encounters physical, social, and psychological problems that may or may not impede the performance of various roles. Analysis of the effect of the problem on normal performance (Llorens, 1976) is both quantitative and qualitative. Is the individual capable of coping with the problem and adapting to or resolving it independently? Is the nature of the problem such that it threatens to disrupt, delay, or impair a person's function? If the problem is sufficient to cause a dysfunction in a person's performance of daily tasks and roles, what resources are available, acceptable, and accessible for assistance?

Within this context, occupational therapists most often work with the following client populations:

1. The acutely ill or injured
2. Persons with chronic diseases or disabilities
3. Children and adults having congenital or acquired conditions that cause developmental disability
4. Persons manifesting emotional, behavioral, or affective disorders, both in acute and chronic phases
5. Persons who are overwhelmed by social stress and trauma
6. Healthy children and adults, particularly those in high risk categories
7. The elderly

An example of the acutely injured population would be a child with severe burns. The long range, systemic effects of burn-associated injuries will both disrupt and delay a child's performance in educational, play, and self-care activities. An occupational therapist also might work with a retired adult who has had a stroke. The residual loss of motor and sensory-integrative functions would affect this person's ability to care for himself and engage in meaningful activities. The mentally retarded child is an example of the client with developmental disability. Poor cognitive function and associated motor and sensory-integrative deficits are likely to cause problems in learning and performance of many play, vocational, and leisure

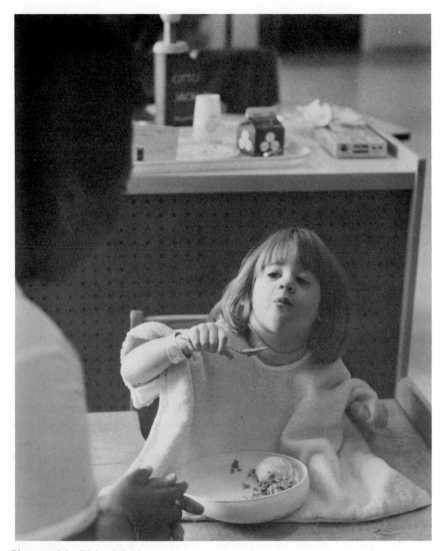

Photograph by Richard Holden.

skills. Opportunities for varied social experiences may be lacking and further reduce competence, often causing behavioral problems as well.

The impact of schizophrenia upon all areas of adult function and interaction is profound and frequently requires the intervention of an occupational therapist. Services also may be provided, with the dual aim of health maintenance and problem prevention, to mothers and fathers of preschool children. Parenting skills may be enhanced through increased awareness of normal growth and development concepts and practice in the functional application of these. Finally, a mother of eight children, living in substandard housing, may lack the skills and resources necessary to alter the overwhelming conditions of her life. She could be assisted by an occupational therapist in the identification of potential strengths and the enhancement of performance skills.

The preceding examples illustrate the approach of this profession in analyzing the effect of a primary problem upon the broader variety of function and performance skill areas. Associated, or secondary problems, frequently emerge to compound the overt dysfunction of a primary problem. Mosey (1974) has written that occupational therapists help people solve problems in living, regardless of age or diagnostic group.

LOCATION AND VARIETY OF OCCUPATIONAL THERAPY SERVICES

The next step after defining the nature of the client's performance needs is to define the nature of occupational therapy services that can be provided to that individual. This is shaped by the specialized knowledge, skills, and

Photograph by Richard Holden.

attitudes of the occupational therapy practitioner and the environment in which service is provided.

Occupational therapy has gone through a continuing process of exploring how to render services that are effective and accountable as well as humanistic. This is similar to the transition experienced by many other human service disciplines. During the past 15 to 20 years, occupational therapy has been extending services into community-based programs from the traditional institutional settings in which the profession developed.

Determination of what services are provided and where is often dependent upon geographic location (urban versus rural), unilateral versus multiple delivery systems, availability of funding and the requirements for obtaining it, professional manpower distribution, priorities within a community, and a host of other related factors. Frequently, the most effective, economically viable, and realistic services can be rendered much more comprehensively within the consumer's local community.

Occupational therapy provides services across the health continuum. It is believed that more desirable, effective, and economical services can and should be provided in prevention and health maintenance, through alternative delivery systems such as home health. Unfortunately, the third party payer mechanism tends to focus reimbursement for services in the acute, episodic, inhospital phases of health care. Services might be better provided through neighborhood health centers, local health departments, home-health services, public and private schools, and social systems such as juvenile and adult correctional programs. Currently, these services must be underwritten by federal research and demonstration funds, state and local legislation, private foundations, or direct consumer payment. These funding mechanisms are often cumbersome or have constrained and limited resources.

Because the orientation of occupational therapists is bio-psycho-social, their services are found in health, educational, and social settings. Traditionally, their services have been identified as part of the rehabilitation component of health care. Table 1 approximates the types and location of occupational therapy services today.

As noted in this chart, a therapist may provide primary, secondary, or tertiary level health care services. An occupational therapist may work with a local health department in cooperation with other disciplines, screening young children for developmental disabilities. Expectant teen-age mothers may be trained in techniques of handling and interacting with a newborn. Some health departments also may provide health maintenance and outreach services. An occupational therapist may be involved in follow-up evaluation of at-risk populations such as low-birth-weight children or adults who are hypertensive.

Table 1.   Comprehensive delivery of occupational therapy services—typical payment mechanisms

PREVENTION/EARLY SCREENING/ INTERVENTION	REHABILITATION $\left\{\begin{array}{l}\text{REACTIVATION}\\\text{RESTORATION}\\\text{REMEDIATION}\end{array}\right.$

Health Departments
Community Health Centers
Well-Baby Clinics
Children and Youth/Maternal and Infant Projects
Health Maintenance Organizations
Private Practice
School Systems
  State Funds/Medicaid
  Private Funds
	School Systems
	Rehabilitation Centers
	Hospitals
	Health Departments
	Visiting Nurses Association
	Correctional/Penal Institutions
	  Research and Demonstration Grants
	  Third Party Payers (limited)
	  Hospital Absorbs
	  Vocational Rehabilitation Agency
	  Private Funds
	  Voluntary/Services Organizations
	  State Funds

HEALTH MAINTENANCE	

Health Departments
Regional Medical Programs
  some State Funds
  Research and Demonstration Grants	

ADULT INTERVENTION $\left\{\begin{array}{l}\text{CRISIS CARE}\\\text{ACUTE EPISODIC}\\\text{CARE}\end{array}\right.$	CONTINUING CARE/HOME HEALTH

Hospitals
  Third Party Payers
  Private Funds
  Local, State, Federal
	Health Departments
	Visiting Nurses Association
	Hospital
	  Third Party Payers (limited)
	  Patients
	  State/Medicaid/Medicare
	  Research/Demonstration Projects—Federal (e.g., NIH-Cancer)

CHILD INTERVENTION $\left\{\begin{array}{l}\text{CRISIS CARE}\\\text{ACUTE EPISODIC}\\\text{CARE}\end{array}\right.$	PREVOCATIONAL EXPLORATION/ VOCATIONAL RETRAINING

Hospitals—General/Specialized
  Third Party Payers
  Private Funds
  Voluntary/Service Organizations
  (often specific diagnosis, e.g., burns)
	Curative Workshops
	Vocational Rehabilitation
	Specialized Centers
	  Private Funds
	  Vocational Rehabilitation Services of HEW
	  Research and Demonstration Grants, HEW

	COMMUNITY OR SPECIALIZED PROGRAMS
	Head Start, Parent Cooperative Preschools Senior Citizens Centers Indian Reservation Schools Housing Developments

Frequently, occupational therapy services are provided in acute hospital settings. An occupational therapist may be involved before, during, and after surgical procedures. For example, a 54-year-old woman who is scheduled for a mastectomy may be assessed preoperatively for comparative purposes to measure the effects of surgery and postsurgical rehabilitation. Postsurgically the therapist will work with the woman to increase muscle strength and range of motion for performance and will assist in the adjustment process associated with the loss of a body part. Occupational therapy services may then extend into the woman's home as part of the continuing care program. To minimize barriers, adaptation of physical space and homemaking equipment may be necessary to facilitate the woman's adjustment and independence.

Occupational therapists often work in public and private residential facilities with the mentally retarded, emotionally disturbed, and chronic physically disabled. These clients also may be followed in residential and day-program facilities for habilitation, rehabilitation, and vocational training.

Community or specialized centers for healthy developmental group populations (e.g., Head Start, senior citizens centers, etc.) often use occupational therapy consultation services. Therapists assist other personnel in the design and evaluation of age-appropriate activity programming.

Often, consumers needing the same general types of services may be offered these programs through different types of agencies in various communities. For example, a child with a specific learning disorder might receive occupational therapy services through the health department, Easter Seals Center, hospital rehabilitation department, or a university-affiliated center. This child also might see an occupational therapist in a public school, a juvenile detention center, a mental health unit, or in a child development center that is publicly, privately, or church supported. Services to this child also might be provided by a therapist in private practice. The referral source can range from physician, psychologist, teacher, and other service professionals to parents themselves. The delivery system is secondary in importance to the fact that service is being provided.

THE OCCUPATIONAL THERAPY SERVICE PROCESS

The sequence and process of occupational therapy service delivery are generally similar in all settings, among all therapists and consumers. An occupational therapist uses a variety of methods and media to evaluate and enhance the performance skills of an individual. These modalities include the use of selected activities, relationships, special techniques, tools, materials, and equipment. Descriptive examples of what and how modalities are used follow to illustrate the general sequence and specific applications of the occupational therapy process.

Screening

The initial contact between a therapist and client generally serves as a screening. It is necessary to determine if the client has problems in occupational performance areas and if referral to additional disciplines and resources is necessary for effective problem identification and resolution. The therapist must decide if occupational therapy intervention would be facilitative or contraindicated.

These decisions are usually made by considering a variety of information. First, the therapist will observe the client, preferably in an activity

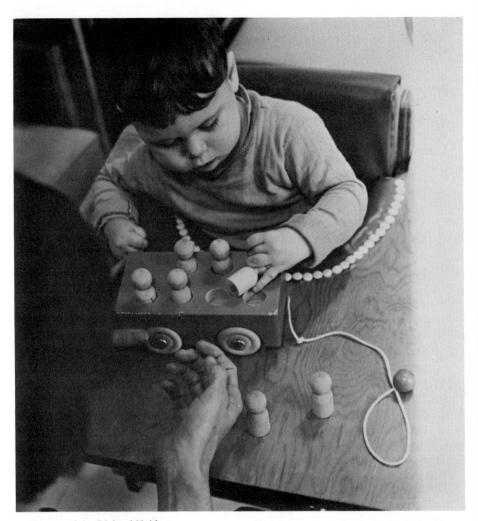

Photograph by Richard Holden.

performance situation (e.g., a four-year-old child, playing with toys, demonstrates difficulty in maintaining balance while using both hands). Whenever possible, the therapist will conduct short interviews with the client, members of the family, and the service delivery team. Next, a performance-based screening test will be administered to the client to identify developmental level, general performance components, capabilities, and deficits. The therapist will then consider the performance requirements of clients in their occupational roles. What should the individual be able to do in order to satisfy self, family, and society? For example, a four-year-old child must be able to maintain standing and sitting balance in order to use both hands skillfully. In turn, skilled coordination of hands is essential to accomplishing a variety of age-level activities that increase school readiness and ability to function as an independent family member.

This preliminary assessment process will guide further evaluation, as the occupational therapist seeks to determine the nature and degree of a client's functional capacities, performance skills, and program goals. Comprehensive occupational therapy evaluation includes (AOTA, 1974):

1. Life Space Data Collection—Through history-taking record review, interviews, and field visits, the therapist defines the client's life roles and environmental, cultural, and performance requirements. External resources, alternatives, and barriers to performance are identified.

2. Evaluation of Performance Components—Formal and informal measures of functional capacity are used to determine why a client has performance problems. This information is collected, both directly and indirectly, by the occupational therapist through record review, administration of standardized or criterion-referenced tests, personal interviews, and consultation with other service providers. Interpretation of the assembled data will provide a picture of the client's capacities and deficits in the five performance component functions. Table 2 provides a description of representative evaluation procedures of the performance components.

3. Evaluation of Occupational Role Performance—The therapist will finally test the client's ability to perform specific activities that are required in daily self-maintenance, play, and/or work roles. The variety of assessment methods is similar to those mentioned above but with the focus on total task performance.

Through this assessment process, the therapist determines client-specific performance disruptions, i.e., what areas of performance require intervention and why. The client's program goals will involve a synthesis of the client's capacities and goals, prognostic analysis of the effect of problems upon goal-achievement, and the availability of occupational therapy and other services. (The general goals of occupational therapy intervention are described above.)

Program Implementation

Following the assessment process, a program of selected activities and assistive modalities is designed and carried out with the client, family or guardian, and other service providers. Most frequently, the initial, short term goals and program will be related to improving performance

Table 2. Evaluation of performance components

Type of function	Commonly used assessment procedures
1. Sensory-Integrative Neurodevelopmental reflex patterns, body scheme and postural integration, form and space perception, sensory discrimination, motor planning	Infant developmental assessments Postural reflexive evaluation Southern California Sensory Integration Test Battery (standardized)
2. Motor Joint range of motion, muscle strength and tone, coordination, endurance, gross and fine motor skill, functional use of body	Functional muscle test (criterion-referenced)
3. Cognitive Time management, problem-solving, conceptualization and integration of new learning, concentration, use of communication skills, ability to follow directions	Job samples (standardized and criterion-referenced)
4. Psychological Object relations, emotional status, coping behaviors, and defenses, self-identity, and self-concept	Projective activity battery (standardized and criterion-referenced)
5. Social Dyadic relationships, group interaction abilities related to task and process, role requirements and performance	Vineland Social Maturity Scale Other criterion-referenced tests

component functions. The long range program plan is likely to be more involved with developing performance in different role activities. At different intervals throughout the intervention process, the therapist will reevaluate and reassess both the functional status of the client and program effectiveness. A few case examples may serve to illustrate the continuing occupational therapy process.

John was 66 years old and recently retired from his job as a mechanical engineer for a large corporation. His first year of retirement was not as rewarding as he had anticipated. Although he and his wife owned their home, both had been actively involved in business and community affairs and had long relied on hiring service persons to maintain their property. When John suffered a mild cerebrovascular accident of the left hemisphere, life seemed to lose all meaning.

Within six weeks poststroke, he showed mild residual hemiparesis of the right arm, trunk, and leg. He had been seen by a physical therapist in the hospital and could walk well with a cane. After discharge, while at home, he was referred to a home health agency for occupational therapy and speech pathology services.

The occupational therapist's first visit with John and his wife took place eight weeks poststroke. The occupational therapist learned that John was walking only between the bedroom, bath, and kitchen. His wife assisted him with all dressing, bathing, toileting, grooming, and eating activities. She seemed depressed and mentioned that her recent trips from the house had been limited to shopping for necessities. John would not talk much, although the speech pathologist's report had indicated that his expressive language dysfunction was minimal.

The occupational therapist arranged for a follow-up visit two days later and suggested that John's wife plan to use part of that time to visit friends. During the second session, the therapist evaluated functional movement patterns and tactile reception in John's arms and legs. John was encouraged to talk about his goals for retirement. Additionally, the therapist asked him to demonstrate a variety of self-care skills. When John's wife returned, the findings were then reviewed with the couple. John's difficulty in coordinated flexing of the hip and knee, plus a mild foot drop, made it difficult for him to change his right leg position without additional support and impaired his ability to climb stairs, use the bathtub, stand up and sit down. His loss of fine coordinated movements of right arm and hand, plus trunk weakness, affected performance of many feeding, dressing, and grooming activities. In addition, the different leisure activities John had hoped to enjoy all required a good deal of manual dexterity. He was fearful of speech lapses and did not wish to risk contacts with former community associates.

During the interim period before the next visit, the therapist discussed these findings with the home health nurse, speech pathologist, social worker, and physician. The therapist contacted the local heart association and arranged to have John visited by a representative.

During the next visit, John, his wife, and the therapist developed the following short term goals and program plan:

1. Restore fine hand function and control of right arm, and increase sensory awareness of involved arm through visual clueing, through involvement in table games, short shopping trips, and kitchen calisthenics.
2. Facilitate recovery of social awareness and skills and reinforce the speech program, through read-aloud sessions with newspapers and current books.
3. Increase independence in self-care activities through training and adaptive equipment, e.g., strategically placed grab bars in bathroom.

Long term goals of occupational therapy intervention included exploration and developmental of leisure interests, use of a graded activity program to protect cardiovascular functions, and training to restore optimal function in daily self-maintenance activities. The program was coordinated within the total care plan of the home health care team.

Joe was a 13-year-old boy in sixth grade. He was being held in a juvenile detention center because of numerous episodes of truancy, vandalism, and running away from home. The occupational therapist from the county health department contacted his school and family. The therapist found that Joe's reading level was less than third grade and that his parents had been divorced when he was seven. He lived with his mother and three younger children. The mother's income as a part-time waitress was supplemented by child support payments. Both his mother and teacher complained of his negative, oppositional behavior.

The therapist talked with Joe and found him distrustful of another guidance counselor. The therapist administered a standardized activity battery to obtain projective and diagnostic information. Media used included clay, paint, mosaic tiles, and plaster (Shoemeyen, 1970). Although Joe remained suspicious and tense, particularly when working with tiles, he enjoyed doing the other activities and demonstrated a natural ability to work with the media. He began to describe his ambivalent feelings about art: although he would like to be a painter, he felt his family depended on him to start work at sixteen. He disliked school, confessing he often could not recognize letters in new words and felt frustrated as the oldest person in his class. He liked art and math but had more trouble in the latter because of required reading.

The therapist's discussions with Joe and with personnel at the school and detention center determined that additional testing should be done to reveal causes of Joe's reading disability and also to explore his skill strengths. A battery of tests to determine sensory-integrative function showed that Joe's weaknesses were in visual and auditory sequencing and discrimination. His visual and manual space and form perception, however, were above average. Prevocational skill testing, done cooperatively with the rehabilitation counselor, showed that Joe had high aptitude and interest levels in art and mechanical skills.

In Joe's case, the occupational therapist developed a program that was carried out primarily by other personnel. The interdisciplinary team felt that Joe should transfer to a technical school where his study program could focus on his special aptitudes. A remedial reading program was recommended to ensure that his reading ability would be sufficient to support his other studies. The therapist worked with a remedial reading specialist to develop a sequence of reading activities that would utilize form and spatial perceptual modes. For a short while, the occupational therapist continued seeing Joe twice a week, helping him to develop more skill in the use of different art media and confidence in his talent. Gradually, Joe was transferred to a small art class in his new school for which the OTR (registered occupational therapist) provided consultant service. As he showed improvement in reading ability, Joe was able to pick up a larger number of fine and manual arts classes.

In working with John and Joe, occupational therapists functioned as members of health, social, and educational service teams. Because John's performance dysfunctions were related to a specific medical problem, his activity program required the close supervision of the occupational therapist. (The requirements for academic and clinical study of medical/surgical disorders in an occupational therapy curriculum sensitize the practitioner to precautions and changes in medical status in response to activity programming.) The therapist who worked with Joe used special expertise in evaluation of performance component functions and exploration of role performance skills. The therapist then shared evaluative findings with other professionals. Their specialized training in remedial reading, art, and counseling helped Joe to develop his role performance skills and subskills in an appropriate educational and peer-group environment.

These two case examples should illustrate that the occupational therapist's special expertise can be used to determine, enhance, and support functional capacities and to relate these to current or new occupational roles. The therapist then can develop a program to provide the client with opportunities to develop skill in play, work, and self-maintenance activities. The occupational therapist would not expect to train clients in all role performance skills. Instead, the client would be referred to a vocational specialist for job training, a special educator for academic skill development, or a physician for remediation of a pathological disorder. The occupational therapist's referral would include objective information about the client's performance of different activities and a professional interpretation of data and reasons for referral. Similarly, referral to an occupational therapist should include a summary of another professional's program and evaluative findings with a client, helpful background information, and reason for referral.

CURRENT ISSUES, NEEDS, AND LIMITATIONS IN SERVICE DELIVERY

The Vacuum Syndrome

Inherent in the use of interdisciplinary intervention strategies is a requirement for an effective and efficient method of collaboration, communication, and cooperation. Dana and Sheps have written that "... interprofessional behavior, in the context in which we view it, is an entity of its own that does not require members of related professions to think alike, but rather to act together" (West, 1969, p. 7). They also suggest that the interdisciplinary team must put the identification and resolution of a client's problem ahead of professionalism, institutional auspices, and other hidden agendas (West, 1969).

Further, if services are to be coordinated and comprehensive, the interdisciplinary model must support the concept of equal input by all disciplines. Communication must flow both horizontally and vertically. For administrative purposes, communication may function best in a line and staff organizational chart pattern. The effective delivery of services to a client, however, requires that all service providers deal with each other directly, respectful of mutual contributions to the intervention process. This is the most basic way to ensure that all service providers are fully knowledgeable in the utilization and reinforcement of each other's special skills. In this way, high quality, total programming becomes possible.

Regretfully, the interdisciplinary model can regress to the less desirable multidisciplinary model. Instead of demonstrating interactive peer relationships, disciplines begin to function as separate entities, each doing its own thing in a well defined but isolated vacuum. "This vacuum exists because of a knowledge gap of what a (specific) discipline has to offer, and because the discipline is unaware of the totality of the agency's program" (Shumlansky, 1975, p. 90).

The Language Problem

One of the major elements of professional education is the acquisition of that profession's vocabulary. In occupational therapy alone, students learn medical terminology, research and statistics terms, and special terminology from the biological and behavioral sciences. These diverse vocabularies are modified and synthesized into the language of occupational therapy. Terms and abbreviations such as "performance," "ADL," "BUE," "orthoses," "play dysfunction," "functional muscle test," etc. creep into daily conversations and documentation. Indeed, competencies in use of professional vocabulary are measured in the certification exam for occupational therapists.

As in any profession, there are several acknowledged schools of thought in occupational therapy. Therefore, in order to communicate with peers, therapists must learn which terms are similar and interchangeable. In encounters with other disciplines, one struggles to translate the other's terms into an occupational therapy concept. What is internalized is the translation. Because of this, future conversations about that concept may actually result in more breakdown of communication than there was the first time around. This happens when both assume that the other has gone through the same translation/symbolization process and that a common pool of interchangeable terms exists.

Discussion, clarification of concepts, and noncompetitive negotiation must take place between and among disciplines if communications are to benefit the client's program. Rather than relying upon false assumptions, it is the responsibility of each service provider to make sure he/she is understood by and understands another. This includes indicating to the other person what one has heard, what translations have been made, and checking on the validity of one's own conclusions.

This responsibility becomes even more critical in direct contacts between the consumer and the provider. It is the authors' belief that each client (consumer, service recipient, student, resident, patient, etc.) should have a clear understanding of the nature and purpose of the program. The explanation of the service should be provided to the client at an appropriate level of understanding and with respect for his/her dignity as a human being. This precludes the use of a patronizing manner and requires that the professional keep in touch with his/her reason for being.

The Mandate Syndrome

To comply with the increasing number of mandates for occupational therapy services, it has become essential for therapists to function in program development and consultative capacities. Frequently, direct programs are then carried out by a variety of paraprofessionals in other health or education areas, under the supervision or consultation of the professional-level occupational therapist (OTR). One problem that has evolved from this model of service delivery is the need to educate the direct care personnel to the realistic scope of services that can be provided without additional training or professional input.

Unfortunately, the unrealistic demands of the mandating system often force paraprofessionals (and professionals) into providing services for which they have not developed adequate competencies. Thus, the therapist becomes a mediator between the demands of the service system, the frustrations of the direct service provider, the decreased quality of care received by the consumer, and his/her own professional ethics.

This is a dilemma common to all human service professionals under the present economic and manpower constraints. A reordering of priorities is needed nationally. A commitment to *qualitative* as well as quantitative service delivery is necessary. A major interdisciplinary issue is the necessity for a united voice that advocates the right of the consumer to obtain quality care, particularly in tax-supported delivery systems.

This issue goes beyond the need for sufficient time to adequately train all levels of service providers before they are required to provide service. It extends to the need for adequate budgeting to employ workers, to buy equipment, to assign space, and to develop programs in an orderly sequence before mandating that program services be provided. When service is mandated before adequate components of the delivery process are available, it is doomed to failure or mediocrity.

The Reality Problem

The reality problem is an extension of the mandate syndrome. Within the regulations of many mandated services is a requirement for individual program plans. These are to include a problem list, goals, and approaches for intervention. Each problem identified by a team must be accompanied by a program plan, usually stated in measurable, behavioral terms.

A majority of persons for whom services are mandated have problems attributable to an underlying pathology. The pathological process itself, whether caused by disease, injury, intrauterine damage, or a lifetime of stress or institutionalization, often precludes changes in the observable behavior of an individual client. An example is a client whose problem is caused by central nervous system pathology. Once destroyed, central nervous system cells do not rebuild. Other cells may provide poor to fair substitutions for lost functions. Typical groups of clients seen with such permanent neurological impairment are children and adults with cerebral dysfunction, adults with Korsakoff's disease, or older persons with cerebral atherosclerosis (organic brain syndrome).

There are many more diagnostic categories that imply *chronic disability* in varying degrees. The process schizophrenic, institutionalized for 20 years or more, may be expected to have muscle bulk loss (atrophy) and loss of skeletal joint flexibility as a result of prolonged periods of inactivity. This person's loss of normal adult work, social, and other learning experiences while institutionalized precludes being able to function adequately in the real world. Placement in a group home, and limited employment in a sheltered workshop would be a highly successful outcome of an improvement program, provided the aging process itself did not further reduce the patient's remaining capacities.

Indeed, a list of problems identified for any client with chronic disability may include some for which there is no current solution. To state that there *is* an approach may be unethical and also may be frustrating to nonprofessional direct service providers who continue to see no change. Other problems may require that an activity be modified so that the client can perform it. Expectations for performance may have to be reduced so that the client can learn to assist the direct care provider in an activity while not being expected to eventually perform the activity independently.

It has become apparent that the less team members know about the pathological process and its implications, the more anger they have about writing and carrying out care plans. Also, the plans tend to be more unrealistic. It is recommended that at least one member of each team possess expertise in the pathological processes of chronic disabilities and that another have special expertise in the human development process throughout the life span. These team members must serve as monitors for appropriate program planning and as interpreters of problems to the rest of the team members. Although federal regulations specify the inclusion of such expertise on service delivery teams, the number of persons with such specialized knowledge is inadequate to meet the needs of the growing numbers of persons who now survive with chronic disability. As a result, minimal consultation services often enable an agency to comply with regulations. One solution may be to use consultant hours largely for inservice education of direct care providers. This detracts, however, from the number of personnel and hours available to provide other mandated services. Thus, one returns to the dilemma of the mandate syndrome.

RESEARCH NEEDS IN OCCUPATIONAL THERAPY

It is believed that the research needs of occupational therapy could, if met, provide some of the answers to the dilemmas discussed in the preceding sections. A good deal of research is reported in the *American Journal of Occupational Therapy* and its international counterparts. As can be imagined by considering the broad variety of client populations served by occupational therapists, the nature and purpose of studies reported are quite diverse. Additionally, because of the nationwide shortage of occupational therapists, those persons who are able to carry out research usually have small population samples. One author's study is rarely replicated by another investigator.

Even if another therapist duplicates a described program, it is unlikely that the second therapist will have the time to prepare the results for publication. More than 70% of practicing occupational therapists are married women; more than half of these women have at least one child (Jantzen, 1972). The population of OTRs is composed largely of persons who perform well in their roles as service providers but are limited in the amount of additional time and energy necessary to perform the added professional roles of researcher and writer. The shortage of academic occupational therapists, involved in university and clinical research programs, is critical.

It is clear the research needs in occupational therapy fall into two major areas: 1) wider standardization of criterion-referenced tests of performance functions and skills, and 2) validation and replication studies determining the effectiveness of different modalities for one or more client-age or problem populations.

In further discussion of the former, most occupational therapists use some type of criterion-referenced measurement of client function. These evaluations are developed by separating roles, tasks, or developmental stages into component parts and sequences. For example, to feed oneself, a person must be able to: reach, grasp a utensil, dip it into food, raise and flex the arm toward the mouth, keep head, neck, and trunk stabilized, open the jaw and mouth, control the tongue, swallow, etc. A variety of neurophysiological mechanisms enables a person to do each of these component processes. The different performance criteria can be referenced in developmental, biological, medical, and behavioral literature. Gradings of normal performance and dysfunction within the steps, according to the client's age and problem, often vary with the therapist's clinical and academic experiences. When these tests are published, standardization is often limited to clients, employees, and residents local to an institution.

For example, Casanova and Ferber (1976) reported on a comprehensive occupational therapy evaluation of self-maintenance activities that they had used with adults in a psychiatric institution. The performance criteria are clearly defined, organized logically, and well documented, and the administrative procedure is well standardized with that population. Until it is standardized on other adult populations, however, it can be used intuitively and no more.

Similarly, comparison and validation of program approaches are sorely needed. It is rare that an occupational therapist has the luxury of a control group for experimental purposes. (Control group is defined here as either a group of clients who can be tested without accompanying occupational therapy service provision or a group of clients who receive no services other than from occupational therapists.) This is likely to remain a fixed limitation in research because the clients referred to occupational therapists cannot ethically and legally be denied service. Also, present third party payer mechanisms frequently do not reimburse occupational therapy as a sole service to the client.

It is not the authors' purpose to argue the above limitations, merely to establish their existence. The primary responsibility of the human service professional is to provide services. Responsible service delivery, however, must always be supported by continued research and evaluation of program approaches and modalities. What can be done are comparative studies that clearly describe the client population and identify modalities used to influence specific functions and skills. Use of consistent pre- and postintervention evaluative procedures is also necessary. Too often a therapist will use one test battery for the initial assessment and another (higher performance level) just before termination of a client's program.

There has been some discussion within the American Occupational Therapy Association regarding the development of a central research data bank to analyze the broad variety of occupational therapy studies and findings. This could prove useful to clinicians, educators, and other service providers. A consulting therapist could use such a data bank to prepare a program for aides or paraprofessionals to implement. Information about effective alternative modalities, when to use these, and different levels of progression within the performance of an activity could be more easily assembled by data banks than by one occupational therapist. The individual therapist might then concentrate on identifying regional differences, documenting replication and results, and providing more input to data banks. At the same time, direct care providers would have clearer guidelines in the absence of the consultant.

HISTORICAL OVERVIEW

The roots of occupational therapy reach back to the early 1900s. In 1917, the National Society for the Promotion of Occupational Therapy was founded. This organization was the forerunner of the present day American Occupational Therapy Association (AOTA). The original founders of the association included a physician, nurse, social worker, architect, and craft teacher. Other early members of the association included people of similar training and other individuals interested in health problems as well as in manual and industrial arts. These founders, although from different disciplines, shared a common philosophy (later postulated by Mary Reilly) that ". . . man, through the use of his mind and body, can influence the state of his health" (Johnson, 1973, p. 203). The original founders also established the first qualifications for membership and training standards for education and training institutions, a joint program that continues today. A national registration also was begun for qualified therapists.

During 1923, the Federal Industrial Rehabilitation Act was passed. It mandated that hospitals involved in treating the industrially injured have occupational therapy provided as an integral part of treatment (Johnson, 1976).

In 1933, AOTA became the first discipline or paramedical organization to seek, obtain, and begin a joint program with the American Medical Association to accredit occupational therapists.

As a result of two World Wars, the psychological and physical rehabilitation needs of veterans placed a growing emphasis on occupational therapy, and federal legislation was passed that provided training for such therapists.

By the early 1940s, all educational programs for the training of occupational therapists were affiliated with colleges and universities. Through the 1940s and 1950s, occupational therapy curricula increased and expanded to the baccalaureate level, requiring basic liberal arts education as well as technical courses. Professional specialization began along with certification for the occupational therapy assistant (Johnson, 1973).

Before the 1960s, occupational therapists were involved with severely and moderately disabled individuals in institutions, rehabilitation centers, and private schools. By the 1960s, therapists began working with those having learning disabilities in the public schools. Occupational therapists also were becoming involved in other community-based programs, such as health departments, mental health centers, university affiliated child development programs, homes for the aged, etc. In 1965, the American Occupational Therapy Foundation (AOTF) was formed by the AOTA as a nonprofit foundation for charitable, scientific, literary, and educational purposes (AOTA, 1967).

Since the late 1960s, more therapists have transferred from medical facilities and have applied their skills in delivery systems of the broader health community. Emphasis is now more often directed to early detection and intervention, education, and treatment in order to prevent or minimize the effects of pathology. In addition to being direct or indirect providers of services, occupational therapists have become increasingly involved as health planners. Graduate level programs in occupational therapy at both the master's and doctoral levels continued to expand.

MAJOR FUNCTIONS OF
THE AMERICAN OCCUPATIONAL THERAPY ASSOCIATION

The major purpose of the American Occupational Therapy Association (AOTA) is set forth in its Articles of Incorporation. "The AOTA is to act as an advocate for occupational therapy in order to enhance the health of the public in its medical, community, and educational environments through research, education, action, service, and establishment and enforcement of standards" (AOTA, 1976, p. 1).

The AOTA has been going through a major reorganization to more effectively address the concerns of members, to anticipate, identify, and resolve emerging issues, and to facilitate, expedite, and interpret decisions into action. The organizational structure includes the Representative Assembly, as the legislative and decision-making body of the Association, which sets policy and procedures for the profession. Representatives and alternates are elected, based on occupational membership distribution among states. Every state has at least one representative. For states having more than 400 members, a population equalization formula is used, so that no state is penalized because of size. There are a number of committees of the Representative Assembly whose functions are to develop policy and procedure statements in specific areas for consideration by the Assembly.

The reorganization has placed certain elected officials (Executive Board) in charge of general association management. There are both voting and nonvoting members of the Executive Board. The voting members, elected by national vote, include the President, Vice President, Secretary, Treasurer, and two Members-at-Large. In addition, officers of the Representative Assembly also are voting members and include the Speaker, Recorder, and the Chairperson of the Committee of State Presidents. Nonvoting members include the Executive Director of the AOTA National Office, the Delegate to the World Federation of Occupational Therapists, and Chairpersons of Standing Committees of the Representative Assembly. The President is the central management person. This individual is charged with carrying out the policies of the Assembly.

The state associations have first line organizational authority to act on local and regional issues affecting occupational therapists. They may also elect to deal with national issues on a local level. The state associations represent membership and elect their respective state representatives to the Representative Assembly. The Council of State Association Presidents is a standing committee of the Delegate Assembly.

The AOTA national office staff provides technical, administrative, and support services for members. They seek to provide resources to the membership and/or state associations so that members are free to carry out policy and programs. The national office staff assists with maintenance activities such as certification, education standards, centralization of public affairs, publications educational support materials, and the archives. In addition, national office staff also represent the association in addressing critical and relevant national issues with the legislative and executive branches of government.

The reorganization of AOTA appears to be strengthening the role of individual members by providing them with support mechanisms that facilitate constructive action on priorities identified by the membership. To assist in this task, an Office of Advocacy was created under the president. The function of the advocate is to assist the membership in identifying, analyzing, and acting upon its priorities. Thus, the advocate is accountable to the membership (Johnson, 1976). This approach frees the national office staff to deal with external forces, including legislative and other issues that do not lend themselves to local or regional resolution.

EDUCATIONAL PROGRAMS IN OCCUPATIONAL THERAPY

Occupational therapy education promotes learning about human and non-human processes, environments, tools, and materials. At present there are four levels of educational programs for the discipline. A person desiring entrance into the field may choose technical level training to become a certified occupational therapy assistant (COTA). At present, this type of educational program is found in junior and community colleges and in a few four-year colleges and universities. Students receive technical skill training as part of a two-year associate degree course. If they already have other college credits, students may opt for a one-year program that includes only the required occupational therapy courses. The graduates of this program are subject to proficiency testing. They will work under the supervision or consultation of an OTR, dependent upon place of employment.

Basic professional education in occupational therapy requires a minimum of bachelor's level academic study and six months of field work experience. The latter is done under the supervision of an OTR with at least one year of professional experience. The student's field work performance is evaluated according to a national rating scale. In addition to meeting general college requirements for the degree sought, students must take courses in occupational therapy and related disciplines. The professional major curriculum must include:

1. Basic human sciences—to understand the structure and function of the human organism and its development from conception to death

2. The human development process—to understand the development, acquisition, and integration of skills, life tasks, and roles essential to productive living and mastery of self and environment
3. Specific life tasks and activities—to understand and perform the processes involved in selected tasks and activities; to identify and analyze the components that make up tasks and activities
4. Health-illness-health continuum—to understand the characteristics of health and illness; to describe and discuss the effect upon the human being of interruptions to, aberrations in, and trauma to the developing human organism throughout the life span
5. Occupational therapy theory and practice—to apply and utilize the theories and principles of occupational therapy, in direct service delivery, consultation, administration, health planning, and research (AOTA, 1973)

These curriculum essentials, along with the field work experience required, are compiled in national standards with which different colleges and universities must comply. The standards for professional education are enforced cooperatively by the American Occupational Therapy Association and the American Medical Association, Council on Medical Education.

Undergraduate students may obtain a bachelor's degree in occupational therapy. Most states have at least one school offering a baccalaureate professional program. A person who has obtained a bachelor's degree in another field may apply for a certificate or a basic master's degree program in occupational therapy. These programs usually require two years to complete. Admission to all programs is competitive. It should be noted that additional graduate study programs in occupational therapy are available for advanced graduate study. All graduates of baccalaureate and master's basic professional programs are required to pass the national certification examination, administered by the Educational Testing Service. Upon successful completion of the exam, graduates are certified to use the initials OTR (Occupational Therapist, Registered).

PROFESSIONAL ORGANIZATION

For further information about occupational therapy and educational programs, contact:

The American Occupational Therapy
   Association, Inc., 6000 Executive
   Boulevard, Rockville, Maryland
   20852

REFERENCES

American Occupational Therapy Association. 1967. Then 1917 and Now 1967. American Occupational Therapy Association, New York.
American Occupational Therapy Association. 1973. Essentials of an Accredited Basic Professional Education Program for the Occupational Therapist. Established and adopted by the AOTA Council on Education in collaboration with the American Medical Association Council on Medical Education. American Occupational Therapy Association, Rockville, Md.
American Occupational Therapy Association. 1974. A Curriculum Guide for Occupational Therapy Educators. American Occupational Therapy Association, Rockville, Md.
American Occupational Therapy Association. 1976. Annual Report. American Occupational Therapy Association, Rockville, Md.
Carlsen, P. N. Human Development Through Occupation: Resources in Occupational Therapy Theory and Practice. In preparation.
Casanova, J. S., and Ferber, J. 1976. Comprehensive evaluation of basic living skills. Am. J. Occup. Ther. 30:101–105.
Jantzen, A. C. 1972. Some characteristics of female occupational therapists, 1970. Part I: Descriptive study. Am. J. Occup. Ther. 26:19–26.
Johnson, J. A. 1973. Occupational therapy: A profession in transition. In J. Hamburg (ed.), Review of Allied Health Education I, pp. 201–229. The University of Kentucky Press, Lexington.
Johnson, J. A. 1976. Newsletter. American Occupational Therapy Association, Rockville, Md.
Llorens, L. A. 1976. Application of a Developmental Theory for Health and Rehabilitation. American Occupational Therapy Association, Rockville, Md.
Mosey, A. C. 1974. An alternative: The bio-psycho-social model. Am. J. Occup. Ther. 28:137–140.
Pelligrino, E. 1973. Preventive health care and the allied health professions. In J. Hamburg (ed.), Review of Allied Health Education I, pp. 1–18. The University of Kentucky Press, Lexington.
Reilly, M. 1962. Eleanor Clark Slagle Lecture. Occupational therapy can be one of the great ideas in twentieth century medicine. Am. J. Occup. Ther. 16:1–9.
Shoemeyen, C. W. 1970. Occupational therapy orientation and evaluation: A study of procedure and media. Am. J. Occup. Ther. 24:1–4.
Shumlansky, S. G. 1975. A look at tomorrow's accreditation. In Home Health Agencies and Community Health Services (ed.), The Issue is Leadership, pp. 89–93. National League for Nursing, New York.
West, W. 1969. The university-affiliated center: History and philosophy. In W. West (ed.), Occupational Therapy Functions in Interdisciplinary Programs for Children. Proceedings of a Conference, August 25–27, 1969, pp. 1–8. United States Department of Health, Education, and Welfare, Maternal and Child Health Service, Rockville, Md.

ORTHOTICS AND PROSTHETICS

Charles Dankmeyer, Jr.

Human lives are at times punctuated by tragedies that give rise to the need for orthotics and prosthetics. The deformities of war, accident, birth, and disease create the need for artificial limbs and braces to reinstate that individual to financial independence, social acceptance, and psychological wholeness.

HISTORY

Orthotics and prosthetics are not new professions. The earliest known reference to orthotics was made about 2500 B.C., while the first mention of a prosthesis dates from about 500 B.C. The oldest known artificial limb in existence, made of wood, leather, bronze, and iron, dates back to the Samnite Wars of 300 B.C. The best known example of a historical artificial hand is that of Goetz von Berlichingen, a German knight of the early 16th century. Goethe wrote one of his dramas around the exploits of this knight who had lost his hand in battle at the age of twenty-three. In the drama, the knight offered his left hand to the monk, Martin. Martin was offended and asked the warrior, "Why do you offer me the left hand? Am I not worthy of knightly courtesy?" Goetz's reply was, "Were you the emperor himself, you must be content with this. My right, though not useless in war, is insensible to the pressure of love. It is a part of my glove; you see, it is iron."

History teaches us that orthoses and prostheses were designed by craftsmen, scientists, and surgeons throughout the 19th century. As technology advanced, the practices of orthotics and prosthetics became more complex and demanding. Following World War II, a great deal of research was instituted to further the development of orthoses and prostheses. This research resulted in an even greater expansion of the technology of orthotics and prosthetics. Today, orthotics and prosthetics are unique blends of medicine, engineering, physics, mechanics, and chemistry.

CERTIFICATION STANDARDS

As development of new materials provided access to more intimately fitting devices, the need to establish credential standards for practitioners became evident. In August 1948, the American Orthotic and Prosthetic Association, in cooperation with the American Academy of Orthopaedic Surgeons, established a credentialing program designed to identify those orthotic and prosthetic practitioners and facilities qualified to render essential public health services in these two disciplines. The program was implemented by the then established American Board for Certification in Orthotics and Prosthetics, a nonprofit corporation.

In addition to its credentialing activities, the Board also seeks to advance the highest levels of competency and ethics in the practice of orthotics and prosthetics in the United States. The American Board for Certification implements the major purposes of its charter through two types of credentialing.

The first is the credentialing of individuals whose education and experience meet established requirements. These persons then are admitted to an examination designed to evaluate their knowledge of orthotic/ prosthetic technology and to assess their ability to fabricate and fit a variety of orthotic and prosthetic devices. Those who successfully complete the examination are issued certificates in the appropriate discipline. These certificates must be renewed annually in order to maintain good standing.

The second area of credentialing is concerned with facilities and educational programs. After site inspections and evaluations, facilities deemed to be capable of providing an acceptable level of prosthetic and orthotic care to patients are accredited by the American Board for Certification in Orthotics and Prosthetics. Educational programs in orthotics and prosthetics that comply with the Board's academic essentials are accredited so that students completing these programs may qualify for examination to establish their professional status. The adoption of the credentialing program for orthotists and prosthetists identifies certified practitioners who are then recognized as professional members of their communities. The adoption of professional standards also serves to protect the general public health and welfare by eliminating those individuals unqualified to provide quality orthotic and prosthetic care to patients in need.

Currently, certification is on a voluntary basis throughout the country with the exception of the state of Georgia. The state of Georgia instituted an Orthotic Practice Act that licenses orthotists in the state. The Orthotic Practice Act reinforces the American Board for Certification program and officially adopts its qualifications. Some certification system is recognized by most agencies involved in the procurement of prosthetic and orthotic devices. Therefore, to practice orthotics and prosthetics as a paid professional, one must be certified.

FUNCTIONS OF THE ORTHOTIST AND THE PROSTHETIST

Orthotist is the term used for the practitioner who provides care by fitting devices known as orthoses to patients with disabling conditions of the limbs and spine. At the direction of and in consultation with physicians, the functions of the orthotist are as follows:

1. Assists in the formulation of prescriptions for orthoses by examining and evaluating the orthotic needs of patients in relation to their disease entity and functional loss
2. In providing the orthosis, creates its design, including the selection of materials
3. Makes all necessary cast measurements, model modifications, and layouts
4. Conducts fittings, including static and dynamic alignments
5. Evaluates the orthosis after its application to assure maximal fit, function, cosmesis, and workmanship
6. Instructs the patient in use of the orthosis
7. Maintains appropriate patient records
8. Keeps abreast of current developments relevant to optimal orthotic patient care
9. Supervises the functions of orthotic assistants and technicians, other laboratory personnel, and laboratory activities related to the development of orthoses
10. Lectures and demonstrates to colleagues and other interested professionals concerned with the practice of orthotics
11. Participates in relevant research

Prothetist is the term used for the practitioner who provides care to patients with partial or total absence of a limb by creating and fitting devices known as prostheses that replace the missing limbs and limb segments. These devices are both functional and cosmetic in their design. Under the direction of and in consultation with physicians, the prosthetist performs the following functions:

1. Assists in the formulation of prescriptions for prostheses by examining and evaluating the prosthetic needs of patients in relation to their disease entity and functional loss
2. In providing the prosthesis, creates its design, including the selection of materials and components
3. Makes all necessary casts, measurements, and model modifications
4. Conducts fittings, including static and dynamic alignments
5. Evaluates the prosthesis after its application to assure maximal fit, function, comfort, and workmanship
6. Instructs the patient in its use

7. Maintains satisfactory patient records
8. Keeps informed of recent developments pertinent to optimal prosthetic patient care
9. Supervises the functions of prosthetic assistants and technicians, other laboratory personnel, and laboratory activities related to the development of prostheses
10. Lectures and demonstrates to colleagues and other interested professionals concerned with the practice of prosthetics
11. Participates in relevant research

Orthotics and prosthetics are two distinctly separate disciplines, although they share similarities in materials used and in design criteria. Approximately one-third of all individuals involved in orthotics or prosthetics are certified to practice both professions.

It should be remembered that while orthotists and prosthetists practice what appears to be a very small and discrete medical specialty, their practice covers virtually all patient age groups and disabilities. For example, an orthotist may be requested to provide a splint for a mild neck sprain, design a splint for an infant with a dislocated hip, or provide a complex system of orthoses to support a paraplegic patient in an upright position. Or, a prosthetist may be asked to provide a prosthesis for a six-month-old child amputated below the elbow, or a prosthesis for a 40-year-old man who has been amputated bilaterally through the hip. The services of orthotists and prosthetists are required by a wide variety of patients of all ages.

SETTINGS OF SERVICE

Orthotists and prosthetists practice from their own independent offices and laboratories. Orthoses and prostheses are individually designed and fabricated. It is essential that the orthotist and prosthetist maintain laboratories sufficiently equipped to provide for the fabrication of each special design. Almost all orthotists and prosthetists are in private practice, while orthotic and prosthetic research laboratories are located in several major universities. These laboratories engage in very little patient care except for those patient services essential to specific research designs.

Most orthotists and prosthetists practice within a clinical setting. Limb prosthesis clinics are divided into three major categories: upper limb, lower limb, and child. Many limb prosthesis clinics do not differentiate and will attend to any level and age group within the same clinic. Most limb prosthesis clinics carry the name of the institution in which the clinic operates, e.g., Johns Hopkins Limb Prosthesis Clinic. The institution may also designate level and age group to identify the patient populations served, e.g., Johns Hopkins Upper Limb and Child Amputee Clinic.

Clinics are not nearly as common in orthotic practice as in prosthetic practice. The clinics in which orthotics are practiced are generally identified by the specific age groups, similar disabilities, or specific disease. Titles for such clinics include: Crippled Children's Clinic, Stroke Clinic, Muscular Dystrophy Center, etc. The delineation is much more general than in prosthetics because the scope of orthotics is much broader. Most orthoses are not prescribed in the arena of a clinic. Orthoses are often needed to release a patient from the hospital. Scheduling for a clinic visit and intrahospital transportation often make waiting for a clinic impractical and expensive.

TRAINING

Orthotists and prosthetists are trained at universities that offer a major in orthotics and prosthetics. Currently, the highest degree obtainable is a Bachelor of Science degree. General areas of study include anatomy, kinesiology, biomechanics, and engineering. This general core of studies is then reinforced and expanded with studies in the professional specialties of orthotics and prosthetics. To be eligible for certification as an orthotist or prosthetist, one must complete the educational requirements of a Bachelor of Science in the appropriate specialty.

CLINICAL TEAM APPROACH

Most orthotists and prosthetists participate on clinical teams. A clinical team usually consists of a physician, a physical therapist, a social worker, and an orthotist/prosthetist who meet for the purpose of defining a treatment mode for individual clinic patients. In the case of an amputee, the normal sequence of events commences with the referral of the patient to a particular amputee clinic by the surgeon who performed the amputation. At the clinic, in most instances, the amputee would first be evaluated by a physical therapist. The therapist then would report the results of the examination, along with a brief medical history, to the physician, the orthotist/ prosthetist, and the social worker. These professionals would then conduct their own evaluations of the patient. Later, all four disciplines would share their individual findings and would plan an individualized treatment procedure. Clinics thus provide an effective and efficient method of supplying patients with the necessary specialized professional services. For the professionals involved, however, working in a clinic can be a time-consuming process.

It must be emphasized that orthotics and prosthetics are extremely specialized fields. Few physicians, few social workers, and surprisingly few physicial therapists are familiar with the nature and scope of orthotics and prosthetics, although they may be aware of their existence. They are generally not familiar enough with the intricacies of orthotics and prosthetics to make prescription recommendations without the assistance of an orthotist/prosthetist. While most clinics are established with the physician as the team leader and all the other disciplines involved on an equal plane, in reality, this approach is generally not followed. In most instances, the findings of the physical therapist and the prosthetist/orthotist define the treatment mode for the individual patient. The physician, as clinic chief, then provides the prescriptions for the prosthetist/orthotist and the physical therapist to follow.

Most social workers become involved with the individual patient after the treatment plan has been selected. In those cases in which a patient requires preprosthetic or preorthotic physical therapy, at the termination of such therapy, the patient will be referred either directly to the orthotist/prosthetist or back to the clinical team. Here, he/she will receive further evaluation before the fitting of an orthosis or prosthesis. The patient is once more evaluated by the orthotist/prosthetist, who will design, fabricate, and fit the appropriate device. Then, use of the device is demonstrated and the patient is given training and practice in its use. Once this training is accomplished, the patient is referred back to the physical therapist for further intensive training in the use of the device. When the physical therapist believes the patient has realized maximal benefit from the device, the patient is evaluated again by the clinical team. At that time, the recommendations of the physical therapist and the orthotist/prosthetist are presented to the physician. The physician generally will examine the patient to ascertain his/her level of functioning with the device. When appropriate, the patient will be discharged subject to various follow-up procedures including periodic visits to the clinic for treatment and examination. The social worker, who has been actively working with the individual patient during the entire training period, will continue to make recommendations directly to the patient and/or the patient's family.

In addition to the clinical team approach, many patients are referred directly from the surgeon to an orthotist/prosthetist and then from the orthotist/prosthetist to the physical therapist.

INTERDISCIPLINARY PROBLEMS

All specialties tend to claim and develop territorial rights. The orthotist/prosthetist believes that the evaluation of orthotic and prosthetic devices for fit, function, and cosmesis are the exclusive province of a certified orthotist/prosthetist. Physical therapists, on the other hand, frequently believe that the evaluation of prosthetic and orthotic appliances for fit, function, and cosmesis belongs rightfully within the domain of physical therapy. Furthermore, orthotists and prosthetists believe that the training of individual patients in the use of orthotic and prosthetic devices belongs within their professional sphere, while many physical therapists believe that training the patient in the use of an orthosis or prosthesis is a function of their own profession. However, while conflicts do arise between members of these professions, for the most part, they are the exception rather than the rule. In the United States, most orthotist/prosthetists design, build, and fit orthoses and prostheses and then evaluate the function and fit of the orthosis and prosthesis on the patient; physical therapists train patients in the use of such devices.

Over the years, orthotists, prosthetists, and physical therapists have learned that criticism of another discipline avails little because it may interfere with the provision of service to the patient and accentuates the lack of interdisciplinary information. The specialties in the allied health professions have become so complex and so specialized that mutual trust and respect among practitioners is essential. When the spirit of mutual respect exists, then orthotists, prosthetists, and physical therapists are able to freely refer patients for service.

The clinical team approach has resulted in the emergence of an unanticipated problem in relation to the efficient practice of orthotics and prosthetics. For physical therapists, physicians, and social workers to become familiar with the needs of patients who require orthotic and prosthetic services, they must see a large number of such patients. Once a hospital establishes such a team, however, other hospitals in the same locale invariably attempt to set up their own clinical program. The resultant proliferation of clinics sorely taxes and exhausts the time of the few orthotists and prosthetists available to act as clinical consultants.

A further sequel to clinical proliferation is a reduction in the patient population examined by each clinical facility. The net result is that the physical therapist, the physician, and the social worker in each clinic receive less exposure and, subsequently, less opportunity to gain the knowledge and skills needed to manage orthotic and prosthetic patients, while the orthotist and the prosthetist spend less time at each of the different clinics. The time spent in consultation significantly affects the cost of services rendered by the orthotist and prosthetist because it diminishes the time available to devote to actual patient management. As a result of this adverse effect on cost, new clinics are being discouraged in many areas.

TERMINOLOGY

The language of orthotics and prosthetics reflects the techniques and principles employed in the appliances being described. General anatomical terms are used abundantly in prosthetic and orthotic language. Most frequently, the area covered, manner fitted, and purpose of the device are merged to form "prostheticisms" and "orthoticisms."

Above knee, plastic laminate, quadrilateral, total contact, suction socket are terms specific to prosthetics and identify a particular segment of a prosthesis recommended for an above knee (AK) amputee. The socket is the part of the prosthesis into which the patient's stump, or residual limb, fits. The above description calls for the socket 1) to be of a plastic laminate as opposed to other available materials, 2) to be quadrilateral in shape, which describes a fitting technique involving varying pressures related to tissue expansion and to consistency with weight bearing on the ischial tuberosity, 3) to provide total contact, i.e., the device should touch all parts of the stump, and 4) to be of the suction variety, which means that the device is fitted with a one way air valve so that once the stump is inserted into the socket, air may exit but not enter the socket, thus producing a vacuum that will hold the prosthesis in place.

The terminology used is specific to the practice. A constant friction knee is one in which the amount of friction during swing phase does not vary. A constant friction knee with an extention assist is one in which the friction is constant during swing phase and extension of the knee is mechanically assisted. There are many available knee systems. Most can best be described by their function rather than their originator. Physicians often will prescribe a Bock knee as part of an above knee prosthesis. Actually, Bock is a manufacturer of knee components that range from swing phase control, through swing and stance phase control, to locked. The prescription of a Bock knee is thus ambiguous, rendering the prescription invalid. Like knee prostheses, hip joints, ankle joints, feet, and suspension systems must be described by the desired function rather than by other identifying characteristics. The upper extremity amputee also requires prescriptions that accurately communicate desired fitting techniques and functions.

Eponyms are common in orthotic terminology, and have all the disadvantages of any eponym, i.e., everyone has a different version of the same device with a different eponym. A great deal of effort has been put forth to eliminate the eponyms from orthotic practice. Because orthoses are provided to support, assist, and protect various body segments, the nomenclature used to describe an orthosis should state precisely what is to be accomplished rather than describe the parts and materials used to produce the device. This can best be illustrated in discussing the spine which is divided into cervical, thoracic, lumbar, and sacral regions. A typical need for a spinal orthosis would result from fractures of lumbar four and five. The most common orthosis used for this condition may carry one of the following eponyms: Knight, Chair Back, Bennett, Modified Bennett, and Goldwaithe. An individual referring to any of these names has no idea what results may be obtained. The correct nomenclature is Lumbo Sacral Flexion, Extension, and Lateral Control Orthosis. Such a description leaves no doubt as to the desired result and is the safest way to communicate intentions when using orthoses. When an orthotist receives a prescription, he/she will usually recognize it as an orthosis with which he/she and the prescribing physician are familiar. Any design changes must be cleared with the prescribing physician.

FITTING TECHNIQUES OF THE PROSTHETIST

Upper extremity amputees are almost always fitted with a terminal device commonly referred to as a "hook." Unlike the stereotype this misnomer implies, the terminal device is not at all like that of Peter Pan's adversary, Captain Hook. Modern day terminal devices may appear to be "hooks;" however, they have a lever or thumb on the side that is connected to a cable. When the cable is retrieved either by motion of the arm or shoulder girdle, activation of a pneumatic system, or an electrical system, the fingers of the hook open wide. The shape of these metal fingers varies depending, in part, upon the desired activities of the amputee.

Terminal devices of this design are preferred over the more cosmetic restorations because they are significantly more functional. A cosmetic hand can be made with fingers and thumb working in several combinations to produce function. They all, however, have two common drawbacks. The first is related to function. The amputee no longer has sensation or proprioception in the terminal device. He/she must be able to see exactly what the device is doing to maintain any degree of control. Hands block essential visibility. A second disadvantage is that hands must be covered with special cosmetic gloves to approximate the texture of skin and the specific color of the individual patient's skin. No cosmetic hand will be a perfect color and texture. None is immune from the effects of soiling from normal use, ink stains, and darkening from sunlight. The life expectancy of this type of glove is approximately three months.

Most upper extremity amputees use a functional two-fingered split hook terminal device for work and replace it with a cosmetic hand and glove only for special occasions. Upper extremity prostheses are almost always designed so that the two types of terminal device are interchangeable with one body prosthesis. As with all areas of prosthetic and orthotic practice, many possibilities exist for wrist design, elbow design, shoulder design, method of fitting, suspension, and control modes. In general, the more proximal the level of the amputation, the less functional mechanical prostheses become and the more apparent the need becomes for utilizing pneumatics and electronics. Both, however, are rarely used. Upper extremity amputees should be fitted early. Unilateral upper extremity

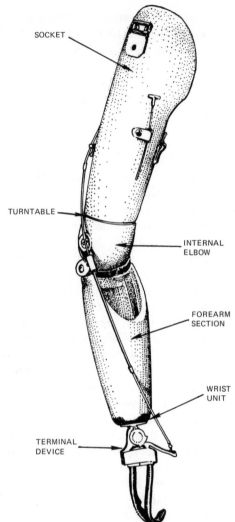

SOCKET

TURNTABLE

INTERNAL
ELBOW

FOREARM
SECTION

WRIST
UNIT

TERMINAL
DEVICE

Figure 1.   Standard above elbow prosthesis.

amputees can often become one-handed in most activities, but they often restrict their activities to what they can easily do with one hand. If fitted early, they adapt more readily to the prosthesis and do not experience the time lag during which one-handedness develops.

Children should be fitted when they are ready to begin trunk balance and sitting alone. They can use their prostheses for sitting balance at first and then to help pull themselves to a standing position. They also can begin to use their prostheses for bilateral grasp. A child who begins in this manner will almost always become a proficient user of the prosthesis. As the child grows older, the ability to perform the finer motor skills may develop at a level equal to his/her peers. It is not uncommon for children to be ardent users of upper limb prostheses until their teen-age years when peer pressure will cause some to cease wearing the prosthesis. This rejection most often occurs between the ages of 13 and 18. When asked to explain this behavior, the teen-ager will often respond, "I look better without it."

Nevertheless, the fine motor skills have already been acquired and will return when social pressure emphasizes performance over appearance. Invariably, a teen-ager who has discarded a prosthesis will return for a new one by the age of 18. Seldom is any training required when these individuals return to their prostheses. Pre-teen-age children often will refuse to remove their prostheses because they are vital to their functioning. Unfortunately, parents, at times, take advantage of this and use the putting away of the arm as a means of disciplinary action.

Upper limb amputees are able to follow a remarkable number of vocational pursuits; they are known to be employed as farmers, physicians, musicians, pilots, and in almost any other skilled or unskilled occupation. Current research is attempting to discover and develop some power source, other than the shoulder girdle through harnessing, to power all segments of the upper limb. While alternate power sources have proved to be successful within research laboratories, they have not been developed for general use. It is hoped that these systems will be released for general use in the near future. Sensory feedback is also currently under study with some successful laboratory applications reported.

Lower limb amputees comprise approximately 90% of the amputee census. Most lower limb amputations are the result of vascular disease, often with diabetes as a contributing factor. In any age group, assuming acceptable cardiac and pulmonary status, patients who are unilateral or bilateral below knee (BK) amputees will be successful in their ability to ambulate. Most unilateral above knee (AK) amputees also will be successful. Individuals who are one AK, one BK, or bilateral AK are limited in their success when they are elderly while they are almost always successful when they are young.

Unilateral hip disarticulation and hemipelvectomy patients are generally successful at ambulation but can walk more rapidly with crutches. Bilateral hip disarticulation or hemicorpectomy patients almost always cannot functionally ambulate. The most common factors limiting performance in lower limb amputees are range of motion limitations because of contracture at the hip and/or knee which limits control of the prosthesis and sensitivity of the stump caused by a variety of sources limiting the wearing time.

Sensitivity factors may include neuromas, arthritic joints, sharp bony prominences, and skin grafts. The age and physical condition of the patient will dictate whether or not preprosthetic therapy or additional surgery can improve the situation. It is not uncommon for initial amputations, done as life-saving procedures, to require revision at a later date. Because prostheses require significantly less energy to use than ambulatory aids, such as crutches and walkers, it is generally concluded that a patient who can use these devices for standing balance will be able to use a prosthesis. In the case of bilaterality, the ability to raise the body up from a chair with the upper limbs is a rule of thumb used to determine minimal strength requirements. This does not take into account the complications of amputation level mentioned earlier.

The optimal amputee will have all of the following factors: good skin coverage with minimal tenderness, well healed wound site, cylindrical or conical stump shape, full range of motion about the remaining joints, no sharp bony prominences good balance with walker or crutches, and acceptable vision. While these are the optimal conditions, success nevertheless is frequently achieved even when complications exist in all the mentioned areas.

To describe all of the possible fitting techniques used in lower limb prosthetics today would require an encyclopedia. It should be noted, however, that children should be fitted as early as possible with six months being the average age to begin. The following represents some of the methods and a brief description of the devices used at various lower limb amputation levels.

1. Forefoot amputations require a molded innersole to support the remaining structures of the foot with a prosthetic segment to fill the forward part of the shoe. The device should allow for a normal bending of the toe joint to simulate the sound side.

2. Some amputations and ankle disarticulations require the prosthesis to accommodate a bulbous distal end. This requires the inner wall of the prosthesis to expand to allow the passing through of the large distal end. This may be accomplished by the construction of a door in the side of the prosthesis that can be opened when applying the prosthesis and then closed for use. (See Figure 2.) A foot that simulates plantar flexion and toe flexion also must be provided.

3. A typical below knee amputee will require a prosthesis to support weight bearing on the stump itself. The patellar tendon and medial tibial flair are considered excellent weight bearing areas. The prosthesis is generally held on with a small strap above the knee over the femoral condyles. This is often assisted with a belt around the waist connected to the strap. Below knee amputees may be fitted with mechanical knee joints and a leather thigh corset to help assist in weight bearing when knee joint instability exists. The foot may simulate ankle motion or an

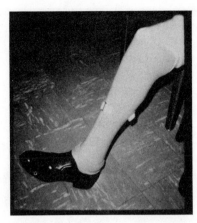

Figure 2.   Prosthesis with side door to accommodate bulbous distal end associated with ankle disarticulation.

actual mechanical ankle may be provided. The typical prosthesis for a below knee amputee is called a PTB (Patellar Tendon Bearing) prosthesis.

4. Knee disarticulation and above knee amputees are almost always fitted with sockets that are quadrilateral in shape and with provision for weight bearing on the ischial tuberosity. A knee mechanism, which could range from a simple hinge to a complex pneumatic or hydraulic control system, must be provided in addition to an ankle and foot mechanism. The prosthesis may be held in place in a variety of ways, the most common being a belt around the hip connected to a hinge approximating the axis of the hip joint. A simple webbing strap, shoulder straps, and vacuum are other examples of the methods used to maintain the AK prosthesis in place.

5. A hip disarticulation prosthesis must provide mechanical hip, knee, ankle, and foot mechanisms. The patient's pelvis is held inside the prosthesis socket and the ischicum is used as a weight bearing point.

Prostheses may be constructed as either exoskeletal (crustacian) or endoskeletal units. The most common is the crustacian type with a hard exterior that is the strength of the prosthesis. Endoskeletal units use tubular inner structures with the necessary mechanical components placed between the tubes at appropriate locations. A soft foam is then attached to the outside of the structure and shaped to match the remaining limb, reversing right and left, as nearly as possible. (See Figure 3.) Endoskeletal prostheses are currently gaining favor for use in above knee amputees in place of the more conventional crustacian designs. Endoskeletal prostheses for below knee amputees are used much less frequently.

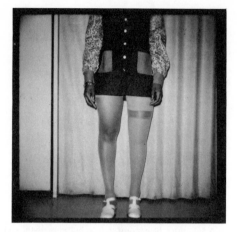

Figure 3.   Finished endoskeletal prosthesis for above knee amputee.

FITTING TECHNIQUES OF THE ORTHOTIST

Orthotists are concerned only with those devices used externally. There are three major anatomical areas requiring their intervention: upper limb, lower limb, and spine. All things applied to the body that have previously been called splints, supports, devices, braces, and calipers are more properly termed orthoses. Unlike prostheses, where the absence of the limb allows free placement and design of joint systems, orthoses must be compatible with the body part that has some functional defect. (See Figure 4.) Design criteria is necessarily significantly different from prosthetics. Orthotists strive to return function, utilizing the least possible system of orthoses. The

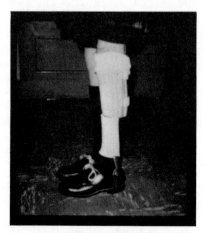

Figure 4.   Orthotic device for patient with perineal palsy and a fractured tibia.

general rule of thumb is to control the very least amount of the body and still allow the patient to function safely.

An example of this is a patient who has a knee extensor weakness and a flail ankle foot. The patient may complain of the need to raise the foot very high to clear the ground without dragging the forefoot. Occasionally, the knee may buckle because of the extensor weakness in combination with the inability to properly place the foot down. To the uninitiated, the orthosis would have to encompass the knee, ankle, and foot to control these joints and provide the function the patient desires. Providing such an orthosis may not be necessary. An orthosis controlling the ankle and foot, maintaining the foot in slight plantar flexion, may be sufficient for a patient with the above complaints. The orthotist seeks ways to design orthoses on a minimal scale so as not to encumber the patient with unnecessary devices.

Orthoses are sophisticated, custom-made devices. The orthosis may be made of any variety of materials. External power, pneumatic and electric, are in common use in upper extremity orthotics. Orthotists frequently work with mobility aids and will modify wheelchairs to suit the needs of individual patients. The techniques used in fabrication and the strength characteristics of many plastics lend themselves to orthotic application. The development of plastic has allowed orthoses to be used more frequently in the management of fractures in the lower limb where intimate encapsulation is necessary in the early stages. As materials change, the number and type of patients able to be helped by the orthotist increase.

PROFESSIONAL ORGANIZATION

To obtain the names of qualified individuals practicing orthotics and prosthetics or for information concerning opportunities and educational institutions training orthotists and prosthetists contact:

The National Office, Orthotics and
   Prosthetics, 1444 N Street, N.W.,
   Washington, D.C. 20005

SUGGESTED READINGS

Edwards, J. W. 1952. Orthopaedic Appliances Atlas. Vol. I. Braces, Splints, Shoe Alterations. J. W. Edwards Publisher, Ann Arbor, Mich.

Edwards, J. W. 1968. Orthopaedic Appliances Atlas. Vol. II. Artificial Limbs, J. W. Edwards Publisher, Ann Arbor, Mich.

Santaschi, W. R. (ed.). 1958. Manual of Upper Extremity Prosthetics. Department of Engineering, University of California at Los Angeles, Los Angeles.

Wilson, A. B., Jr. (ed.). 1973. Orthotics and Prosthetics. American Orthotic and Prosthetic Association, Washington, D.C.

PEDIATRICS

Robert B. Johnston

Pediatrics is that medical specialty which provides a broad scope of health care services to children from birth through adolescence. It has as its main goal the maintenance of physical and mental health toward the realization of full adult potential.

SCOPE OF SERVICES

The nature of endeavors in pediatrics has evolved as the nature of its challenges has changed. Initially, pediatrics was mainly concerned with maintaining life and function against the deleterious effects of malnutrition and infectious diseases such as smallpox, polio, and diphtheria. With the advent of improved nutritional technology, antibiotics, and effective immunization procedures, the frequency and severity of these problems diminished. These factors have allowed time for efforts to be expended toward other pressing concerns.

Pediatrics, then, has progressed in several directions: specialization of efforts, concern for mental as well as physical growth and development, and increasing involvement in the care of chronic illnesses. There are now pediatric subspecialists in such diverse areas as cardiology, nephrology, neurology, hematology, and allergy, to name a few.

The pediatrician's role also has expanded into fostering psychological and emotional development not only among well children but among sick children with illnesses that have far reaching implications for growth and development.

Thus, while continuing to provide for acute health needs, the pediatrician has become increasingly involved in long term developmental concerns for both normal and chronically ill patients. This effort has opened the door to the utilization of a number of services outside the traditional medical spheres that enhance and improve pediatric intervention. For instance, a child with a chronic pulmonary disease, such as cystic fibrosis, lives longer now than in the past because of advances in therapy. This chronic illness may well require the services of not only the physician but also the nutritionist, physical therapist, social worker, educator, and psychologist. Likewise, the child with arthritis, diabetes, or chronic kidney disease may require various disciplinary interventions throughout the course of the chronic illness.

Intervention with a group of conditions known as developmental disabilities best reflects the trends in pediatrics toward specialization, concern for mental and physical development, chronic care, and the incorporation of interdisciplinary services. Throughout this chapter specific reference is made to the relationship of pediatrics to developmental disabilities as examples of pediatric involvement. This new specialty of pediatrics called developmental pediatrics is, however, only one sample taken from the broad scope of special interests within the profession of pediatrics.

Traditionally, the thrust of pediatric services has been directed toward prevention, diagnosis, and therapy. A brief explanation of the nature of each follows.

Prevention

Pediatrics is concerned with both the factors influencing physical health and growth and those factors that might interfere with the psychological and emotional development of children. Prevention, then, refers to the removal of interfering insults before their negative effect and is a key issue in pediatrics.

Better nutrition, immunizations, early prenatal care, removal of environmental poisons, and effective counseling are examples of preventive measures. In addition, early identification of abnormalities and early interventions, in themselves, are approaches that are geared to prevent progressive damage and ensuing complications of a particular disability for an affected child and his/her family.

Diagnosis

The pediatrician is concerned with identifying the underlying condition that is affecting a patient's life. The primary purpose for establishing this diagnosis is its implication for treatment. The etiology or cause of a given condition in many instances must be understood and appreciated before appropriate therapies can be commenced. Yet, in some cases, conditions are such that this typical medical approach is not applicable and does not allow for the most efficient utilization of resources.

The pediatrician is trained to work within the medical model as an approach to illness. Basically, this model calls for sequential establishment of a diagnosis, implementation of appropriate therapies, and the ultimate provision of a cure. Although this disease-oriented model stands up well in a large number of cases, it has its weaknesses, particularly when involved in those interventions having to do with the chronically disabled child. Examples of a few points of conflict follow.

The pediatrician's need to establish an etiology is in apparent conflict with other disciplines' "Etiology Be Damned" (EBD) approaches (Cohen, 1973). EBD espouses the implementation of therapy, such as improved pedagogic or behavior modification techniques, without regard to etiology. Medicine, on the other hand, seeks to determine a cause of the dysfunction so that preventive measures can be developed and specific therapy can be directed to the actual underlying deficiency. For example, treatment of fever without determining its cause would result in the indiscriminate use of antibiotics, which could reduce the fever as a secondary effect of removing an underlying infection, but be of no use in those fevers of other origin. Although these two approaches appear to be diametrically opposed, it is possible to accept them as means to mutually shared goals, and they may be juxtaposed through intensive interdisciplinary effort and cooperation.

Rigid adherence to the model sometimes becomes counterproductive with regard to therapy. Modification of approach is sometimes necessary, particularly in the chronic handicapping conditions such as developmental disabilities, because therapeutic trials may be necessary before etiology and specific diagnosis can be established. In fact, the nature of the response to the therapy may often aid in establishing categorization and diagnosis.

Within the scope of health services provided, the establishment of an early diagnosis for an abnormal condition is fundamental to effecting efficient intervention. If the condition is identified early in its course, it may very well be easier to treat. The one professional that sees a large number of children on a routine basis during the first five years of life is the primary care physician, whether a family practitioner or a pediatrician. It is unusual for a child to be seen initially by a speech and hearing therapist or a psychologist during these early infancy years. The physician, then, is in a key position to identify significant deviations in health and/or development and to initiate necessary therapeutic programs and interventions.

Therapy

The role of the pediatrician in therapy is a broad one. He/she can act as medicator, counselor, advocate, and, at times, coordinator of services.

Certainly, medications play a key part in many cases. Advances in this area have been great, such as in the control of infections and the replacement of deficiencies. In most cases, however, medication is only one part of the overall therapeutic program. The pediatrician also plays a vital role in counseling and supporting patients and their families in matters pertaining to health and disease. The pediatrician is called upon frequently to act as an advocate for pediatric clients and families, especially in the field of learning disabilities, mental retardation, and other developmental disabilities. In addition, the pediatrician often serves as a source for referrals and consultations with other professionals who are integrated into overall therapy programs and, at times, serves as a coordinator of these interdisciplinary efforts.

Finally, the medical model seeks cures and the removal of disease. The cure-oriented pediatrician will be extremely frustrated in the field of chronic handicaps. Not only will efforts be considered fruitless, but he/she will look upon the efforts of other disciplines as rather superfluous. "There is *nothing* to do. . . ." When, however, the goal is to ameliorate and habilitate, not to cure, the efforts of all take on more significant meaning, and the roles and contributions of each discipline can be better appreciated.

NATURE OF CLIENTS

Pediatrics is rather unique in that a large segment of its client population is healthy, underscoring its interest in prevention. Well-baby checkups are geared to provide general parental guidance and counseling on the maintenance of health and the avoidance of disease, to monitor the child's physical and mental growth and development, and to provide necessary immunizations. On the other hand, children with a wide variety of conditions and diseases are served through the pediatrician's diagnostic and therapeutic efforts.

Those children with developmental disabilities generally have one or a combination of aberrant neurological functions that are present during the developmental years. Deficiencies may be present in motor, intellectual, language, and/or personal-social skills. Specific conditions involving these functional spheres have been identified. *Cerebral palsy* primarily involves abnormalities in motor function having to do with defective tone, control, and/or strength and may also include deficits in other spheres such as intelligence. *Mental retardation* refers to aberrant intellectual development which globally affects all other spheres of function. Specific *language* and *learning disorders* are characterized by abnormalities in understanding and/ or expressing the spoken or written word and include such disabilities as aphasia, dyslexia, and agraphia. There is wide spectrum of developmental *behavioral abnormalities* with autism and psychosis representing the most severely affected segment. In addition, there is an increased incidence of *epilepsy* (convulsions) in this entire population because of underlying neurological abnormalities.

Children with nervous system birth defects, such as *meningomyelocele* (open spine), have a wide variety of abnormalities, at times involving ambulation, bladder and bowel control, and intelligence. Frequently they require interdisciplinary services of the pediatrician, physiatrist, urologist, psychologist, educator, physical therapist, and social worker.

SETTINGS FOR SERVICES

Pediatric services are available in the private and public sectors, with primary and consultative specialized care provided in both. Primary pediatric care addresses broad health needs emphasizing prevention, identification, and treatment measures. These services may be provided in the office of the private practitioner who may be practicing alone or, more commonly, in a partnership or group arrangement. Group practices range from specialty groups (pediatrics alone) to larger multispecialty groups with a variety of physicians represented that may include pediatricians, surgeons, internists, and family practitioners. In addition, there are a variety of clinical settings supported by local, state, or federal health programs that provide a number of general pediatric services and comprehensive care.

Consultative services are provided through subspecialty clinics that supplement primary care intervention through their more intensive focus on diagnosis and treatment of complex medical problems. Examples are clinics devoted to cystic fibrosis, allergy, leukemia, and growth problems. These facilities are often based at large medical complexes, usually, but not exclusively, in association with medical schools.

In the area of developmental disabilities, there are numerous service settings. State Crippled Children's Services, the United Cerebral Palsy Association, and the National Foundation support a variety of services for this population. Larger communities often have growth and development clinics where the needs of the developmentally disabled are assessed and services rendered.

Within the recent past, the federal government, through the Maternal and Child Health Division of the Department of Health, Education and Welfare has provided extensive programmatic support for regional facilities throughout the country. These centers are charged with the responsibility of providing a broad range of interdisciplinary services necessary for the care of the developmentally disabled. In addition, these University Affiliated Facilities (UAF), through their extensive training programs, provide the professional manpower needed to deal with this expanding field. Considerable amounts of research are being pursued by these centers seeking better understanding of and intervention in developmental disabilities. The UAF, then, stands as an example of the importance placed on the interdisciplinary nature of services, training, and research efforts in developmental disabilities and is an important proving ground for the effectiveness of this approach.

SPECIALIZED TECHNIQUES

Pediatric intervention involves an investigative process that establishes a diagnosis, followed by selection of appropriate treatment modalities and careful monitoring of responses. The pediatrician has developed a rather large "bag" of diagnostic tools and therapeutic approaches to assist in his/her intervention. These techniques have been invested with a specialized jargon that, unfortunately, often is a barrier to interdisciplinary understanding.

Diagnostic Techniques

The diagnostic investigation is approached by acquiring a medical history, performing a physical examination, and obtaining certain laboratory and technical data.

The *history* starts with information concerning the nature of the pregnancy, labor, delivery, and early newborn period, focusing on the presence of "at risk" factors. It proceeds with a delineation of developmental milestones, family history, significant illnesses, operations or injuries, and a review of body systems (status of the heart, lungs, kidneys, etc.). A careful review of the presenting problem rounds out this complete historical perspective.

In the physical examination, the physician assesses the integrity of the body's several systems by listening, touching, and looking. For instance, among other things, he/she listens to the heart and lungs, feels the skin and abdominal contents, looks at the ears, nose, and throat, places the joints through their range of motion, and elicits certain responses and reflexes from the nervous system. In addition, the physician pays particular attention.to growth by measuring head circumference, height, and weight.

Particularly significant in children with developmental disabilities is the assessment of the nervous system. Two different approaches are taken: the *classical neurological exam* and the *neurodevelopmental assessment*. The traditional neurological exam monitors motor movement and coordination, sensations such as touch and pain, the cranial nerves which service many complex functions in and around the face, and the deep tendon reflexes. The neurodevelopmental assessment notes the degree of function in gross motor, adaptive, language, and personal/social skill areas. This developmental approach takes into consideration the dynamic nature of the child's acquisition of abilities and takes particular note of the fact that skills expected at one age may very well be absent at an earlier age. Developmental norms are readily available for monitoring this progression of skills during the first five or six years of life. Further maturation is less well documented in the school-age child, who is continuing to make progressive but subtle gains in motor, sensory, and laterality spheres. Assessment of these developmental functions often uncovers deficiencies that are termed soft signs when they represent a level of function that is below that expected for a given age.

The age of technology has provided the physician with several aids that assist in diagnosis. Extensive information is obtained through a number of procedures, e.g., analysis of blood and urine can depict several metabolic and biochemical abnormalities, bacterial cultures can determine the nature of many infectious diseases, and x-rays of various parts of the body can yield invaluable information in assessing functional impairments. The study of each of the body's systems utilizes an increasingly sophisticated array of technical advances and is beyond the scope of this chapter. A review of some of the tests involved in the study of the nervous system, however, may offer an example of the variety of approaches that are available.

The *electroencephalogram* (EEG) depicts the brain's electrical activity and can be of significant value in the study of seizure problems. Its limitations, however, are significant. It does not measure thought processes or personality traits, and it certainly cannot be used to depict the presence or absence of brain damage, as it is often mistakenly called upon to do. A *spinal tap,* or lumbar puncture, is a procedure that removes from the spinal canal a small amount of fluid that then can be subjected to a number of tests. Because the fluid bathes the brain and the spinal cord, studies analyzing bacterial and cellular content and protein and sugar levels can often reflect the condition of the nervous system. The *brain scan* depicts the brain's uptake of small amounts of radioactive material that have been injected into the bloodstream. Gross abnormalities, such as brain tumors or abscesses, can be suggested through this test. The *arteriogram,* which shows the outline of the blood vessels in and around the brain, and the *pneumoencephalogram,* which outlines the ventricular canals within the brain, have been virtually replaced by the *EMI scan,* which, in a noninvasive way, through computer technology, produces pictures of the brain at various levels.

Although these technical advances assist in discerning gross functional and anatomical deviations, they are of little help in a large number of neurological problems that are caused by more subtle types of brain dysfunction. These advances are fraught with technical difficulties and overutilization. No test is perfect, and oftentimes one test result in isolation can be quite misleading. Clinical judgment on the part of the physician remains a prime necessity in condensing and sifting all the information that is obtained during this investigative process. It is the use of clinical judgment, then, that leads one to the synthesis of a diagnosis and permits medicine to remain an art as well as a science.

Therapeutic Techniques

The pediatrician as *medicator* has at his disposal a wide array of drugs and medication regimens that assist in treatment. These medications relate to a wide number of abnormalities. In general, advances in medication technology are sought for symptomatic relief of a number of afflictions, control of infections, replacement of deficiencies, and support of systemic weaknesses. Examples of drugs within these categories are antihistamines, anti-inflammatory agents, antibiotics, insulin, growth hormone, thyroid replacement, and cardiotropic medications such as digitalis. Continued research provides new drugs and regimens that improve the quality of medical intervention.

Medications are beginning to play a more relevant role in the field of developmental disabilities. The use of anticonvulsants in a wide variety of seizures is improving and providing better control. Psychotropic drugs are used in conjunction with other approaches, such as psychotherapy and behavior modification, toward ameliorating many dysfunctional behaviors. There is considerable interest in the stimulant drugs that appear to enhance attention and diminish inappropriate motor activity in some hyperkinetic children. Finally, progress is being made in the development of effective medications to decrease muscular tone and to diminish involuntary movements.

The pediatrician's role as *counselor* is enhanced by other technical advances that allow parents to be better advised as to the suspected presence or absence of a specific condition. The *karyotype* is a laboratory study that depicts the nature of the cell's chromosomes, the carriers of genetic information. The finding of abnormalities in gross structure and/or number can be instrumental in understanding the basis and nature of a child's disorder and can·allow the physician to counsel in an enlightened manner. In addition, *amniocentesis* is a procedure that removes a small amount of fluid that is bathing the developing fetus in the uterus. Study of this fluid and its cells can define the presence or absence of a few specific metabolic, chromosomal, or anatomical defects.

PROFESSIONAL TRAINING

Most pediatricians attain their M.D. degrees through four years of premedical undergraduate work and four years of medical school. From that point, further training consists of three additional years of residency training, which incorporates the traditional internship year. Following these three years of post-M.D. training, many pediatricians begin private practice while some continue with one or two years of additional training in a subspecialty area. Pediatricians who are interested primarily in the field of developmental disabilities pursue these two additional years of subspecialty training.

Each physician must obtain a license to practice from the state in which he/she is working. The American Board of Pediatrics provides certification for those pediatricians who fulfill the basic training requirements and demonstrate competence by passing a number of examinations.

RESEARCH NEEDS

In general, the field of pediatrics is involved in research in a number of critical areas. Again, specific reference to research needs in the field of developmental disabilities serves as an example of the types of studies that are being pursued.

Research in developmental disabilities is centered in the areas of etiology, prevention, diagnosis, and intervention. Preventive measures having to do with prenatal diagnosis, nutritional needs, and the psychosocial effects on the developmental process are currently being highlighted. Continued work in early diagnosis, as it relates to the effectiveness of early intervention, is undergoing research scrutiny. The broad spectrum of intervention strategies is undergoing constant review and modification through research efforts. The development of more effective medication regimens, as well as the evaluation of various controversial therapies in the developmental disability field (megavitamins, diets, patterning, etc.) is necessary.

CURRENT ISSUES REGARDING INTERDISCIPLINARY COOPERATION

The pediatrician (physician) is a latecomer to the interdisciplinary scene. This member's presence on the team appears to have engendered more controversy and concern than most new members, except, perhaps, for that of an exorcist. The pediatrician, not unlike an exorcist, brings a unique set of attitudes, role perceptions, approaches and rituals to the team setting. He/she meets a set of attitudes and disparate role expectations on the part of the other team members. In addition, many are mystified by the jargon and procedures of his/her rituals. Whether the interaction is between the pediatrician and only one other discipline or with a number of disciplines, these factors influence the extent of interdisciplinary cooperation and the ultimate success of the effort.

Basic to interdisciplinary cooperation is the establishment of *mutual respect* among disciplines. Without it, the true interdependent nature of the involved disciplines cannot be realized nor their unique contributions appreciated. Mutual respect is fostered when an individual discipline has established its own competency and self-worth. In addition, each discipline must acknowledge the worth and equality of other team members, removing any element of elitism and hierarchy of status within the team. Open and frank dialogue and effective management planning can best be accomplished when members meet on an equal footing. This is not to say that each discipline is expected to always contribute equally to planning and management, because each case requires a different distribution of inputs according to specific needs. When, however, the atmosphere is such that one or a number of disciplines works from a relative position of alleged or apparent weakness, the team effort often is sabotaged by power struggles and subsequent defensive postures and maneuvers.

The following discussion addresses those dynamics that affect the pediatrician's interaction within the team and influence the establishment of mutual respect, so important to the concept of interdisciplinary cooperation.

Attitudes Toward the Pediatrician

The pediatrician is met with a variety of reactions from team members that impede effective interaction, ranging from awe and submission on the one hand to antagonism and resistance on the other.

For centuries, the physician has enjoyed a position of awesome authority and esteem from which he/she dispenses care and cures. This healer-patient, authority-child relationship which highlights dependency upon the physician may be beneficial in the therapeutic setting. When, however, this omniscience and omnipotence are translated to the interdisciplinary conference table, they wreak havoc with the team's interactional dynamics.

On the other side of the coin, there are varying levels of resentment toward physicians demonstrated by team members based on their prior negative personal or professional experiences. Depending upon the source, the physician has at one time or another been thought of as closed-minded, arrogant, self-aggrandizing, money-hungry, intolerant, cold, and/or unfeeling. Whether justified or not, these prejudicial opinions do impede effective interaction and deter the growth of mutual respect.

Attitudes of the Pediatrician

The pediatrician's training does not provide adequate preparation for an interdisciplinary role with nonmedical disciplines. He/she has learned to interact and consult with medical specialists on complicated medical problems. Exposure to other disciplines usually has been limited to a few consultations *to* the discipline during which advice was decreed or knowledge imparted but without significant interaction on a give-and-take basis.

Thus, the pediatrician learned that life was composed of medical and *para*medical disciplines, implying that the latter are associated with medicine in a subsidiary or accessory capacity, hardly a boon to the development of mutual respect. Logic would dictate, however, that any profession with a capacity for independent function, with established membership standards, and with a set of identified abilities and skills, need not be considered "*para*-anything." On the other hand, the pediatrician is rightfully indignant when referred to as a member of a paraeducational discipline, despite the fact that pediatrics does not play as key a role as education in certain learning disability problems.

Fortunately, the time is ripe for effecting a change in these detrimental attitudes. Most disciplines have finished experiencing their growing pains and have gained recognition for their roles and contributions. Medical training is beginning to recognize the necessity of approaching health care from a broader perspective, incorporating a spectrum of necessary services that are outside the traditional medical sphere. It will, however, take time to effect a change in older physicians whose attitudes toward and understanding of other disciplines are based on experiences that took place in a setting and at a time vastly different from the present.

Jargon

There is no doubt that the physician's language is oftentimes incomprehensible to those outside the field. Although the presence of specialized medical jargon has its base in medicine's early beginnings in the Greek and Latin languages, it is intensified and highlighted by technological advances that have foisted yet another element into medicinese. The implication of this as an impediment to interdisciplinary communication is obvious.

The language of the pediatrician, as well as that of the other disciplines, can impede interdisciplinary understanding and communication when it is used to establish and maintain turf and status. Examples abound in the confusion caused by the complexity and technical nature of these languages. A glossary of terms frequently used in interdisciplinary dealings has been established (Johnston and Magrab, 1976).

The contrasting uses of language can reflect subtle differences in approach by individual disciplines. For instance, the recipient of attention is referred to as the patient by the pediatrician, the client by the social worker, the student by the teacher, the subject by the experimental psychologist, and the resident by the extended care facility worker. In addition, what was once known as an arm to most everyone is termed an upper extremity by the pediatrician and the physical therapist or an appendage by the anatomist.

Another use of language that raises concern is that of labeling. Pediatricians are often accused of excessive use of labels which may stigmatize a child and may lead to limited role expectations and stereotyped approaches. While it is generally agreed that labels are to be avoided, it should be noted that the purpose of the classification is not to categorize an individual so that he/she remains within that fixed category. The child who is identified as functioning in the trainable range of mental retardation is classified as such for the purposes of current, not necessarily future, interventions. Continued monitoring and assessment are needed as the child's further developmental progress evolves. Likewise, the pediatrician's penchant for syndrome analysis and the identification of characteristic features of syndromes represents an attempt to clarify the nature of the condition and to provide treatment and counseling based on wide experience with other individuals within that syndrome.

Role Expectations

Disparate role perceptions, most evident when mutual respect is lacking, jeopardize interdisciplinary intervention. Interactional squabbles result and, more important, available resources are used inefficiently. Problems arise mainly when a given discipline is underutilized because of an excessively limited role perception or when a given discipline usurps too broad a role and begins to function out of its area of expertise. For instance, the pediatrician is underused when called upon only to dispense medication. On the other hand, when the pediatrician attempts to incorporate the methods and skills of other disciplines into his/her own diagnostic and therapeutic repertoire, this represents a misinterpretation of roles. This transdisciplinary approach disregards the clinical acumen and judgment that necessarily accompany a given discipline's practices and techniques that evolve after years of training and experience.

In summary, the pediatrician is an important and often essential component of most interdisciplinary efforts. His/her unique expertise and knowledge are undoubtedly invaluable for a number of interventions involving prevention, diagnosis, and treatment. The pediatrician's effectiveness as a team member can be realized to its fullest extent when the milieu in which the team functions is free of attitudinal and perceptual handicaps on all sides of the table. The team's potential for overall success can be measured by the level of mutual respect within it that serves to moderate disagreements and facilitate solutions.

REFERENCES

Cohen, S. A. 1973. Minimal brain dysfunction and practical matters such as teaching kids to read. *In* F. F. de la Cruz, B. H. Fox, and R. H. Roberts (eds.), Minimal Brain Dysfunction, p. 302. New York Academy of Sciences, New York.
Johnston, R. B., and Magrab, P. R. (eds.). 1976. Developmental Disorders: Assessment, Treatment, Education, pp. 503–515. University Park Press, Baltimore.

SUGGESTED READINGS

Bartram, John B. 1975. The physician and the child with a permanent handicap. *In* V. C. Vaughan and R. J. McKay (eds.), Pediatrics, pp. 139–142. W. B. Saunders Company, Philadelphia.
Bryant, K. N. and Hirschberg, J. C. 1961. Helping the parents of a retarded child— The role of the physician. Am. J. Dis. Child. 102:52–66.
Gesell, A. J. and Amatruda, C. S. 1974. Developmental Diagnosis. H. Knobloch and B. Pasamanick (eds.), 3rd Ed. Harper and Row, New York.

Haslam, R. H. A. (ed.). 1973. Symposium on Habilitation of the Handicapped Child. Pediatr. Clin. N. Am. 20:1–272.

Johnston, R. B. 1976. Medicine. *In* R. B. Johnston and P. R. Magrab (eds.), Developmental Disorders: Assessment, Treatment, Education, pp. 129–148. University Park Press, Baltimore.

Kenny, T. J. and Clemmens, R. L. 1975. Behavioral Pediatrics and Child Development. The Williams and Wilkins Company, Baltimore.

Paine, R. S. and Oppe, T. E. 1966. Neurological Examination of Children. Clinics in Developmental Medicine. Vol. 20/21. Spastics Society Medical Education and Information Unit, William Heinemann Medical Books, Ltd., London.

PHYSICAL MEDICINE AND REHABILITATION

Lewis J. Goldfine

PURPOSES AND GOALS

Rehabilitation may be defined as a process directed at restoring an individual to a healthy condition and/or useful and constructive activity. The Latin derivation is *habilitas* meaning ability. Those trained in the art and science of medicine, the social and behavioral sciences, and the arts represented by music, dance, and art become involved in restoring disabled individuals to their former useful and constructive places in society.

Even though civilization has progressed from its primitive tribal beginnings, when the disabled were objects of scorn and rejection, to more enlightened levels, where man has more respect for his fellow beings, the disabled still occupy an unenviable place in society. In this modern age, some degree of discrimination still exists, particularly in regard to the difficulties faced by a rehabilitated disabled person preparing to enter the job market and become, once again, a useful member of society. Progress, obviously, depends on full acceptance of the disabled individual back into the social mainstream. A broad common goal of all involved disciplines is to restore the disabled person to a useful and respected social role.

A recent (1976) American Medical Association definition of medical rehabilitation services reads:

> . . . a coordinated, multidisciplinary approach to disability under a qualified physician who directs a plan of management of one or more of the categories of chronic disabling diseases or injuries, specifying realistic goals for maximum recovery. That approach may include, if required, several or all of the following services: skilled rehabilitation nursing care, physical therapy, occupational therapy, speech therapy and audiology services, prosthetic and orthotic devices and services, social, recreational and psychological services.

The physician who specializes in physical medicine and rehabilitation (the physiatrist) must work in concert with various members of the team of allied health professionals involved in the rehabilitation process. Most people would agree that, at least in the initial stages of a patient's rehabilitation, the physiatrist or a physician caring for that patient should assume a leadership role because the ultimate medical and legal responsibility lies with him/her. A major reason for this approach is that in order to plan properly a path of rehabilitation leading to a constructive future, an expert evaluation of the disability must be conducted first. An attempt to correct the problem or myriad of problems can then be undertaken. Incomplete or improper evaluation of the cause and results of the disability can only lead to confusion and frustration in treatment and management. For example, if it is *not* recognized that a patient with a stroke may have lost the right or left half of the visual field in each eye (homonymous hemianopsia), the patient's true level of functioning may be underestimated and the patient required to undertake daily activities involving the blind side, e.g., eating food, using a telephone, or getting in and out of bed on the visually affected side.

The evaluation must be a composite one, and those in the various specialized areas must contribute to a thorough evaluation before planning an appropriate program and setting realistic goals. The setting of goals is a well established practice in educational areas and clinical practice. It is recognized, however, that goals set initially may not be achieved and, at other times, may be surpassed. Experienced professionals in all branches of this field appreciate that it is often more practical to set limited areas of achievement initially and then proceed in a stepwise fashion, resetting the goals as the patient's progress merits.

The patient's previous educational and occupational experience, personality, and age before the onset of the disabling illness or injury are all factors to be considered. A severe disability may bring to light aspects of personality previously unrecognized. The frustration and depression precipitated by the disabling event must be recognized, dealt with, and managed with sensitivity and understanding.

TYPES OF PATIENTS AND THEIR PROBLEMS

The patients seen by a physiatrist present many problems. The nature of the disability may be a modifying factor, thus making an accurate diagnosis of the utmost importance. Does the patient have a static, recurrent, or progressive condition? An amputation resulting from trauma has different implications from that which is a consequence of peripheral vascular disease, although the rehabilitation principles for both kinds of patients may be the same at any one time. Similarly, the patient with a head injury resulting in paralysis of one side of the body (hemiplegia) presents a different situation from the point of view of prognosis than the patient with cerebrovascular disease with hemiplegia, although the immediate management may be essentially the same. The patient with cerebrovascular disease may have further strokes in the future. Similarly, the ultimate goals for patients with progressive illnesses, such as muscular dystrophy and multiple sclerosis, may have to be modified or redefined depending on the extent and progress of the disease and its functional effects.

Spinal Cord Injury

Spinal cord damage results in paraplegia (paralysis of the lower extremities) or quadriplegia (paralysis of both upper and lower extremities), depending on the level at which the spinal cord is involved by injury, disease, or tumor. In addition to the muscular paralysis that follows insult to the spinal cord, the functioning of the bowel, bladder, and sexual organs becomes disordered. Sensory loss also occurs below the level of the lesion.

The physiatrist must determine the level of spinal cord involvement in order to predict the ultimate functional level of the patient. Will the patient walk unaided; will he/she require the help of bracing, canes, or crutches; or will he/she achieve independence at the wheelchair level? Bowel and bladder training can usually be accomplished so that these systems function on a reflex basis. Rehabilitation efforts are directed at independence in activities of daily living, e.g., washing, dressing, and feeding; strengthening intact muscle groups; preventing contractures of joints; preserving skin integrity by preventing breakdown (decubitus ulcer); and the prescription of appropriate splints, braces, and assistive devices such as wheelchairs to aid ambulation.

Soft Tissue, Spinal, and Joint Disorders

Musculoskeletal disorders, which may or may not be associated with metabolic or systemic diseases, cause considerable numbers of people, 144,000 annually in the United States, to be *disabled* from rheumatic disorders alone. These disorders include rheumatoid arthritis, ankylosing spondylitis, and osteoarthritis.

Rheumatoid arthritis usually affects several joints of the upper and lower extremities. Efforts, in addition to controlling pain and inflammation caused by involvement of the joint lining (synovium), are directed at preserving range of motion of joints, preventing joint deformity (contractures), and preserving and improving muscle strength of those muscles weakened by the involvement of the joints they control.

Ankylosing spondylitis predominantly affects the spine causing loss of mobility and deformity. When there is involvement of the rib cage, lung function may be affected leading to a reduction of lung capacity. Treatment is aimed at preserving the upright posture and as much mobility as possible, particularly of the cervical spine and hips which, when involved, may be the cause of severe disability. Breathing exercises also may be indicated.

Degenerative or osteoarthritis involves the spine and weight-bearing joints of the lower extremities (hips and knees). Again, rehabilitation efforts are directed at maintaining mobility of joint motion and strengthening appropriate muscle groups.

Patients with very serious joint involvement, in addition to the above measures, may need various forms of bracing, assistive devices for walking, and, in certain cases for the severely impaired, wheelchairs. Various aids for simplifying work activities may be required. A home program presented in detail by physicians and therapists is extremely important.

Trauma to the musculoskeletal system varies from the minor, such as sprains and various forms of tendinitis, to the major, exemplified by amputation of a limb, a fracture, or severe burn. Each resultant injury will require a specific plan for rehabilitation involving one or more team members, depending on the severity of the injury.

A variety of causes for loss of an extremity exists. Estimates are that one in 300 people have had a major amputation as a result of such conditions as trauma, peripheral vascular disease, chronic infection, tumor, or congenital absence. Replacement of the extremity, partially or wholly with a prosthesis, is an involved process involving several members of the team including the surgeon, physiatrist, physical therapist, occupational therapist, prosthetist, and vocational counselor.

Disorders of the low back range from strains of ligaments and muscles to involvement of nerve roots secondary to pressure from a ruptured or protruded disc. Back problems account for a large group of disabled persons. Nerve root involvement can produce significant pain and weakness in parts of the lower extremity. While other injuries may be more disabling, a disproportionate amount of time is lost from work by people with back disorders.

Rehabilitation efforts are aimed at initial relief of pain with rest and analgesics, establishment of an exercise program directed at restoring mobility and strengthening muscle groups, and temporary bracing of the back. Normally, bracing is discontinued when supporting muscular groups regain their optimal strength. The exercise program should probably be continued indefinitely at home on a maintenance basis. Increasing activity on a graded scale with regard to work activities is begun at the appropriate time. Modification in work may be necessary and, in extreme cases, change of occupation may be desirable. In the chronic case, various psychological factors may be an added complication, and psychiatric evaluation and counseling may be required. Financial therapy (compensation) may have a dramatic effect.

Cerebrovascular Disorders (Stroke)

Various kinds of stroke syndromes with differing patterns, depending on the territory of the cerebral vessels involved, usually are associated with paralysis of the upper and lower extremities on one side of the body (hemiplegia). In addition to the paralysis, sensory deficits involving speech, hearing, vision, and sensation to touch and position, can cause even more disability. Other factors complicating motor function are spasticity and rigidity, both causing increased stiffness of extremities and ataxia (loss of balance and coordination).

Rehabilitation is essentially aimed at having the patient acquire skills that have been lost as a result of the stroke. His/her eventual functional level depends on the degree of recovery of the area of the brain affected by the stroke. In older patients, diffuse cerebrovascular disease with intellectual deterioration (organic brain syndrome) may present added problems in restoration of functional activities. Persistence of incontinence of bowel and bladder heralds a poor prognosis.

A left hemiplegia with associated perceptual dysfunction, as opposed to a right hemiplegia (usually accompanied by speech loss or dysfunction), presents less chance of successful functional recovery because of the perceptual-motor deficit, even if there is good return of motor function. Patients with good return of speech, language, and motor functioning may demonstrate serious cognitive handicaps including an inability to make independent judgments.

Patients who have had a technical or professional background may more easily be returned to a suitable vocation than those who have been essentially unskilled workers. Reversal of roles in the home may sometimes be appropriate: the patient becomes the homemaker, and the partner seeks employment out of the house.

Muscle Diseases

The group of diseases known as the muscular dystrophies are hereditary disorders and usually involve a fatal outcome. This prognosis is not inevitable: one of the disorders, facio-scapulo-humeral dystrophy, is associated with a normal or near normal life span. Patients affected with any of the muscular dystrophies are not usually helped by formal physical therapy but should be encouraged to do as much as possible in their daily activities as a form of exercise. They usually follow a downhill course from being able to ambulate normally, although their manner of walking (gait) may be abnormal (waddling). Eventually, bracing and assistive devices may be needed for ambulation, then a wheelchair, and finally bed at the end stage of the disease. This deterioration may take several years and can be slowed by rehabilitation efforts such as those designed to prevent contractures. In facio-scapulo-humeral dystrophy, where the life span approaches the normal, long range goals can be established.

Myasthenia gravis, a disorder probably caused by abnormal destruction of the chemical transmitter (acetylcholine) released at the junction of nerve and muscle, causes muscle weakness. Recovery can be achieved with appropriate drugs. Rehabilitation efforts emphasize the psychological and vocational areas.

Other Neurological Diseases

A group of diseases, having effects on muscle function similar to those of muscular dystrophy, are the progressive muscular atrophies. In this group of diseases, the nerve fibers degenerate as they arise from cells in the spinal cord. The resultant paralytic effect is seen in the muscles supplied by affected nerves. Examples of this type of disorder are the childhood disorders: Werdnig-Hoffmann disease and amyotonia congenita (which can have a more favorable course). Amyotrophic lateral sclerosis, a nonhereditary disease, occurs in adults.

Multiple sclerosis is a disease of the nervous system that produces varying degrees of disability ranging from severe paralysis to minor sensory changes. The goals of rehabilitation will depend on the individual case and on progress or remission of the disease. Lack of coordination (ataxia), as well as muscle weakness, may be a serious problem, and spasticity may add to the patient's difficulties.

Cerebral palsy is a term used for a group of diseases that affect brain function in varying ways and occur in the prenatal, natal, and postnatal periods of childhood.

Peripheral Nerve Disorders

Disorders of peripheral nerves (neuropathy or neuritis) produce dysfunction of the muscles supplied by these nerves; accompanying sensory deficits also contribute to disability. Numerous causes of peripheral nerve involvement include trauma, metal poisoning, metabolic disorders (including diabetes mellitus), chronic alcoholism, vitamin deficiency, infectious disorders, and disorders of unknown cause. Rehabilitation is directed at preventing contractures of joints and splinting or bracing in positions of function. It should be remembered peripheral nerves regenerate at a rate of 1–1.5 mm per day or one inch per month, on the average, so that recovery may take a lengthy period of time.

Specific problems include peroneal nerve involvement resulting in foot-drop or inability to raise the foot upward and ulnar nerve lesions causing paralysis or weakness of the small muscles of the hand, impairing fine movements. Radial nerve damage causes a wrist drop and results in the inability, when the back of the hand faces upward, to straighten the fingers and move the hand in an upward direction. It also prevents a grip from being used in an optimal fashion.

Cardiorespiratory Disorders

It is now well recognized that patients with ischemic heart disease caused by coronary artery disease benefit from exercise programs that are directed at improving exercise tolerance. Obviously, careful evaluation by a physician, prescription of activities to be undertaken by the patient, and regular follow-up by the physician are extremely important.

Similarly, rehabilitation medicine plays a definite role in the management of patients with chronic obstructive pulmonary disease (COPD) usually resulting from chronic bronchitis and/or emphysema. Chest physical therapy can certainly benefit and, at least, help to maintain, if not actually improve, respiratory function.

Cancer

Disability related to cancer in its various forms can be modified, and rehabilitation principles can be applied to the individual case. Degree of involvement and stage of disease are helpful for prognosis and setting of realistic goals. Psychological factors need to be managed as well as social and vocational aspects.

It should be remembered that major advances have been made in the treatment of various types of cancer and that patients may have several years of survival in front of them, while in some a complete cure may be effected. Accordingly, it is not unreasonable to encourage these patients to continue their previous occupations or train for another suitable vocation, if that becomes necessary. Certainly, the diagnosis of cancer does not, as in past years, carry with it a total sense of hopelessness, and all efforts to rehabilitate patients should be encouraged.

THE EVALUATION PROCESS

It cannot be stressed too emphatically that an appropriate evaluation of the patient is the basis upon which a constructive plan for rehabilitation of the patient depends. Augmenting the conventional medical history and examination, additional aspects of the examination are emphasized in the physiatrist's evaluation. When the patient has some disorder affecting mobility, strong emphasis is placed on the neurological and musculoskeletal part of the evaluation. Details contributing to the patient's functional state are extremely important in these cases, in contrast to the routine medical examination in which this information is often given scant attention.

Observation of the gait and testing of muscle strength add valuable information to the evaluation. Muscle strength is measured according to an international set of grades ranging from zero to normal. Detailed evaluation of joint mobility (measured in degrees) also is made whenever appropriate. These aspects are further evaluated by the physical therapist.

Assessment of activities of daily living is made, including bed and wheelchair activities, toileting, dressing, and feeding. Also included is an evaluation of the home with a view to modifications that might need to be made in light of the person's disability.

Psychiatric, psychological, and perceptual-motor evaluation, as well as speech and hearing and vocational assessment, all contribute to the basic examination of the disabled patient. These assessments combine to form the basis for the team's plan of rehabilitation.

A special area that is an adjunct to examination of muscle and nerve function is electrodiagnosis. This includes electromyography, a technique that involves inserting a needle electrode into muscle and recording and interpreting the electrical changes taking place. Using the same apparatus, it is possible to measure the velocity of nerve conduction (nerve conduction studies) in peripheral nerves or segments of these nerves. Only physicians trained in this technique should undertake the performance of electrodiagnosis.

To perform the above techniques satisfactorily and to obtain meaningful information, a detailed neuromuscular evaluation by the physician must be conducted to determine which areas of muscle and nerve should be studied. This necessitates that the physician be educated in depth in the evaluation of the neuromuscular system. It should be appreciated that technicians, however skilled in the actual techniques, cannot perform this type of examination adequately, because it requires training in the medical diagnosis of neuromuscular disorders.

These techniques aid in the diagnosis of peripheral nerve injuries and disease (neuropathies), muscle disease, disorders of nerve roots, and diseases of the cells from which nerves arise, i.e., the anterior horn cells in the spinal cord.

After all the necessary information is obtained, the physician and team of allied health professionals have a sound basis for embarking on the complicated process of rehabilitation and for setting realistic goals so that the person may return to a useful role in society.

INSTITUTIONS AND SOURCES OF SERVICES

Most of the serious problems causing disability, at least initially, need to be assessed, and the management begun in an institutional setting. The majority of university hospitals usually, but surprisingly not always, have a department of rehabilitation medicine (or physical medicine and rehabilitation). One advantage of this location is that all other specialized branches of medicine and surgery are found within such an institution and may be called upon to help in the evaluation and management of rehabilitation problems. Some large community hospitals also have sections of physical medicine and rehabilitation.

Certain institutions, such as the Institution of Rehabilitation Medicine, which is a part of the New York University Medical Center, one of several excellent facilities, are renowned for care of patients, teaching and training of physicians and allied health professionals, and research.

The Veterans Administration provides comprehensive rehabilitation services for the disabled veteran. Other institutions deal with specialized problems of rehabilitation; for example, the Craig Hospital, a rehabilitation center in Denver, Colorado, provides comprehensive care for patients with spinal cord injuries and brain damage.

There are also several institutions that do not fall into the acute hospital or nursing home categories and may be called intermediate care facilities. Patients suitable for this type of hospital are usually stable with regard to their general medical condition but need prolonged rehabilitation because of the nature of their disability, such as a complicated stroke problem or spinal cord injury. In these cases, because of increased expense and lack of need for acute medical services, the intermediate care facility is preferred to the acute general hospital.

As patients progress in their rehabilitation efforts, the emphasis changes to a vocational one. Patients are then best managed on an outpatient or a residential basis, accomplished in certain centers jointly funded by state and federal agencies. Such rehabilitation centers are located in various areas of each state.

Once the rehabilitation process is over or nearing completion, vocational training and evaluation may be accomplished at such facilities as Goodwill Industries, which is a sheltered workshop type of environment. National agencies, such as Easter Seal, United Cerebral Palsy, Muscular Dystrophy Association, and others, also provide rehabilitation assistance, and other services.

RESEARCH NEEDS, TIME, AND COST OF SERVICES

In keeping with the desire to improve the quality of medical care for the patient, continuing efforts to evaluate and improve methods of management are desirable.

Accurate evaluation of the degree of disability is lacking in many disorders of the neuromuscular or musculoskeletal type. Diagnosis does not necessarily reflect the level of the patient's disability. The same disease may incapacitate individual patients to varying degrees. Further study is needed to delineate the functional level of the patient in an accurate and uniform way. This is most important in the assessment of claims for compensation and disability pensions. As an example, a patient suffering a stroke may be disabled to a catastrophic degree, and yet another may make an almost complete recovery with negligible disability and the ability to continue former employment. This situation points to the extremes of a condition; the problem is evaluation of the patient who falls in a category between these two extremes.

Studies have been performed in which patients with a variety of disorders are exposed to the rehabilitation process. After several years of follow-up, the findings of these studies indicate that these patients function at a better level than those who had not had the benefit of a rehabilitation program. The older patient who has had a stroke and has returned home or to a nursing home without any rehabilitation efforts may fare worse than a counterpart who has had the benefit of a rehabilitation program. Patients whose families have become involved in the treatment program will often show significant functional improvement. Further study in these areas is in order.

Studies have attempted to demonstrate that good home treatment programs may indeed be as beneficial as prolonged hospital or nursing home treatment. This would obviously be an important factor in these times of rising health care costs. Further studies are needed to determine whether or not long term home-management programs produce results as salutary as those reported in repeated institutional program evaluations.

Is medical education becoming regressive? Recent studies have shown that physical medicine and rehabilitation, while offered in 80 of 87 medical school curricula in 1969, was only provided to students in 81 of 113 schools in 1975. Thus, there seems to be a paradox between improving the quality and breadth of health care, on the one hand, and educating individuals who are being trained to perform this, on the other. To clarify this situation, ongoing research in this educational area would seem to be appropriate.

Attempts to assess the psychological effects and their impact on physical disability, though well documented, also need further study.

Quality of medical care is difficult to assess, but it should be borne in mind that the quantity of treatment does not necessarily improve the end result. How much? By whom? Where? Each of these aspects needs to be assessed, preferably by the physiatrist and the other professionals involved.

Studies of the contributions that industry can make to the disabled in terms of job availability need to be made. It is well known that every dollar used for vocational evaluation and training, in the first five or so years of subsequent employment, produces a fivefold return of tax dollars by the disabled person.

CURRENT PROBLEMS OF THE DISCIPLINES INVOLVED

Many of the problems relating to the area of rehabilitation arise from lack of cooperation among the various disciplines participating. This failure is often a result of inadequate communication of which physicians, family, and health professionals may all be guilty. Sometimes the patient may be under the care of several people, instead of under the primary direction of one physician using input from the rest of the team. Allied health professionals may assume care of medical problems and evaluate situations for which they are not specifically trained.

How can this be avoided? There is general agreement among concerned professionals that the rehabilitation process should be guided by a physician, trained in this field, who should be responsible for coordinating the activities of the various allied health professionals. Accepting that, there may be greater emphasis at varying times on physical therapy, occupational therapy, or vocational aspects, all of which will depend on the stage of the patient's rehabilitation. The physician, however, should always be aware of what is happening to the patient so that a logical progression of events in the restorative process may take place.

In summary, if all the team members are aware of their roles, accept their own limitations, and coordinate their activities, the rehabilitation process should be a constructive and productive experience for the patient who, after all, is the principal member of the team and for whose benefit the team effort is made.

Consumer groups, i.e., disabled people, should have input in the rehabilitation process. Consumer pressures account for the progress that has been made in this country in the construction of doorways adequately sized for wheelchair patients, in the placement of telephones within easy access in public buildings, and in the modification of curbstones to enable easier passage.

Congress must legislate to adequately fund comprehensive programs for rehabilitation of the young, the working population, and the old who suffer from disabilities. The government should not fall short in this task by underfunding these programs in order to support other areas of need. If there is to be comprehensive health legislation in the future, it should encompass all aspects of medical rehabilitation.

No doubt progress will be made to overcome not only the architectural barriers that exist but also the philosophical, psychological, and sociological barriers that the disabled patient faces.

PROFESSIONAL TRAINING, LICENSURE, AND CERTIFICATION

Before beginning speciality training in physical medicine and rehabilitation and becoming a physiatrist, one must obtain the degree of Doctor of Medicine which requires attendance at a recognized college to obtain the Bachelor's degree before entering medical school. Upon completing medical school, the physician is required to train in a recognized residency program, approved by the American Medical Association and the American Board of Physical Medicine and Rehabilitation. This period of postgraduate medical training in physical medicine and rehabilitation is usually three years and follows a one-year internship, either medical or rotating in several major areas such as medicine, surgery, and pediatrics. In special circumstances, the internship and residency training can be accomplished in a total of three years following graduation from a medical school in the United States.

After completing this residency training, the physician is qualified to sit for Part I, a written examination, set by the American Board of Physical Medicine and Rehabilitation. Successful completion of Part I of the examination and one year of practice in the specialty entitles the physician to take Part II, an extensive oral examination. If successful, he/she can become a Board-certified specialist in Physical Medicine and Rehabilitation: a physiatrist.

PROFESSIONAL ORGANIZATIONS

American Academy of Physical Medicine and Rehabilitation, 30 North Michigan Avenue, Chicago, Illinois 60602

American Congress of Rehabilitation Medicine, 30 North Michigan Avenue, Chicago, Illinois 60602

SUGGESTED READINGS

Athelston, G. T. 1976. Rehabilitation of the severely disabled. How are we doing? Where are we going? Arch. Phys. Med. Rehab. 57:486–488.

Krusen, F. H., Kotke, F. J., and Ellwood, P. M., Jr. (eds.). 1971. Handbook of Physical Medicine and Rehabilitation. 2nd Ed. W. B. Saunders Company, Philadelphia.

Lehmann, J. F., Feinberg, S. D., and Warren, C. G. 1976. Undergraduate education in rehabilitation medicine: Trends in curriculum development and the impact on specialty manpower and delivery of service. Arch. Phys. Med. Rehab. 57:497–503.

Licht, S. (ed.). 1968. Rehabilitation and Medicine. E. Licht, New Haven, Conn.

Rusk, H. A. 1971. Rehabilitation Medicine. 3rd. Ed. The C. V. Mosby Company, St. Louis, Mo.

PHYSICAL THERAPY

Ruth M. Latimer

FUNCTIONS, GOALS, AND LIMITATIONS

Physical therapy is a health profession, ancient with respect to the background of some modalities used but new and perhaps "unborn" in many of its roles and functions. What is physical therapy? How does it differ from and overlap with nursing, occupational therapy, respiratory therapy, physical education, and other human services?

This question may be approached by first considering the role and function of a physical therapist who is primarily engaged in direct patient care through the interrelated activities of therapy, evaluation, program planning, and goal setting. A second consideration could be the physical therapists who perform these clinical roles and also function in areas of administration, research, consultation, planning, and education.

Direct Patient Care

Therapy The therapeutic care of the sick and disabled falls into three broad areas: surgical, pharmaceutical, and physical. The latter pertains to physical therapy which is treatment by using certain physical means such as heat, cold, light, water, electricity, massage, ultrasound, exercise, and functional training. Other health professionals also use these physical means to a lesser extent but not as the focus of their disciplines.

1. Heat therapy or thermotherapy is a method used wherein the patient's tissues are warmed to a tolerable level by the four basic methods of conduction, convection, radiation, and conversion.
   a. Conduction is the direct transfer of heat from a solid or semisolid source that is warmer than the skin temperature. The source could be a hot water bottle, an electric heating pad, a hot moist pad, or a paraffin bath.
   b. Convection is heating the body by warm dry air such as a sauna, moist air, or water (hydrotherapy).

279

    c. Radiation uses infrared energy transmitted from a natural source, the sun, or from an artificial source, an infrared or heat lamp. The infrared energy absorbed by the tissues becomes heat.

    d. Conversion is the changing of three types of energy into heat within the tissues and is a deeper method of thermotherapy than either conduction, convection, or radiation. The three energies used are high frequency alternating currents (shortwave diathermy), higher frequency microwave energy (microwave diathermy), and high frequency sound above the audible range (ultrasonic diathermy).

2. Cold therapy or cryotherapy is a method used wherein the patient's tissues are cooled to a tolerable level by the abstraction of body heat. This might be done by conduction (use of ice or cold moist pad) or convection (water or air).

3. Light therapy specifically means the use of nonvisible "light" called ultraviolet therapy or actinotherapy. It is used for the chemical and biological effect on superficial parts of the body, primarily the skin. A natural source of ultraviolet energy is the sun; an artificial source is an ultraviolet lamp.

4. Water therapy or hydrotherapy has been mentioned previously under thermotherapy and cryotherapy. In addition to thermal qualities, the hydrostatic and hydrodynamic properties of water make it an excellent body-supporting and exercise medium.

5. Electrotherapy employs the use of low frequency alternating and direct currents. Procedures such as galvanism and iontophoresis cause the movement of ions under the influence of a direct current. Drugs in an electrolytic form may be introduced into the tissues. Percutaneous electrical stimulation of muscles and nerves can be used to reduce pain and cause muscle contraction for neuromuscular education.

6. Massage has different purposes and definitions. In physical therapy, it is a form of manual therapy done to increase circulation, decrease pain, and reduce tight scar tissue. Closely allied is traction to joints, performed either manually or with equipment.

7. Therapeutic exercise and functional training are the most encompassing and important aspects of physical therapy. Therapeutic exercise includes assisting or teaching the patient body positions and exercises or movement procedures.

    Patients primarily seen by the physical therapist are those who have problems or disabilities relating to the neuromuscular or musculoskeletal systems that reveal deficits in strength, endurance, balance, coordination, sensation, and joint range of motion. These problems, often accompanied by pain, are demonstrated by an inability to perform normal motions or by degrees of abnormal activity.

    Techniques used to stimulate activity or reduce untoward move-

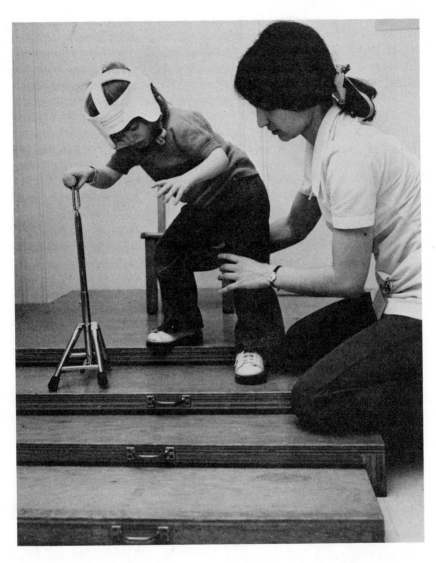

Photograph by Richard Holden.

ments and states include various peripheral neuromuscular facilitations or inhibitory procedures advocated by Rood (1954), Knott and Voss (1968), Brunnstrom (1970), Bobath (1971), and others. Physical modalities such as ice, vibration, and biofeedback also may be employed. In biofeedback, an electromyograph is used as a teaching tool by which the patient attempts to increase or reduce the audiovisual presentation of muscle action potentials.

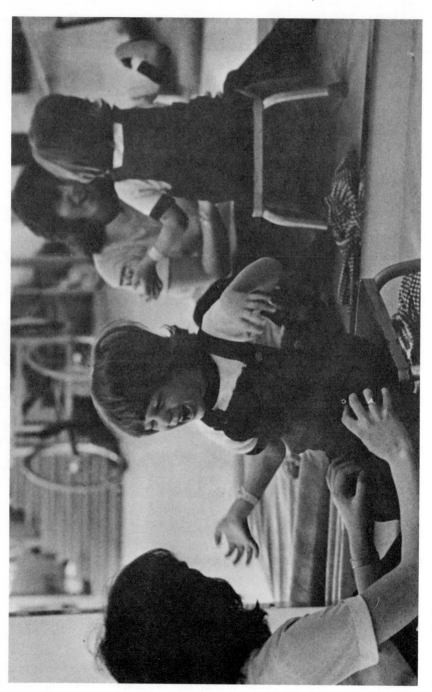

Photograph by Richard Holden.

Photograph by Richard Holden.

Closely in line with therapeutic exercise is functional training, which includes assisting or teaching the patient in ambulation, use of assistive and supportive devices such as crutches, prostheses, and braces, and self-care or activities of daily living that may include the use of special aids for dressing, eating, etc. appropriate to the patient's disability.

Occupational therapy also is used for patients with neuromuscular and musculoskeletal problems, but the approach of exercise is usually in conjunction with performing some task or craft. In contrast to a physical educator, the exercise program is aimed at the abnormal or the pathological rather than the normal.

Patients with cardiovascular problems also are instructed in appropriate exercises. Some procedures are passive and include positioning, supportive bandaging, and the use of intermittent venous occlusion. The patient undergoing cardiac rehabilitation is advised of and instructed in a progression of activities and exercises.

Chest therapy for patients with respiratory problems, as performed by a physical therapist, is somewhat different from that performed by professionals specializing in inhalation or respiratory therapy. The primary modes used are those of positioning, manual percussion, and teaching or encouraging changes in the respiratory pattern.

8. Certain procedures may be performed by a physical therapist that are adjunctive to the primary ones. They are less exclusively in the domain of physical therapy. For instance, there is aseptic bandaging, as used for wounds, and supportive bandaging for body parts. For more stable support and fixation of joints, casts of various materials are made and applied. Before the fabrication of a permanent prosthesis or orthesis by a specialist, the physical therapist often makes a temporary pylon for the amputee or a brace to assist the weakened or paralyzed extremity or trunk.

Evaluation   Before treatment, and periodically after treatment, a health professional should perform and record the results of various evaluative procedures 1) to ascertain a baseline of the patient's problems, 2) to establish a therapeutic plan for reducing or eliminating these problems, and 3) to evaluate the success of the plan in order to make indicated changes and reconsider progression toward goals.

The evaluative procedures performed are in close alignment with the therapeutic procedures and are usually conducted to determine the patient's disability relating to the neuromuscular and musculoskeletal systems. However, they also can relate to the respiratory and cardiovascular systems. Some of the many tests performed are noted below.

1. By manual muscle testing or analysis, the physical therapist not only attempts to find out if there is a deficiency in the function and strength of gross movements but also tries to determine the specific function of one muscle as a primary mover in relation to others as secondary movers, synergists, antagonists, and stabilizers. Evaluative grades are assigned (Kendall, Kendall, and Wadsworth, 1971; Daniels and Worthingham, 1972). If the patient presents an abnormal static or dynamic posture or is unable to perform certain activities, the physical therapist is faced with the challenge of identifying which muscles are not functioning normally.

2. Posture, both static and dynamic, is further analyzed by observation and measurements of alignment, symmetry, rhythm, and pace. The latter would incorporate gait analysis of patients with lower extremity amputations using prostheses or analysis of patients using braces, crutches, and canes.

3. Goniometry employs the use of a special protractor or other means to measure the patient's passive and active joint range of motion to assess both muscle strength and joint mobility and stability.

4. Bilateral measurements of extremity girths and lengths are often-made

to ascertain asymmetry caused by edema, atrophy, alignment, and joint-bone pathology.

5. Important to motor function is an assessment of various types of sensory perception. Using appropriate stimuli, the physical therapist tests for abnormalities in feeling, pain, touch, temperature, and proprioception.

6. Electrophysiological testing includes the percutaneous electrical stimulation of nerve and muscle tissue and the observation of muscle reaction visually or with an electromyograph. Recordings are made of the muscle contraction (threshold, quality) and of the presence and velocity of nerve conduction. Electromyography is the recording, both visual and auditory, of muscle action potentials.

7. Overall assessments of the patient's sensorimotor system include the testing and observations of the following: perceptual motor ability, abnormal motor patterns and reflexes, the presence of spasticity, rigidity, and athetosis, the ability to assume and maintain various postures, and the existence of abnormal superficial reflexes.

8. Another evaluation task is to observe and record the patient's general functional ability as he/she attempts to perform simulated vocational and daily activities (Lawton, 1963). Activities range from the ability to feed one's self to gait analysis, including checking out the use of an appliance such as a prosthesis.

9. Assessments of the autonomic nervous and vascular systems include tests of sweating by either chemical or electrical means and evaluation of vasomotor mechanisms. In the latter, the therapist observes the appearance, color, and temperature of the skin and checks for the presence of lesions or edema. These observations might be made before and after the patient is subjected to various positions and exercises and to hot and cold applications. To measure the peripheral circulatory rate, an oscillometric test is performed.

10. Tests of vital signs (blood pressure, pulse, and respiration) are conducted to determine the patient's reaction to thermal agents and the stress of exercise. These basic procedures are necessary for the judicious care of the patient and for determining the cardiac and respiratory ability to cope with a planned exercise program. For the patient with specific thoracic problems, measurements of chest expansion and vital capacity are indicated.

11. In a very cursory way, the physical therapist determines the patient's psychological, cognitive, and emotional behavior.

12. Other evaluations that might be carried out by the physical therapist are those of bowel and bladder function and, by palpation, the location of hypersensitive areas in the dermal layer that may cause local or referred pain.

Program Planning and Goal Setting The above therapeutic and evaluative procedures are concurrent with periodic determinations of treatment plans and realistic short and long term goal setting. Generally, the process is 1) to evaluate, 2) to plan for treatment and set goals related to the evaluative results, 3) to perform a succession of treatment combinations, 4) to reevaluate, 5) to replan, etc. Concurrent with the process, the therapist requires the consent of the referring practitioner, consultation with other professionals concerned, and the willingness and motivation of the patient to participate in the program.

Goals and Limitations The goal of the physical therapist is not unlike others in the health professions, particularly those in habilitation and rehabilitation. The end objective is to help the patient meet the functional demands of his/her daily activities or to maintain or return to as normal functioning as possible. To achieve this end result, earlier procedures attempt to reduce or eliminate abnormal pathology, to treat the symptomology, and to enhance more normal function of the various systems.

The limitations of reaching these goals are numerous. First, there is the reality that many disabilities are irreversible and many pathologies incurable. Second, because most physical therapy is performed by the patient, with the therapist acting as an evaluator, motivator, and instructor, the mental and psychological state of the patient is extremely important. Therefore, the therapist must be skilled in receiving and transmitting verbal and nonverbal communication and in setting realistic goals for the patient. In addition to the importance of patient-therapist communication, a successful program depends on communications with the family and other health professionals. The physical therapy program must be part of a total treatment program, in concert with contributions from others.

Other limitations are financial and geographic. The chronically and severely disabled patient is probably not able to support extensive and long term appointments. There are even limitations exerted by third party payers (e.g., Medicare and Medicaid). Many patients are therefore placed on a home program in which they are expected to follow instructions and manage periodic checkups. The continued home program is applicable for many patients because of geographic problems, namely, the difficulty of traveling to an appropriate hospital or other treatment facility.

Another limitation concerns the dependency of the physical therapist on the referring practitioner, usually a physician. By law and professional ethics, a patient must be referred to the physical therapist. Interdisciplinary awareness of the availability and the role and restrictions of the physical therapist, therefore, is important. Continued educational changes in the total health team concept and improvement of the professional services and public relations of the physical therapist should reduce this limitation.

Other Roles and Functions

The role of a physical therapist may encompass other than direct patient care. Administration of the physical therapy services covers areas common to directors and supervisors of similar organizations. These include personnel management, budget planning and accounting, establishing and directing policies within the service that are compatible with the larger organization, purchasing and conducting inventories of equipment and supplies, and communicating with other services and agencies.

The physical therapist is responsible for maintaining professional knowledge and skills by continuing education, both within and without the employing institution. A professional commitment also exists to participate in the education of others, e.g., in training supportive personnel such as physical assistants and aides who assist with patient care. The physical therapist is responsible for offering direction and supervision to supportive personnel in their services. Some physical therapists are primarily educators of students pursuing a physical therapy curriculum.

The clinical physical therapist should advance the knowledge of the profession by participation in clinical research. It is unfortunate that many clinicians fail to tabulate, analyze, and report their findings. Research is often left to those in an academic setting.

Many physical therapists are consultants and participate in overall planning and evaluation of health care management. These personnel are employed by local governments (county and state health departments), by the federal government, or by various private health agencies and organizations. In these positions, or as individuals representing the profession, they are active in the community as members of various organizations and public and private boards. Often they participate in the legislative process as it relates to state licensure, health care issues, and the promotion of the needs of the handicapped.

PATIENTS AND SERVICE

Types of Patients

As discussed above, patients who might benefit from the service of physical therapy are not only those with problems relating primarily to the neuromuscular and musculoskeletal systems but also those with problems relating to the cardiovascular and pulmonary systems. Treatment of diseases and lesions of the skin is sometimes aided by physical therapy. These problems can be primary or secondary to disease, injury, or surgery involving other body systems, e.g., a neuropathy which is a secondary result of diabetes, pain and muscle weakness resulting from kidney surgery, or hysterical paralysis as a symptom of a psychological problem. The type of patient who might be seen by a particular physical therapist covers a broad spectrum, with limitations peculiar to the therapist's place of employment, services he/she provides, and the referring practitioner. The referring practitioner is usually a physician or surgeon, but, in some states, the physical therapy statute allows referrals from dentists and osteopaths. In one study (Worthingham, 1970), the referring practitioner was primarily the orthopaedic surgeon. Other specialties, in descending order of referral, were identified as physical medicine, internal medicine, general practice, surgery, neurology, pediatrics, neurosurgery, and plastic surgery.

The severity of the patient's problem may determine whether he/she receives the services of a physical therapist. The problem may be so minor that the physician feels formal physical therapy is not needed or recommends only one visit to receive a check-out and home instructions. On the other hand, the problems may be so disabling and multifaceted that long term and comprehensive health care, including physical therapy, is indicated.

Places and Methods of Employment

A physical therapist dealing in direct patient care is usually employed in one facility and salaried. Most physical therapists work in hospitals but are involved in a combination of places and occasionally work on a contractual basis. Most hospitals now offer physical therapy services; utilization of these services doubled in the 10 years between 1965 and 1975 (Magistro, 1975). Physical therapy service within the hospital is usually a fairly autonomous unit but may be a part of the department of rehabilitation.

The types of hospitals employing physical therapists vary. These hospitals are usually classified as general but may be specialized as to the age of the patient (pediatric and geriatric), longevity of the patient's hospitalization (acute or chronic), or particular disease entities (orthopaedic, pulmonary, psychiatric, etc.). In these institutions, service is offered to both hospitalized and ambulatory or outpatients.

Some physical therapists are connected with extended care facilities or nursing homes. The service within a particular facility may be part-time, with the physical therapist employed at a set salary, by contract, or through direct billing to the patient. In addition to offering direct patient care through therapeutic and maintenance programs, educational and consultative services are frequently offered to the staff.

Other areas of employment include private and publicly supported rehabilitation centers, physicians' offices, and clinics and agencies that offer health care to ambulatory patients. These types of organizations, e.g., a county health department, and therapy given in the patient's home offer a partial solution to the delivery of services to patients living in less populous areas.

To meet the needs of the handicapped student, physical therapists are often employed by public school systems, private schools, or health departments. In these situations, the student receives both therapy and education while attending school.

Another ever-increasing segment of the profession are the self-employed therapists, who are either in individual or group practice. These therapists also offer services upon the referral of a physician while acting as the managers and administrators of their own service. Usually services are offered in the therapists' offices; however, self-employed practitioners may see patients in nursing homes, health centers, and in a patient's own home.

Physical therapists, as other health professionals, are not yet sufficiently involved in prevention programs that offer the first step in good health care. Blood (1975) cites the future needs for the physical therapist to get more involved in schools, industry, and health maintenance organizations.

Cost of Service and Methods of Payment

The physical therapy service is usually a financially viable unit within an institution. The fee may be incorporated in the daily hospital rate or handled as an additional billing. For hospitalized and nonhospitalized patients, the fee schedule is usually graduated and based on a formula related to type and time required for treatment or evaluations. Patients may be required to pay their own bills but are more likely to have them paid by governments, insurance companies, private organizations and agencies, or by the third party payers of Medicare and Medicaid.

As in most service-oriented occupations, the cost for service is primarily for the salaries of employees. The physical therapist's income ranks in a range similar to that of other health professionals with equal education. A report of 6,709 physical therapists in 1973 indicated a median income of $11,617 for salaried therapists and $20,077 for those who are self-employed (APTA, 1973).

Supportive Personnel

To assist in the administration of physical therapy service and care of patients, supportive personnel are often employed. Of these, the most closely involved with the patient is the physical therapist assistant who works under the direction and supervision of a physical therapist. The degree of this supervision and direction varies in different services. Usually, the physical therapist is responsible for evaluating and planning the treatment program, while many of the treatment procedures are carried out by the physical therapist assistant.

Most departments do not have the service of physical therapist assistants but usually do have aides and orderlies who help with transportation, maintenance, and some supervised patient-related activities. The department also may require the service of typists, clerks, secretaries, and a receptionist. Volunteers often participate in the physical therapy service, especially in specialized centers such as those providing pediatric service.

EDUCATION

Basic Professional Education

Past and Present   In the early part of the 20th century, the people who offered physical therapy services had obtained their knowledge and skills as apprentices working with physicians. During World War I, formal education was initiated and all of the personnel involved were women called Reconstruction Aides. By 1940, educational programs had increased in number and were usually located within a college or university. Casualties of World War II and the outbreak of large poliomyelitis epidemics for several years around 1950 created a greater need for physical therapists, resulting in a further increase in the number of schools.

In 1976, there were 78 schools in the United States, including Puerto Rico, which offered basic professional physical therapy programs. These schools had a total enrollment of approximately 5,000 students and graduated 2600.

The schools vary in their administrative organization. They may be departments of colleges or hospitals or, occasionally, schools within a university. They are more likely, however, to be departments or divisions of schools, such as allied health professions, medicine, or arts and science, located within a university.

The 78 schools offer 92 basic educational programs consisting of four distinct types. Seventy-one admit freshmen or juniors for four- or two-year undergraduate programs and award the baccalaureate degree; 13 require a bachelor's degree for admission to a certificate program of approximately one-year duration; six also require students to have an undergraduate degree and offer a two-year program leading to a master's degree; and two, which are located in a hospital setting, offer a certificate with the undergraduate degree being awarded by an affiliated college or university. Thus, the four types of programs require the professional physical therapist to have from four to six years of postsecondary education and to have, at a minimum, a bachelor's degree.

The various educational programs include, either as prerequisites for admission or within the professional curricula, courses in the humanities and liberal arts, physical sciences (math, physics, chemistry), social sciences, biological sciences (anatomy, physiology, pathology), medical specialties, and physical therapy (didactic and clinical experience).

Future Trends As noted previously, many of the educational programs are administratively located in a school or college of allied health professions or similar designation. The trend, beginning about 1950, for universities to develop a separate college or school for the education of two or more of the various allied health professions continues. More of these interdisciplinary schools are predicted for the future. Some of the advantages of grouping several allied health educational programs under one administrative unit are:

1. Facilitation in the coordination and communication of matters concerning curricular development and research efforts
2. Improvement in obtaining institutional funding and governmental grants
3. Sharing of facilities
4. Enhancement of core curricula for several disciplines
5. Opportunity for students, who will later work together, to learn together

Within the last 20 years, there has been a trend toward an increasing number of baccalaureate degree programs and a decreasing number of certificate programs. The master's degree preparation program began at Western Reserve University in 1959. Only six schools in the ensuing 15 years have inaugurated graduate level basic physical therapy education; consequently, the trend toward postbaccalaureate professional preparation has been slow. Daniels (1974) supports the requirements of a master's degree in the education of a physical therapist. Master's level skills involve increasing responsibility in patient management, competency in patient evaluation and programming, proficiency in supervision, and ability to communicate easily with health professionals at all levels. Most educators admit the difficulty of obtaining both a basic and a professional education in four years. Although students may meet the minimal standards of performance in four years, it is unlikely that there would be sufficient depth and breadth to their didactic and clinical education. Others question whether salaries received by physical therapists warrant attending college for six years; some feel that greater professional competency would yield a higher financial return. At present, the undergraduate physical therapy programs are usually longer than the traditional four academic years, and the postbaccalaureate certificate programs require a minimum of five years.

Graduate and Continuing Education

As true for all professionals, a physical therapist must constantly continue his/her educational experiences to maintain and enhance knowledge and skills. The education may or may not be obtained through formal courses for credit.

For a professional seeking employment in educational, administrative, and consultative positions, a graduate degree beyond the basic preparation is usually required. Consequently, many physical therapists are obtaining master's and/or doctorate degrees in areas appropriate to their professional goals such as physical therapy, education, administration, public health, or the biological sciences of anatomy or physiology. Of the 78 institutions offering a basic physical therapy program, 17 also have curricula for the physical therapist seeking a master's degree.

Continuing education through short term courses, seminars, and workshops is becoming increasingly popular. In some states, legislation that would mandate participation in continuing education programs as a requirement for maintaining licensure is under consideration.

In 1970, the American Physical Therapy Association began to investigate and promulgate a plan for continuing education. Guidelines were published (APTA, 1972) that defined continuing education and set criteria for such programs. There are now procedures through which a sponsoring institution or organization may offer programs that allow participants to receive credit for continuing education units.

Supportive Personnel

Of the supportive personnel employed by physical therapy services, the physical therapist assistant (originally called the physical therapy assistant) receives formal education before employment. The educational programs are located at two-year colleges having a curriculum of general, technical, and clinical education. The graduate receives an associate degree (APTA, 1970).

The introduction of physical therapist assistant programs began in the 1960s. These programs have expanded rapidly along with the explosion of the community and junior college systems in the United States. As of 1977, there are 41 programs with an enrollment of approximately 1,600 students and 800 graduates per year. They are primarily located in, or affiliated with, two-year colleges. Five are under a university system, and two of these offer a professional physical therapy program.

Other supportive personnel utilized in a physical therapy service have usually not received formal college education. The physical therapy aide, assigned to some patient-related activities, is a nonlicensed worker who has completed an on-the-job training program (APTA, 1967).

ACCREDITATION, CERTIFICATION, LICENSURE AND OTHER REGULATORY MECHANISMS

As the health care educational and delivery systems in the United States have grown more formalized and complex, so have the various interrelated public and private mechanisms regulating the institutions and the practitioner, especially at the professional level.

The four categories of health care regulations and the regulating mechanisms are as follows:

1. Accreditation of both the educational institutions and their programs and the service institutions (hospitals, etc.) is determined by voluntary organizations and agencies.
2. Certification or registration of the practitioner also is regulated by a private organization and is available to all persons meeting general requirements or persons qualifying for a specialized certificate.
3. Licensure, which is sometimes called registration, is regulated by the laws of the particular state.
4. There are various other regulatory mechanisms, some for the specific institution and its employees, and some, such as codes and standards, for a specific discipline. This broad category of regulations may have been initiated by a particular organization or institution or may be a result of federal or state laws.

The overall purpose of these various regulatory mechanisms is the protection and welfare of the public, meaning client or patient, by assuring competency of the practitioner and quality care offered by the institution and its personnel. Inherently, the processes act as self-evaluating mechanisms and offer protection for the profession and the professional.

Accreditation

In addition to institutional accreditation by the regional Association of Colleges and Secondary Schools, the basic professional physical therapy educational program must be accredited. The American Physical Therapy Association (APTA) has been active in varying degrees in accreditation since 1929. Beginning in 1934, the American Medical Association (AMA) became involved, first (1934–1956) with the APTA acting only in an advisory capacity. In 1956, a collaborative arrangement of the two organizations was initiated. There are presently 24 allied medical occupations accredited by the collaboration of the AMA through its Council of Medical Education and the organizations representing the various occupations. A document, "Essentials of an Acceptable School for Physical Therapists" (AMA, 1956), has been used as the primary guide for educational institutions and by the survey teams and committees of the two organizations in the evaluation and reevaluation processes.

For several years, representatives of the APTA and the AMA attempted to bridge the areas of philosophical differences and to develop a co-equal consortial arrangement and a new document to replace the 1956

"Essentials." The situation reached an impasse. Subsequently, the 1976 House of Delegates of the American Physical Therapy Association adopted a resolution:

That the American Physical Therapy Association:

1. terminate participation in the AMA–APTA collaborative process for accreditation of educational programs for physical therapists effective December 31, 1976;
2. implement its program of accreditation for physical therapy educational programs effective January 1, 1977;
3. seek recognition by the U.S. Office of Education and the Council on Postsecondary Accreditation as the accrediting agency for physical therapy educational programs; and
4. seek to collaborate with other recognized organizational and accrediting agencies for the purpose of advancing the quality, improving the efficiency and enhancing the coordination of the accrediting process (APTA, 1976b).

Subsequently, petitions for recognition of the American Physical Therapy Association as an independent accrediting agency were submitted September 1, 1976 to the U.S. Office of Education and the Council on Postsecondary Accreditation, the latter being the nongovernmental recognizing body of accrediting agencies.

In the summer of 1977 the American Physical Therapy Association was recognized as an accrediting agency for physical therapy educational programs, including those for physical therapists and physical therapist assistants. The American Medical Association was also recognized to continue as a separate accrediting agency for six months.

To carry out the new accreditation process the American Physical Therapy Association has made procedural changes to include:

1. An Advisory Council on Educational Standards consisting of 12 members (scientists, educators, clinicians, consumers, students)— reviews and makes recommendations to the American Physical Therapy Association's Board of Directors regarding standards for physical therapy education (APTA., 1976a).
2. An On-Site Evaluation Team consisting of three members (physician, clinician, and educator)—serves for fact finding and consultative purposes to the Committee on Accreditation in Education.
3. A Committee on Accreditation in Education consisting of 10 members representing the concerns of physical therapist and physical therapist assistant education, institutions, health care facilities, physicians, and the public—has the responsibility to determine accreditation of physical therapist and physical therapist assistant educational programs.

Some institutions in which physical therapists are employed are also evaluated for the delivery of quality patient care. Hospitals are reviewed by standards formulated by the Joint Commission on Accreditation of Hospitals. Within the accrediting document are standards pertaining to physical therapy.

Certification

Unlike some health professional organizations, the APTA has not been involved in national certification or registration of physical therapists. Before 1970, the American Congress of Rehabilitation Medicine maintained an American Registry of Physical Therapists which listed qualified graduates who had passed an examination and were paying an annual fee. With the increasing emphasis on specialization, a certification program of professionals meeting specific criteria may evolve.

Licensure

As mentioned, rather than seeking certification or registration by a voluntary organization, the field of physical therapy has chosen to allow the laws of the states and, therefore, the public, through its legislative and judicial system, to be the legal regulator of the practitioner.

Beginning in 1913, various states adopted physical therapy practice acts. All states, plus the District of Columbia, Puerto Rico, and the Virgin Islands, now have regulations on the practice of physical therapy. The law is administered and eligibility for licensure is determined by boards consisting of physicians and/or physical therapists and sometimes consumers.

In addition to being a graduate of an approved school and paying a fee, the applicant must pass a written examination. In 1953, states began to use a written examination prepared by the Professional Examination Service (PES), an organization that prepares examinations for health related fields and by the American Physical Therapy Association. All states now use the PES with the exception of Hawaii. Endorsement among states has been facilitated by the fairly universal use of the PES and an Interstate Reporting Service. Some of the states have other requirements for licensure such as an oral examination and practical demonstrations. Perhaps in the future, competency-based examinations will be used initially for licensure, and continuing education credits will be required for relicensure.

Beginning in 1971, a few states also incorporated into their law a mechanism for the licensure of physical therapist assistants. The PES and the Interstate Reporting Service are also available for these individuals.

Some people favor institutional credentialing of all practitioners at each particular institution. It has been advocated that the licensing of personnel and facilities under one unit would provide better regulation for quality patient care. Most health professions, however, including physical therapy, envision problems of unequal criteria among institutions and the self-employed individual and are therefore opposed to this method.

Other Regulatory Mechanisms

Physical therapists, as members of the American Physical Therapy Association, are guided in their professional conduct by the organization's Code of Ethics. There is also a document for the physical therapist assistants who are affiliate members of the organization.

Realizing that the statements in the Code of Ethics are rather broad, the national organization and some state chapters have developed documents pertaining to standards of practice for the physical therapy service and the practitioner. These documents address the essentials of quality service and care with statements on organizational structure, administration, physical plant, communications, fiscal management, continuing education, personnel, research, and means of patient referral-evaluation-treatment. They may be used by the practitioner or may serve for self-evaluation by a chapter's peer review committee.

An institution, whether it be a hospital agency, school, or other type of organization, will have specific requirements and regulations regarding employees. The organization, by law, may require not only physical therapy licensure but, in addition, specific prerequisites of education, experience, and an examination.

To improve quality care and to enhance accountability, the institution and its sections, including physical therapy, may use mechanisms of patient audit and peer review. These mechanisms also improve disciplinary and interdisciplinary communications. To help in the latter, some institutions use the problem-oriented medical record which lists the patient's various problems. It is hoped that all personnel involved with the patient will approach and communicate on these problems collectively and comprehensively.

National and local (state, city, and county) governments have laws and regulations affecting the physical therapist indirectly and directly. Some of these may be incorporated into the regulations of the institution, licensed by the state.

On the national level, there are regulations of the Social Security Act covering funding for patients receiving Medicare and Medicaid benefits. The regulations are very specific as to the referral mechanism and the documentation of proper utilization of physical therapy for quality care. There are also regulations on health and safety pertaining to the physical facility. To date, The Occupational Safety and Health Act of 1970, administered by the U.S. Department of Labor, has primarily been a regulator of industry. It is anticipated that, in the future, standards will be developed to cover health agencies and institutions.

The Department of Labor is requesting competency statements on various types of employment. The American Physical Therapy Association is currently studying this challenge, but statements have not been finalized and published.

There are considerable governmental pressures and regulations on all health occupations, including physical therapy. They will not diminish. It therefore behooves the profession to act before it has to react in opposition to regulations developed by persons outside the field.

RESEARCH NEEDS

One criterion of a profession is that its members contribute to and expand upon the body of knowledge attributable to that profession. As noted by Fowler (1969), research in the field of physical therapy provides a scientific framework and improves both individual patient care and the delivery of health services.

The lack of physical therapy participation in basic, applied, and clinical research continues to be evident, even though there has been some improvement. There are several possible reasons for this: 1) As an allied health professional, the physical therapist has been too content to believe what is handed down and leaves investigation to others, especially those in medicine; 2) educational programs have offered limited opportunities for experiences to learn about the method and logic of experimental design and statistical analysis; 3) there has been restricted funding and time for professionals in the academic environment to carry out research. With better educational curricula and improved technology to monitor studies, contributions to the knowledge and skills of physical therapy are increasing and are of higher quality.

Many areas are yet to be fully researched and documented. Three, which are discussed below, are: 1) education and performance of physical therapy personnel, 2) some basic patient problems, and 3) equipment and appliances.

Education and Performance of Physical Therapy Personnel

Educational institutions, including physical therapy, continue to view admission requirements as a predictor of future success. Among the criteria used to select students for admission are the grade-point average, an Allied Health Professions Admission Test, letters of recommendation, personality-interest inventory, and an interview. Which combination of these criteria is the better predictor of future academic and professional success is not well documented.

As discussed previously, there are three types of physical therapy educational programs: baccalaureate, certificate, and master's. Studies are needed to guide institutions in determining the appropriate competencies and curricula that will better meet the professional needs of the future.

More analysis is needed in differentiating between the performance of the physical therapist and that of the physical therapist assistant and in determining how the utilization of these personnel compares with their respective educational programs. At the University of Florida, various studies have been made on the utilization of rehabilitation personnel. Dumas and Muthard (1970) studied various tasks performed by the clinical physical therapists and concluded that persons with less education could have performed, with or without supervision, some of the tasks that required 32% of the physical therapists' time.

Basic Patient Problems

As discussed earlier, the majority of the patients seen by a physical therapist will have diseases and injuries directly or indirectly causing an abnormality of neuromuscular or musculoskeletal functions. For deficiency in muscular strength, endurance, and speed of motion, more studies are needed to support the advantages of the isokinetic method of training versus the isometric or isotonic.

Various neurophysiological approaches of facilitation and inhibition are used for the patient with upper motor neuron pathology. All have had some clinical success in reducing problems of spasticity, athetosis, and ataxia. Physiological explanations of the various approaches are often theorized. The need for more understanding of the therapeutic uses of reflex patterns, proprioceptive and extroceptive reflexes, the muscle spindle, and perceptual motor learning is indicated. Research to better explain how the normal person learns basic skills might benefit clinical research by enhancing an understanding of the methods of relearning in the pathological state.

Pain is often a major component of the problems of patients seen by a physical therapist. Thermal modalities of both heat and cold applications are used, and some clinical success with both methods challenges researchers to pursue a better explanation of the underlying rationale for this success. The ancient use of electricity for pain is being revived and is now called transcutaneous nerve stimulation. The postulated gate theory is questioned, but other explanations of clinical benefit are not yet forthcoming. Future research in the use of biofeedback and acupuncture for pain also is indicated.

A variety of modalities such as water, ultraviolet and infrared radiation, and electricity have been tried on patients with decubitus ulcers. Again, there is a need to establish better clinical methodology, explanations, and relative usefulness.

Equipment and Appliances

The patient and the physical therapist are dependent on the usefulness, safety, and cost of the equipment and the appliances they use. For instance, the wheelchair, so important for some handicapped persons, still needs substantial improvement. The modern one of metal and leather (or synthetic substitute) is far better than the old wooden type. Further improvements, however, could yield better design to decrease the weight, enhance the safety, and offer adaptations for the specific patient. Motorized wheelchairs offer limited utilization to the handicapped person because of their weight and difficulty in driving. To solve these problems, manufacturers need to consult more with bioengineers and physical therapists. Also, before wheelchairs and other patient-utilized equipment and devices are placed on the market, they should be tested by the types of patients who will ultimately be the consumers.

Physical therapists need to continue contributing to the research of developing better prosthetic and orthotic devices. The lower extremity prosthesis is far more functional than the various electrical and mechanical means designed to replace the amputated upper extremity.

Most of the equipment used in physical therapy clinics needs improvement in safety, usefulness, and clinical validity. For example, a generator used for electrical stimulation and diagnosis frequently has a variety of currents and controls that only confuse the user and compromise its benefit. There is also the need to validate the claims for pulsed versus continuous shortwave and for ultrasonic diathermy and electrical stimulation combined with ultrasound.

CURRENT ISSUES AND PROBLEMS

A profession without problems to solve and issues to confront is static. Many current problems in physical therapy were here yesterday and still lack solutions. Similar problems or new ones will be here tomorrow because a solution to one problem often opens the door to another. A few issues are specific for physical therapy, but most have relationships with, or implications for, other human services, especially the health professions. In other words, they are interdisciplinary issues.

Of the current issues and problems relating to physical therapy, six are discussed below: referral mechanisms, specialization, interdisciplinary overlap and communications, accreditation, education and utilization, and socioeconomics.

Referral Mechanisms

From a legal viewpoint, the physical therapist works as an agent of a referring practitioner, usually a physician. Three questions arise:

1. Should the referring practitioner be only a physician and only of a particular specialty? The physical therapy profession has taken the stand that all persons licensed to practice medicine or surgery and, if the state law permits, others, such as dentists, may be referring practitioners.
2. What should be the requirements of the referral mechanism? Should there be a fairly specific prescription or order, or should the referral be only a request for service with guidelines as to patient's problems,

goals, and precautions? Again the profession has taken the more liberal approach that the particular state law should be limited to delineating the referral mechanism.

3. Should there be alternate patterns for initiating physical therapy services? The professional association now has under study the legal and ethical implications of initial patient evaluation without practitioner referral. An area to be addressed is that of the physical therapist's participation in preventive health care such as screening programs in schools. Another area is an extended care facility where the physical therapist would collaborate with the nursing service in a maintenance program for all the residents. Another question confronting the physical therapist is how to handle the patient who is self-referred or referred by other nonmedical professionals (teachers, counselors, social workers, etc.)

The appropriate response to these questions is less a problem for those health professionals who are not so closely aligned by law and ethics with the physician and who may see clients without a referral.

Specialization

Specialization is also an area of controversy. Most clinical physical therapists, especially in their earlier years of practice, consider themselves generalists. Some, through interest, experience, and additional education, begin to concentrate in specific areas of disability and/or therapeutic approaches. The American Physical Therapy Association now has sections for members with special interests. Under consideration by the APTA is some sort of recognition for specialization. Questions arise. What should be the areas of specialization? Should the APTA have a program of specialized certification? If so, what should be the criteria to obtain a certificate? What implications will certification have for the employee, the profession, the patient, and state laws?

Interdisciplinary Overlap and Communications

With the multiplicity of health disciplines, the delineation of the scope and responsibilities of specific disciplines continues to be an ongoing issue. For instance, there is overlap between physical therapy and the fields of respiratory therapy, nursing, corrective physical education, occupational therapy, speech therapy, and others. Not adhering to strict lines of demarcation as to who does what may be advantageous to the patient. Most institutions do not have the broad spectrum of health professionals available, so the talents and responsibilities of one discipline may need to encompass a larger scope. Many problems, however, arise with regard to the competency of the service, professional jealousies, and the adherence to legal and ethical principles.

As a result of the increasing number of health disciplines, there is, to some extent, the problem of insufficient communication between the various persons involved with a particular patient's care. As discussed by Michels (1971), comprehensive health services may exist in the larger health care facilities but not comprehensive health care. One continues to hope that more interdisciplinary education will result in better interdisciplinary care for the patient. To make collaborative health care a reality, physical therapists and all health participants must continue to inform others of their services and, in turn, be cognizant of the contributions of others.

Accreditation

The accrediting of physical therapy education programs is a current issue. As discussed previously, the proposed new method is to have the American Physical Therapy Association serve as the accrediting body. There has been insufficient time thus far to realize the benefits and the liabilities of this changed mechanism. Will the input from physicians be adequate? Will the APTA have sufficient funding and personnel to administer quality accreditation? For several years, the greatest concern of those in physical therapy and other professions has been the proliferation and duplication of accrediting bodies for the ever-increasing number of health professions. To study this problem, a commission was formed with representation from the American Medical Association, Association of Schools of Allied Health Professions (now American Society of Allied Health Professions), and the National Commission on Accrediting. The commission published a report commonly called SASHEP (1972) with recommendations that are still under study by various accrediting bodies.

Another issue pertaining to accreditation is within the standards promulgated by the Joint Commission on the Accreditation of Hospitals. Consistent with the philosophy that a physical therapist should be the administrator of the clinical service (department, clinic, unit) and that the service should be available to all referring practitioners, not just one medical specialty, the professional organization has objected to the standard that limits the administrative autonomy of the physical therapy service. In reality, the standard is not enforced, because in most hospitals physical therapy is an independent service accepting patient referrals from all practitioners recognized by the hospital.

Education and Utilization

As alluded to previously, the quality and the quantity of physical therapy educational programs continue to be issues of concern. Questions remain as to the appropriateness of each of the three types of physical therapy programs and how they relate to those programs for the physical therapist assistant. In fact, the advent of a second level of physical therapy personnel, the assistant, has created many issues such as utilization, separation of responsibilities, supervisory relationship, membership in the professional association, and licensure. There are many persons who question the need for personnel educated at the associate degree level, especially because the majority of physical therapists are baccalaureate graduates.

Appropriate supply to meet the demand for physical therapy services continues to be a problem. In the past there was a universal shortage. Today the situation is reversed in some sections of the country. Perhaps the number of existing positions is being exceeded by the increasing number of schools and graduates. In contrast, the potential for utilizing physical therapists with the development of new and expanding programs, changes in the health delivery system, and an improved economy would increase the demand considerably.

Socioeconomics

The labor movement has expanded into the unionization of hospital personnel. Usually, professional and management personnel, including physical therapists, have been exempt from compulsory membership. When necessary, the professional organization, both nationally and locally, has attempted to establish physical therapy as the collective bargaining unit for the involved personnel.

Another socioeconomic problem facing the profession is related to the Medicare Amendments of 1972, P.L. 92-603, section 251c. Under the salary equivalency regulation, the physical therapist offering service to a patient under Medicare is being compensated inadequately. The APTA is working for a unit of service systems with more equity and flexibility in financial reimbursement.

In summary, there are numerous issues and problems that challenge the individual physical therapist and the profession collectively. Some will not be solved easily, and new ones will evolve. As the health care delivery system improves, conditions will become more complex, especially for the practitioner and the organizations with which they associate. It is hoped that physical therapy will continue to make its rightful contributions to the interdisciplinary approaches to human services.

PROFESSIONAL ORGANIZATIONS

The American Physical Therapy Association, 1156 15th Street, N.W.
  Washington, D.C. 20005

1. History—began in 1921 as the American Physiotherapy Association
2. Headquarters staff—Executive Director and 37 personnel

3. Membership—over 26,000 in six categories: active, life, affiliate, student, student affiliate, and honorary
4. Structure
   a. House of Delegates—annual meeting of 411 chapter delegates to decide on Association policies
   b. Board of Directors (15), Executive Committee (5)—officers and directors to carry out policies as determined by the House of Delegates
   c. Committees (16)—standing and special—to study specific areas and problems
   d. Sections (11)—special interest groups that meet biannually with a total membership of 6,000
   e. Chapters (53)—50 states (some with districts), District of Columbia, Puerto Rico, and the Virgin Islands
5. Functions—to represent the profession of physical therapy in the United States with participation in matters relating to education, service, research, legislation, and socioeconomics
6. Regular Publications
   a. *Physical Therapy*—professional journal published monthly with 26,000 subscriptions
   b. *Progress Report*—a monthly membership newsletter
   c. *Government Relations Bulletin*—special monthly publication for subscribers, Chapter Presidents, and Section Chairmen

Related Organizations

The American Physical Therapy Association has representation in the following:

1. American Association for the Advancement of Science
2. American Hospital Association
3. American Medical Association—Advisory Committee on Education for the Allied Health Professions and Services
4. Association of American Medical Colleges
5. Coalition of Independent Health Professions
6. Joint Commission on Accreditation of Hospitals—Accreditation Council for Facilities for Mentally Retarded
7. MEDICO
8. National Association for Foreign Student Affairs
9. National Association for Home Health Agencies
10. National Health Council—Organizational Member and Committee on Health Manpower
11. National League of Nursing, Inc.
12. World Confederation of Physical Therapists

Some organizations wherein physical therapists have individual membership:

1. American Alliance of Health, Physical Education, and Recreation
2. American Association for the Advancement of Science
3. American Association of University Professors
4. American College of Sports Medicine
5. American Public Health Association
6. American Society of Allied Health Professions
7. Arthritis Foundation, Allied Health Professions Section

8. National Athletic Trainers Association
9. National Education Association and Council of Exceptional Children of NEA
10. National Rehabilitation Association

ACKNOWLEDGMENT

This chapter is presented with an expression of appreciation to Mrs. Elsie McDaniel for her editorial assistance.

REFERENCES

American Medical Association. 1956. Essentials of an Acceptable School for Physical Therapists. American Medical Association, Chicago, Ill.

American Physical Therapy Association. 1967. Training and utilization of the physical therapy aide. Phys. Ther. 47:33.

American Physical Therapy Association. 1972. Guidelines for continuing education for components of APTA. Phys. Ther. 52:405–407.

American Physical Therapy Association. 1970. Guidelines for physical therapy assistant programs. Phys. Ther. 50:535–541.

American Physical Therapy Association. 1973. Income Survey of Membership. American Physical Therapy Association, Washington, D.C.

American Physical Therapy Association. 1976a. Handbook of Information Concerning the Accreditation Process of Physical Therapy Educational Programs. American Physical Therapy Association, Washington, D.C.

American Physical Therapy Association. 1976b. Resolution on accreditation of educational programs. Phys. Ther. 56:1245.

Blood, H. 1975. The administrative environment. In R. J. Hickok and APTA (eds.), Physical Therapy Administration and Management, pp. 1–23. The Williams and Wilkins Company, Baltimore.

Bobath, B. 1971. Abnormal Postural Reflex Activity Caused by Brain Lesions. William Heinemann Medical Books Ltd., London.

Brunnstrom, S. 1970. Movement Therapy in Hemiplegia. Harper and Row, New York.

Daniels, L. 1974. Tomorrow now: The master's degree for physical therapy education. Phys. Ther. 54:463–473.

Daniels, L., and Worthingham, C. 1972. Muscle Testing: Technique of Manual Examination. W. B. Saunders Company, Philadelphia.

Dumas, N. S., and Muthard, J. E. 1970. A Methodology for Optimizing the Training and Utilization of Physical Therapy Personnel. Regional Rehabilitation Research Institute. University of Florida, Gainesville.

Fowler, W. M. 1969. Physical therapy and research. Phys. Ther. 49:977–982.

Kendall, H. O., Kendall, F. P., and Wadsworth, G. E. 1971. Muscles: Testing and Function. The Williams and Wilkins Company, Baltimore.

Knott, M. and Voss, D. 1968. Proprioceptive Neuromuscular Facilitation. Harper and Row, New York.

Lawton, E. B. 1963. Activities of Daily Living for Physical Rehabilitation. McGraw-Hill Book Company, New York.

Magistro, C. M. 1975. Department planning, design and construction. In R. J. Hickok and APTA (eds.), Physical Therapy Administration and Management, pp. 143–183. The Williams and Wilkins Company, Baltimore.

Michels, E. 1971. The 1971 presidential address. Phys. Ther. 51:1183–1190.

National Commission on Accrediting. 1972. Study of Accrediting of Selected Health Educational Programs: Commission Report. Washington, D.C.

Rood, M. S. 1954. Neurophysiological reactions as a basis for physical therapy. Phys. Ther. Rev. 34:444–449.

Worthingham, C. A. 1970. Study of basic physical therapy education. V: Request, prescription or referral for physical therapy. Phys. Ther. 50:989–1031.

PSYCHIATRY

James P. Connaughton

Human services have been characterized as "those service occupations in which the interpersonal relationships between the provider and recipient of the service play a central role. The goals of human services involve change in the clients, person or situation, aiming at a better adaptive equilibrium or greater creativity" (Rogawski, 1974, p. 59). While the range of services that could be included under such a definition would be endless, Rogawski has included mental health, welfare and social services, some aspects of medical care, components of education or rehabilitation, public services, and services related to law enforcement, correction, probation, and parole.

Differential professional and paraprofessional staffing patterns are often without clear role definition, thus conjuring up a series of perplexing images, bewildering possibilities, and vague horizons concerning questions of a professional, economic, social, political, and even a legal nature. The form in which collaborative ventures between disciplines can take place is particularly difficult if a consensus philosophy is the *modus operandi*. The difficulty is heightened further by the fact that, currently, everyone seems to have a stake in the human service market, even business entrepreneurs.

These comments are in no way intended to demean the value of an integrated team approach, particularly as it relates to the problems of the multihandicapped child or adult, or, for that matter, its contribution to professional growth and development. The comments are intended to raise serious questions about the wisdom of promulgating an interdisciplinary consensus approach as a panacea for all human services problems. When there is, however, a clear definition of the interdisciplinary team in relation to a specific human service task or problem, and when the participating professionals are secure in their respective roles, the patient or client stands to gain immeasurably by such an integrated approach.

Psychiatry is best identified as a human service discipline in its clinical and social or community roles. Among the many who have defined psychiatry are Sullivan (1953), who called it a science of human relations, Meyer (1957), who considered it a study of the biology of the psyche, and Redlich and Freedman (1966), who saw psychiatry as a medical specialty concerned with the study, diagnosis, treatment, and prevention of behavioral disorders. Probably the most widely accepted definition is that of Noyes and Kolb (1958, p. 1) who characterized modern psychiatry "as that branch of medicine which is concerned with genesis, dynamics, management and treatment of such disorders and undesirable functioning of the personality, as to distort either the subjective life of the individual, his relationships with others or with society." Psychiatry in their opinion deals with the immaturities, disorganizations, and disintegration of personality and, as such, is concerned with morbid personality and psychopathology.

Currently, most psychiatrists view their brand of medicine as lying within a model similar to that of Erickson's (1963) which includes a psychosomatic, an interpersonal, and an intrasocial dimension.

CHANGING TRENDS IN
PSYCHIATRIC FOCI AND PROFESSIONAL TRAINING

The dual origin of psychiatry, with its roots in the biological and behavioral sciences, is reflected both in the criteria for admission to a residency training program and in the form and content of the training provided. To gain admission to a residency training program in psychiatry, the candidate must have completed medical studies and have graduated. There is also the requirement that an internship be completed at an accredited hospital. This requirement has been waived for the past several years, but it is believed that it will be shortly reinstituted.

The content of psychiatric training has changed markedly over the years, primarily because of significant advances in the field of behavioral science and the related field of neuroscience. In 1961, when Carmichael (1962) presented an outline suggesting the ideal learning experience for the general psychiatrist, he included: 1) an adequate range of clinical experiences with appropriate clinical materials, 2) suitable case conference, and 3) basic theoretical and clinical didactic instruction with an eclectic orientation. The neurological requirements included preparation in clinical assessment and diagnosis and treatment of neurological disorders. No attempt was made to specify course content or sequence or training experience. It was suggested, however, that topics such as dynamics of mental illness, supervision in psychotherapy, somatic therapies, consultation and teaching experience, psychosomatic medicine, social psychiatry, and elective opportunities in research and special learning in pertinent basic science areas be included. Because there was considerable freedom academically, each training program was free to interpret how its residents should be trained. During the 1950s and early 1960s, the directors of these programs were predominantly psychoanalysts, and, consequently, much of the training took place within the psychoanalytic model. Individual psychotherapy was the major therapeutic modality of that era. One of the most frequent criticisms leveled at psychiatry was that the psychoanalytic forms of training tended to prepare the trainees more for private practice. This pattern resulted in a marked deficiency of psychiatric manpower needed to deal with the more global problems of psychiatric disturbance in the general population, particularly in lower socioeconomic groups.

Since Carmichael's original formulation, there have been considerable advances in the behavioral sciences and in the neurosciences. New psychotherapeutic modalities and their variations were introduced, with family therapy and group therapy dominating the field. This resulted in the modification of the highly individualized intrapsychic approach to the patient, in the direction of transactional analysis and systems theory. In the process, individual psychotherapy took on a role of lesser importance in the training of residents, and a greater premium was placed on social and community psychiatry, which had become a major force in the field of mental health.

Since the original formulation of training requirements by the American Board of Psychiatry and Neurology, psychiatric training has become increasingly complex in light of the advances in the behavioral and biological sciences. The movement of psychiatry into the community heralded activism in the field, and, with it, there was also "a pullulation of basic biological research into mental illness and for the first time, the nineteenth century dream of rapproachment between the neurological sciences could be considered closer to realization" (Ransom, 1973, p. 841). Coincidental with these advances came an increasing formalization of program content that was no longer left to the philosophical whims of training directors. Pressures for change were reflected in, and brought about by, the range of knowledge required for board certification. A candidate currently must demonstrate knowledge and competencies in 1) psychiatric diagnosis, 2) psychopharmacology, 3) somatic therapy, and 4) psychotherapy (individual, family, and group). Over the past decade, behavioral therapies have been increasingly included in training programs, with a consequent significant impact on research as reflected in the marked increase in professional publications related to epidemiology, psychotherapy, psychopharmacology, and genetics.

Because of advances in the neurological sciences, these subjects have received increasing prominence in training programs. There are very few professional journals in the field that do not devote significant attention to the neurosciences of neuroanatomy, neurophysiology, neurochemistry, neuroendocrinology, neuropharmacology, and neurogenetics.

Increased understanding of biological rhythms and biofeedback also has generated considerable excitement about their potential application to the field of psychiatry. These areas hold further promise of a holistic approach to the understanding and treatment of mental illness.

For the purposes of certification by the American Board of Psychiatry and Neurology, the trainee must have completed three years of training, followed by two years of additional training or clinical experience, before application can be made to take the certifying examinations. Additional training and further examination are required for certification in subspecialties of child, administrative, and the more recently established forensic psychiatry.

MANPOWER

Currently, about 1,000 graduates of U.S. medical schools enter the field of psychiatry every year. Until recently, this figure represented 9-10% of all graduates; however, this percentage has recently dropped by one percent because of the increase in the number of medical school graduates (Brown, 1976).

There are approximately 27,000 trained psychiatrists in the United States with a projected figure of 30,000 by 1980. The professional distribution, however, is quite uneven and ranges from five per 100,000 in 11 states, including South Dakota, Wyoming, and Alabama to 55 per 100,000 in the District of Columbia (Arnhoff and Kumbar, 1973).

It is quite apparent from these figures that, even though there has been a rapid acceleration in the growth of psychiatry in this country over the past 40 years, and particularly over the past decade, the numbers and distribution of psychiatrists in this country fall far short of meeting the needs of the increasing reservoir of psychiatrically disturbed individuals in our society. This gap will widen even further because of recent governmental decisions that markedly restrict the number of foreign graduates entering the United States. The reduction in the number of foreign graduates will have a decided impact on state hospital staffing because state hospitals are predominantly, or even completely, manned by foreign graduates.

Epidemiology

It is estimated that at any given time in this country, approximately 25% of the population experiences some disturbance in psychological functioning. The great majority of these individuals seeks help from a variety of sources which includes family, friends, clergymen, family doctors, and mental health facilities. A further indication of the national level of psychiatric disturbance is reflected in the growth in the utilization of mental health resources. In 1955, approximately 1.7 million U.S. citizens had contact with a mental health care facility. In 1971, 2.4 million availed themselves of the service. The projected figure for 1975 was set at 6.0 million (Ozarin and Taube, 1974).

The incidence of psychiatric disturbance in children needing specialized intervention has been recorded rather consistently as 8% of the child population. This figure represents the number of children who evidence disturbance of a sufficient degree to require professional intervention. The number of children exhibiting transitional disturbance is much greater. When one considers that over one-half of the U.S. population in the early 1970s was under 25, the extent of disturbance in the youth of our country becomes obvious and represents a serious public health concern. Yet, of the nation's children, a very small number was receiving active psychiatric intervention. This is illustrated best by the fact that less than one-tenth of the mental health clinics in the country provide children's services. Moreover, of those who attend, the majority receive only diagnostic service, with a mere 40% receiving any active treatment.

HISTORICAL AND PHILOSOPHICAL BASES OF PSYCHIATRY

Psychiatry today is greatly influenced by forces within the current social matrix, while its theory, philosophy, and treatment are inextricably tied to the history of its past. To paraphrase Santanya, those who are not acquainted with history are doomed to repeat its failures. Had such an axiom been applied to some of the recent developments in the field of psychiatry and mental health, many of the errors made and failures experienced might have been obviated.

Traditionally, the history of psychiatry has been written from two main perspectives: 1) the organicist approach which traced the development of the field from the time of the advent of modern medicine in the 16th century, and 2) the inductive or Whig (Butterfield, 1931) approach which considered the earlier history of psychiatry, favorably or unfavorably, in the light of current knowledge. The latter was the approach adopted by Zilboorg (1941), who, in his overview of psychiatric development, compared it with the psychoanalytic approach to the field. Both the organicist and the inductive approaches to the history of psychiatry generally have been written with a primary focus on major figures who contributed to the development of the field and often with little recognition of the role that social forces contributed to these advances. "The fact remains, that the spirit of the times (*Zeitgeist*) must be ready before certain ideas can take shape and embody certain expressions in particular men" (Mora, 1967).

There is no more illustrative example of the *Zeitgeist* than the case of Pinel who freed the mentally ill from their chains at Bicetre. The fact that he released the inmates at the height of the Reign of Terror during the

French Revolution gave even further recognition to his act as one of great courage. In keeping with the concept that particular advances or innovations take place in the context of changing patterns and ideas within a social system was the fact that Louis XVI, before his demise, had already established a commission to inquire into the deplorable conditions of the mentally ill in institutions in Paris. While Pinel received considerable recognition for his actions, overshadowing his act of valor was the fact that he was, first and foremost, a pragmatic clinical psychiatrist who understood the iatrogenic features of institutional care and who, in his treatment of his patients, planned for their return to the community in a manner that anticipated current concepts of social psychiatry.

Psychiatry today is a product of the past 200 years; its current theories and practices are shaped by a confluence of social, cultural, political, philosophical, and economic forces. As a discipline, psychiatry is imbedded in an ever-changing social matrix, its progression and retrogressions closely mirroring societal changes, particularly in its humanistic dimensions. Consequently, psychiatric theory and practice have been continuously influenced by changing concepts of the mind and the mind-body interaction, and by changing philosophical concepts of the individual in relation to society.

PREINSTITUTIONAL CARE OF THE MENTALLY ILL

Psychiatry, until the third decade of this century, was practiced predominantly in an institutional setting. This is not to suggest that the evolution of the discipline is synonymous with institutional care of the mentally ill, although the writings of medical historians would tend to convey that impression.

In essence, psychiatry, as a profession, arose from a combination of circumstances, the most predominant of which was social need. The earliest pattern of care of the mentally ill in this country took place within a community setting during colonial times. The predominantly rural distribution of the population resulted in each small community taking care of those considered dysfunctional. Individuals who presented behavioral disturbances, who were considered a threat to public safety, or who were indigent because of their idiosyncratic patterns of behavior were taken care of within the community as part of its obligation. The approach to the management of those considered mentally disturbed ranged from foster care to supplementary stipends for families who cared for the individual in his/her own home. This did not, in any way, mean that the predominant care was necessarily humane even in the case of those in foster homes. Many of the deranged individuals were victimized, some were run out of town, and others were confined and even shackled in their own rooms or in the rooms in which they were boarded.

There was, in colonial times, no identifiable treatment of mental disturbance because it was not recognized as an illness in itself; rather, it was conceptualized within a moral and judgmental context.

EARLY INSTITUTIONAL PSYCHIATRY

Grob (1973), in tracing the evolution of psychiatric institutions in this country, observed that the earliest identifiable development came at the beginning of the 19th century. This movement was ushered in by significant demographic changes in the population which included: 1) a significant population growth, 2) a sharp rise in immigration of persons who were poor and impoverished, and 3) increasing urbanization of the population.

The earlier hospitals for the treatment of the mentally ill were founded on private philanthropy. The stimulus for their development arose from an increased humanistic concern for those afflicted, as well as from significant developments in medical and psychiatric thought catalyzed by developments on the European continent. It was also the belief that treating the mentally ill was not only beneficial to the patient but, in the final analysis, to the community.

The medical directors of these institutions might best be described as visionary. They were extremely humanistic in their approach to the inmates of their respective institutions. Their methods of treatment were highly individualized; each institution took on the image and philosophy of its director. Despite limitations of available therapeutic tools, patients benefited immeasurably, and, even by current day standards, the rate of success of these therapeutic interventions was high. These hospitals served as prototypes for the early public mental health hospitals developed in the ensuing decades. The traditional referral patterns were maintained, i.e., those identified as in need of care because of behavioral patterns that were a threat to society and those who were indigent and, therefore, dependent because of idiosyncratic behavior or infirmities were referred.

Because of the rapid growth of the population and the increase in numbers of those defined as mentally ill, the private philanthropic institutions could no longer take care of the broad-based population they had served, regardless of economic circumstances. These institutions gradually began to take on the quite different function of providing care mainly for those who had the economic resources to pay for it. Many of the private hospitals founded during that period are in existence today, e.g., McLean Hospital in Boston, Bloomingdale in New York, and Hartford Retreat in Connecticut.

At present, there are 180 private psychiatric hospitals in the United States with a bed capacity of 15,000 (Houck, 1975). These are found predominantly on the east and west coasts and provide about 6% of all inpatient care episodes in this country.

The public mental health institutions came into being when the private hospitals could no longer meet the growing need for institutional care because of the rapid growth in population. Consequently, the public sector began to assume a greater responsibility for the mentally ill. The early public institutions closely followed the paradigm of the private institutions, and, accordingly, their pattern of care was highly individualized and their philosophy therapeutic.

The therapeutic philosophy was fostered by the superintendents of these early institutions who, fortuitously, were highly gifted physicians, preeminent in their profession, and who brought to the field their professional knowledge, a missionary zeal, and a compassionate concern for the mentally ill. The therapeutic philosophy and individualized care of their patients were further enhanced by the fact that the public institutions then were not plagued by bureaucratic entanglements.

The humanistic concerns for the mentally ill and the therapeutic intent of these early public institutions did not mean that the modalities of treatment used could, by contemporary standards, be considered humane. Quite the contrary, the persistent purging of patients, the use of emetics, the frequent blood letting, and the shaving and blistering of the scalp were considered part of acceptable medical practice. Many of the other innovations, including the special chair designed by Rush to elevate a bound, agitated patient in the air in order to improve his/her cerebral circulation, would today be considered primitive.

Much of the treatment of that era was formulated from a moral and quasi-scientific basis. While organicity was postulated as a possible cause of mental illness, the majority of disturbances was considered to originate from lack of an orderly relationship between the individual and nature or between the individual and society brought on by unsanitary habits, immorality, and improper living. Hence, the goal of treatment was to restore that balance. During these early days, fear was viewed as an essential element in the treatment of patients. This tenet was later dispensed with in favor of kindness, and much positive benefit accrued.

Because of the highly personalized quality of care given, the early institutions were extraordinarily successful in their treatments even by today's standards. This was reflected in the short length of stay and rapid return to the community.

Like so many other innovations in the area of human services that are proved effective, the tendency existed then, as it does now, to generalize the pattern of care to larger populations, whether applicable or not. Unfortunately, in doing so, all too often the philosophy and therapeutic intent of the program are lost sight of, to its eventual detriment as a modality of care. Such is the case when one examines the early institutional care of the mentally ill as compared with later developments in this care system.

The public mental hospital movement grew until each state had at least one large institution. Many states had additional institutions located in large metropolitan areas. Several of them recorded patient populations in the thousands, with a resultant loss of the highly personalized quality care provided in the early days. Subsequently, there was a marked shift in these hospitals from a primary focus on individual care to the administrative needs of institutions. Not surprisingly, then, the institutions deteriorated in terms of both humanistic care and therapeutic intent and became increasingly identified as receptacles for society's outcasts. They became the forerunner of the modern day "snake pit."

From the 1870s on, the voices of protest were heard vilifying the institutional care of psychiatrically disturbed individuals; many of the charges are similar to those that are even more stridently echoed today. The roots of the difficulties at that time, no more than now, did not arise purely because of a significant multiplication in the number of patients needing care or because of incompetency on the part of psychiatrists running these institutions, although the blame was partially theirs. Societal changes that brought increasing bureaucratization of hospitals and their operation, legislative practices, and changing social attitudes toward those needing institutional care also contributed to the problem.

The mental hospitals then, as is the case now, became increasingly subject to the vagaries of public policies and legislative, legal, administrative, and financial practices. As a result, many difficulties arose that persist to this day. These difficulties involve the increasingly blurred lines that exist among health and welfare agencies and the courts with respect to the inmates in institutions (Grob, 1973). Mental institutions, then, took on increasingly pluralistic functions, which are best summarized as follows:

> They (mental hospitals) continued to care for a heterogeneous population which included a significant portion of the poor, inadequate, the geriatric patient, and individuals considered a danger to society. In addition these hospitals had the major responsibility with respect to the acutely disturbed psychiatric patient in addition to housing a large population of chronic psychotic and dysfunctional patients (Grob, 1975, p. 41).

Not surprisingly then, state hospitals have come to be identified with all that is bad in psychiatry. This, in itself, is a paradox because legislative, economic, and legal practices have had more influence on the form institutions have taken than has the psychiatrist in establishing philosophies for their operation. If there was, however, one identifiable reason why psychiatry as a profession deserves criticism vis-à-vis public mental health institutions, it is that psychiatrists had acceded to unrealistic expectations and unreasonable demands placed upon them.

CURRENT STATUS AND PROBLEMS OF MENTAL HOSPITALS

Mental hospitals today might best be described as beleaguered institutions because of the broad spectrum of assaults launched against their credibility in caring for the mentally ill. While the basis for these attacks has its roots in the history of the field (i.e., the perception society has had, historically, as to their function and the consequent patterns of referral), these assaults are now being reenacted in a variety of settings and forms. Problems include: 1) funding, 2) a proliferation of critical reviews and reports, 3) the new consumerism, 4) renewed antipsychiatric attitudes, 5) antihospital dialectic, and 6) a vivid sensitivity to civil liberties. All of these, according to Brill (1975), have made the future of mental institutions quite uncertain and planning for them extraordinarily difficult.

The general philosophy behind a variety of court actions relevant to public institutions has been to promote the right to treatment and to protect the civil liberties of individuals, especially as they relate to involuntary commitment. These court decisions have resulted in directives that a state institution cannot retain a patient, even though committed, if adequate treatment is not provided. At the same time, the rights of patients have been defined to include the right to refuse treatment proferred, even though he/she is institutionalized. Danger to society seems to be the one major acceptable determinant in commitment procedures. It is unclear at this point whether or not danger to oneself constitutes a basis for involuntary hospitalization.

Ennis (1972) of the American Civil Liberties Union (ACLU), who has led the fight on public mental health institutions and their practices, observed that 95% of their patient population did not constitute a threat to society. He set as a goal the closing of all such institutions with the expectation that alternative and less restrictive forms of care would be made available.

The overall results of such endeavors have been mixed in character. These efforts put increasing pressure on the institutions to provide more adequate care for the mentally ill. They also have prompted attempts to provide less restrictive forms of care in communities across the country, including daycare hospitals, halfway houses, and community foster homes. An assessment of the current situation would lend considerable support to the belief that, for some, particularly the chronically psychiatrically disturbed individual, the cure has been worse than the disease.

In response to court directives, the great majority of states are systematically reducing the population in the public mental institutions. In 1973, California set as its goal the closing down of all state institutions for adults within a five-year period and of all facilities devoted to the care of children by 1982. The timetable was, in a large part, on the way to being realized, and by 1974 there were only 7,000 beds still in use. At that point, however, the public and the legal sector became concerned about the potential dangers presented by the return of a large number of the mentally ill to local communities (Aiguist, 1974).

Similar experiences were encountered in Massachusetts and New York where the *New York Times* reported public alarm in its editorial columns. The alarm was prompted primarily by the fact that, in New York, large numbers of patients were being turned out of the public institutions without adequate alternative planning. It was estimated at one point that as many as 100,000 chronically ill psychiatric patients were wandering the streets of New York, eventually ending up in locations such as the Bowery, sharing habitation with prostitutes, drug addicts, petty criminals, and other predators. There, they were perceived as either threatening or assaultive. More commonly, they were the victims of assaults, robberies, and exploitation (Reich and Siegel, 1973).

Even when alternative accomodation was provided, as for example in nursing homes, in group-care homes, or even motels, these individuals were exploited and often were so disorganized and unmotivated that they were unable to avail themselves of the follow-up care provided by the community. This was particularly ironic in light of the fact that the philosophy behind the concept of community mental health has been to provide follow-up care for this very population. The issue becomes even more critical when one considers that the available treatments, particularly the drug treatments (major tranquilizers, trycyclic antidepressants, and lithium) have proved effective in moderating the course of severe psychiatric disturbance, and the chronically psychotic would have been maintained more adequately in the community had they availed themselves of clinical services. Many of these unfortunate individuals settle in areas reserved for the outcasts of society. Such was the case in Los Angeles where, in one small section of a ghetto area, 1,100 individuals with chronic psychiatric disturbance congregated and, in a sense, established their own institutional system with its own unique iatrogenic features. The history of the case of the mentally ill, and particularly, the chronically psychotic had apparently gone through one complete cycle, and their circumstances echoed many of the descriptions of the preinstitutional era.

GENERAL HOSPITAL PSYCHIATRIC UNITS

The significance of the role of the psychiatric unit in community hospitals is reflected by the fact that in 1971 and in part of 1972 these units had a total of 542,642 admissions or 31% of all admissions to psychiatric settings in this country (Ozarin and Taube, 1974). Yet, despite this rather impressive statistic, their role in the care of the mentally ill has received limited recognition and has been overshadowed by the significance of public mental health institutions and community mental health centers in providing for the psychiatrically disturbed.

Psychiatric units in general hospitals are mainly a post-World War II phenomena; their development paralleled the growth of the private practice of psychiatry in the community. Approximately 66% of the psychiatrists in this country are in full- or part-time private practice (Lebensohn, 1975). A further impetus for the development of psychiatric units was the availability of Hill-Burton funds for hospital construction that allowed general hospitals, as part of their obligation to the community, to provide beds for psychiatric admissions. Further funding provided under the Mental Health Act of 1964 allowed for the expansion of services. Some hospitals developed the full range of services required for the purpose of being identified as a community mental health center.

The psychiatric services currently provided by general hospitals are traditional in nature and generally are based on a medical model of psychiatic illness. These services include inpatient (short term, usually adult and adolescent) and outpatient (adult, adolescent, and sometimes child psychiatric) services. In addition, many of the general hospitals have drug abuse and alcoholic units. The range of services provided in these settings includes: 1) diagnostic services, 2) crisis intervention, and 3) consultation services. The range of treatment offered includes: 1) psychotherapy (individual, family and group, short term, and intensive), 2) somatic therapies, including electroconvulsive therapy, and 3) pharmacotherapy or drug treatment. The staffing of these units usually follows a traditional pattern: psychiatrists, psychologists, psychiatric social workers, and nurses who are psychiatrically trained. These units generally follow a private practice model and operate on a fee-for-service basis, limiting much of their service to those who are sufficiently affluent and motivated.

COMMUNITY PSYCHIATRY

Community psychiatry originated in the early 1960s, and its development evolved through a confluence of forces, including: 1) an increasing disenchantment with state psychiatric institutions and their role in the treatment of mental disorders, 2) a changing concept of psychiatric disturbance with increasing adoption of a sociocultural model (this put the major focus on environmental determinants as the basis for psychiatric disorders), 3) a recognition of the limitations of the traditional modes of therapy, more specifically the psychoanalytic forms of treatment that used the dyadic model, which is not applicable to the more global mental health needs of the population, 4) the increasing recognition that economic limitations prevented the great majority of the population from receiving adequate mental health services and 5) the election of a president who was committed to improving the lot of the psychiatrically disabled and the mentally retarded.

The concept of community psychiatry was by no means an original one and, in fact, had already been anticipated by some of the pioneers in the field of mental health even as early as the turn of the 20th century. Clifford Beers (1939), who founded the Society for Mental Hygiene in the early decades of this century, called for lay social action to further the interest of those who were afflicted with emotional disturbance. During the same era, Meyer (1952) proposed education as a route to preventative psychiatry and suggested that general practitioners be included in the care of their patients in psychiatric institutions so that they might more effectively be able to help them in adjusting upon their return to the community.

Querido (1969), in the early 1930s, in response to a directive to reduce the number of institutionalized psychiatric patients in Amsterdam, Holland, adopted a triage approach to those who became acutely ill psychiatrically. Through prompt intervention, he managed to maintain patients in the community who would otherwise have been hospitalized.

In 1963, the Community Mental Health Program was ushered in when President Kennedy (1963), in response to the findings of the Joint Commission of Mental Illness and Health (1961), proposed legislation to establish a new mental health program encompassing the concept of comprehensive community care for the mentally ill and retarded. Reflecting on these new proposals as an alternative to the "outmoded types of institutional care which now prevail," he suggested, "We need a new type of facility, one which will return the care of the mentally ill to the mainstream of American medicine." He observed further, "Reliance on large Mental Hospitals will be supplemented by the open warmth of community concern and capability."

Just as had been the case in Amsterdam in the 1930s and in Great Britain in the early 1960s, it was recommended that the number of institutional beds in the country should be reduced by 50% within the decade. The Community Mental Health Act of 1963, which incorporated President Kennedy's proposals, was adopted by Congress in 1963. Under this new law, it was proposed that a series of mental health centers be set up, each serving a geographic area of 75,000 to 200,000 population. These centers were to be comprehensive in character and were required by regulation to provide the following five basic services with other service categories apparently optional: 1) inpatient services, 2) outpatient services, 3) emergency services, 4) partial hospitalization (e.g., a day hospital), and 5) consultation and educational services. Surprisingly, no specific requirements were made that these centers should provide diagnostic services, rehabilitation services, children's services, or services to the alcoholic and drug addict. It was only through supplementary legislation that additional funds were provided for these services.

The failure to require diagnostic, children's and rehabilitative services during the early planning of these centers, even though they were essential to the whole concept of preventive psychiatry, symbolized the failure of an integrative approach to the whole field of comprehensive mental health care, a failure that has plagued its development ever since.

At the time of the initial legislation it was envisaged that 2,000 mental health centers would be constructed. To date, however, approximately 591 have been built, and the future of the rest is uncertain.

WHAT IS COMMUNITY PSYCHIATRY?

Community psychiatry has been defined as "that body of knowledge (that is, theories, methods, and skills in research and service) required by psychiatrists who participate in organized community programs for the promotion of mental health through prevention and treatment of psychiatric disorders" (Caplan and Caplan, 1967, p. 1499). It includes, in addition, rehabilitation within the community of those psychiatric patients who were formerly institutionalized.

The sociocultural theory on which the practice of community psychiatry is based conceptualizes psychological health and disturbance as originating from a complex series of dynamic interreactions between the biopsychological forces within the individual and the social fields of force in which he/she is enmeshed. It also incorporates a unified concept of health and disease in which psychological disturbances are viewed as on the basis of a continuum with health, with no clear line of demarcation between what might be considered healthy as opposed to disturbed. This allows for transient phases of disturbed functioning without actually labeling an individual disturbed. As opposed to the medical model of psychiatric disorders that categorizes psychiatric symptoms and designates discrete disease entities, sociocultural theory tends to view the manifestations of disturbed functioning as being in a continued state of flux, their character at any time being determined by the social fields of force (e.g., family, school, military, or community), with which the individual is interacting at any given time. Community psychiatry, then, rather than placing primary emphasis on disturbance within the individual, interprets disturbed functioning in terms of whether social fields of force operate in the interest of health promotion or contribute to psychological dysfunction.

While community psychiatry represents a significant departure from traditional psychiatric practice, which in the past was mainly conducted within the walls of a hospital or a private office, its concepts were anticipated in the child guidance movement of the early 1930s and in the later family and group therapy movements. All of these to some degree interpreted disturbance within the individual as reflecting patterns of disturbed relationships within the family and in the individual's own culture. Consequently, therapeutic focus was placed, in both group and family therapy, on correcting distorted patterns of interaction that were self-defeating in character.

Family and group therapies as modalities of treatment have been questioned on the basis of whether intrapsychic pathology is always translatable into interpersonal problems. Questions also have been raised as to whether these therapies conducted in an office away from the individual's life space or social milieu can reconstruct adequately the difficulties the individual is having in day-to-day life experiences. The community psychiatrist endeavors to counter these arguments by moving out from behind the walls into the community and there exploring health and disturbance in their latent or established form (in vivo).

The practice of community psychiatry is based on a public health concept of prevention and early intervention. Its endeavors are directed toward:

1. Reducing the incidence of disturbance by identifying and eliminating factors in the social milieu that contribute to disturbance. Further, by the provision of societal services in relation to need, it is hoped that individuals within the community may, in turn, experience a greater sense of mastery. Educational programs also are directed toward better role definition in the population or segments of the population, thus allowing its members to perform more effectively with respect to an individual task, e.g., programs directed toward more effective parenting or toward combating alcoholism and drug abuse.
2. Seeking to attenuate the course of a disturbance and, in the process, reducing the level of psychological dysfunction within the community, through the process of case finding and prompt intervention.
3. Providing adequate follow-up for those who are psychiatrically disturbed so as to prevent further episodes of decompensation. In this context, too, the rapid return of patients who have been hospitalized to the community is facilitated by providing follow-up which in turn offsets the negative features of prolonged hospitalization. Interim contact with the families of these patients prevents a restructuring of the family unit in a manner that would exclude the patient on his/her return.

The psychiatrist in a community center has four identifiable roles:

1. *Clinical.* A high degree of traditional clinical skills are required in the areas of: 1) diagnosis, 2) treatment, i.e., short term therapy, crisis intervention, and drug therapy, and 3) rehabilitation.
2. *Consultation.* This role is by far the most important because it is the goal of the community psychiatrist to utilize his/her skills over the

widest possible arena. This is accomplished by identifying the network of helping agencies (public, private, and voluntary) and helping them promote mental health and manage acute episodes of disturbance. The consultation is primarily directed toward increasing the professional understanding and objectivity of the caregivers in those agencies by imparting principles of mental health that might be applicable to their specific areas of work. The goal, ultimately, of consultation services in the field of community psychiatry is to provide service in such a way that other professionals will make optimal use of the psychiatrist's expert knowledge while retaining their own sense of identity, commitment, and responsibility.

3. *Public health role.* This role is also clearly the function of the community psychiatrist, and it is the premise on which his/her whole operation is based. It involves primary, secondary, and tertiary forms of intervention, ranging from identifying factors that contribute to dysfunction in a population to providing educational programs relative to these particular findings to case finding and treatment of those discovered to be disturbed to the rehabilitation of those identified as psychiatrically ill.

4. *Research.* This is also viewed as an essential role of the community psychiatrist; yet, it has received lesser emphasis. Ordinarily subsumed under this role is research into: 1) epidemiology, 2) the development of new modes of intervention in the community, 3) various patterns of interrelationships in social networks, including models of community organization, and 4) family relationships and attitudes.

While there is little question that the community psychiatry model has contributed much to the understanding of psychiatric disturbance, particularly its community or environmental roots, the overall results have not been as dramatic as had been hoped. Certainly, the therapeutic millenium that had been conceptualized by the earlier innovators in the field is far from being realized. Yet, the statistics on the number of patients serviced by 591 community mental health centers in this country are impressive. In 1975, there were 232,000 annual inpatient admissions, 1,123,000 annual episodes of outpatient treatment, and 104,000 episodes of day treatment.

The major areas in which these centers have failed in their mandate include: 1) the failure to develop a viable model for the management of the chronic psychiatrically disturbed, particularly those who have been released in large numbers in recent times in response to a variety of court decisions, 2) the failure to provide adequate children's services and to preserve the family therapy model in the treatment of child patients, 3) the politicization of the community mental health movement that saw many of its professionals involved in social action and political manipulations for which they were totally unequipped and in the process neglecting the needs of the patient population of many of these centers, and, 4) confusion on the part of the public and legislators as to professional roles because of the egalitarian image projected by many of the centers. The demarcation lines between professional and paraprofessional became quite blurred, with the result that it was difficult for many who used those centers to identify the level of care they were receiving.

A frequent criticism leveled at the community mental health movement has been that it has been dominated by psychiatry; yet, in a recent overview, Glasscote (1975) found the reverse to be true. Several of the centers were inimical to the participation of psychiatrists in their operation. When one considers that of the 40,000 persons employed in community mental health centers around the country, psychiatry has but a 6% representation, questions arise regarding the ability of many of these centers to meet the diagnostic and medical treatment needs of their patient population, particularly those who are chronically disturbed.

CHILD PSYCHIATRY

Child psychiatry, as we know it today, is a very young discipline with its origins dating back only 60 years. Its development paralleled and grew out of more enlightened social attitudes that gave increasing emphasis to the child as an immature and vulnerable human being who should be afforded protection. The changing social attitudes were reflected in the passage of legislation promoting the welfare of children. They included laws related to: 1) child labor, to prevent the exploitation of children in sweat shops, 2) child abuse, to protect children against abuses within their families, 3) education, to require mandatory attendance at school, and 4) legal modification of the court system, to provide for the management of youthful offenders within a paternalistic rather than an adversarial framework.

The emergence of psychoanalytic theory as propounded by Freud contributed much to the modification of the structural organic or moralistic perspective of childhood disturbances. For the first time, professionals in the field had a theoretical framework that allowed them to look beyond the manifest behavior for the origin of disturbance. The psychoanalytic concept that adult neurosis could not exist without a preexisting childhood neurosis shifted investigative focus to early childhood development on the assumption that it would provide clues to the origins of later developing psychiatric disturbances. This in turn led to an increasing acceptance of the child as a psychological being with a psyche, however immature, and permitted the exploration for psychological causality in the origin of childhood disturbance. Behavior disorders in children were no longer interpreted as evidence of constitutional deviation or degeneracy. The approach now adopted to the management of the disturbed child was a psychological one, as opposed to the moral sanctions and retributions in the form of punishment that had been the method adopted previously.

Child psychiatry as a discipline evolved from multidisciplinary roots with contributions coming from the fields of psychiatry, psychology, pediatrics, education, and neurology. Much of its present knowledge represents an integration of contributions by these various professional groupings to the changing concepts of child development.

It was Stanley Hall who first introduced the concept of child development and Wundt and Binet who first devised concrete measures for the assessment of intellectual development and functioning in the child. Itard and Sequin were pioneers in their endeavor to reach the retarded child, their case study of The Wild Boy of Aveyron being considered a historical landmark.

Guggenbuhl challenged the homogeneity of mental efficiency by describing Cretinism as reflecting a deficiency state, and Langdon described Down's syndrome (mongolism). Tay-Sachs described amaurotic family idiocy. Heller, an educator, described a progressive neurological disorder very similar to autistic syndrome, as described by Kanner (1943), but which had a somewhat different clinical and prognostic course. All of these contributions questioned the validity of mental deficiency as a uniform entity.

It has only been over the past 50 years that an endeavor has been made to identify, classify, and treat psychiatric disorders in children, despite the individual contributions made by Emminghaus, Ireland, Maudsley, and Spitzka in the 19th century. The only reference to childhood disorders by Krepelin in his monumental classification of psychiatric disorders was to early idiocy in children, which he suggested might be equivalent to dementia precox occurring in childhood.

The child guidance movement represented the earliest endeavors in the treatment of psychiatric disturbances in children. This movement had its beginnings in the early 1920s and was sponsored by the Commonwealth Fund which set up a series of demonstration centers throughout the country where parents, teachers, and social agencies could confer on the treatment of children with emotional problems. These centers were identified by a rather rigid collaboration between psychiatrists, psychologists, and social workers which initially excluded other professionals such as pediatricians, neurologists, educators, jurists, and public health officials. This exclusion was subsequently remedied. Major criticisms directed toward the child guidance centers concerned: 1) their tendency to remove themselves from other professional groupings, particularly their isolation from medical centers, 2) their restrictiveness on the type of mental handicap treated, and 3) the treatment focus in these centers which was so child-focused that the parents and families were seen as an extension of the child's therapy.

Subsequent developments in the field of child psychiatry led to the establishment of a series of child psychiatry departments in major pediatric centers across the country. These centers were sponsored by the Joshua Macey Foundation, and the earliest of these was developed at The Johns Hopkins Hospital under the direction of Dr. Leo Kanner in 1931. The goal of these centers was to establish a close liaison between the pediatrician and the child psychiatrist in the management of the multiplicity of disorders encountered in pediatric practice, both inpatient and outpatient.

THE FAMILY MOVEMENT

This movement arose, in part, because of the frustration experienced with the rigidities of the child guidance model, by which heavy emphasis on the child resulted in the exclusion of the family's needs and the role the family played in promoting health or creating dysfunction in the child.

Ackerman, a psychoanalyst and child psychiatrist, is credited with being the founder of the family movement. The family movement arose out of his belief that there was a need for greater study of the role environment played in the evolution of disturbance in the child. He noted that, in the child guidance model, therapists acted as missionaries dedicated to the rescue of the hurt child, and the child, consequently, was given the services of the psychiatrist while the mother was assigned a second class role. Ironically, child psychiatry failed to adopt the family approach, and, in the process, "It missed a unique potential for intervening in a natural group which offered an opportunity for new advances into the theory of personality and new models for conceptualizing mental illness" (Ackerman, 1967, p. 13). With this loss of initiative, the more systems-oriented family therapy developed by Sager and Kaplan (1972) began to dominate the field, and it has become one of the central modalities of treatment in community mental health centers. Unfortunately, many of the current models of family therapy, except for the one adopted by Minuchin (1965), have tended to operate in the direction of excluding children. Furthermore, Zilback (1974) has questioned the possibility of having true family therapy, particularly because the traditional division between adult and child psychiatry departments precludes family therapy that does not fit into one or the other model.

Reference has already been made to the incidence of disturbance in children. The 8% figure suggested, however, is believed to be a conservative one because of the many contacts disturbed children have with multiple agencies, each diagnosing the child according to its own frame of reference. Through attendance at a psychiatric clinic, a child may be diagnosed as having unsocialized aggressive reaction. At the same time, the same child may be considered as having a specific learning disability with behavioral difficulties in a school setting. The Department of Social Services may consider the child in need of supervision, or the child may be diagnosed as delinquent by the Department of Juvenile Services.

Other significant epidemiological factors include a suicide rate of 2,268 in the population ages 12–19 and 4,000 in the 15–24 age group (Cantor, 1975). There were 25,000 fatal accidents in the same population. Alcohol was a contributing factor in 50% of those accidents. The incidence of alcoholism is markedly rising in the teen-age population, rapidly replacing drug abuse as a major public health concern (Chafetz, 1974).

CHILD ABUSE

Child abuse is growing at an alarming rate in this country; it is estimated that there were 1,000,000 cases of abuse, with a projection of another 1,000,000 unreported cases, in 1976. The potential for many of these children to become abusing parents, represents a vast reservoir of future psychopathology.

Teen-age pregnancies also contribute to the incidence of disturbance in the child population not only because of the pregnant adolescents' own problems but also because the problems of their offspring contribute significantly to the steadily increasing population of handicapped children. In 1973, of the 600,000 teenage girls who gave birth, 210,000 were unmarried. This population is biologically at risk in child-bearing, with a 25% incidence of low birth weight, which makes the offspring susceptible to mental retardation and other handicapped conditions (Millar, 1975).

Finally, an area of increasing concern in recent years has been the fate of children where one or both parents are psychotic and living at home. Unfortunately, the current policy of returning severely disturbed schizophrenic patients to the community after they have returned to the state of marginal functioning has resulted in a large number of young children growing up in grossly dysfunctional environments. This dilemma has been heightened further by recent court decisions that have allowed floridly psychotic patients, who formerly would have been maintained in hospitals, to return to their homes. These families represent yet another large reservoir of children who have a significantly increased potential for manifesting psychiatric disturbance at a later date. It further illustrates the often encountered difficulty of devising treatment programs for both children and adults, particularly when the psychiatric treatment and planning for one may not be compatible at all with the well-being of the other.

HOW IS EMOTIONAL DISTURBANCE DEFINED?

One of the earliest definitions characterizes childhood disturbance as an aberration from the norm stemming from the growing child's relationship to self and environment. Biological and environmental factors condition the child's response, and the child's individuality and life's vicissitudes determine the form of expression. In the final analysis, there are three characteristics identifiable in all emotionally disturbed children: 1) lack of a steady state, 2) lack of stable internal images of the environment, and 3) excessive and persistent anxiety.

In the short history of the field, more than 40 classifications of childhood disorders have been proposed. Any classification of disturbances in children must take into account the developmental immaturity and plasticity of the child. This is best reflected in the Group for Advancement of Psychiatry (GAP) (1966) classification which encompasses psychosomatic, developmental, and psychosocial dimensions. It allows for the consideration of: 1) heredity, 2) family and environment, 3) developmental capacities and vulnerabilities of the child, and 4) plasticity of the child.

Because of the very nature of their patients, child psychiatrists, in the practice of their profession, must adopt an approach very different from the dyadic one of the adult counterpart. The field of exploration required for the purposes of evaluating the child inevitably leads to interdisciplinary involvement because it not only includes an assessment of the designated patient but also incorporates information provided by the family and agencies such as a health clinic and school. Only by adequately assessing the range of the child's life participation can one complete a diagnostic picture and plan meaningfully for the child's treatment. Consequently, the practice of child psychiatry not only involves the diagnosis and treatment of psychiatric disorders in children but also involves consultation with a variety of agencies, including hospitals (inpatient and outpatient services), other health clinics, schools, therapeutic daycare programs, departments of social services, and juvenile court systems. In all of these areas, the child psychiatrist contributes significantly not only by evaluating individual children but by promoting the mental health of children through assisting the professionals in these agencies to help children more meaningfully during periods of crisis.

EDUCATION IN CHILD PSYCHIATRY

The increasing numbers of disturbed children found in the general population raise serious questions as to how their needs are to be met, particularly when one considers that only 9% of the psychiatrists in the United States are involved in the care of children. The recognition that child psychiatry cannot meet the growing need for service has resulted in a proliferation of other professionals (nonmedical) in the field. The result has been that child psychiatrists have often found themselves competing with other

professionals who are as skilled or more skilled than they in psychotherapeutic procedures.

One of the factors that seems to militate against more diversified training in child psychiatry is that many programs have as their goal the
preparation of the trainee for private practice in the subspecialty. This
single-track training is believed by McDermott (1974) to account for the
fact that, despite an annual average of 750 child psychiatrists in training
over the past 15 years, there are fewer than 1,000 graduates of these programs who are Board-certified in the subspecialty of child psychiatry.

Sonis (1974), in a survey of 32 divisions of child psychiatry in academic
settings, found some uncertainties concerning the direction the subspecialty
should take. There seemed to be reasonable agreement on the range of
clinical experiences offered the trainee; these included: inpatient, outpatient,
daycare, emergency, pediatric liaison, and adolescence. Less clear was the
direction that should be taken in the area of research, which reflected the
fact that 24% of the programs had clinical research, followed by 67% with
developmental research, and 38% with operational and pharmocological
research. Currently, most authors agree that the image of the child psychiatrist of the future should be forged from: 1) a foundation in the biological
sciences, 2) a broad knowledge of the social sciences, 3) experience in
pediatrics, 4) training in child neurology, 5) a high level of skill in psychiatric diagnosis, and 6) a functional knowledge of psychotherapeutic techniques and their adaptations.

TRENDS IN RESEARCH

Despite frequent criticism leveled at child psychiatry, a considerable body
of research has been and continues to be conducted in the areas of: 1) epidemiology, 2) genetics, 3) child development, 4) neuropharmocology, and 5)
clinical psychiatry. Chess, Thomas, and Birch (1967) have investigated the
innate disposition of children as it relates to the vicissitudes of their
development, including parental responses and their outcome with respect
to the child. Fish (1976) more recently carried out a prospective investigation to determine the identifying characteristics of children who are likely to
become psychotic later in life. There has been a wide range of investigations
relating to patterns of parenting and their impact on child development, in
addition to a reappraisal of foster care and its role in promoting the well-
being of children. Institutional care of children has come under further
scrutiny, particularly with respect to the characteristics of those institutions
that prove beneficial to children, as opposed to the global condemnation of
the past.

A variety of intervention programs has been studied to enhance parent-
child interaction in the interest of furthering cognitive growth in the child.

Biological rhythms of children and adults and their effect on the individual's physical and psychological functioning have been studied. The bearing of biological rhythms on the medical management of patients, particularly as they relate to the optimal time for providing the appropriate pharmacological agent, also has been explored. Finally, increasing investigations in the field of neurotransmitters and psychoneuropharmocology have raised hope that an array of pharmacologicals will be forthcoming that will moderate significantly, if not cure, psychiatric disturbances in children and adults.

INSTITUTIONAL CARE OF CHILDREN

While institutions have played a role in the management of child disturbance, they have not been as widely used as in adult psychiatric disturbance. Again, institutions have been the object of vilification, often justifiably, considering the devastating impact on children of the early and current impersonal institutions. Increasing focus on the quality of care in modern institutions has reduced some of the extreme objections to the institutionalization of children. The modification of patterns of institutional care of children has closely followed changes in the adult sphere. Increasingly, the trend is toward short term care with increasing amounts of residential treatment provided in the community. Despite the major thrust to return the psychiatrically disturbed child to the least restrictive setting in the community, it is likely that a small but significant proportion will need traditional, although upgraded, residential care. Many of the endeavors to provide the benefits of a residential treatment setting for the psychiatrically disturbed are being further abridged by the increasing support of children's rights. There are at least four states at this time that have laws that give a minor the right to refuse treatment and/or hospitalization, despite the wishes of the parent. In effect, a minor has all the protection under the law, in relation to commitment procedures, that has been afforded an adult.

CURRENT ISSUES

Psychiatry today is confronted by a series of issues that not only affect its current practices but that also will significantly influence future directions in the field. The issues, although not necessarily discrete, relate to psychiatry as an identifiable profession, to the clinical practice of psychiatry, to psychiatric education, research, and to funding.

Over the past decade, the proliferation of professional and paraprofessional groupings that qualify their activities with the term "psychiatric" or use the prefix "psycho" has resulted in considerable confusion for the uninitiated. The plethora of such titles in the mental health market place has resulted in much confusion in the minds of the public and among those high in government. Even when governmental officials can discriminate among professional groups, they often choose not to for reasons of fiscal convenience. Unfortunately, this practice has filtered down to some hospital administrators whose primary goal is to fill beds rather than provide adequate professional care. This practice has all too often resulted in paraprofessionals being the main providers of care in the wards of mental hospitals and in the inpatient units of community hospitals.

A further complication in the rather confusing picture is the fact that many psychiatrists function exclusively as psychotherapists, and, as a result, there is no longer any clear differentiation between their role and that of lay therapists. The psychiatrist (Freedman, 1974), as a physician trained in the biological and behavioral sciences, is to be identified by the professional skills employed in the clinical assessment of patients. These skills are based on 1) competence in judging biological and psychosocial processes affecting the patient, 2) a perspective on the range of disorders from transient to severe, organic, and functional, 3) expertise at recognizing particular constellations of complaints, and 4) skill in the management of behavioral emergencies when etiology is obscure. The role also includes selecting appropriate therapeutic regimes for the patient and ensuring competent delivery. The psychiatrist's professional role is bound by codes of ethics promulgated by both the American Medical and American Psychiatric Associations. These professional organizations prescribe guidelines regarding individual practice and regulate the manner in which associations with other professionals (nonmedical) are established.

Over the past decade, clinical psychiatry has experienced increasing encroachments on its field of practice. A series of court decisions have endeavored to define commitment procedures and the rights of patients when hospitalized. There also have been court endeavors to clarify issues related to informed consent and confidentiality, particularly when competing interests have been involved, such as the rights of parents versus those of a child.

There have been several other areas in which the courts or legislative bodies have taken specific action in regulating clinical practice; the most prominent of these are related to the use of electroconvulsive therapy and psychosurgery.

The inexorable intrusion of the federal government into the field of medicine, purportedly in an attempt to relate cost effectiveness to quality care and to curb runaway inflation in the field of health care, has resulted in the establishment of a network of Professional Standard Review Organizations (PSROs). With the support of the AMA, these PSROs oversee and regulate patterns of health care within the Medicaid and Medicare programs. This innovation is considered a harbinger of procedures to come and presages the large bureaucracy that inevitably will result from the passage of national health legislation. Already the impact of the PSROs is being felt across the country because of the powers with which they have been invested, allowing for the regulation of hospital admissions, length of stay, and the character (not synonymous with quality) of treatment provided. Psychiatry, in particular, is affected by this trend because the PSROs, as a consequence of their focus on cost effectiveness, often interfere with meaningful planning for the psychiatrically ill.

In keeping with the forebodings as to the future, particularly in the field of psychiatry, are the observations of Gibson (1974). In his review of the many proposals for national health insurance, he noted that most had as their goal, not only to change the physician payment system but also, through financing, to control the delivery of services. Most patients in need of psychiatric care would be forced or induced, because of financial necessity, to obtain service within an organized system of care, e.g., the Health Maintenance Organization (HMO), which, selectively, would offer a much wider range of psychiatric coverage, at the same cost, than could be provided by the private psychiatrist. This, in effect, would result in serious encroachment on the private practice of psychiatry and would most probably provide a further stimulus for expansion of the community mental health center, a model as yet unproved as to either its therapeutic or cost effectiveness.

The use of finances as a mechanism of control in the field of medicine also raises serious question about the future of medical training programs and the direction they should take. There are many who believe that residency training, which has long been a basis for preparing highly skilled physicians for practice, will, as national health insurance becomes more and more a reality, become less possible in its present form. The HMO model, which puts a premium on outpatient as opposed to inpatient hospital care, will markedly limit the range of experiences that a hospital-centered program can provide. This is of considerable import to the field of psychiatry in which training, because of the nature of psychiatric patients, has always been hospital- or institutionally based. It is difficult to envision training programs being located primarily in community mental health centers, as has been proposed. In a recent review of psychiatric residency programs and the quality of their education, it was found that community mental health center ownership was not often associated with programs of a high quality. Training programs of higher quality were generally to be found in locations where there were well defined admission procedures that were thoroughly and seriously followed by both faculty and current residents. Those programs deemed superior included well defined child psychiatry training, continuity in the case of patients over the entire period of training, a close association with a medical care system (particularly in university settings), and the presence of other service systems, e.g., social, educational, and legal (Daniels et al., 1977).

Finally, research, which is the life blood of the development of any science or medical discipline, has in the case of psychiatry fallen on difficult times, particularly with respect to funding. Brown (1977) noting the difficulties that arose because of the traditional role of the National Institute of Mental Health in overseeing the holy triad of research, training, and service, observed it was time to more discretely define the research component of the institute. He reported that, between 1967 and 1977, there was a significant reduction in the funding of research from 103.8 million dollars in 1967 to the current figure of 95.9 million dollars, a drop that far exceeds 7.9 million dollars, when one considers the impact of inflation. Some of this reduction arose, in part, out of confusion concerning the various roles of the National Institute of Mental Health, a confusion that has been traditional. Even though there have been considerable advancements in the field of psychiatric research, the criticisms of both the service and training aspects of the Institute often have been used to reduce funding for research.

Brown concluded by commenting,

> The present Mental Health research crisis is not merely an economic and administrative debate the resolution of which will entail either a recouping of research resources or a downgrading of research and isolation. Rather it is now believed that the decline in research support, with all its contributing dynamics is hinged to the cohesiveness and success of the total Mental Health Program in this country (1977, p. 120).

Psychiatry today, despite significant advances in the field, is faced with considerable uncertainty as to its future course. This uncertainty has arisen after almost two decades of testing and validating its theoretical formulations, through their applications to the understanding of psychobiological, intrapsychic, interpersonal, sociocultural, and sociopolitical phenomena. While the origin of this uncertainty is in part a natural byproduct of an evolving science, it also is rooted in complex social changes that have resulted in the emergence of the egalitarian ethos and a significant change in public thinking as to the right to health care. The egalitarian stance, which seeks instant explanations and comprehensions of the most complex of issues, has demanded immediate relief from distress through instant mental health (Vanderpool, 1973). The refusal of the public to continue to accept the lack of adequate mental health care as a misfortune, but instead to view it as an intolerable injustice, has resulted in the right to treatment becoming enshrined in our jargon (Freedman, 1974) and being mandated by the courts, e.g., *Wyatt* v. *Stickney* (Stickney, 1971).

The task of providing for the mental health needs of the population is a formidable one and can only be realized through a concerted multidisciplinary approach to the problem. Yet, there are specific factors that create some uncertainties as to the way psychiatry might participate in such an ambitious endeavor. Already, concerns are being voiced about the dwindling number of available psychiatrists, despite the many optimistic statements by the National Institute for Mental Health. There also have been governmental efforts, past and present, to redistribute unrealistically the role of the psychiatrist to primary care physicians, to other mental health professionals, and even to paraprofessionals. Many ill-conceived national health insurance bills have excluded psychiatric care under the guise of being actuarily unsound, and even those that include some coverage have abridged the patient's right to the freedom of contracting a psychiatrist of his/her choice for mental health services. All have created a significant danger that quality psychiatric care may become the province of the elite and the wealthy.

Finally, the move toward the elimination of all training grants by the Washington bureaucracy has placed increasing pressures on training directors to seek out alternative sources of funding. There also has been an increasing emphasis on paying patients as the basis of training. Modalities of treatment are being fostered that are fiscally sound. This represents a return to the private practice model and a move away from the eclectic and diversified psychiatric training so necessary if the mental health needs of the nation are to be met. Hopefully, a more enlightened government will address this problem and return support at least to those programs whose interests lie in the mental health needs of the total population.

REFERENCES

Ackerman, N. W. 1967. The future of family psychotherapy. *In* N. W. Ackerman, F. L. Beatman, and S. N. Sherman (eds.), Expanding Theory and Practice in Family Therapy, pp. 3–16. Family Service Association of America, New York.

Aiguist, Senator A. E. 1974. Final Report: Senate Select Committee on Proposed Phase Out of State Hospital Services. State of California, Sacramento.

Arnhoff, F. N., and Humbar, A. H. 1973. The Nation's Psychiatrists—1970 Survey. American Psychiatric Association, Washington, D.C.

Beers, C. W. 1939. A Mind that Found Itself. Doubleday, Garden City, N.Y.

Brill, H. 1975. The mental hospital and its patients. Psychiatr. Ann. 5:352–359.

Brown, B. S. 1976. The life of psychiatry. Am. J. Psychiatry 133:485–495.

Brown, B. S. 1977. The crisis in mental health research. Am. J. Psychiatry 134:113–120.

Butterfield, H. 1931. The Whig Interpretation of History. G. Bell and Sons, London.

Cantor, P. 1975. The effects of youthful suicide on the family. Psychiatr. Opin. 12:6–11.

Caplan, G., and Caplan, R. B. 1967. Community psychiatry: Basic concepts. *In* A. M. Freedman and H. I. Kaplan (eds.), Comprehensive Textbook of Psychiatry, pp. 1149–1516. The Williams and Wilkens Company, Baltimore.

Carmichael, H. 1962. The American Board of Psychiatry and Neurology—Some Comments and Perspectives. Presented to Texas Neuropsychiatric Association.

Chafetz, M. E. 1974. Adolescent drinking and parent responsibility. Newsletter. Parent Council of Washington, Washington, D.C.

Chess, S., Thomas, A., and Birch, H. G. 1967. Behavioral problems revisited—Findings of an anterspective study. J. Acad. Child Psychiatry 6:321–331.

Daniels, R. S., Abraham, A. S., Carcie, R., and Wilkinson, C. 1977. Characteristics of psychiatric residency programs and quality of education. Am. J. Psychiatry 13(suppl):7–10.

Ennis, B. 1972. Prisoners of Psychiatry: Mental Patients, Psychiatry and the Law. Harcourt, Brace and Javanovich, New York.

Erickson, E. H. 1963. Childhood and Society. W. W. Norton and Company, Inc., New York.

Fish, B. 1976. An approach to prevention in infants at risk for schizophrenia. J. Child Psychiatry 1:62–82.

Freedman, A. M. 1974. Presidential address: Creating the future. Am. J. Psychiatry 131:749–756.

Freedman, D. X., and Gordon, R. P. 1973. Psychiatry under seige: Attacks from without. Psychiatr. Ann. 3:10–34.

Gibson, R. 1974. The use of finance to control the delivery of services. Psychiatr. Ann. 4:22–41.

Glasscote, R. 1975. The future of the community mental health center. Psychiatr. Ann. 5:69–80.

Grob, G. 1973. Mental Institutions in America: Social Policy to 1875. Free Press, New York.

Grob, G. 1975. Psychiatry and mental hospitals in the nineteenth century America: Interpretation. Psychiatr. Digest 36:36–44.

Group for Advancement of Psychiatry. 1966. Psychopathological Disorders in Childhood: Theoretical Consideration and a Proposed Classification. Formulated by the Committee on Child Psychiatry. Vol. VI. Report No. 62. Mental Health Materials, New York.

Houck, J. H. 1975. The private psychiatric hospital. Psychiatr. Ann. 5:25–36.

Joint Commission on Mental Illness and Health. 1961. Final Report. Action for Mental Health. Basic Books, New York.

Kanner, L. 1943. Autistic disturbance in affective contacts. Nerv. Child 2:217–250.

Kennedy, J. F. 1963. Message for Mental Illness and Mental Retardation. U.S. Congress, 85th Session. Washington, D.C.

Lebensohn, Z. M. 1975. Private psychiatric practice. Psychiatr. Ann. 5:56–68.

McDermott, J., Jr. 1974. Certification of the child psychiatrist. What is special about the specialist? J. Child Psychiatry 13:196–203.

Meyer, A. 1952. How Can Our State Hospitals Promote a Practical Interest in Psychiatry Among the Practitioners? Collected Papers of Adolf Meyer. Vol. 4. The Johns Hopkins Press, Baltimore.

Meyer, A. 1957. Psychobiology, A Science of Man. Charles C Thomas, Springfield, Ill.

Millar, H. E. C. 1975. Approaches to Adolescent Health Care in the 1970's. U.S. Department of Health, Education and Welfare. Publication No. (HSA) 75-5016. Rockville, Md.

Minuchin, S. 1965. Conflict resolution and family therapy. Psychiatry 28:278–286.

Mora, G. 1967. History of Psychiatry. Current Issues in Psychiatry. Science House, Inc., New York.

Noyes, A. P., and Kolb, L. C. 1958. Modern Clinical Psychiatry. W. B. Saunders Company, Philadelphia.

Ozarin, L., and Taube, C. 1974. Psychiatric in-patients: Who, where and the future? Am. J. Psychiatry 131:98-104.

Querido, A. 1969. The shaping of community mental health care. Int. J. Psychiatry 7:300-311.

Ransom, A. J. 1973. Social psychiatry: An overview. Am. J. Psychiatry 130:841-849.

Redlich, F. C., and Freedman, D. X. 1966. The Theory and Practice of Psychiatry. Basic Books, New York.

Reich, R., and Siegel, L. 1973. The chronically mentally ill: Shuffle to oblivion. Psychiatr. Ann. 3:35-55.

Rogawski, A. S. 1974. The new paraprofessional's role in mental health. Psychiatr. Ann. 4:59-71.

Sager, C., and Kaplan, H. 1972. Progress in Group and Family Therapy. Brunner/Mazel, New York.

Sonis, M. 1974. Pilot study of division of child psychiatry in 32 schools of medicine. J. Child Psychiatry 13:604-617.

Stickney, S. 1971. Wyatt vs Stickney. The right to treatment. Psychiatr. Ann. 4:32-45.

Sullivan, H. S. 1953. Interpersonal Theory of Psychiatry. W. W. Norton and Company, Inc., New York.

Taube, C. A., and Redlick, R. W. 1973. Provisional Data on Patient Care Episodes in Mental Health Facilities. Statistical Note. National Institute of Mental Health, Division of Biometry, Rockville, Md.

Vanderpool, J. 1973. The quest for instant mental health. Arch. Gen. Psychiatry 29:134-137.

Zilback, J. J. 1974. The family in family therapy. J. Child Psychiatry 13:459-467.

Zilboorg, G. 1941. A History of Medical Psychology. W. W. Norton and Company, Inc., New York.

PSYCHOLOGY

Alfred M. Wellner

Psychology as a health and human service profession has grown substantially in the past three decades (Schofield, 1969, 1976; Garfield, 1974; Rabin, 1974; Reisman, 1976; Woods, 1976). Psychologists currently are providing a variety of services in hospitals, mental health centers, private practice, group practices, university health centers, correctional facilities, family service agencies, school systems, and other areas. It is difficult to identify a human service arena in which psychologists do not participate and contribute.

The field of psychology is rooted in the behavioral sciences, and the psychologist has functioned as a scientist practitioner. Psychology is somewhat unique among the health professions in that the education and training of psychologists has generally been attained in graduate schools of arts and sciences rather than professional schools. The development of professional schools of psychology granting the Psy.D. (Doctorate of Psychology) degree is a relatively new experience; the California School of Professional Psychology established in 1969 was the first such program.

According to the standards of the profession, a doctoral degree is required for the title of psychologist. The doctoral degree in psychology indicates that the psychologist has gained special and extensive training in research and experimental design and has acquired a scientific attitude toward problems. Study for the doctorate has provided the psychologist with the opportunity to continually evaluate the nature of services rendered and to modify approaches based on the effectiveness of those services. This data-oriented approach or penchant for inquiry and skepticism is often the hallmark of a fully functioning professional psychologist. The professional psychologist completes a 4–5-year graduate academic program leading to the doctoral degree and also serves a one-year intensive internship. This represents a 5–6-year period (after four years of undergraduate work) of concentrated work and experience focusing on the science of psychology and its application to human welfare.

The psychologist then must balance the application of skills and techniques in service delivery with the scientific rigor demanded of all behavioral scientists, sometimes not an easy balancing act. Although much of the growth in the field and the contribution that psychology has made in the human services field may be a consequence of this balance and combined strength, it has also placed psychologists in difficult dilemmas and priority challenges. Some of these dilemmas and challenges are reflected in the interactions between psychologists and their professional colleagues in which the psychologist may be viewed as somewhat distant or unwilling to devote full energies to service deliveries. In such cases, the scientific or research value systems are viewed as encroachments on the service delivery time. Depending on the psychologist's general orientation and his/her interpersonal skills in handling these exchanges with colleagues, the outcome can be a very fine and effective integration of research and service delivery.

THE PROFESSION OF PSYCHOLOGY—
SOME BACKGROUND INFORMATION

The American Psychological Association (APA) is the national professional association of psychologists with approximately 45,000 members in 1977 (APA, 1977a). Full membership in the APA requires a doctoral degree in psychology. The 33 divisions of the APA attest to the diversity of specialized interests of psychologists:

General Psychology
Teaching of Psychology
Experimental Psychology
Evaluation and Measurement
Physiological and Comparative
   Psychology
Developmental Psychology
Personality and Social Psychology
The Society for the Psychological
   Study of Social Issues
Psychology and the Arts
Clinical Psychology
Consulting Psychology
Industrial and Organizational
   Psychology
Educational Psychology
School Psychology
Counseling Psychology
Psychologists in Public Service

Military Psychology
Adult Development and Aging
Society of Engineering Psychologists
Rehabilitation Psychology
Consumer Psychology
Philosophical Psychology
Experimental Analysis of Behavior
History of Psychology
Community Psychology
Psychopharmacology
Psychotherapy
Psychological Hypnosis
Humanistic Psychology
Mental Retardation
Population and Environmental
   Psychology
Psychology of Women
Psychologists Interested in Religious
   Issues

The range of activities reflected in the division titles also suggests the diversity of activities in which psychologists are engaged. For example, the industrial psychologist may be involved in managerial selection, personnel development, or conflict resolution at a manufacturing plant. The physiological psychologist may be engaged in laboratory research, may be teach-

Photograph by Richard Holden.

ing in a graduate university, or may be consulting in a medical school on issues relating to stress. The clinical psychologist may be engaged in research on intervention approaches, may be providing diagnostic and other assessment procedures in a mental health center, or may be engaged in the full-time private practice of psychology (APA, 1975; Wellner and Mills, 1977). It is important to stress the diversity of interests and educational backgrounds of psychologists and the different specialties of psychology while recognizing that all psychologists have a common educational background in the general science of psychology.

The APA provides the profession with the general standards of professional educational preparation and practice. For example, the APA reviews and accredits university doctoral programs in clinical, counseling, and school psychology. These have been the traditional applied or professional programs in psychology. APA accreditation of a program implies that the program has met the standards established by the profession for sound professional education in psychology (APA, 1973). There are now approximately 120 university doctoral programs in the fields mentioned above that have met the APA accreditation criteria.

In addition to reviewing and accrediting university training programs, the APA Committee on Accreditation also accredits internship training programs. There are currently over 120 APA-approved internships. These are one-year, full-time internships, typically served in hospitals, mental health centers, university health or counseling centers, etc., in which the psychologist as part of his/her doctoral training spends a full year, full-time, under the careful supervision of senior psychologists in the application of psychological principles and techniques in the delivery of health and human services.

The APA accreditation system has provided the profession with a mechanism for establishing appropriate standards of professional education while maintaining a reasonable degree of academic freedom. Programs are evaluated in terms of the goals set, permitting a range of training models and orientations. The accreditation system also has provided a professionally established mechanism for testing innovative approaches, techniques, or theories within the professional marketplace before establishing them as reasonable, usual, or acceptable professional psychological practices.

The APA also has established a set of ethical standards by which all psychologists must abide (APA, 1977b). In addition, a code of standards for providers of psychological services (APA, 1977c) has been developed recently which provides another set of benchmarks for professional practices. The Ethical Standards and the Standards for Providers offer both the profession and the public statements of principles for psychological practices and for interactions with other professions, consumers, and clients of services.

These Standards represent the attainment of a goal towards which the Association has striven for over twenty years; namely, to codify a uniform set of standards for psychological practice that would serve the respective needs of users, providers and third-party purchasers and sanctioners of psychological services. In addition the Association has established a standing committee charged with keeping the *Standards* responsive to the needs of these groups, and with upgrading and extending them progressively as the profession and science of Psychology continue to develop new knowledge, improved methods and additional modes of psychological service. These *Standards* have been established by organized psychology as a means of self-regulation to protect the public interest (APA Standards, 1977c, p. 2).

LICENSING/CERTIFICATION

The title and practice of psychology is restricted through statutory legislation in 49 states and in the District of Columbia. Only the state of Missouri has nonstatutory certification of psychologists for practice which is handled by the state Psychological Association. Any psychologist who holds himself/herself out to the public must be licensed or certified in the state for such practice. The license or certificate is generally obtained after passing a written examination and a review of credentials. The examination covers the general field of psychology and some of the applied professional areas. General groundwork in psychology is a requisite for passing the examination and for obtaining the license or certificate to practice.

Currently there are approximately 25,500 licensed or certified psychologists in the United States (Wellner and Mills, 1977). Because the licenses or certificates to practice are generic (i.e., they cover all specialties in psychology), this number does not reflect the total number of service providers in the country. It is not necessary for someone to be a member of the APA or the state Psychological Association in order to obtain a license to practice. Clearly then, there are a number of members of the APA who are not licensed or certified to practice and there are also a number of licensed or certified psychologists who are not members of the APA (Wellner and Mills, 1977).

In the licensing of psychologists, a stage agency, typically the state Board of Examiners of Psychology, has the responsibility for reviewing the credentials, administering the examination, and passing on the qualifications for licensure in that state. There is an increasing tendency now to include public members (nonpsychologists) on the boards of professional examinations. This is true for other professions as well as for psychology.

The state Boards of Examiners of Psychology grew out of the public demand for some control over the delivery of psychological services. The state Boards are designed to protect the public from persons who hold themselves out as psychologists but do not meet the professional standards established by the Board. Typically, the license or certificate is obtained if the individual has a doctoral degree in psychology and one or more years of supervised experience in the field.

THE NATIONAL REGISTER OF HEALTH SERVICE PROVIDERS IN PSYCHOLOGY

In view of the generic nature of licensing, it has been extremely difficult to identify the number of health providers from among all of the licensed/ certified psychologists. The Council for the National Register of Health Service Providers was established at the request of the APA Board of Directors in 1974 (Council for the National Register, 1975; Zimet and Wellner, 1977). Its purpose was to establish a system by which psychologists who are licensed or certified to practice can more readily be identified. The National Register, using the established criteria of the profession and the statutes covering the title and practice of psychology in the states and the District of Columbia established the following criteria for listing in the National Register:

1. A license or certificate from the state Board of Examiners in Psychology
2. A doctoral degree from a regionally accredited university
3. Two years of supervised experience in health services

A grandfather/mother clause (effective until January 1, 1978) has permitted persons who have been in practice for some time and who are licensed or certified to also apply for listing in the National Register without the doctoral degree, provided they have at least six years of experience.

The 1976 National Register and Supplements (1977) include approximately 9,000 psychologists, 88% of whom have the doctoral degree. These are psychologists who have applied voluntarily for listing in the Register and who meet the stated standards for such listing. The National Register has become recognized as a major professional resource for identifying qualified health service providers. A number of insurance and third party payers have formally recognized the Register for reimbursement purposes.

On the basis of a recently conducted national survey of all licensed/ certified psychologists, the National Register has determined that there are approximately 18,000 licensed/certified psychologists who are health service providers. This represents approximately 74% of all licensed/ certified psychologists (n = 25,500) (Wellner and Mills, 1977). The data indicate that, of that group, approximately 25% are in full-time private practice, with over 55% in part-time private practice.

Other information compiled by the National Register relating to the services of psychologists in private practice indicate that approximately 90% of these psychologists provide individual psychotherapy services. Approximately 72% of all psychologists in private practice offer diagnostic or assessment services. Close to one-third of all psychologists in private practice offer group therapy, and more than 50% provide consultative services.

AMERICAN BOARD OF PROFESSIONAL PSYCHOLOGY

The American Board of Professional Psychology (ABPP) was established in 1947 to grant the diplomate status to psychologists who apply for examination and who have achieved high degrees of competencies in their services. To be eligible for the examination, the psychologist must have the doctoral degree and at least five years of postdoctoral experience. Very few states had licensing laws in the late 1940s, and ABPP was a procedure developed by the profession to identify practitioners. ABPP has granted the diplomate in four fields: clinical, counseling, school, and industrial/organizational psychology. There are almost 2,400 psychologists in the country who hold the diplomate. (APA, 1977a). Most of the diplomates ($n = 1,605$) have been granted in the clinical specialty. Although the diplomate remains a significant credential available to the practitioner in psychology, there are mixed feelings in the field regarding the diplomate and its examination procedure. The examination for diplomate, noted for its high anxiety-inducing effects upon applicants, involves review by peers of activities, cases, and specific services.

ABPP has been engaged recently in promoting continuing education programs for psychologists and has helped develop the Council for the National Register of Health Service Providers in Psychology.

AMERICAN BOARD OF PSYCHOLOGICAL HYPNOSIS

The American Board of Psychological Hypnosis (ABPH) grants diplomates in clinical hypnosis and experimental hypnosis. Currently, there are approximately 100 diplomates in hypnosis.

SPECIALTY AREAS OF PSYCHOLOGISTS

Of all psychologists who are members of the APA, the primary employment setting is the university, with over 30% of all APA members working in such a setting. Approximately 15% of the APA members have identified hospitals and clinics as their primary employment setting.

In terms of specialty areas in psychology, the clinical and community psychologist represents the largest group with over 30% of all APA psychologists identifying that as an area of specialty. Counseling and school psychologists comprise approximately 15% of the specialty areas of psychologists who are members of the APA. The other specialty areas identified are: 1) developmental, personality, and social psychology (15%); 2) experimental physiological psychology (approximately 12%); 3) engineering, industrial and organizational psychologists (approximately 8%); educational psychologists (8%); and 4) systems methodology and techniques (approximately 7%) (APA, 1975).

SERVICES PROVIDED BY PSYCHOLOGISTS

Within a set of functions identified as appropriate to psychological services, there, no doubt, are a number that would seem to be unique to the profession of psychology as well as a number of other functions that may be shared with other professional groups. Particularly in the area of human services and attempts to deal with "the whole person" it is very likely that different professional groups provide comparable services, and, indeed, some of the specific techniques may be very similar. Each profession, however, has a fund of knowledge and a basic core of information upon which it builds applications of that field. Psychological services obviously are related directly to the basic science of psychology. The application of psychological services, therefore, is related directly to psychological theory and practice. If one searches for unique characteristics or unique contributions provided by psychologists, they will be found in the relationship of the services rendered to the theory and science of the field of psychology.

Psychology is, of course, the science of behavior, and the field of psychology focuses on the understanding of behavior and on an understanding of the conditions or environment that lead to certain kinds of behaviors. This basic knowledge can then be applied by the professional psychologist to change or modify an individual's behaviors, adjustment, or overall coping effectiveness. An understanding of the conditions that lead to an existing behavior or an existing set of abilities in an individual may be viewed as a diagnostic or assessment function. The changing of maladaptive, disturbed, or disturbing behaviors or coping mechanisms may be viewed as treatment.

The psychologist's basic fund of knowledge generally covers the following fields of psychology: learning, motivation, perception, human development, physiological systems, statistics, research methodology, neurological functions, measurement, and group processes. These subjects form the basic core of general psychology. The scientific data that have evolved in these fields are the bases upon which the psychologist has developed procedures, skills, and techniques to deliver a variety of human services.

In addition to this basic core of psychology, the professional psychologist who delivers human services also has mastered the basic applied principles. These include abnormal behavior (psychopathology), interviewing, the use of measurement for diagnosing and assessing the range of human functions (including intelligence, intra- and interpersonal functioning, memory, thinking, behavior deviance, etc.), principles of psychotherapy, counseling and behavior change, the application of the scientific method for developing program evaluation systems, and basic research.

The applied psychologist, then, in contrast to the basic science psychologist, uses the fund of knowledge of the science of psychology in delivering human services. There are numerous scientific publications in psychology that provide the psychologist with updated scientific information on the basic principles of the field. The applied psychologist's special strengths are the integration and application of the science with methods and procedures for dealing with human problems.

The internship experiences are, of course, the clearest example of how the basic science and application are integrated. It is during the internship year that the psychologist is continually reminded that what he/she does needs to be verifiable or validated by the science. If the psychologist administers a standardized test to an individual and proceeds to interpret the test, the psychologist must be able to provide substantial evidence that the interpretations are based on studies in the field that have been found to be reliable (consistent) as well as valid (appropriate to the problem). Thus, the psychologist continually refers to the literature in developing the skills and procedures necessary to do a competent job. It is obviously clear that to be able to maintain this approach, continuing professional development is essential. As the field changes and grows, the psychologist must be able to maintain his/her skills based on emerging knowledge.

With a field as diverse and extensive as psychology, it is difficult to comprehensively cover all the appropriate services. It is evident that, in view of the diversity of the field, different psychologists with different professional educational backgrounds and specialties may offer different services. Some of the human service functions provided by psychologists include:

1. Psychotherapy
2. Behavior change
3. Diagnostic/evaluation assessment
4. Consultation
5. Program evaluation

6. Teaching
7. Basic research
8. Program administration
9. Program planning
10. Career counseling
11. Organizational development

The focus in the following sections is on those direct service functions that are most frequently identified with psychological services. Woods' (1976) volume, *Career Opportunities for Psychologists,* identifies a number of emerging functions and services of the field. Review of any recent professional journal in psychology also will reflect the very significant diversity of services and functions of psychologists.

Psychotherapy

Psychologists are skilled and trained in the delivery of psychotherapeutic services. Psychologists who provide psychotherapy include the whole range of psychotherapeutic orientations. There are psychologists who are psychoanalytically oriented, neo-Freudians, rational emotive therapists, client-centered therapists, Gestalt practitioners, behavioral practitioners, and others. Both through university doctoral programs and through internship activities, the psychologist typically has had considerable experience in dealing with individuals in both one-to-one and group therapy situations. Increasingly, psychologists also are involved in marital, conjoint, and family therapy activities.

The therapy provided by the psychologist will vary depending on the nature of the client's or patient's problems as well as on the general orientation of the therapist. Therapy can be of a short term, time-limited nature or a more extended, therapeutic interaction.

It is in the area of delivering psychotherapy to individuals and groups that the fields of psychology and psychiatry have often been in conflict. Psychiatrists have often maintained that only an individual trained in medicine can assume responsibility for the psychotherapy of an individual. However, the psychologist's training and skills in psychotherapy and behavior change generally have led the psychologist to effectively deliver psychotherapy and assume responsibilities for such services to large numbers of people.

The psychiatrist and the psychologist have different perspectives on an individual's problems and behaviors. The psychologist is familiar with how an individual learns to do what he/she does and can identify the conditions under which such patterns will emerge. To provide service for the vast majority of clients who have adjustment problems, training in medicine for the psychologist to provide services is unnecessary; most of the behavior and adjustment problems presented by individuals are not related to medical or physical problems requiring medical diagnoses and medication. An excellent article developing this point has been written by a psychiatrist (Mariner, 1966). Over the past two decades, it has become fairly well recognized that psychologists are able to competently provide psychotherapy and can assume full responsibility for their professional practice.

As mentioned above, approximately 90% of all psychologists in private practice offer psychotherapy services. Psychologists are trained to work with individuals with mild behavioral problems as well as with those who have more severe impairments. Psychologists will assume responsibility for the management of the course of treatment when appropriate. Of course, in group settings or interdisciplinary situations, the responsibilities can be shared or apportioned depending on the nature of the problem and the availability of resources. It is important to emphasize, however, that the professional psychologist is well trained to handle the full range of responsibilities for patients in therapy.

Behavior Change

One of the principal components of professional education in psychology is the field of human learning. How an individual learns and how an individual's behavior is related to that learning are issues at the core of the psychologist's training. The general scientific orientation of the field also encourages the psychologist to deal with observable events. The field of behavior change has received widespread attention over the past decade. "Behavior modification" has become a catchword. The identification of specific behaviors or patterns of behaviors that need to be modified or changed has become an important activity in a range of human service settings. The use of behavioral approaches to work with the retarded, to control substance abuse, to deal with bizarre behaviors, to allay phobias, anxieties, etc. has grown phenomenally over the past few years.

The origins of the behavioral approaches are embedded in general psychology. From Skinner's early work in operant conditioning, a whole field of behavior analysis has emerged. Applications of behavioral approaches have been made in hospitals, clinics, school systems, correctional facilities, parent education programs, and all other human service activities. There is hardly one human service function or area that has not been involved in testing behavioral approaches. The growth of behavior analysis has been, in fact, a revolutionary development.

The value of behavioral approaches is that it permits the pinpointing of a problem area and the development of strategies to deal with that behavior. Behavioral approaches also have built-in evaluative systems in that they demand a high degree of data collection and recording. The widespread use of behavioral approaches is, in part, the result of the efficacy of the procedure. If the factors that are reinforcing to an individual can be identified, the conditions that will change that individual's behavior can be established.

Although the use of behavioral approaches has become widespread, there also have been widespread abuses. The application of appropriate procedures for the reinforcement of certain behaviors requires a substantial amount of knowledge about learning, conditions of reinforcement, and the individual. It is not a simple procedure in which all one has to do is dispense M&Ms. Too many programs have failed because of the lack of professional knowledge regarding behavior and behavior change. Furthermore, issues also have been raised regarding the rights of individuals in the implementation of behavioral programs.

Behavioral approaches can be very effective instruments in assisting individuals to cope more effectively. This is true for a range of human service problems and with persons of all ages. *It is not, however, a panacea. The blind application of behavioral technology should be avoided.* The technology and procedures, if used appropriately and with good professional resources, can be very helpful. Psychology and psychologists have much to contribute to the effective application of behavioral programs.

The questions relating to the personal rights of individuals in a behavior change program have received increasing attention. Some of the procedures used in public settings (mental hospitals, prisons, and juvenile delinquency homes) have included questionable practices. For example, we know that, if we deprive someone of a needed commodity (food, sleep, water), the presentation of that commodity will be all the more powerful in developing behavior patterns. If food is to be a reinforcing stimulus, it is important that the subject be hungry, otherwise food has no impact. These principles have been generally demonstrated in the laboratory with both animals and humans. In order to deal dramatically with some of the problems in some of the institutions, there have been occasions in which the staff has deprived individuals of what have generally been accepted as basic human needs. Although the goal is for rehabilitation or the person's own benefit or even society's benefit, the ethical question arises as to whether or not society has the right to deprive an individual of his/her basic needs, however noble the cause. Even when informed consent is received, the validity of that informed consent may be questioned on the basis of the very nature of the situation. How much choice for example, does a prisoner have? How meaningful is an informed consent from a retarded person or even from the guardian of a retarded person? The guardian faces the special dilemma of making a judgment for his/her relative or trustee without some of the technical knowledge of the issues related to the treatment program. States, the federal government, and institutions have been grappling with this question, and standards for appropriate practices are being developed. It seems clear that a consensus has been emerging that encourages and/or directs the use of voluntary, open participation, informed consent, full disclosure, and the avoidance of deprivation states.

Diagnostic Evaluation/Assessment

Psychologists are widely known and regarded as professionals trained in the assessment of personality, intelligence, academic achievement, perceptual/ motor functioning, vocational adjustment, behavioral performance, and other areas of functioning. Indeed, there are a number of human service professionals who tend to have a limited view of psychologists as "testers." Although the psychologist is particularly trained in the application of testing procedures, it is but one of several professional functions.

The value of sound psychological testing is that it provides an opportunity for a reliable method of evaluating the client's status, strengths, and weaknesses in a well controlled situation. The test results then can be compared to standards of performance (norms) or can be evaluated over a period of time on the same person for determination of changes. The standardized testing situation is an essential diagnostic procedure in assessing the individual's difficulties as well as his/her areas of (potential) strengths. There are a number of excellent texts on the subject; the reader is referred to *Clinical Methods in Psychology* (Weiner, 1976), as an example.

Psychological testing, although proved useful in a variety of situations in the human services field, also has come under considerable criticism. Concerns have been raised regarding the applicability of some of the testing procedures to the clients served. Potential abuses of testing procedures have led to some public antagonism. At times, misinformation or distortion of information has led to sharp criticisms of testing procedures in school systems and elsewhere. Some of the criticism leveled at the psychological testing methods and their uses has been justified. Indeed, there have been occasions in which psychological tests have been misused or conclusions drawn from test results that are unwarranted on the basis of the reliability or validity of the test itself.

There is a singular appeal attached to the idea of having someone "tested." Psychologists often find it extremely frustrating to respond to the request for a child's IQ score when the score may be meaningless and some of the other characteristics of the testing situation may be much more significant in terms of understanding the child. Society and other professionals sometimes demand simplistic answers and become impatient with what are perceived to be uncertain or vague responses. *Professional psychologists, however, are very mindful of the nature of the diagnostic procedure and the limitations of the tests and results.* Some of the criticisms of testing have resulted from the severe demands made on psychologists for simple answers, especially in terms of numbers. In an effort to be responsive to requests from colleagues, psychologists have at times been too willing to provide simple responses. It has been convenient to avoid identifying all of the shortcomings and problems by providing simple numbers, answers, or descriptions of people, their thoughts, behaviors, attitudes, skills, etc.

Another significant problem has been that psychological testing has often been carried out by persons not fully trained as professional psychologists. Unless the professional is well versed in the concepts and theories underlying the testing situation and the diagnostic procedure itself, the results can be misinterpreted or simply misunderstood. In view of the press of time, it is all too easy to simply identify some of the scores rather than the behaviors and the implications of the behaviors in the standardized situation.

The most effective way of gaining the maximal benefit from psychological skills in diagnostic situations appears to be for professionals to present the situation or problem to the psychologist and then provide the psychologist with the opportunity to exercise his/her judgment as to the best procedure for answering the questions posed. Predetermining the nature of the tests or the nature of the responses serves only to oversimplify the problem and increases the likelihood of distortions, misunderstandings, and possible abuse. The range of tests available to psychologists is extensive, and it is essential that the tests be selected in terms of the client and presenting problem.

Consultation

Particularly in view of the focus on, and interest in, interdisciplinary approaches, it is important to emphasize the consultative services offered by psychologists. Consultation is emerging as a major service function of psychologists. In view of the limited number of professional psychologists available and the value in assisting other helping professions in the delivery of services, it has become essential for the psychologist to develop skills in program and case consultation. The consultation can be in the form of support services to an ongoing treatment program or for clarifying difficult diagnostic problems. Psychologists provide a significant amount of consultation in hospitals, clinics, mental health centers, schools, and other service programs. For example, speech therapists often find it helpful to obtain the consultation of a psychologist to assess the degree of psychological impact of the speech problem on the patient as a "total" person. Often, the psychological factors can impede or otherwise interfere with the therapeutic approaches. It is through the comprehensive understanding of the total person that the most effective treatment can be rendered.

Many psychologists, for example, are involved in consultation activities to school systems in which they serve as resource personnel. Some of the problems presented by teachers or guidance counselors to the psychologist include behavioral disruptions in the classroom, learning disabilities, interpersonal conflicts, and the enhancement of the overall learning environment. Although the psychologist may not be directly involved in interaction with students, the psychologist can participate with the school personnel in evaluating problems and in identifying possible strategies for intervention. Using his/her knowledge of learning, motivation, perception, and behavior change, the psychologist can explore alternative approaches with school personnel to identify those that are most consistent with the overall goals of the institution. It is always essential that the strategies developed be appropriate to the institution and to the values of the personnel involved.

Consultation skills require high level professional expertise. The consultant inherently works collaboratively with others. The consultant must be well aware of the situation, the environment, and the availability of resources. Nothing is more detrimental to effective interdisciplinary cooperation than to have a consultant identify solutions that are impractical, impossible, unworkable, overly expensive, or otherwise ineffective. Progress in small discrete steps is often a major advantage over attempting to restructure a system totally and quickly. Handling the interpersonal stresses that often occur in consulting relationships is also a difficult and demanding skill.

Consultation functions, therefore, although highly desirable and significant, also provide difficult challenges. It is potentially a very rewarding service, but it can also be a very frustrating one for both the consultant and the consultee. A willingness on the part of the consultee to be open and frank about the nature of the consultation and its value to the consultee is essential.

Program Evaluation

The psychologist's special training in research methodology and experimental design and the general data orientation of the psychologist provide for a very effective program evaluation service. There are many concerns in the human service field accompanying the development of sound evaluative procedures for a range of treatment approaches. How effective is the treatment? How effective are the integration of services and the delivery of services? Are there alternative methods of dealing with the service delivery system? These and other questions of significance to a treatment program and to any specific service can be addressed by psychologists trained in research methods.

Program evaluation has become a significant aspect of all human service systems. In part because of the "crunch" of federally supported programs, as well as because of the need to assess the viability of ongoing services, it has become essential for all human service programs to carefully monitor their activities. Quite often, existing personnel in a human service setting are unfamiliar with the necessary research procedures or lack the skills needed to develop and implement an appropriate program evaluation system. Professional psychologists are particularly well trained in looking at service delivery systems or components of such systems and developing methods or strategies for determining the extent to which the programs are effectively meeting their goals, serving clients, rehabilitating, helping to educate the retarded, or providing any one of a number of other service activities. The scientific grounding of the psychologist in the field of behavioral sciences provides the psychologist with an overall appreciation of the scientific method and data collection systems. The biggest hurdle in developing an evaluation system is to identify the problems in measurable terms. The training in research methodology and statistics and the data orientation of the psychologist permits him/her to apply those skills and that knowledge to design and implement an evaluation system.

A SPECIFIC EXAMPLE OF
PSYCHOLOGICAL SERVICES IN ONE SETTING

It is not possible to comprehensively cover the field of psychological services in a short chapter. Given the array of psychological specialties and the settings in which psychologists serve, only a minimal amount of data can be presented. A recent paper by Drotar (1977) presents a specific example of one aspect of psychological practice. Drotar describes the general setting and services of the psychologist in a pediatric hospital. He presents a good example of the kinds of services one specialist psychologist can provide in an interdisciplinary situation. The unit described by Drotar is in a 220-bed teaching hospital at Case Western Reserve University School of Medicine. Drotar points out that nearly half of the pediatricians' referral questions concerned intellectual development of the children. Other referrals related to the patients' adaptation to physical disease and handicaps, depression, ward management, and parental adjustment. Approximately 20% of the referrals involved psychological factors in somatic systems. Other problems related to behavioral difficulties and social withdrawal. Psychological services also included assessment in a multidisciplinary diagnostic situation and a variety of interventions. Drotar described the value of the interdisciplinary approaches to diagnostic workups:

> Multidisciplinary diagnostic and treatment planning conferences supplemented formal testing. Pediatricians, nurses, childlife workers, and occupational and physical therapists contributed valuable observations concerning intellectual functioning, social development and parent child interactions. In addition, colleagues from child psychiatry and social work contributed to assessment (Drotar, 1977, p. 74).

Drotar's report is a good description of the extent and value of interdisciplinary approaches to the comprehensive management of children in a medical pediatric setting. He also points out the need for coordination between the hospital and community agencies dealing with specific kinds of pediatric problems. The psychologist in a pediatric setting then combines a variety of therapeutic services with diagnostic skills.

PSYCHOLOGY AS AN
INDEPENDENT HUMAN SERVICE PROFESSION

The recognition of professional psychology as an independent profession has grown dramatically in the last decade. Psychologists have been identified in various articles of federal legislation as independent health care providers. These include Vocation Rehabilitation services, Health Maintenance Organizations, the Federal Employees Health Benefits Act, and the Comprehensive Employment and Training Act. The Civilian Health and Medical Program of the Uniformed Service (CHAMPUS) recognizes the independent practice of qualified psychologists by the Department of Defense. Psychologists listed in the National Register are identified as qualified providers under CHAMPUS as well as under the Blue Cross/Blue Shield Federal Employee Benefit Program.

State statutes have been enacted in over 20 states to ensure that an insured consumer has the choice between psychiatric and psychological services when mental health services are covered. That is, the consumer, or patient, has the freedom of choice in selecting the professional most appropriate to deal with the presenting problem. The Health Insurance Association of America also has formally recognized psychologists as independent providers of health care.

Psychologists have been appointed as directors of community and local mental health centers and also have held positions of significance as the mental health authorities (i.e., Commissioners) of a number of states. There have been a number of court decisions that have recognized the services of psychologists as expert witnesses in areas of determining a person's competencies and general mental condition.

The above examples of the identification of psychology as an independent health profession attest to the recognition gained by the field as a responsible profession. It also provides further evidence of the contributions of psychologists in a range of situations dealing with the individual and his/her adjustment and general well-being.

SOME PROBLEMS IN
EFFECTIVE INTERDISCIPLINARY FUNCTIONING

One of the major impediments to effective interdisciplinary functioning is the view of the patient as turf to be owned or controlled. It has been too easy for some of the professions to interact competitively in terms of status, prestige, control, power, and money rather than to behave cooperatively for the patient's benefit. The competitive spirit is, of course, well ingrained in American society, and it is not surprising that such competition spills over into service delivery systems. This may be particularly true in those situations in which the professions or the providers have been engaged in grueling preparation activities that have demanded sacrifices of time, energy, and money to achieve qualifications as professionals. When the prize is difficult to reach and highly sought, it is to be expected that it will be embraced and held onto tightly.

It seems very reasonable to believe or to advise that each profession should focus on its own skills and areas of expertise and provide services relevant to that specialty field or problem. Although that advice makes empirical sense, it is difficult to follow. It is difficult primarily because a number of professions have overlapping areas of competencies and skills. Moreover, it is particularly difficult when dealing with human beings if one views the client or patient as a "whole" person. The recommendation that each profession "stick to its field," at times, can go counter to the view of the patient as a whole person. The kidney specialist who does not consult the hematologist, the psychiatrist who does not consult the neurosurgeon, or the psychologist who does not consult the special education expert will find himself/herself treating one part of the whole person while another professional may be counteracting that therapeutic endeavor.

It is obviously difficult to achieve maximum cooperation efforts without establishing various kinds of hierarchical structures or without dealing with some of the basic anxieties of each of the individual professionals involved. Issues of turf arise, in part, because of the anxiety of relinquishing some responsibilities to someone else, of trusting someone else, or of feeling that somehow one's own position will be diminished as a result of that experience.

There are strong values and benefits to be derived from reasonable open discussions by the various members of the treatment team. These discussions allow for maximal benefit from each of the specialties involved and reduce some of the anxieties and competitiveness in dealing with the problems. Mutual respect for professional training and expertise is a *sine qua non* of good interdisciplinary functioning.

REFERENCES

American Psychological Association. 1973. Criteria for Accreditation. American Psychological Association, Washington, D.C.

American Psychological Association. 1975. Careers in Psychology. American Psychological Association, Washington, D.C.

American Psychological Association. 1977a. Membership Register. American Psychological Association, Washington, D.C.

American Psychological Association. 1977b. Ethical Standards of Psychologists. American Psychological Association, Washington, D.C.

American Psychological Association. 1977c. Standards for Providers of Psychological Services. American Psychological Association, Washington, D.C.

Council for the National Register of Health Service Providers in Psychology. 1975. National Register of Health Service Providers in Psychology. Council, Washington, D.C.

Drotar, D. 1977. Clinical psychological practice in a pediatric hospital. Prof. Psychol. 8:72–80.

Garfield, S. 1974. Clinical Psychology: The Study of Personality and Behavior. Aldine Publishing Company, Chicago.

Mariner, A. 1966. A critical look at professional education in the mental health field. Am. Psychol. 22:271–281.

Rabin, A. (ed.). 1974. Clinical Psychology: Issues of the Seventies. Michigan State University Press, East Lansing.

Reisman, J. 1976. A History of Clinical Psychology. Irvington Publishers, New York.

Schofield, W. 1969. The role of psychology in the delivery of health services. Am. Psychol. 24:565–584.

Schofield, W. 1976. The psychologist as a health professional. Prof. Psychol. 7:5–8.

Weiner, I. (ed.). 1976. Clinical Methods in Psychology. John Wiley and Sons, Inc., New York.

Wellner, A., and Mills, D. 1977. How Many Health Service Providers in Psychology? Finally, an Answer. Register Report #1. Council for the National Register of Health Service Providers in Psychology, Washington, D.C.

Woods, P. (ed.). 1976. Career Opportunities for Psychologists—Expanding and Emerging Areas. American Psychological Association, Washington, D.C.

Zimet, C., and Wellner, A. 1977. The national register of health service providers in psychology. In B. Wolman (ed.), International Encyclopedia of Psychiatry, Psychology, Psychoanalysis, Neurology, pp. 329–332. Van Nostrand-Rineholt-Aesculapius Publishers, New York.

REHABILITATION COUNSELING

Brockman Schumacher

Rehabilitation counseling is best understood as an outgrowth of the rehabilitation movement that started in the first quarter of the 20th century. Although charitable organizations and a few states had given attention to the handicapped before World War I, the first nationwide effort in rehabilitation began in 1918, under the Smith-Sears Veterans Rehabilitation Act. The early concern of national and state legislation was vocational training for disabled veterans. In 1920, Congress passed the Vocational Rehabilitation Act which provided for federal grants to the states for the purposes of providing vocational training, counseling, and job placement for disabled civilians. These programs were to be administered by a state vocational rehabilitation agency operating within the framework of a state division, commission, or board of education. A matching system of federal and state expenditures was proposed and continues to this day. Succeeding years saw Congress extend the program and rehabilitation as a reflection of the concerns of the American public (Oberman, 1965). Also, during this period, schools of physical therapy and occupational therapy were developing curricula that recognized the value of administering a rehabilitation program concurrent with medical treatment of the handicapped. Social workers in medical settings also recognized the need for early contact with the disabled client with home care as part of a comprehensive rehabilitation program.

Legislation and public concern has continued on a federal level as well as among private agencies and public organizations. Between World Wars I and II, it became increasingly obvious that rehabilitation of the physically disabled could not be the concern of a single discipline and would always require the work of many disciplines. A definition by the National Council on Rehabilitation in 1942 proposed rehabilitation as the "restoration of the handicapped to the fullest physical, mental, social, vocational, and educational usefulness of which they are capable." The field of medical rehabilitation was growing. Counseling and guidance toward specific adjustment and performance goals and the need for specialized facilities and equipment was being recognized. The needs for testing, vocational training, the development of work readiness, job placement, and follow-up also were recognized for long term rehabilitation of the disabled. Furthermore, the rehabilitation movement needed an awakened public interest, attention to progressive legislative reaction, community planning, and public education. Rehabilitation, then, in its early conception was seen as being not only the services and techniques of restoration for the paralyzed, blind, or stroke victim but also the involvement of many disciplines and the public toward a common goal. For the disabled patient, goals became more than simple restoration. There was a positive element: to assist the individual toward maximal growth where his/her own commitment and cooperation were vital in the return to self-sufficiency.

By World War II, it was known that successful rehabilitation should be a concern at the onset of a disability. Early planning and contact with the client with concern for competitive employment were combined with goals toward effective living and self-actualization. Modern rehabilitation emerged with great vigor following World War II. Military casualties were greater than in any previous war. There were significant advances in surgical techniques and drug therapy. The Veterans Administration medical care and rehabilitation programs intensified interest and commitment to job placement and training of the returning veteran which led to increased use of handicapped workers in industry. Advanced methods of restoration and treatment made it possible for many soldiers to survive the crises of the early phases of a disability. Thus, disabled veterans were discharged back to their communities where they still faced many physical and psychological adjustment problems. The increased importance of effective job placement was emphasized by Public Law 16, passed by the 73rd Congress. This made provision for increased vocational rehabilitation opportunities for disabled veterans. Later amendments by way of the Barden-LaFollette Act of the 78th Congress paralleled these efforts and significantly expanded and improved vocational programs for civilians. Rehabilitation services were expanded to all persons by way of the identification of one public function and one state agency for the multiple services required for rehabilitation. Services could be purchased or given directly. Subsequent legislation also led to the extension of these services to persons with mental disabilities including the mentally retarded.

From this brief description, it can be seen that development in the public domain and the gradual enlargement of services to the handicapped were partly federal in nature. However, private groups, hospitals, clubs, and national organizations such as Goodwill Industries and rehabilitation workshops also were involved. Rehabilitation now includes multiple services such as institutional care, medical treatment, corrective therapy, testing, counseling, work evaluation, home-bound care, manual arts therapy or training, mobility training for the blind, and job placement. These and other services in rehabilitation are found to be most effective in the hospital, rehabilitation center, facility, or workshop. The modern concept of rehabilitation, then, is of a process providing a comprehensive program of services deemed appropriate to the needs of disabled or handicapped persons and designed to enhance the disabled person's physical, social, psychological, and vocational potential for useful and productive activity. With this expanded view, the number of professions involved in rehabilitation is large. One also can identify the institutions providing rehabilitative services such as hospitals and their rehabilitation departments, rehabilitation centers or institutes, sheltered workshops, vocational training schools, and special institutions or schools for particular disabilities, e.g., blindness or deafness.

The development of rehabilitation counseling follows the growth of the rehabilitation movement. Although the fields of vocational guidance and school counseling had existed in school systems and in specialized institutions, the specific area of counseling in relation to the handicapped was identified at a national level by the Vocational Rehabilitation Act of 1920. This led to the present form of the state-federal programs. These counselors in the state agencies were and are the key to the successful operation of the state-federal programs. They evaluate the needs of the disabled client and coordinate the client's rehabilitation by way of the purchase of services ranging from physical restoration to training, tools, and certification. They also assist the disabled client in finding employment. They give guidance, support, and counseling.

These counselors rehabilitate over 300,000 clients a year. Other professionals concerned with the human services will have contact with these counselors when the client's rehabilitation planning is needed. The state agency is usually identified as the Division of Vocational Rehabilitation (DHEW Federal Register, 1974). A sampling of services provided or arranged by these agencies follows:

1. Evaluation of rehabilitation potential, including diagnostic and related services, incidental to the determination of eligibility for, and the nature and scope of, services to be provided
2. Counseling, guidance, and referral services
3. Physical and mental restoration services
4. Vocational and other training services, including personal and vocational adjustment, books, and other materials
5. Maintenance during rehabilitation, not exceeding the estimated cost of subsistence
6. Transportation in connection with the rendering of any vocational rehabilitation service

7. Services to members of a handicapped individual's family when such services are necessary to the adjustment or rehabilitation of the handicapped individual
8. Interpreter services for the deaf
9. Reader services, rehabilitation teaching services, and orientation and mobility services for the blind
10. Telecommunications, sensory, and other technological aids and devices
11. Recruitment and training services for handicapped individuals to provide them with new employment opportunities in the fields of rehabilitation, health, welfare, public safety, and law enforcement, and other appropriate public service employment
12. Placement in suitable employment
13. Postemployment services, including follow-along
14. Occupational licenses, tools, equipment, and initial stocks and supplies
15. Such other goods and services that can reasonably be expected to benefit a handicapped individual in terms of his/her employability

FUNCTIONS OF THE REHABILITATION COUNSELOR

The emergence of rehabilitation facilities and workshops, with the increased sophistication of the state-federal vocational rehabilitation system and advances in academic training, have served to enlarge the role of the counselor. Today, the rehabilitation counselor represents a link between the experiences of the handicapped and the world of personal, social, and vocational performance. Today's rehabilitation counselor has ". . . the role of a change agent for a society that resists social integration of its deviant members" (Jaques, 1970). While previously he/she was primarily concerned with vocational goals, the counselor is now expected to expand objectives and goals to include not only vocational objectives but the coordination of medical, social, economic, family, and psychological needs of the client as well. This represents an organized attack upon the residuals of the disability. It involves a recognition of the problems and the actions necessary to resolve them that are based on the evaluation of all assets and liabilities of the client. Instead of a primary concern for perhaps one or two techniques in the restoration process, the counselor is concerned with the broad development and integration of a rehabilitation plan for the individual client. The counselor, therefore, becomes the interpreter of services, facilities, and strategies necessary for rehabilitation. As a counselor, he/she is able to help the handicapped client confront his/her abilities and limitations and to engage in activities leading to a more productive and gratifying life.

The counselor often functions as a member of a team in conjunction with other professionals such as physicians, psychologists, therapists, social workers, teachers, and others. In addition to coordination by way of purchase and referral of services for the client, the counselor will maintain contact throughout the entire rehabilitation process from initial testing and interview to job placement and follow-up. As a team member, he/she coordinates or assists in the coordination of services from the onset of the disability through job placement and ultimate adjustment and follow-up. Furthermore, in his/her expanded role, the rehabilitation counselor gives direct services. He/she may directly work with the client in personal and affective counseling, group counseling, teaching, vocational guidance and career planning, medical referral, evaluation and test administration, and related functions. As discussed here, the counselor, by way of referral as well as by way of direct services to handicapped clients, works toward restoration and development of the disabled person's maximal potential for coping with the social and employment environment (U.S. Dept. of Labor, Occupational Outlook Handbook, 1970). The functions of the counselor are commonly accepted in the profession and include the 12 areas discussed below.

Case Finding

Case finding refers to the counselor's attempts to make his/her services known to agencies and potential clients. Often, the counselor working in an institution such as a mental hospital or correctional facility may have occasion to identify appropriate clients as a part of the treatment or rehabilitation team.

Eligibility Determination

The rehabilitation counselor must determine whether or not the client with his/her problem or configuration of problems is eligible by agency policy and its funding capability.

Restoration Provision

Especially in the state-federal system, i.e., the Divisions of Vocational Rehabilitation, the cost of artificial limbs, hearing aids, mobility training for the blind, supply of wheelchairs or other implements, and appropriate medical services related to restoration are contracted by the rehabilitation counselor.

Training Provision

Preparation for the world of work is a central concern of the rehabilitation counselor. The identification of transferable skills in instances of traumatic injury may be an initial task. In instances where there are no existing skills, training potential must be identified and appropriate vocational training may be purchased or defined by the rehabilitation counselor. He/she may use a number of resources to achieve this. The client may first be assigned to work evaluation, performance testing, or situational evaluation to make the best possible choice. The counselor may use a variety of sources of occupational information and other means to appraise the client and mutually search for training possibilities. The appropriateness of the training, the availability of employment, and allied problems may be reviewed during the provision of training. The selection of an appropriate school for vocational or academic training is usually crucial. This process may include consideration of such factors as the presence of architectural barriers, attitudes of instructors, and, of course, the physical limitations and capabilities of the client. Allied considerations by the counselor include a concern for the motivation of the client and his/her intellectual capacity to respond to vocational or academic training. In the state-federal system, the provision of training may include assistance with such items as transportation, equipment, books, and continued medical support.

Provision of Support Services

Generally, throughout the rehabilitation process, support services may range from the provision and follow-up of medication through continued individual and group counseling. The counselor may have occasion to maintain contact with the family and also with other professions involved, such as therapeutic recreation, psychiatry, or social work, to ensure that the client is developing in personal, emotional, and interpersonal areas while he/she is receiving training or workshop services.

Employment Placement

The counselor may give direct instruction and assistance to the client as he/she begins to seek employment through the use of public resources, employment agencies, and personal resources of the client. In addition the counselor may use his/her skills and knowledge in employer contact and in developing on-the-job training or employment opportunities directly for the client.

Planning

This function may continue from the evaluation throughout the delivery of services. From the point of view of planning, the counselor has the primary task of relating a series of goals or options to services that will be needed. The mentally retarded client may need a series of work-readiness experiences by way of minimal stress tasks in a protected workshop. This may be paralleled with selected educational goals and a series of experiences in skills of everyday living that could be contracted from a local agency. Family and other interested persons in the community may be sought to be of assistance and to phase the mentally retarded client into reasonable employment or back into community living after return from an institution. The recent amputee may require continued attention and medical referral as well as referral to physical therapy. Contacts with the employer may be required to ensure that there is a minimum of architectural barriers and that the employer is ready to assist the amputee in readjusting to the work situation. Family contacts may be planned to ensure that the recent amputee may return to satisfying family living. Thus, the planning process includes many dimensions and many disciplines. Two important objectives of planning are that the client should participate equally in the process and that the plan should move the client from a recipient to an initiator of services as he/she returns to the community. Therefore, the ability of the rehabilitation counselor to make the planning process one of mutual effort is a most desirable skill.

Counseling

Counseling within the rehabilitation process has been given various definitions. Basically, the rehabilitation counselor engages in a face-to-face or a group relationship with the client to assist the disabled person to understand both his/her problems and potentialities. The counselor helps the client carry through with activities enhancing personal, vocational, and social adjustments to the end that he/she will find the best possible means of dealing with his/her handicap. It is often a continuous learning process involving interaction in a nonauthoritarian fashion through which the counselee learns new attitudes and ways of appraising the realities of his/her situation. It may assist the client in discovering his/her unique assets and liabilities. Counseling at one level may be involved with vocational planning or the specifics of adjustment. At another level, the rehabilitation counselor may be concerned with reducing anxiety, augmenting the client's sense of control over his/her own life, building motivation, and/or strengthening other personal attributes (Renzaglia, 1962). The counselor may, for example, deal with the sexual problems of a paraplegic, the actual adjustment, depression, and mourning following an acute or traumatic injury, or problems of accepting supervision and responding adequately to training. This process may continue with varying degrees of intensity throughout the entire rehabilitation effort.

Evaluation

The rehabilitation counselor's main effort in evaluation is devoted to combining the medical data, psychological data, direct observation and interview results, psychosocial vocational information, and work sampling and work evaluation information, and to scrutinizing this information with the goal of formulating a workable plan. Although evaluation usually follows the determination of eligibility, it may be a continuing and self-correcting process throughout all of the strategies the rehabilitation counselor may use. The counselor may refer to the appropriate disciplines for evaluation. He/she also has the skills for evaluation in the areas of academic, vocational, intellectual, and psychomotor competence. The end result of the evaluation, in most instances, is for the counselor with the client to arrive at a rehabilitation plan that can continue with modifications throughout attempts to return him/her to full, effective functioning in the community and in the world of work.

Agency Consultation

The rehabilitation counselor possesses skills in communication with agencies on matters of client concern. The communication may have to do with referral, follow-up for the client as he/she receives vocational training, joint planning, purchase of a variety of services, or combined efforts for job placement.

Public Relations

Rehabilitation counselors, particularly those working in smaller agencies and communities, will often assume the varied tasks involved in general community contacts. For example, the counselor may meet with employer groups and support groups who need to learn about available services or need to be informed of the problems and prospects of a particular disability group. He/she may meet with appropriate agency personnel to provide assistance in the development of rehabilitation measures for public offenders. The counselor may have occasion to meet with private or public school directors to discuss architectural barriers or the special problems in counseling of the handicapped young adult. The counselor takes on the role of advocate for rehabilitation at large as well as for the individual client.

Follow-Along

Follow-along is, of course, a continuing activity crucial to the successful rehabilitation of the handicapped. The rehabilitation counselor has continued contact with employers, trainers, and agencies who are giving parallel services and also keeps in touch with the client. The handicapped person is usually making a complex adjustment in crucial areas of recreation and interpersonal and social contact, as well as in physical or emotional well-being.

CLIENTS

At this point, it is appropriate to ask who are the clients. All persons with disabilities, an estimated 35 million, are potential clients. There are three major groups. As described above, the physically handicapped were the first clients of the rehabilitation counselor. In a general rehabilitation setting, the rehabilitation counselor may work with persons with paraplegia, quadriplegia, stroke disorders, diabetes, spinal cord injuries, cerebral palsy, epilepsy, Parkinson's disease, and many disabilities. A number of counselors specialize in a particular area of rehabilitation; some may work almost exclusively with the blind, alcoholics, drug addicts, or the deaf.

The emotionally disturbed comprise the second major group. Some counselors work in institutional settings with psychotic and severely psychoneurotic clients. Others may work in workshops or protected employment settings with this group. Still others are located in mental health clinics or outpatient clinics, or they may work in a coordinated community program that provides outpatient services, after-care, protected workshops, and social living settings.

The third client group may best be described as the socially disabled. These persons often have disabilities that are exacerbated or represent special difficulties in rehabilitation because of their economic or social situation. Counselors assisting this group may work in correctional institutions, probation and parole settings, special programs for adolescent public offenders, or antipoverty programs.

The mentally retarded are receiving increasing attention from rehabilitation counselors who have specialized in this area. Here the counselor may have occasion to follow the client from special education settings or institutions into vocational planning, counseling, and employment, sometimes in protected settings.

SETTINGS AND INSTITUTIONS

Some summary can be made of settings and institutions in which rehabilitation counselors work. Approximately 20,000 persons work as rehabilitation counselors, almost one-half of whom are in state Divisions of Vocational Rehabilitation. About 800 rehabilitation counselors work for the Veterans Administration and many state and private psychiatric hospitals have rehabilitation counselors who work on the psychiatric team. An increasingly larger group of counselors works in rehabilitation facilities and sheltered workshops. These workshops may carry out such functions as work evaluation, work adjustment services, living skills training, and vocational training. In these settings, the counselor works cooperatively with vocation evaluators, job placement specialists, and work adjustment specialists. Rehabilitation counselors also may be found in labor unions, insurance companies, special schools for the mentally retarded, training schools for the blind and deaf, and other public and private agencies with rehabilitation programs. Of special note is the trend toward use of the rehabilitation counselor by industry. Often, this counselor is a specialist in such areas as drug abuse and alcoholism. As many industries move toward affirmative action programs in employment and work adjustment of the handicapped, the rehabilitation counselor will be used more frequently.

PROFESSIONAL SKILLS AND TRAINING

The array of skills and knowledge utilized by the rehabilitation counselor in performing the functions described in this chapter includes the following:

1. An understanding of human growth and development
2. Some understanding of human anatomy and physiology, including the effects of disease or injury on body structure, function, behavior, and personality
3. Understanding of the mental and emotional conditions affecting social and vocational adjustment
4. The ability to understand and detect the relationship of vocational and social adjustment to mental and physical disability
5. Familiarity with medical information, therapy, prostheses, and equipment design used to minimize the effects of the disability
6. The ability to use various methods of evaluation, including case studies, vocational and psychological testing, and reporting, and to adapt these procedures to the practices of employing agencies
7. The ability to establish and maintain a productive counseling relationship
8. The ability to use occupational information to assist in vocational counseling (this includes knowledge of the world of work)
9. The ability to analyze occupations in terms of skills, physical and psychological factors, training requirements, and working conditions
10. An understanding of relationships of aptitudes, skills, interests, and educational background to occupational requirements
11. An understanding of community organizations, workshops, and other facilities (this includes knowledge of referral procedures, functions, and staff)
12. The ability to make use of available community services and resources
13. An understanding of the relationship of administrative policies and procedure to the work of the rehabilitation counselor
14. The ability to use support services both within and without the rehabilitation agency staff
15. The ability to utilize national, regional, and state reports on industrial, occupational, and labor trends and to analyze specific community job information and opportunities
16. The ability to orient and prepare employers for the employment of disabled persons
17. An understanding of federal, state, and local laws and related social legislation pertaining to rehabilitation

18.   The ability to interpret agency policy, regulations, and functions to clients and others

From the above list, it can be seen that training for the professional rehabilitation counselor encompasses a broad range of techniques and skills. Often, as a matter of customary practice, many persons with the bachelor's degree and training in the social services have working titles as rehabilitation counselors in agencies and facilities. However, employers are placing increasing emphasis on the master's degree in rehabilitation counseling. The professional level for rehabilitation counselors is the master's degree. This is a two-year program of study requiring both course work and supervised field training. Courses include counseling theory and practice, vocational guidance, medical and psychosocial aspects of disabilities, evaluation and assessment, research in rehabilitation, occupational information and the world of work, job placement, and legislative aspects. Practicum and internship in a rehabilitation setting also are required. The doctorate in rehabilitation is offered by approximately 30 schools. Completion of the doctoral degree requires between four to six years of graduate study beyond the baccalaureate. Persons holding the doctorate are usually teachers, administrators, or research personnel.

ACCREDITATION AND CERTIFICATION

Accreditation of rehabilitation counselor education programs started in 1975. Master's degree training programs have responded vigorously so that already approximately 40 of the 80 rehabilitation counselor education programs are accredited (Schumacher, 1975). Certification has developed at a similar rate, with the first certification of field counselors taking place in 1976. There are now about 13,000 certified counselors. Certification is based upon an extensive examination conducted by the National Commission on Rehabilitation Counselor Certification (McAlees, 1975). The master's degree with varying amounts of field experience, from one to two years, is required for admission to the examination. The bachelor's degree with four to five years of experience is also acceptable for admission. Subscription to the Commission's Code of Ethics is an additional requirement.

RESEARCH

From the range of activities and goals of the rehabilitation counselor and of the rehabilitation movement at large, one can expect a varied, applied, and interdisciplinary approach to research. A consideration of research in rehabilitation might best be approached in terms of the major topics or themes. The first of these is research dealing with client characteristics.

Studies are conducted in such areas as sexuality of the paraplegic, changes in self-concept of the recent amputee, or motivation of the schizophrenic client. The concern of this type of research is often to suggest guides and approaches to working with or understanding disability groups. The second research theme is the investigation of the effectiveness of various techniques. Examples are the usefulness of biofeedback in control of blood pressure, the effectiveness of temporary job placement and work trial for the mentally retarded, and the usefulness and effectiveness of job-seeking groups. The third theme is in the area of service delivery. Configurations of service delivery are often investigated. The effectiveness of interdisciplinary teams including welfare, rehabilitation, and community workers in enhancing the job placement of the handicapped are examples. Studies of the effectiveness of decentralized offices and services for the economically deprived and the use of peer counseling in adjustment to higher education for the handicapped are further examples. A fourth theme in research may be termed operational. Here, ongoing problems or designs within an organizational framework are given attention. This is often evaluational research, such as an investigation of the mission of sheltered workshops and the degree of program effectiveness, or the determination of the effectiveness of a halfway house for rehabilitation of psychiatric patients. Perception of the goals of a rehabilitation facility by client and counselor is another example. A final theme in rehabilitation research is the focus upon counselor characteristics. Such topics as task analysis of counselor functions compared to level of education and experiences required or investigations into differences between counselor and agency expectations of roles and "role strain" would fall into this category.

In addition to these five general themes, newer research is emerging on the client with multiple handicaps. Considerable emphasis in current and future research will be given to service delivery for this group. The dangers of physical or psychological relapse are always present, and the environment within which adjustment to the community occurs is sometimes hostile or indifferent. Often, there are problems in simply maintaining contact with the client and ensuring that services that are already planned are actually delivered. The client with multiple handicaps will require increasing sophistication for successful rehabilitation.

CURRENT ISSUES

Current issues in rehabilitation occur in several areas. The first area is increased interest and concern for "habilitation." An increasing number of handicapped persons who have had no effective level of functioning and for whom vocational skills have not emerged are now receiving services. The largest group are the mentally retarded. This expansion of services places additional demand on the already heavily committed skills and resources of the rehabilitation counselor. As is obvious with this group, the handicapping consequences of mental retardation are extremely varied (Malikin and Rusalem, 1968). Some mentally retarded are limited in terms of academic tasks, while others may be impeded in almost everything they do. Intellectual limitations may be more disabling in some types of activities than others. Uneven patterns of social and behavioral adjustment are encountered frequently. There is general agreement that a classification of mental retardation is often as much a function of the environment as of the individual. Interdisciplinary work is always needed. Close communication with schools is needed. Family support of the client and a workshop or halfway house may be needed. The closer the client gets to the community and the better his/her response to rehabilitation, the greater the counselor's responsibility will become. Therefore, as the mentally retarded client moves into the community, the counselor takes increasing responsibility to deal with the employer, sometimes on a day-to-day basis, as well as with the family and professionals in other disciplines.

Another issue, partly as a result of recent federal legislation, is the increasing emphasis on the severely and multiply handicapped. Although these groups have always received services from the rehabilitation counselor, state and federal legislation has increased the demand for more services. Demands of the multiply handicapped individual require increased amounts of medical support and close coordination among disciplines concerned with almost every area of the individual's life. Family support must be maintained and special arrangements for employment and training must be carefully developed and followed. Attention must be paid to avocational and recreational needs. Problems of transportation, architectural barriers, communication, etc. become most intense. The counselor often must meet this increased demand for services with the same money resources and time allocations as he/she has had previously. The requirements for helping this group also will lead to increased specialization among rehabilitation counselors. Heavy allocation of new resources and increased training in this area will characterize the remainder of this decade.

A third issue for the remainder of the 1970s is the increased professionalization of rehabilitation counselors. Acqusition of the skills of the professional rehabilitation counselor requires at least two years of training to the master's degree level. The emergence or emphasis of additional handicapped groups will leave increasingly less time to train counselors in the requisite skills. Parallel to this problem is the importance of articulating the skills of the rehabilitation counselor in the various agencies and workshops, as well as in public institutions. Approximately 30% of rehabilitation counseling graduates are employed in settings that have never had a rehabilitation counselor. Each counselor is faced with the need to articulate his/her role or position within the service or treatment team. The current advances in accreditation and certification are a step in the direction of articulating the role of the rehabilitation counselor to other disciplines at a national level. Local acceptance by agencies and institutions is now needed.

An event that will gain increasing attention for the remainder of this decade is growing consumer involvement. This has been a concern to almost all human service disciplines. Society and individuals are becoming more sophisticated, and the possession of a professional degree is no longer a passport for automatic credibility. In the field of rehabilitation, one result has been the passage of federal regulations requiring more client participation. Most significant is the development of a contract or statement of understanding between the rehabilitation counselor and the client in the state agencies. The individualized, written rehabilitation plan must be co-authored and signed by both parties with mutual statements of responsibility.

A second and even more crucial development in the area of consumer involvement is the emergence of numerous militant organizations of the handicapped themselves. The handicapped are increasingly using public and political persuasion by way of lobbying, political action, and direct demands for effective services. A recent consequence of this effort was the passage of the Rehabilitation Act of 1973, which requires state agency accommodation of consumer participation and advisory groups in various governing boards.

The last emerging issue may be characterized as the increased "nationalization" of the rehabilitation movement. The Rehabilitation Act of 1973 sets conditions by which all contractors with the government must show evidence of affirmative action programs for the handicapped. This will require employers to make special efforts to employ and incorporate the handicapped in their industries or businesses (President's Committee on Employment of the Handicapped, 1976). They must show evidence of support services and modifications in hiring policy. The implications within industry and other institutions are enormous. The amount of resources and funds to be used, the expertise required, and the shift in public attitudes in the business sector cannot yet be envisioned. The role of the rehabilitation counselor will now, in its broadest definition, address itself to the 35,000,000 handicapped in this country.

PROFESSIONAL ORGANIZATIONS

In view of the current issues in rehabilitation counseling, the activities in most professional organizations have increased. A list of professional organizations follows:

American Rehabilitation Counseling Association, 1607 New Hampshire Avenue, N.W., Washington, D.C. 20009

Association of Rehabilitation Facilities, 5530 Wisconsin Avenue, Suite 955, Washington, D.C. 20015

Commission on Rehabilitation Counselor Certification, 520 North Michigan Avenue, Suite 1504, Chicago, Illinois 60611

Council on Rehabilitation Education, 520 North Michigan Avenue, Suite 1504, Chicago, Illinois 60611

National Council on Rehabilitation Education, 1522 K Street, N.W., Washington, D.C. 20005

National Rehabilitation Association, 1522 K Street, N.W., Washington, D.C. 20005

National Rehabilitation Counseling Association, 1522 K Street, N.W., Washington, D.C. 20005

President's Committee on Employment of the Handicapped, Washington, D.C. 20210

SELECTED PUBLICATIONS ON REHABILITATION

Journal of Rehabilitation
National Rehabilitation Association
1522 K Street, N.W.
Washington, D.C. 20005

Performance
President's Committee on Employment of the Handicapped
Washington, D.C. 20210

Psychological Aspects of Disability
Div. 22, American Psychological Association
3519 Germantown Rd.
Fairfax, Virginia 22030

Rehabilitation Counseling Bulletin
American Rehabilitation Counseling Association
1607 New Hampshire Ave., N.W.
Washington, D.C. 20009

Rehabilitation Literature
National Easter Seal Society for Crippled Children and Adults
2023 W. Odgen Ave.
Chicago, Illinois 60612

The Social and Rehabilitation Record
Social and Rehabilitation Services, H.E.W.
Government Printing Office
Washington, D.C. 20402

REFERENCES

Jaques, M. E. 1970. Rehabilitation Counseling: Scope and Services. Houghton Mifflin Company, Boston.

Malikin, D., and Rusalem, H. 1968. Counseling the mentally retarded. *In* D. Malikin and H. Rusalem (eds.), Contemporary Vocational Rehabilitation, pp. 157–174. New York University, New York.

McAlees, D. 1975. Toward a new professionalism: Certification. Rehab. Counseling Bull. 18:160–163.

Oberman, E. C. 1965. A History of Vocational Rehabilitation in America. T. S. Denison Co., Minneapolis.

The President's Committee on Employment of the Handicapped, Affirmative Action to Employ Handicapped People. 1976. The President's Committee, Washington, D.C.

Renzaglia, G. 1962. Counseling the psychiatric client. *In* B. Schumacher (ed.), Problems Unique to the Rehabilitation of the Psychiatric Patient, pp. 75–111. St. Louis State Hospital, St. Louis.

Schumacher, B. 1975. Toward a new professionalism: Accreditation. Rehab. Counseling Bull. 18:163–165.

U.S. Department of Health, Education and Welfare. 1974. Federal Register. Vol. 39, No. 103. Department of Health, Education and Welfare, Washington, D.C.

U.S. Department of Labor. 1970. Occupational Outlook Handbook. Bulletin No. 1450. Department of Labor, Washington, D.C.

SOCIAL WORK

William J. Hersey, Jr.

PHILOSOPHY AND GOALS

Social work means different things to different people. Readers who only peripherally know the profession may be aware of social work as associated with poverty and relief, foster care, and protective services. The profession covers a wide range of activities, the principal thrust of which is assisting people to enhance the quality of their lives in their social relationships.

A very broad definition of social work and social work practice is found in the Annotated Code of Maryland:

> "Social Work" means the professional act of helping individuals, groups or communities to enhance or restore their capacity for social functioning, and creating societal conditions favorable to this goal. "Social Work Practice" means the professional application of social work values, principles, and techniques for the purpose of helping people obtain tangible services, counseling with individuals, families and groups and helping communities or groups provide or improve social and health services (Article 43, Number 863, p. 597).

The profession of social work proudly acknowledges historical roots and basic philosophy in the Judeo-Christian heritage of aiding those in need. The prescriptions of Christ to bury the dead, visit the sick, feed the hungry, clothe the naked were expressions of this heritage. Martin Luther later admonished that, without good deeds, man could not enter the kingdom of heaven. Individualized efforts at charity began to be organized in the early church through parishes and the monasteries. Later, with the social change brought about by the Reformation and the Industrial Revolution, there were modifications in the manner in which social work was organized and in the way it was practiced. The Elizabethan Poor Laws of the 13th century set the precedent for governmental responsibility for social services. Social changes brought by industrialization were accompanied by increased potential for individual and community deterioration.

Charity workers of the 19th century, clergymen of many faiths, volunteers (friendly visitors from upper and middle classes), and wealthy or influential citizens, as well as agencies or state boards of charities and other institutions and paid charity agents, were the precursors of modern social workers. These individuals, however, were associated only in their common efforts to aid the needy, without a common bond of education, training, or purpose. In recognition of this, the first schools of social work began to appear in the early 20th century. Knowledge and techniques, derived from many fields of art and science, were proposed in the solution of social problems. They became the bond that distinguished the first professional social workers.

Social work has come to represent society's attitude of responsibility toward its less fortunate members. It is a profession concerned with those activities that improve the social functioning of people as individuals and as members of families or other groups as they relate to society at large. Concern for the individual is articulated in social work values such as belief in the value and dignity of people. The capacity of people to change and the right of individuals to determine their own destinies were enunciated by the first social workers. The emerging profession articulated a philosophy of responsible willingness to implement society's concern for the welfare of its members.

The profession has further articulated this responsibility by a code of ethics that contains the following provisions:

1. I regard as my primary obligation the well-being of the individual or group served. Inherent in this obligation is action for improving social conditions and the quality of life.
2. I give precedence to my professional responsibilities over my personal interests.
3. I will provide services without violation of the client's human rights. I will not discriminate because of any personal characteristics or group identification. I recognize my responsibility individually and in concert with others to combat institutional restrictions which limit the fullest attainment of economic, racial and social justice.
4. I hold myself responsible for the quality and extent of the services I perform and am accountable to the client, to the community and to my professional colleagues.
5. I respect the privacy, autonomy, and rights of those I serve. I treat as privileged, information I receive in my professional capacity. I make clear to clients how information will be used, with their informed consent. I actively support protection against unwarranted intrusion upon the privacy of all people.
6. I treat with respect the findings, views, and actions of all colleagues and express my critical assessments responsibly.
7. I practice social work as a composite of professional knowledge, values, and skill, and recognize their dynamic and interacting qualities.
8. I support the principle that professional practice requires professional education and disciplined experience.
9. I continually seek to improve the level of my professional competence through continuing education.

10. I accept responsibility to add my ideas, experience, and findings to the body of social work knowledge and skill.
11. I accept responsibility to help protect the community against unethical practice by any individual or organization engaged in social welfare activities.
12. I provide appropriate professional service in emergencies.
13. I distinguish clearly between my public statements and actions as an individual and as a representative of any organization or association.
14. I support the principle that clients should be represented in the program planning and policy development processes of social work.
15. I share with my professional colleagues the responsibility for creating and maintaining conditions that enable social workers to conduct themselves in keeping with this code (National Association of Social Workers (NASW) Task Force on Ethics, 1977, p. 4).

PROFESSIONAL SCOPE

Social work is practiced in a variety of settings. In some, such as child welfare and family service agencies, social workers carry out the major functions of the agency. Child welfare agencies provide services that substitute for impaired parental care. These services range from homemaking and daycare to substitute care in foster homes and the establishment of a new legal family through adoption. The programs of family service agencies include marital and family counseling, family life evaluation, problem solving assistance in various areas of living, and referral to and intervention with official institutions on behalf of clients.

In other settings, such as schools, child guidance clinics and hospitals, social work plays an auxiliary role. In schools, social workers help students when personal or family problems interfere with education. Social work practice in schools includes work with pupils and their families, people and organizations in the community, faculty, and staff. Social workers participate in much the same way in child guidance clinics, hospitals, and psychiatric institutions. In hospitals, medical social work practice, whether casework, group work, or other mode, aims to make it possible for the patient to use available health services more effectively. For example, a hospital admission can evoke anxiety about such matters as finances and child care, thus impairing the client's ability to think through and deal with the admission problem. Another example is the case of a pregnant mother with high blood pressure who is asked to remain in the hospital for a few weeks until her problem is resolved. A social worker can arrange for foster care or homemaker services and thus avoid the situation in which the father must take time off from work, and possibly lose income or the job itself in order to care for the children.

Social workers in hospitals provide other social work services, such as individual counseling related to the illness or marital counseling when a disturbed marriage may be affecting the course of treatment. Medical social workers also will be found in the community involved in the development of nursing homes, home-care programs, and similar programs that decrease the need for inpatient hospital care.

Courts and penal institutions employ social workers in their diagnostic and rehabilitation activities. In youth agencies, community centers, and settlement houses, social workers act as group leaders, administrators, and program planners. Public welfare departments utilize social work in delivery of income-maintenance services as well as other services that maintain social functioning, such as adoption, foster care, family services, and service to the elderly.

Social workers are commissioned in the military services. They deal with the prevention of mental and physical disabilities as well as the treatment and rehabilitation of mentally and physically disabled servicemen and women. They perform functions akin to family service agencies and child guidance clinics.

Social workers, trained in social strategy or community organization skills, also are employed in business and industry. Industry has found it useful to employ social workers to help resolve problems that lead to absenteeism. This assistance can operate at a direct service level such as problem recognition and resolution where the worker helps the employee deal with the cause of his/her absenteeism. It can also be at a planning level when the absenteeism is considered a joint employer-employee problem.

Various policy-making and planning agencies of local, state, and federal governments employ social workers who have skills at the many levels of expertise required for program implementation. Social workers with skills in social strategy or community organization are trained in planning, program development, and implementation. They are employed in such offices as the U.S. Department of Health, Education and Welfare, or in a mayor's program for volunteerism in a specific community.

PROFESSIONAL TRAINING

At the present time in the United States, a professional social worker is required to have a master's degree from an accredited school of social work and three years of supervised experience. He/she must be a member of the National Association of Social Workers and the Academy of Certified Social Workers. As in all new professions, there are a variety of exceptions to this rule. In the early days of social work, for instance, the master's degree was earned in one year. With the development of higher standards, these individuals were included in the National Association of Social Workers under grandfather clauses.

An accredited school of social work is one accredited by the Council on Social Work Education. Such a school offers a two-year basic course of study at the graduate level. This study consists of classwork and field experience. The National Association of Social Workers has a voluntary certification system that relies on peer recommendation for membership, three years of professional supervision, and successful completion of an examination.

Not all social workers meet the qualifications required by the profession. In many departments of social services, for example, it has been customary to employ individuals directly out of undergraduate education to fill entry level positions. These individuals have a baccalaureate degree in social welfare and, increasingly, this is a requirement for employment. The B.S.W. was developed to meet the heavy demand for the delivery of human services. Various levels of skill have been identified as necessary in the delivery of such services. The emphasis of the B.S.W. is on the development of a sector of manpower trained to help people work their way through the maze of service delivery systems. The social worker at this level of competency should understand the motivations, needs, and desires of people and also know when to refer clients to a higher level of care.

A field of practice also has been identified for paraprofessional positions in the field. Persons with a two-year undergraduate community college or associate of arts degree in social work, or its equivalent, are eligible for employment at this level.

Holders of the doctoral degree in social work may work in administration, research, or clinical practice. The National Association of Social Workers and the Council on Social Work Education have encouraged the doctoral degree for competitive and credibility standards when working with administrative and research disciplines.

At the present time, attempts are underway to formulate an educational design that will enable students and workers to move through different levels of career advancement to positions requiring progressively higher competencies. In addition to formal academic education, training programs are offered by many agencies. These programs are directed specifically to the people in the field of social work who do not have the training required and defined by the profession as the minimum for professional standing. These individuals are increasingly incorporated into the professional organization by being awarded professional status.

LICENSURE AND CERTIFICATION REQUIREMENTS

As indicated above, the professional association has a voluntary certification system. A professional social worker is admitted to the Academy of

Certified Social Workers after three years of supervised practice and examinations. In most states, this certification is sufficient for practice.

Some states have adopted licensure procedures for social workers. For example, the Maryland Code requires:

1. The Board shall issue a license as a social work associate to an applicant who:
   a. Has a baccalaureate degree from an accredited college or university, including completion of a social work program accredited by the Council on Social Work Education; and
   b. Has passed an examination approved by the Board for this purpose.
2. The Board shall issue a license as a graduate social worker to an applicant who:
   a. Has a master's degree from an accredited college or university, including completion of a graduate social work program accredited by the Council on Social Work Education; and
   b. Has passed an examination approved by the Board for this purpose.
3. The Board shall issue a license as a certified social worker to an applicant who:
   a. Has a master's degree from an accredited college or university including completion of a graduate social work program accredited by the Council on Social Work Education and has two years of social work experience, under supervision of a certified social worker, but if supervision is unavailable this provision may be waived upon request of the applicant; or
   b. Has a doctorate in social work including completion of a graduate social work program accredited by the Council on Social Work Education; and
   c. Has passed an examination approved by the Board for this purpose.
   d. For any academic requirement approved by the Board for this purpose, the Board shall by regulation provide general standards of acceptable equivalents, including completion of related academic curricula such as psychology and counseling, and practical experience in a related field of work properly supervised and documented (Annotated Code of Maryland, Article 43, Number 863, p. 598).

More information can be obtained by writing to either of the professional organizations listed at the end of this chapter.

SPECIALIZED TECHNIQUES AND LANGUAGE

One of the major characteristics of social work is inherent in its basic value and belief in the dignity of man. Working with this philosophy, a social worker frequently has to yield to the client's self-determination, accepting the individual as a person of worth who chooses to act in contradiction to the dictates of others or the larger society. In such an authoritative setting as the military, a social worker may demonstrate his/her respect for a client who chooses to go AWOL or break some other regulation.

The social worker acts as a broker for the individual who is unable to deal with social institutions. At a basic level, the brokerage role is to help direct and advise the client with regard to the available options so that the client may make decisions relevant to his/her particular life-style. This brokerage role enhances the client's ability to make his/her investment pay off and/or bring about constructive change. As a client advocate, the social worker is engaged in action to bring about change in adverse conditions. This advocate role may include speaking up on behalf of the client in quest of a needed service or bringing to the attention of authorities the needs of a group of clients. As an agent of social welfare, he/she also helps clients live constructively within current societal values. That these goals conflict is a limitation of the profession.

Another characteristic of social work is its change of focus and method in response to societal change. In its early years, social work, in response to the influence of the Protestant ethic and other values, was engaged in character reform. The paternalistic approach yielded to involvement in reform movements in face of the adverse social conditions of the late 19th and early 20th centuries. Emphasis has since moved to the consideration of the psychological or sociological causation of human problems. The philosophies of Freud and his followers highly influenced the profession of social work to look at and work with the inner feelings of people as sources of maladaptive behavior. Increasingly, since the mid-20th century, with new developments in sociology, economics, psychology, and the other behavioral sciences, social work has paid renewed attention to social causal factors. The result of this reponse to changes in society is that social work has been identified with a number of foci in a very short period.

Social work has broadened its activities in search of more effective ways to carry out its original mandate. It has borrowed knowledge, ideas, and intervention techniques from a number of disciplines with the result that it is difficult to define what is unique about social work. The most striking example of this is social work's identification with Freudian psychology during the 1920s. Some schools of social work today are referred to as Freudian. Identification with this practice has led to confusion among the other helping professionals so that social work is frequently difficult to distinguish from mental health counseling or the counseling of a public health nurse. To some, the social worker may be accused of acting in a field in which he/she may not be competent (Chaiklin, 1976).

Chaiklin, in consideration of the inherent dilemma, suggests that social work should be defined, not in terms of its differences from other professions, but rather in terms of its behaviors. These behaviors are not unique or exclusive to social work, but, taken together, they identify a group of activities that can uniquely be called social work practice. Chaiklin believes that a set of activities exists that characterizes all social workers. His definition of the social worker's role includes the following functions:

1. Works at the physical, social, emotional and cultural factors that influence a client's behavior
2. Works with all the problems the client presents
3. Examines the social situations in which problems present themselves
4. Works with the problems in an individual, family, group, or policy context.
5. Knows the community and its resources
6. Coordinates services
7. Meets a need without requiring attitudinal change (Chaiklin, 1976)

The emphasis, then, is on the external conditions causing behavior rather than on the individual internal motivation of that behavior. Social work practice is not defined in terms of a theory of human behavior, although a mastery of at least one theory is essential for practice. The social worker relates to human feelings and social factors that influence behavior.

SOCIAL WORK METHODS

Social work objectives and goals have been separated into three basic concentrations: clinical methods, social strategy, and administration. Each sphere is concerned with the dignity of people. Each is concerned with helping people help themselves. Each is concerned with the enhancement and restoration of the client's capacity for social functioning and, depending upon the setting, may be concerned with the individual or with groups. Inherent in all social work methods are the qualities of nonjudgmental attitudes, empathy, and recognition of the client's right of self-direction.

Clinical Methods

Clinical social work is one of the oldest methods and the one performed by most social workers today. It is an individualized technique of helping people to make use of their own resources and the resources of the community in solving problems that interfere with social functioning. It requires knowledge of social resources, human capabilities, and the role that unconscious motivation plays in determining behavior. It assists individuals, families, or small groups in acquiring greater human realization by freeing psychosocial potential and functioning. Clinical social work is the traditional method of providing one-to-one service. A clinically trained social worker works directly with a client and/or his/her family. Clinical social workers also have skills of working with individuals in a group setting in which the worker guides the interaction and peer support toward helping the group members.

Social Strategy

From the earliest through contemporary experiences, social workers have viewed the community as a setting that needs to be planned for in order to ensure the fullest development of clientele. Community organization or social strategy came into being as a social work method. Social work perceives the community as a client in need of individual respect and the right to self-direction. Community organization and social strategy methods help the development and implementation of programs providing human services to people in need.

Community organization was originally concerned with developing and financing social welfare services in the voluntary agencies and institutions in the community. Activities such as the United Fund or Community Chest were organized by a community that sought means to coordinate fund-raising activities. Councils of social agencies developed to coordinate and to avoid duplication of services and to ensure a minimum of gaps in service. Through these experiences, social work developed sufficient community experience to address other community problems. This expertise was used to broaden its own theoretical base as well as to contribute to the development and policies of the Great Society legislation, under the Johnson administration, and of such groups as the Urban League. The increase in scope is now referred to as the method of social strategy.

Administration

The social work method of administration was not recognized until the 1960s. It has been identified and singled out as a method of practice and sequence taught in many schools of social work. Social work has been associated with large social agencies as well as small. Those workers who have moved into administrative roles of supervision, planning, and direction have caused administration to be formally identified as a social work method. As the profession has broadened its knowledge of community-based programs, it has acquired the sophisticated knowledge to administer them. Social welfare administration clearly blends social work values and the various techniques of budgeting, personnel management planning, and decision making.

SOCIAL WORK TECHNIQUES

Social work is a problem-solving process. The client can be a person, a group, a community, or an agency. Given the client and the method of practice, there are social work techniques that, with appropriate modification, are germaine to all social work methods.

The social history or case history is developed by logical, common sense, inductive, and deductive methods of inquiry. The study seeks to identify the nature of the presenting problem. What is it the client wishes to overcome or achieve? The study seeks to identify the significance of the problem. How important is it in terms of psychological and social implications? The worker looks for antecedents, causes, and effects in operation. What coping efforts has the client made? What resources does the client have? The worker seeks to determine why the client has sought help and what solutions are expected. This inquiry is made, with the goals and purposes of the actual agency in mind, to determine whether the appropriate resources for the particular problem are being used.

Resource finding is a social work problem-solving skill based on unique knowledge of community resources. Sometimes, with sufficient help, a client can make use of community resources. At other times, provision of a resource, such as financial assistance, may prolong or present another problem.

Teaching enhances a client's problem-solving potential. Explaining the system and defining the limitations and opportunities help to provide the client with a road map of how to get where he wants to go.

Interpretation helps the client understand underlying causes and/or how various events fit together.

A social worker may offer the *psychological* or *physical support* a client may need before beginning to tackle a problem or during the solution of it.

Ventilation is a technique used to help a client air or relieve himself/herself of overreactions or very strong feelings.

Partialization assists the client who is overwhelmed with the magnitude of the problem or with a multiplicity of problems. The client is assisted in working with one thing at a time.

Frequently, workers promote exercises in *problem solving* to increase client independence.

Clinical social work, social strategy, and administration employ orderly, systematic methods basic to effective thinking, feeling, and action. The solution takes place by and through the persons involved in the problem. Social work attempts to help its clientele to understand themselves and their situation.

In recognition of the way powerful emotional factors may prevent a client's functioning, the worker provides a supportive and objective relationship in which the client finds ways to overcome or cope with the problem. The experts do not unilaterally provide solutions by which the client is reduced to consumer: on the contrary, the client is encouraged to produce the solution himself/herself. Thus, the client's self-responsibility and independence are strengthened.

INTERDISCIPLINARY EFFORTS

Interdisciplinary team efforts on behalf of clients in trouble are highly valued by professional social workers. In such efforts, social workers see themselves as representing the unique individuality of the client, that which makes him/her different from any other "case." For example, in the days when tuberculosis was treated in sanatoriums, social workers dealt with a group of AWOLS, typified as alcoholics, who left the hospital for a drinking binge. For these cases, precipitating elements were usually discovered, such as the patient's loneliness for his/her family or complete misunderstanding of the treatment regime. With such evidence available, the team frequently tested novel treatment plans such as more frequent visits by family or even lean-to tents outside the home to avoid the separation of family members.

Social work frequently finds itself in a position to influence the interdisciplinary team toward change when the team recommendations make unnecessary demands on the client. Professionals who espouse middle class values, for instance, can be influenced to react in a receptive manner to values of a different class. The social worker's optimistic dedication to the capacity of man to change can be particularly refreshing to a team when working with a seemingly immutable client.

For example, wealthy South American families often have a maid for each child. A team had long recognized that these maids tend to infantalize children, keeping them well below their self-care potential. In this particular case, a seven-month-old handicapped baby was so dependent that he was no source of joy to his parents. The team had increased his abilities to eat higher level food, to smile, and to use other means of communication than crying, but the team insisted on training the maid. She, however, did not want a child capable of making higher demands. The social worker recognized parental willingness to defy traditional practice of having a maid care for the child, in spite of their initial attempt to institutionalize the child. The parents responded to the child's new capacities and took over his care personally. Thus, in interviews with the parents, the social worker was able to help the parents defy tradition; the worker had sensed their willingness to do so. Other members of the team could have helped but this assistance was the social worker's assigned task.

Currently, a frequent problem presented to members of an interdisciplinary team is that of child abuse. By most state laws, anyone hearing of such abuse is bound to refer the case to legal authority and a protective service division of the local department of welfare. This is usually a repugnant task unless the referee is aware of the benefits of such a referral. The social worker knows what help protective services can offer a family and can interpret the benefits of such a referral. He/she can even suggest that most reported persons are grateful for the referral. The social worker's knowledge of community resources and his/her familiarity with such social problems as child abuse help the team deal with individual cases and establish methods to deal with future situations.

Even though social workers favor the team or interdisciplinary approach, workers do have common problems. The profession is so frequently identified with services to the poor that workers feel they are only called in when the client is disadvantaged by poverty and social ills associated with poverty. As a matter of fact, most "social work" in the United States is practiced in welfare agencies and by personnel who are not professional social workers. Persons with high school education do eligibility interviews; others with B.A. degrees in English, music, etc. carry out service functions. Much heroic work is done by these individuals but they are not professional social workers.

Frequently, social workers complain that they are only called on to do resource finding. The solution to this type of identification lies with the worker who defines his/her role and demonstrates the capability to carry out other services.

A social worker's insistence on the rights of the individual to make his/her own choices may place the worker in the position of resisting a team recommendation. In the army, a worker identified a soldier as continuously opposing army regulations. This soldier had maintained a good record, but it was attributable primarily to his need to please his father. The father had died recently, and the soldier began breaking regulations. Until the soldier was able to make his own choice to serve well, the social worker had to accept continued infraction of rules.

Advocacy is probably one of the most difficult roles for the team social worker. This role is increasingly expected of the worker by the team and by himself/herself. Social workers have not had training in the sensitization needed for advocacy, nor in the appropriateness of advocacy. They require more training in law as it applies to individual rights and entitlements, more knowledge of service delivery systems that impinge on people's lives, and more knowledge and skill in reaching and using the influence and power systems in a community. Although such activities were part of the beginnings of social work, the profession left this field of action and is only recently resuming interest in these elements. The worker may hesitate to assume an advocacy position against the team. A team may essentially infantalize a mentally retarded person by calling him/her by a childhood nickname, by encouraging an adult to carry a stuffed toy, or by relying on an outdated IQ score. The worker realizes a call for advocacy in these situations, but is in conflict each time these situations arise as to what course of action to take lest he/she break an established working relationship with a team. At times, social workers observe aides or other professionals ignoring the rights of patients and/or families. Social workers are accustomed to roles with clients that are facilitative and nonjudgmental. They generally do not give advice. They accept a client as he/she is. On the interdisciplinary team, workers may relate to members in much the same way, and thus be viewed as passive, noncontributing members of the team.

At times, the worker may be aware that different team members are communicating different messages to the family. He/she may be using all efforts to get the psychologist and psychiatrist together for a meeting to clarify directions when it appears that a family may be confused by team disagreement. This type of facilitation in a team meeting is often misunderstood, with the worker being identified as meddling.

Social workers do not have chemical analyses, developmental scales, or other standardized tests with which to confidently present an assessment of a social situation. Confidence and competence are imperative in order to function within a team.

Interdisciplinary activity is favored and fostered by social workers because this approach offers clients opportunities to examine all the facts as he/she develops an appreciation of a problem. Not only are the facts given to the client, but they are given without the bias of any one discipline, and he/she is encouraged to participate in an enlightened way to solve the problem. The team looks at the whole person and makes its recommendations from that perspective. Because interdisciplinary teams can be made up of professionals who have come to know each other well, time and energy are not wasted in dysfunctional differences among disciplines. The client then becomes the recipient of a harmonious team effort.

PROFESSIONAL ORGANIZATIONS

Council on Social Work Education, 345 East 46th Street, New York, New York 10017

National Association of Social Workers, 1425 H Street, N.W., Washington, D.C. 20005

REFERENCES

Annotated Code of Maryland—Social Workers Article 43, 1975, Number 859–870, pp. 17–18, 597, 598.

Chaiklin, H. 1976. Needed: A Generic Definition of Social Work Practice. Paper presented at the National Conference of Social Welfare, Washington, D.C.

National Association of Social Workers Task Force on Ethics. 1977. Proposed revised code of ethics. NASW News 22:16–17.

SUGGESTED READINGS

Kahn, A. (ed.). 1959. Issues in American Social Work. Columbia University Press, New York.

Towle, C. 1965. Common Human Needs. Rev. Ed. National Association of Social Workers, New York.

SPEECH, HEARING, AND LANGUAGE PATHOLOGY

Audrey S. Hoffnung

The purpose of the field of speech, hearing, and language pathology has been stated in a variety of ways. Informally, one might acknowledge the writing of Emily Dickinson who expressed the sentiment,

If I can ease one life the aching . . .
I shall not live in vain.

More formally, the purpose, as it has been stated by the American Speech and Hearing Association is:

. . . to encourage basic scientific study of the processes of individual human communication, with special reference to speech, hearing, and language, promote investigation of disorders of human communication, and foster improvement of clinical procedures of such disorders; to stimulate exchange of information among persons and organizations thus engaged; and to disseminate such information (American Speech and Hearing Association, 1975, Directory, VII).

Speech, hearing, and language pathologists attempt to relieve suffering and to aid in developing, correcting, or restimulating speech and language patterns so that humans can successfully communicate with each other. It is the specific ability of language that allows man to acquire and to utilize the knowledge of the past, to create theories, and to impart the nuances of emotion. It is these specific abilities that differentiate man from other members of the animal kingdom.

SCOPE OF THE FIELD

Definition

The title, "speech therapy," has been semantically detrimental, placing artificial limitations on a field that has many aspects and many spheres of interest and influence. Speech therapists have alternately been referred to as speech correctionists, speech pathologists, speech and hearing therapists, communication therapists, and communicalogists. The oral communication system is based on speech, hearing, and language, and therefore the term speech, hearing, and language pathologist is used in this chapter to support that premise. A new organization has chosen the title New York City Speech, Hearing, and Language Association. In contrast, the Legislative Council of the American Speech and Hearing Association has endorsed "speech-language pathologist" as the official title for professionals providing speech and language services to persons with communicative disorders (Healey and Dublinske, 1977).

Oral communication

The oral communication of others is relayed via hearing. The development of symbolic oral communication or language is based on physical readiness (Lenneberg, 1967) and on cognition (Piaget, 1963; Bloom, 1970) which fosters the development of the rules of language (Chomsky, 1965; Jakobson, 1967). Rules apply to the development of the sound system (phonology), to grammar (syntax), and to the meaning of words (semantics). The time is past when each of the above elements is considered an entity unto itself (Cutting and Kavanagh, 1975). Language, the symbolic code, is considered unitary (Berry, 1969). No one aspect of language is acquired in its entirety before the other, e.g., "ba" (bat), an utterance of a child, requires the phonemes /b/ + /a/. The /b/, according to the distinctive feature theory, is formed by simultaneous occurrence of the rules, e.g., + consonant, + voice, and + interrupted, and + grave (Jakobson, Fant, and Halle, 1967). The semantic referent is an inanimate object and the syntactic category operates under the restrictions of a noun phrase. The entire sound system, e.g., /l, r, v, or s/ has not necessarily been developed nor has the entire semantic or syntactic system; however, the basic elements of each have been incorporated to produce a meaningful utterance. Separation of the areas of speech and language is impossible.

Evidence is available to support the hypothesis that there is a correlation between disorders in speech, language, and hearing and other language skills such as reading (Shankweiler, 1968) and writing (Nazarova, 1952; Myklebust, 1973). Many of the problems encountered in the syndrome of learning disabilities have a high correlation or a causal relationship with the development of normal speech, language, and hearing. Disturbances in other areas such as neuromotor maturation and emotional development are related to disturbances in the areas of speech and language.

The full realization of the importance of speech, hearing, and language to the individual and to society has provided impetus to scientific and creative study in all areas of communication, whether normal and/or deviant,

Photograph by Richard Holden.

Photograph by Richard Holden.

artistic and/or therapeutic, or research-based and/or clinically oriented. The field has burgeoned, knowledge has increased, instrumentation has become more sophisticated, techniques have become more structured, and remediation has become more theoretically based.

Pathology

People with communication problems, stemming from a wide range of recognized etiologies to symptoms that defy etiological definitions, seek and receive therapy from speech, hearing, and language pathologists. Lack of development, arrest, or dissolution of the nervous system produces syndromes that are classified, for example, as cerebral palsy, aphasia, or mental retardation. There are other problems that are alternately labeled functional or organic and some that appear to develop solely from a functional background. For many of the disabilities, the profession seeks to identify and describe the syndromes, even though specific neurological examinations have not produced definitive proof of neurological involvement. Parts of syndromes overlap. A person may have a number of problems in varying stages of severity (quantitative aspect) with subtle qualitative differences. It is difficult to establish lines of demarcation between syndromes. The speech, language, and hearing problems encountered by persons with problems such as aphasia, cerebral palsy, stuttering, autism, cleft palate, and voice disorders are discussed in this chapter. Overlapping features of each are interwoven in the presentation.

Aphasia Goldstein, Landau, and Kleffner (1958) noted that electroencephalographic (EEG) examination of children diagnosed as having childhood aphasia revealed that only 40% of the children had positive EEG findings. The language problems of these children are developmental and may be quite severe; yet, definitive signs of neurological involvement are absent. The problems affect not only symbolic oral communication but gestural communication, reading, writing, and learning as well. Problems exist in the processing and production of spontaneously produced utterances (possibly caused by impairment in the sequencing or retention of sounds, words, or phrases), in the development of categories, in the rapid timing required for the comprehension and production of language, or in the integrating of the desired word with the vocal mechanism. For instance, in the production of, "I want to go home with you for lunch," 24 sounds (phonemes) must be processed. Lenneberg (1967) estimated that 14 phonemes are produced per second, illustrating that processing must be rapid. It is sometimes suggested that severe speech and language problems may be on the same continuum as childhood aphasia, dyslexia, and dysgraphia.

In recent years, programs for the development of language have evidenced the field's interest in the transfer of meaningful information. These studies are concerned with imitation of language (Fraser, Bellugi, and Brown, 1963; Hoffnung, 1974), reception and comprehension of language (Lowe and Campbell, 1965; Shipley, Smith, and Gleitman, 1969; Ruder, Smith, and Herman, 1974), production of language (Bloom, 1970; McReynolds and Huston, 1971), and training of language (Stremel and Waryas, 1974; Holland, 1975). These problems are not separated from speech. The therapist works with multifaceted problems as they occur.

Aphasia does not occur only in children. It is found in adults who have incurred a cerebral vascular accident (commonly called a stroke) through hemorrhage, embolism, thrombosis, tumor, trauma, or other factors that disturb the circulation within the brain, damaging the brain and producing problems in the comprehension and production of language symbols. Many persons with aphasia describe this condition as one in which words are locked up inside, the key is lost, and the words cannot be retrieved (Schuell, Jenkins, and Jiménez-Pabón, 1967). Immediate therapy is needed to stimulate both receptive and expressive language, to motivate the depressed and frustrated patient, and to counsel the family. Concern for the family, family relationships, and family involvement is a major factor in providing therapy for both young and old patients.

Cerebral Palsy   Cerebral palsy results from neurological damage to the brain. The problems are usually multiple and range from mild to profound disabilities. Initially, the speech, hearing, and language pathologist operates as a member of a rehabilitation team and is concerned, along with the physical therapist and the occupational therapist, with the neurodevelopmental training of the individual. The neurodevelopmental approach seeks to inhibit abnormal reflexes and to facilitate the normal development of patterns that have been retarded or arrested (Bobath, 1966; Mysak, 1968; Mueller, 1972), e.g., persistence of the mouth-opening reflex may prevent lip closure, while weakness of the muscles of the lips will reduce the strength of the lip closure. Both problems will hamper the production of the bilabial (b,m,p) sounds. When teaching speech skills, a full understanding of the development of normal and abnormal reflexes is essential.

Alternate means of communication are being taught to those who are so neurologically disabled that they are not able to produce intelligible oral communication. If the person can minimally control his/her arm, eyes, head, or shoulder, he/she may be able to communicate without the use of vocalization. The individual may be taught to use one of the many types of communication boards that can be utilized to send a message to the listener by touch or eye movement. A simple board may have pictures pasted on it of members of the family or of everyday occurrences. A more complicated board may be color-coded to limit the area of the board under scrutiny and then have numbers to indicate the specific line in that color coded-section having the information the person wants to convey. To transmit a message, the individual looks at one of the colors placed along the edge of the board and then looks at a number. As the client learns to read, words are substituted for pictures and later the person may spell words with his/her eyes by looking at the letters. Electrical devices based on the same principles may be faster and more efficient and may be used by those who are severely restricted in voluntary movements. They are also more expensive. A comprehensive compilation of the nonvocal communication techniques and aids, plus an excellent bibliography and a list of manufacturers, can be found in a book edited by Vanderheiden and Grilley (1976).

For clients who do develop language, the physical disabilities of the individual must not distract the pathologist from analyzing other facets of speech, hearing, and language. Problems may exist above and beyond those caused by actual dysfunction of muscles. The pathologist should always be alert to the person's intellectual limitations, auditory and visual acuity and perception, limiting psychological attitudes, and delayed language development. Attention also should be focused on distortion of speech sounds that may lead to poor auditory discrimination and faulty comprehension. Inadequate proprioceptive feedback, for example, is believed to have a significant impact on the comprehension of oral language and on the ability to read. Liberman et al. (1962) stated that the articulation of the speaker provides feedback that aids the perception of speech. The production of consonants is categorical as is their perception. Chalfant and Scheffelin (1969) believe that the movements of the articulators are used by young children, when reading or writing, to analyze the sound composition of words. Nazarova (1952) found that, if the production of language is prevented in young children, the number of errors in writing increases. In addition to the relationship between speech and reading, it is recognized that reading is dependent on the development of language, language being a linguistic skill (Mattingly, 1972; Stark, 1975).

Intellectual limitations may delay the course of language development because cognitive restrictions may prevent the development of the basic rules of language, i.e., those rules that exist in sounds, words, and grammar. There is a direct correlation between intelligence level and the speech and language patterns developed. The speech, hearing, and language pathologist works with the child not only to help with the production of sounds but also with the development of structure, concepts, and generalizations.

Hearing loss at any age causes speech and language problems. In conjunction with cerebral palsy, hearing loss usually creates additional obstacles to the development of speech and language. Certainly, the age of onset, type, and degree of severity of the hearing loss are important determinants of speech and language skills and problems that one will observe. If the child was born deaf, the impairment of normal development of speech and language usually is greater than if the child was born with a hearing loss of a lesser degree. Speech and language arise through stimulation from the environment. People talk to and around the child. The child selects from that abundance of stimuli and then perhaps uses his/her Language Acquisition Device (McNeill, 1966) to develop language. Congenitally hard-of-hearing and deaf children are not able to do this with facility. They do not hear the stimuli and thus are not able to build a meaningful and useful oral communication system. They may turn to other means of communication to reduce frustration and to help them in establishing relationships with other human beings. Pathologists may use an alternate system of communication such as fingerspelling or sign language as facilitators of oral language or as a substitute for oral communication (Bender and Valletutti, 1976). Mayberry (1976, p. 223) suggests the use of ". . . educational-manual systems which are based on American Sign Language, Signing Exact English, Signed English and Linguistics of Visual English." These systems or some adaptation of them may be used with children who have problems in the areas of autism, mental retardation, hearing impairment, and cerebral palsy.

Others lose their hearing as they grow older because of such problems as industrial noise, otosclerosis, presbyacusis, and Ménière's disease. In such cases, the pathologist will evaluate hearing acuity and perception, help the patient select an appropriate hearing aid, train the individual in the use of the aid, offer experiences in aural rehabilitation, i.e., speech reading and auditory training, and provide speech and language therapy to prevent deterioration of the existing but vulnerable system of oral communication. If the patient does not receive auditory feedback, sound production may be slurred, diminishing speech intelligibility. Techniques utilizing proprioceptive feedback aid the patient in retaining an acceptable standard of speech and language production. A total program must be established based on proper evaluation of the hearing problems, the needs of the patient, the environmental conditions the patient encounters (e.g., riding on trains, being with groups of people, talking on the telephone, functioning in a job situation), as well as the mental and psychological capabilities/weaknesses of the individual. When a person has a hearing problem in addition to cerebral palsy or mental retardation, the task of the pathologist increases, and the demands on the patient are exacting.

Stuttering   Theoretical discussions of causality of stuttering still engage the profession. Stuttering is a disorder in rhythm or fluency evidenced by a blockage or repetition of a speech sound or word (Bloodstein, 1969). The pathologist must be acquainted with various theories relevant to etiology and should be sensitive to and discerning of the actual speech performance, such as blockages, repetitions, and additional compensatory mannerisms (e.g., closing of eyes, tensing of neck muscles, and tapping of foot) of those who stutter. Therapy may be based on one or a number of theories. These theories may be organized into functional classifications including: 1) learning theories (Wischner, 1950; Sheehan, 1958; Brutten and Shoemaker, 1967), 2) psychological theories (Barbara, 1954; Glauber, 1958; Van Riper, 1973), and 3) organic theories such as the delayed auditory feedback theory (Soderberg, 1969), the biochemical theory (West, 1958), and the cerebral dominance theory (Travis, 1931). Some theories are combinations of the above, e.g., when the child is considered to be predisposed genetically to a breakdown in speech, but the actual breakdown occurs because of severe environmental pressures (West and Ansberry, 1968) or when the child's speech pattern breakdown is in response to severe communicative failure (Bloodstein, 1958, 1969). In both theories of severe communicative failure, the child's self-image is said to be poor. He/she views speech as demanding or difficult. Stuttering is self-identified when, under communicative stress, fragmentation or normal dysfluency in speech pattern is perceived as a failure in communication.

New methods of therapy are constantly being introduced based on new ideas and instrumentation. Many authors are interested in operant conditioning; thus, their studies evaluate the effects of reward or punishment on stuttering blocks (Martin and Siegel, 1966a, 1966b; Costello, 1975). Others suggest that monitoring equipment such as an auditory biofeedback unit, should be used (Hanna, Wilfling and NcNeill, 1975). This unit alerts the person who stutters to the degree of laryngeal tension present. The person must then learn to control this tension to reduce the stuttering blocks. Goldiamond (1965) and Perkins (1973a, 1973b) utilized delayed auditory feedback (DAF). DAF was used by Goldiamond as a negative reinforcer, while Perkins used it to slow and control the speech of a stutterer. Klinger (1976) spoke of Webster's use of a voice monitor to help in the control of vocal loudness. This device, with the aid of techniques to control gentle onset of speech and smooth transitions, is offered as a program of therapy for stutterers. In each of these methods, the person must work hard and be willing to exchange the stuttering blocks for normal fluency. The recent emergence of a journal whose articles pertain only to stuttering is proof of the strong, continued interest in the field.

Autism   Regardless of whether a biological or an affective causation is supported, the speech, hearing, and language pathologist is interested in altering the behavior of autistic children and in opening the channels of communication. These children have minimal physical and eye contact with people in their environment, have abnormal behaviors, may not use meaningful speech and language, or may use them in unusual ways (Irwin and Marge, 1972). They may whisper or speak in a monotone or a high pitch. They may repeat words just heard (echolalia), omit or misuse pronouns (pronominal reversal), or use expressions very literally (Rimland, 1964). The language used may be of prognostic value. At one time, autistic children were thought to have good general intelligence, but this is now being questioned. Autistic children seem to use the information they receive in a different way than do normal or nonautistic subnormal children, which may signify a difference in the cognitive processes underlying language (Cromer, 1974). Programs, many of which have been based on operant conditioning, have been developed to aid these children (Lovaas et al., 1966; Wolf and Ruttenberg, 1967).

Cleft Palate   Children who have a cleft palate comprise another area of interest. Cleft palate, when it exists without a cleft lip, is not visible to the casual observer. It is only when communicating with the person that the disability may become discernible. Genetic factors, vitamin deficiencies, viral factors, or accidental deviant development may be linked to this disorder. One of the problems presented to the speech, hearing, and language pathologist is extreme hypernasality, which results in unintelligible speech. To speak normally, the child must be able to close off the nasal passage and emit air through the oral cavity (mouth) for all but the three nasal consonants (m, n, ŋ (-si*ng*)). Sophisticated equipment and techniques, such as cinefluorography, are now employed to examine the adequacy of this closure (Moll, 1960). Recent studies have suggested that the oral communication problem is not one of speech alone but that language deficiencies may be present. Researchers have found that cleft subjects perform more poorly than noncleft subjects on language tests. Philips and Harrison's (1969) results indicated that language deficiency occurs on both the receptive and expressive level while Smith and McWilliams (1968) learned that children with cleft palate "tend to show depression in those areas of language sampled by the Illinois Test of Psycholinguistic Ability" (p. 242). Morris (1962) stated there were language differences between normal subjects and subjects with cleft palate in structural complexity and mean length of utterance. Speech and language therapy is essential in aiding the child in understanding the nature of the problem, in strengthening the muscles, and in stimulating language development. Additional psychological problems, such as poor development of social relationships, must be considered in establishing a total therapeutic approach to habilitation.

Voice Speech and language are said to reflect one's personality, attitude, emotions, and intellect. It is easy to understand why some of the voice problems encountered by the speech, hearing, and language pathologist may have, as their precipitating cause, the occupational or emotional situation of the person as, for example, salesmen and teachers who are dependent upon oral communication for long periods each day. They present ideas to somewhat reluctant listeners. The voice is used to create needs, stimulate thinking, and then to convince. Omnipresent tension, in a parent and a child who have a hostile relationship, may affect the voice, resulting in hoarseness, huskiness, and stridency. Many times, these functional problems irritate tissue over a long period of time and result in singer's nodules (nodes on the vocal cords), polyps, or contact ulcers. The vocal cords, then, have been physically altered by long abuse. Therefore, functional problems can become organic ones (Moore, 1971). The true organic voice problem may occur subsequent to an accident that results in paralysis of the vocal cords or subsequent to a malignancy of the vocal cord or the entire larynx. The otolaryngologist refers patients with voice problems to the speech, hearing, and language pathologist to avoid surgery or after surgery has been performed. Together, the pathologist and patient analyze the voice production and the situations that cause vocal abuse. Application of therapeutic techniques to modify phonation are then employed. In situations in which the malignancy necessitates the removal of the larynx (voice box), the patient is guided in the establishment of a new manner of speaking. The pathologist must understand the mechanics of voice production: the movements of the cords, the respiratory mechanism supporting phonation (sound production), and the components of resonance. The pathologist also must understand the person: the tensions, the pressures, and the vocal needs.

Speech, hearing, and language pathology provides programs for all of the disabilities listed above and for many others. For each of the services offered, the pathologist is prepared to offer an integrated program based on knowledge of 1) normal and deviant development, 2) linguistics, 3) psycholinguistics, 4) anatomy, 5) physiology, 6) personality factors, 7) techniques of learning, and 8) therapeutic theories and methods. Speech, hearing, and language pathology is aided by the allied field of speech and hearing science which furnishes research data with practical applications.

SPEECH AND HEARING CENTERS

A list of centers that offer diagnostic and rehabilitation services may be found in such publications as *A Guide to Clinical Services,* published by the American Speech and Hearing Association, and *Directory of Services for the Deaf in the United States,* published by Gallaudet College. Some local communities publish booklets that provide similar information. For example, *Sourcebook: Speech and Hearing Services,* published by the New Jersey Leigh Foundation, offers an index of clinical services in the New York/New Jersey metropolitan area (Fenton, 1976). In this instance, the metropolitan area is defined as the five boroughs of the city of New York, New York's Nassau and Suffolk counties, and the northeastern part of the state of New Jersey.

Facilities that offer speech and hearing services may be found in a variety of settings:

1. In hospitals
    a. In speech and hearing departments
    b. In specialized team-oriented programs that offer speech, hearing, and language therapy as part of a total program, e.g., a cleft palate center
    c. In speech and hearing centers that are part of a department of physical medicine and rehabilitation. These centers usually serve patients with aphasia, Parkinson's disease, muscular dystrophy,

cerebral palsy, and, often, language-disturbed children with associated learning disabilities.

2. In speech and hearing centers that are part of a college or a university training program. These centers may offer services to the community while providing clinical experience for their students.

3. In special school programs within the public school system that limit their population to students with particular problems, e.g., a school for the deaf

4. In special private day-school centers that provide educational and therapeutic programs for particular problems or problems related to specific etiologies or specific age groups

5. In school bureaus created by the education system for a particular area, e.g., a bureau of the hearing-handicapped

6. In special nonprofit centers specifically formed to provide multidimensional programming for a specific problem area for all age groups, e.g., the New York League for the Hard-of-Hearing

7. In state institutions that house patients with a particular type of disability, e.g., the Willowbrook Developmental Center in New York, that provides residential care for mentally retarded persons

8. In centers formed through the efforts of an association that is committed to research and to treatment of individuals troubled by a particular syndrome, e.g., the United Cerebral Palsy Association, Inc.

9. In private residential accommodations for the elderly, where 24-hour care and rehabilitation services are offered

10. In centers formed by particular religious groups but which are usually secular in their admission policy, e.g., the Catholic Charities Office for the Handicapped and the Institute for Retarded Children—Shield of David

11. In private therapy centers that are the enterprises of a particular individual or group of individuals who are licensed or certified and who offer services to the speech-, hearing-, and language-handicapped person

EQUIPMENT AND TECHNIQUES

Speech, hearing, and language centers are equipped with items that are in general use in evaluation and therapy sessions and with items that are specific to a particular type of disorder being treated.

Each center should be replete with equipment for diagnostic testing in hearing, speech, language, auditory discrimination and perception, and concept development, to name only a few areas of concern. If this equipment is not available, the center should then refer the patient to other centers for these evaluations. Standardized tests should be available to aid therapists in evaluating the problems of the child or adult, in establishing a training program, and in determining whether growth has occurred. Diagnostic teaching involving the continual reevaluation of the client during therapy is mandatory (McGinnis, Kleffner, and Goldstein, 1956). Many times informal procedures used by an able clinician offer invaluable information and insight into the patient's problem and are superior to more formal procedures.

An audiological evaluation before the initiation of therapy is essential. This is usually a routine practice in speech, hearing, and language centers. Many children who are slow learners, hyperkinetic, and/or disruptive may suffer from an undetected hearing loss. Referral to an otolaryngologist, followed by a short period of therapy, may be all the remediation necessary. When the speech and language patterns improve, behavior may improve, and the child may then be able to function in the classroom. Other patients may require hearing aids, auditory training with an auditory training unit, speech reading, and speech and language therapy. Some patients do not have a pure tone hearing loss but experience difficulty in the perception of language. This problem is more difficult to judge, and research is continually directed toward probing this area. Hearing evaluations, even the most basic kind, require extensive equipment, such as a sound-treated room, pure tone and speech audiometers capable of doing site-of-lesion testing, an acoustic impedance bridge, a sound level meter, hearing aids, and batteries.

Equipment used fairly universally in therapy centers include: tape recorders, which enable a patient to better understand and analyze speech problem(s) through auditory feedback; a phonic mirror, a type of tape recorder that offers immediate playback and good fidelity; articles such as chairs and tables of appropriate height and size; stationary or removable mirrors to heighten visual cues; tongue depressors; and applicators. Learning materials are used during therapy sessions, and these can be created by the therapist or purchased. Materials, whether objects, pictures, books, records, games, or puzzles, used skillfully can motivate the patient and can serve as the bases upon which to build a productive session. There are companies that manufacture items that cater to the speech, hearing, and language pathologist. Other companies catalogue materials that can be modified by the therapist to provide the stimuli needed for a particular lesson. The names of companies whose items are suitable for therapy are included at the end of this chapter.

The field of speech and hearing science is a branch of the fields of speech pathology and audiology. The three divisions are integrally intertwined because many speech and hearing science majors were speech pathology and/or audiology majors at the undergraduate and master's levels. Therapeutic approaches have been developed as a result of the research of speech and hearing scientists on such subjects as formant or energy patterns of the voice, acoustic variables of sounds, voice prints (which law enforcement personnel would like to see perfected), cinefluorographic analysis of nasopharyngeal valving, synthetic production of speech, masking, and delayed auditory feedback. For many persons in the field, no professional division exists; they actively engage both in therapy and in scientific research. In various locations, the speech, hearing, and language therapist, the audiologist, and the speech and hearing scientist work together, each offering particular skills to advance the delivery of service to the patient in need.

The basic instrumentation of speech and hearing science is designed to "... control, store, produce, measure, and modify sound" (Hanley and Peters, 1971, p. 65). A list of instruments used may be found in the appendix of a very extensive chapter on instrumentation by Hanley and Peters (1971). They have stated that the basic instruments for a speech and hearing laboratory are microphones, amplifiers, loudspeakers, receivers, oscillators, signal generators, high fidelity recorders, voltmeters, and sound-level meters. Specialized laboratories, such as laboratories for laryngeal research or for speech synthesis, are equipped with instruments that allow for specific and exact types of measurements. Because of the similarity among subdivisions of the field, there is great overlapping of the instrumentation at various laboratories. A researcher, for example, to achieve his/her goal, may find it necessary to examine the larynx, thus requiring cinefluorographic equipment for x-ray motion pictures, a strobolaryngo-scope to aid in lighting the laryngeal area, and stroboscopic laminagraphy (STROL) to provide coronal aspect x-rays of the vocal cords during various phases of vibration. The human respiratory mechanism has a direct relationship to phonation (sound production), and, therefore, researchers examine aerodynamic phenomena such as air capacity, air flow, subglottal pressure, and muscle movement. They may use a spirometer to measure respiratory capacity and an electromyographic recorder to measure changes in the diameter of the thoracic and abdominal walls during speech or to measure the movement of a specific muscle. Researchers interested in speech analysis and synthesis may be involved in acoustic analysis of phonemes (sounds of the language) and prosodic features (inflections and stress patterns of the language) as performed by a sona-graph, a sound-spectrum analyzer. A fundamental frequency indicator, which automatically extracts the fundamental frequency for a sound utterance (the normal pitch of the voice), and a vocoder or pattern playback for analysis of the intonation patterns or articulatory features of speech, respectively, may be employed. The findings of these machines are displayed by spectrographic analysis. A phase vocoder, which may be used to compress or elongate time (Flanagan and Golden, 1966), may have practical application when working with the hearing-impaired who require rates of processing different from those of the normal speaker.

The audiology center, interested in hearing processes, pathologies, diagnostic testing, remediation, hearing aid testing, and aural habilitation and rehabilitation, may require sophisticated and complex laboratories. Various types of audiometers are used to measure the type and severity of the hearing impairment. Pure tone and speech audiometry are used in diagnostic audiology. Functional grouping of audiometers specifies: ". . . clinical research models; and the Békésy type of automatic units; and instruments for pure-tone threshold and screening usages" (Hanley and Peters, 1971, p. 119). A special warbling type of sound may be used to test infants who are too young to voluntarily indicate whether a sound is heard. Electrodermal or psychogalvanic skin response tests may be used for the young or for those who are not able to cooperate during a more traditional type of test. Anechoic chambers are used for free-field testing and for calibration of instruments. In free-field testing, the sound of a particular frequency and intensity is introduced into the room through loudspeakers. The tester observes the child for a change in behavior that would signal the reception of sound, e.g., the cessation of activity. Electroencephalographic audiometry may be used with patients who are extremely difficult to test. Researchers, asking searching questions and using elaborate, sophisticated instrumentation or simple material, have produced information that has resulted in constant reexamination of the methods used in the practice of speech, hearing, and language therapy. Hixon, Mead, and Goldman's (1976) study of the thoracic and abdominal cavities during breathing for speech has led to a modification of the traditional abdominal approach to voice therapy. Abbs, Folkins, and Sivarajan (1976) used electromyographic signals to measure the motor production of muscles that were anesthetized and found that they had diminished capability for rapid movements. This would suggest that those with a sensory deficit also will have a motor (production) deficit. Tallal (1976) varied fundamental frequency of two 75-millisecond complex tones with dysphasic and normal populations. She found that dysphasic children processed nonverbal auditory stimuli more slowly than did the normal population. This suggested that the slow rate of processing was in direct correlation with poor reception of language. Knowing the cause of the problem is the first step in finding the solution.

PROFESSIONAL REQUIREMENTS

The American Speech and Hearing Association (ASHA), which was organized in 1925 and has held annual conventions since then, is the major professional organization that has represented the areas of speech pathology, audiology, and speech and hearing science. The standards for membership and certification in these fields are set by this association. The Certificate of Clinical Competence (CCC) must be acquired by those who wish to offer clinical services. The requirements are different for speech pathology and for audiology, but a member may hold dual certification. The CCC may be granted only to members of ASHA. The requirements for the CCC can be found in the ASHA Directory.

To gain membership in ASHA, an individual must hold 1) a master's degree or its equivalent, with a major emphasis in speech pathology, audiology, or speech and hearing science or 2) present evidence of active research, interest, and performance in the field of human communication (ASHA, 1975a, Directory, VII). The areas of study and clinical practicum are specific and detailed.

Courses

If the applicant is interested in receiving the CCC in the major area of speech pathology, 60 academic hours must be completed in the areas of normal aspects of communication, developmental disorders, and clinical techniques for evaluation and management of such disorders. Twelve of the 60 hours must be taken in the areas of normal development and the use of speech, language, and hearing. These courses normally include such topics as: anatomy and physiological development related to speech, language, and hearing; physical bases and processes of production and perception, e.g., acoustics, phonology, and perception; and linguistics and psycholinguistics. Twenty-four hours must relate to understanding, training, evaluating, and managing communication disorders. Among the courses appropriate for this category are those with subject matter including aphasia, cerebral palsy, language disorders, cleft palate, voice disorders, diagnosis, and rehabilitation of speech and language. Six hours must be pursued in the minor area of audiology with emphasis on the study of pathologies, assessment, and those habilitative or rehabilitative procedures of speech and language problems associated with hearing impairments.

If the major professional area is audiology, 24 of the 60 hours must be in audiology and should include the study of auditory disorders, pathologies of the auditory system, assessment of auditory disorders, habilitative and/or rehabilitative procedures (i.e., selection and use of amplification and evaluation and management of speech and language problems of the hearing-impaired), conservation of hearing (i.e., noise control in schools, military installations, and industry), and instrumentation (i.e., electronics and calibration). Six credits should be taken in the minor area of speech pathology and should cover speech and language pathology in disorders other than those specifically related to hearing impairment.

Students are encouraged to study in allied fields to complete the 60 hours. Areas suggested are statistics, administration, theories of learning and behavior, and the sensory, emotional, and intellectual development of the child.

Clinical Practicum

In addition to the academic requirements, the student must complete an academic clinical practicum that consists of a minimum of 300 clock hours of supervised direct clinical experience under the supervision of a person who holds a CCC in the area in which the supervision is provided. The hours are specifically categorized so that 150 hours must be earned on the graduate level; 200 of the 300 hours must be in the student's area of specialization. The types of disorders the applicant is to experience are mandated, so that, for the major professional area in speech pathology, 50 hours must be earned in evaluation, 75 hours in management of language disorders in children and adults, 25 hours in the management of problems such as voice, articulation, and rhythm (stuttering and cluttering), and 35 hours in audiological assessment and management of speech and language problems associated with hearing impairment.

For the major professional area in audiology, 50 hours must be spent in identification and evaluation of hearing impairments, 50 hours in the habilitation or rehabilitation of communication handicaps, and 35 hours in the evaluation and management of speech and language problems not related to hearing impairment.

Examination

An applicant must pass a national examination in speech pathology or audiology. An applicant's academic and clinical practicum record must be approved before he/she is allowed to take the required national examination. A satisfactory record means that the applicant has passing grades in all pertinent academic subjects and has the signature of the director of the speech and hearing center where clinical requirements were completed satisfactorily. If the center is accredited by the American Board of Examiners in Speech Pathology and Audiology (ABESPA), the application for the CCC will be accepted automatically.

Clinical Fellowship Year

After completion of the academic clinical practicum and the national examination requirements, the applicant must complete a Clinical Fellowship Year (CFY) under a supervisor who holds the CCC in the professional area in which the applicant is working. The applicant must be involved in direct clinical work with patients for no less than a nine-month period.

Thirty hours a week is considered full employment. If the employment is part-time, 15–19 hours per week is required over an 18-month period of employment; 20–24 hours per week requires 15 months of employment, and 25–29 hours per week requires 12 months of employment. All of these hours must be spent in direct contact with the patients, with no hours granted for record-keeping or for conferences. The Clinical Fellowship Year must be completed in a maximum of 36 consecutive months. After the CFY has been approved, with the payment of dues, the applicant receives the Certificate of Clinical Competence.

After all the requirements have been met, the member is encouraged to take short courses that are offered at ASHA conventions and in other settings.

The ABESPA establishes standards, conducts examinations, and determines the certification of individuals, organizations, and institutions. ASHA adheres to a code of ethics and has an ethical practice board that enforces the code of ethics. ASHA operates under a set of by-laws that determines membership, dues, governing boards, committees, professional standards, and ethical practices.

Licensing

Thirty states now mandate licensing of the speech pathologist and audiologist and usually require that the applicant be in possession of the American Speech and Hearing Association's Certificate of Clinical Competence in Speech Pathology and/or Audiology (Boone, 1976). In addition, these states require that the applicant be at least 21 years of age, be of good moral character, be regularly employed as a speech pathologist or audiologist, and have been engaged in the practice of speech pathology or audiology for at least two years. If the applicant does not meet these requirements he/she must file for licensure by examination, be examined by the Board, have a master's degree or its equivalent, and have his/her relevant experience evaluated by the Board.

STATISTICS

As of December 31, 1975, ASHA had 23,295 members. In 1975, the greatest increases, by 100 or more, listed in descending order, occurred in California, New York, Illinois, Texas, Pennsylvania, and Iowa. Membership has doubled in the past six years. Ninety-three percent of the members hold advanced degrees: 10% hold doctoral degrees, and 83% hold master's degrees. A small percentage of members are doctors of medicine or dentistry who also have Ph.D. degrees.

Salaries for speech and language therapists start at approximately $10,000 for those who hold a M.A. and a CCC and reach a maximum of approximately $19,000. This varies in different regions and in different settings.

EMPLOYMENT

The largest percentage of individuals are employed in elementary schools or secondary schools, with speech and hearing centers ranking second, followed by colleges and universities. A number equal to those working in speech and hearing centers work in private practice on a full- or part-time basis. Unemployment declined from 10.4% in 1971 to 6.5% in 1976 (ASHA, 1975b).

In recent years, the specific environment in which speech, hearing, and language pathologists work in the parochial and public schools has been altered. In some districts, they serve a number of schools and may spend one day or a half-day at each school. Much of the work in this type of setting is with articulation problems, speech and language problems of the moderately hearing-impaired, and problems of stuttering, voice, and cleft palate. Pathologists also may serve children in centers for the multiply handicapped and those children who are considered to have learning disabilities. Speech, hearing, and language pathologists are particularly suited for work with individuals with learning disabilities, because, in fulfilling their academic and clinical practicum requirements, they have learned to evaluate, test, plan, and execute programs of therapy and are sensitive to the needs of the whole child. Services are provided in articulation and language testing and in language development and correction. It is recognized that the child's competence in oral language influences all other academic skills. Pathologists are cognizant of the interrelationships among speech, language, hearing, cognition, and emotional and physical development.

Evaluation and placement programs that are being provided in some vicinities are examples of programs that can be offered by speech, hearing, and language pathologists and are excellent examples of the advantages that accrue from offering a team approach to the handicapped individual. In this type of program, the individual, after being evaluated by a team consisting of a speech, hearing, and language pathologist, a social worker, a psychiatrist, and a neurologist, is referred to a center that can best meet his/her major problem. Services are offered at these centers to those who are classified as brain-injured and to those who have retarded mental development, cerebral palsy, aphasia, hearing impairment, and/or emotional disturbances.

Many school districts are structured so that speech centers are housed in a particular school. Students with severe speech problems are taken to the speech center where they receive their academic school work and speech and language therapy five days a week. The pathologist at these speech centers generally treats students who are multiply handicapped.

Many pathologists are full- or part-time private practitioners who maintain their own offices and may receive referrals from schools, physicians, or dentists in their area. Many states now require that they be licensed. The Committee on Private Practice (ASHA, 1976b) presents workshops that provide material and information to those pathologists who wish to set up a private practice. Private practice may offer flexibility to the pathologist to allow time schedules to be determined by the needs of the patient and the clinician.

Working at a clinic in a college or university is particularly stimulating because the environs of higher education offer opportunities for a free exchange of ideas concerning research, new theories, and their practical, therapeutic applications. Many academic settings house training programs for both undergraduate and graduate students. The course work is integrated with therapy sessions. This type of environment offers a high degree of stimulation to the staff and students as the eagerness and motivation of the students blends with the knowledge and experience of the staff, producing an atmosphere conducive to learning, skill development, and research. The patients receive the benefits of this collaborative effort. Despite these advantages, there may be some reluctance to work in this type of setting because the pay scale is low and the therapist usually does not receive employee benefits such as sick days, vacation, or other fringe benefits.

LEGISLATION

When one reviews the legislation that has been enacted in recent years, it is clearly evident that the federal government supports the fields of speech pathology, audiology, and speech and hearing sciences. The Health Profession Educational Assistance Act (Public Law 94-484) provides Public Health Service (PHS) support for graduate speech and audiology training. As of October 1, 1977 (fiscal year 1978), grants and contracts are available for projects and programs in speech pathology and audiology (ASHA, 1976d). Under this law, the fields of speech pathology, audiology, and speech and hearing science are listed among the health professions for which the Department of Health, Education and Welfare collects, compiles, and analyzes data. The National Health Service Corps (NHSC) makes scholarships available, on a competitive basis, to graduate students in audiology and speech pathology. The students pay back the awards by serving the NHSC for two or more years.

The expanded benefits mandated by the Social Security Amendment of 1972 became effective under Medicare, Part B. Speech and hearing centers, which under this law are considered to be rehabilitation agencies, may provide Medicare patients with outpatient speech pathology services (ASHA, 1976c). Under Medicare, the agency must be approved by the health department and the patient must be referred by a physician. Patients may receive therapy on an inpatient or outpatient basis, or from a home health-care visitor. The initial referral must be provided by a physician in all three instances. For inpatient care, the patient is responsible for a deductible amount which, at this time, is $124 for the first 60 days. He/she is scheduled for speech therapy along with other essential services. For outpatient care, the patient receives 80% of the allowed charges, after a $60 deductible. For home health-care, the patient is allowed up to 100 therapy sessions by a visiting pathologist. The physician must renew the prescription every two months. The support provided to the patient by this legislation is limited, however, and efforts should be concentrated to increase this coverage. Many patients with neurological problems, e.g., those with aphasia or Parkinson's disease, require long term treatment for rehabilitation or maintenance. The licensed speech and language pathologist should have the authority to determine the need for therapy. Coverage for extended periods of therapy based on the judgment of a qualified pathologist is one of the goals of the field. For information concerning therapy under Medicare contact:

Home Health and Outpatient Physical Therapy Section, Bureau of Health Insurance, Social Security Administration, Baltimore, Maryland 21235

Determination Policy Section, Division of Provider Reimbursement and Accounting Policy, Bureau of Health Insurance, Social Security Administration, Baltimore, Maryland 21235

or send for:

Outpatient Physical Therapy Provider Manual (HIM-9), Provider Reimbursement Manual (HIM-15), Social Security Administration, Publication Distribution Office, Baltimore, Maryland 21235

Medicare Audit Guide ($4.00), Audits for Voluntary Health and Welfare Organization ($4.00), American Institute of Certified Public Accountants, 1211 Avenue of the Americas, New York, New York 10036

Speech therapy also may be provided under Medicaid when the patient's eligibility has been established. Treatment is provided in clinics and in the home. Speech and hearing clinics may give primary treatment (testing) and secondary treatment (rehabilitation) to the hard-of-hearing person. These centers are staffed by audiologists. Under Medicaid, a physician must prescribe the treatment. The audiologist may diagnose, evaluate, and provide aural rehabilitation for the patient. At this time, the dispensing of hearing aids for profit by audiologists is a controversial subject.

Attention is being given to the formulation of a clear definition of the hearing-handicapped because the present definition is ". . . inadequate for legal description of, and compensation for hearing handicaps . . ." (ASHA, 1976c, p. 241). Contact with governmental agencies on the federal, state, and local levels is an ongoing process to ensure competent, reliable, and beneficial treatment of hearing aid purchasers. Concern for the hearing acuity of the entire population has been the driving force behind the New Federal Noise Standard, effective as of January 1, 1978. Adherence to this law, it is estimated, will reduce traffic noise by 24% in 1990 (ASHA, 1976a). ASHA has been seeking cooperative endeavors with other groups. Liaison has been established with the American Academy of Ophthalmology and Otolaryngology to form a statement of cooperation on occupational hearing conservation and with the Joint Commission on Accreditation of Hospitals to establish standards for the Rehabilitation Section of the Manual. In addition, the American Association of Dental Schools and ASHA (ASHA, 1975b) have established a position statement on tongue thrust therapy.

CURRENT ISSUES

Although the School Services program of ASHA works with the Bureau of Education for the Handicapped, education of those in other disciplines as to the strengths, abilities, and contributions of this discipline to the education and service of the handicapped must be continued and expanded. Seminars and workshops that include members of the field of special education are mutually beneficial in fostering understanding and in setting a firm foundation upon which to build the programs of the field.

General public awareness of the contributions of this discipline also must be heightened. A program has been initiated to alert the public to the nature and scope of the profession. Two thousand radio, television, and newspaper spot announcements were bought in 1976 to inform the public of speech, hearing, and language services (Boone, 1976). This program of education is being extended to include the medical profession, many of whom are not aware of the benefits that the patient will receive from a program in speech, hearing, and language pathology. Postgraduate courses in medical schools reflect the need for this type of education. A workshop for those in allied professions, i.e., psychologists, physical and occupational therapists, speech, hearing, and language pathologists, nurses, and physicians, was recently convened at New York University Graduate Medical School to study cognition and perception of brain-injured patients (e.g., those suffering from aphasia or senility). Members of ASHA were active participants in this joint workshop. Many physicians in the fields of neurology, pediatrics, otolaryngology, physiatry, internal medicine, and general medicine refer clients to speech, hearing, and language pathologists. It is hoped that the number of physicians who are cognizant of and receptive to this area of rehabilitation will increase.

ASHA must continually work with legislators to gain their understanding and support for the profession in health insurance and educational programs. Coverage under Medicare and Medicaid must be expanded; therapy must be considered an essential service in education. Legislators are being contacted and asked to focus their attention on the communicatively handicapped. These contacts are imperative because legislative bills relating to the field are constantly being introduced. If the national health insurance program becomes a reality, speech, hearing, and language services must be specified. These services should be available to all in need.

SOURCES OF MATERIAL FOR THERAPY

American Guidance Service, Inc., Publishers' Building, Circle Pines, Minnesota 55014

Cleo Learning Aids, 3957 Mayfield Rd., Cleveland, Ohio 44121

Communication Skill Builders, Inc., P.O. Box 6081-k, Tucson, Arizona 85733

Consulting Psychologists Press, 577 College Avenue, Palo Alto, California 94306

Developmental Learning Materials, 7440 Natchez Avenue, Niles, Illinois 60648

Dormac, Inc. P.O. Box 752, Beaverton, Oregon 97005

Ed-U-Cards Manufacturing Corp., P.O. Box 43, 1100 Church Lane, Easton, Pennsylvania 18042

Educational Activities, Inc., Box 392, Freeport, New York 11520

Incentive for Learning, 600 West Van Buren Street, Chicago, Illinois 60607

Learning Concepts, Inc., 2501 North Lamar Street, Austin, Texas 78705

Milton Bradley, 1500 Main Street, Springfield, Massachusetts 01115

Modern Education Corp., P.O. Box 721, Tulsa, Oklahoma 74101

Playskool Press, Chicago, Illinois 60618

The Psychological Corp., 757 Third Avenue, New York, New York 10017

Sound Materials, P.O. Box 452, Knoxville, Tennessee 37901

Teaching Resources, 100 Boylston Street, Boston, Massachusetts 02116

Word Making Productions, 70 West Louise Avenue, Salt Lake City, Utah 84115

REFERENCES

Abbs, J. H., Folkins, J. W., and Sivarajan, M. 1976. Motor impairment following blockade of the infraorbital nerve: Implications for the use of anesthetization techniques in speech research. J. Speech Hear. Research 19:19–35.

American Annals of the Deaf. 1968. Directory of Services for the Deaf in the United States. Gallaudet College, Washington, D.C.

American Speech and Hearing Association. 1971. A Guide to Clinical Services in Speech Pathology and Audiology. American Speech and Hearing Association, Washington, D.C.

American Speech and Hearing Association. 1975a. Directory. The Interstate Printers and Publishers, Danville, Ill.

American Speech and Hearing Association. 1975b. Joint Commission on Dentistry and Speech Pathology-Audiology. Position statement on tongue thrust. Asha 17:331–337.

American Speech and Hearing Association. 1976a. Capitol highlight. Asha 18:868.

American Speech and Hearing Association. 1976b. Committees and Boards of the American Speech and Hearing Association. Asha 18:253–259.

American Speech and Hearing Association. 1976c. 9030. Asha 18:241.

American Speech and Hearing Association. 1976d. 9030. Asha 18:433.

Barbara, D. A. 1954. Stuttering: A Psychodynamic Approach to its Understanding and Treatment. Julian Press, New York.

Bender, L. 1960. Autism in children with mental deficiency. Am. J. Mental Deficiency 63:81–86.

Bender, M., and Valletutti, P. J. 1976. Teaching the Moderately and Severely Handicapped. Vol. II. University Park Press, Baltimore.

Berry, M. 1969. Language Disorders in Children. Appleton-Century-Crofts, New York.

Bloodstein, O. 1958. Stuttering as an anticipatory struggle reaction. In J. Eisenson (ed.), Stuttering: A Symposium, pp. 1–69. Harper and Row, New York.

Bloodstein, O. 1969. A Handbook on Stuttering. National Easter Seal Society for Crippled Children and Adults, Chicago.

Bloom, L. 1970. Language Development: Form and Function in Emerging Grammars. The M.I.T. Press, Cambridge, Mass.

Bobath, K. 1966. The Motor Deficit in Patients with Cerebral Palsy. The Lavenham Press, Ltd., Lavenham, Suffolk, England.

Boone, D. J. 1976. Our profession—where is it? ASHA 18:415.

Brutten, E. J., and Shoemaker, D. J. 1967. The Modification of Stuttering. Prentice-Hall, Englewood Cliffs, N.J.

Chalfant, J. C., and Scheffelin, M. (eds.). 1969. Central Processing Dysfunctions in Children: A Review of the Research. National Institute of Neurological Disease and Stroke. Monograph No. 9. U.S. Dept. of Health, Education and Welfare, Bethesda, Md.

Chomsky, N. 1965. Aspects of the Theory of Syntax. The M.I.T. Press, Cambridge, Mass.

Costello, J. 1975. The establishment of fluency with time-out procedures: 3 case studies. J. Speech Hear. Disorders 40:216–231.

Cromer, R. F. 1974. Receptive language in the mentally retarded: Processes and diagnostic distinctions. In R. L. Schiefelbusch and L. L. Lloyd (eds.), Language Perspectives—Acquisition, Retardation, and Intervention, pp. 237–267. University Park Press, Baltimore.

Cutting, J. E., and Kavanagh, J. F. 1975. On the relationship of speech to language. Asha 17:500–506.

Eisenberg, L. 1957. The fathers of autistic children. Am. J. Orthopsychiatry 27:715–724.

Federal Register. 1976. Education of Handicapped Children, Assistance to States: Proposed Rulemaking. Part III. U.S. Dept. of Health, Education and Welfare, Office of Education, Washington, D.C.

Fenton, E. R. 1976. Sourcebook: Speech and Hearing Services Metropolitan New York Area. New Jersey Leigh Foundation, New York.

Flanagan, J., and Golden, R. 1966. Phase vocoder. Bell System Tech. J. 45:1493–1509.

Fraser, C., Bellugi, U., and Brown, R. 1963. Control of grammar in imitation, comprehension and production. J. Verbal Learn. Verbal Behavior 2:121–135.

Glauber, I. P. 1958. The psychoanalysis of stuttering. In J. Eisenson (ed.), Stuttering: A Symposium, pp. 71–119. Harper and Row, New York.

Goldiamond, I. 1965. Stuttering and fluency as manipulatable operant response classes. In L. Krasner and L. P. Ullman (eds.), Research in Behavior Modification, pp. 106–156. Holt, Rinehart and Winston, New York.

Goldstein, R., Landau, W. M., and Kleffner, F. R. 1958. Neurological assessment of deaf and aphasic children. Transactions of the American Otologic Society. 46:122–136.

Hanley, T., and Peters, R. 1971. The speech and hearing laboratory. In L. E. Travis (ed.), Handbook of Speech Pathology and Audiology, pp. 75–140. Meredith Corporation, New York.

Hanna, R., Wilfling, F., and McNeill, B. 1975. A biofeedback treatment for stuttering. J. Speech Hear. Disorders 40:270–273.

Healey, W. C., and Dublinske, S. 1977. Notes from the school services program. Language, Speech, and Hearing Services in Schools 8:67–71.

Hixon, T. J., Mead, J. and Goldman, M. D. 1976. Dynamics of the chest wall during speech production: Function of the thorax, rib cage, diaphragm, and abdomen. J. Speech Hear. Research 19:297–356.

Hoffnung, A. 1974. An analysis of the syntactic structures of children with deviant articulation. Unpublished doctoral dissertation. City College of New York, New York.

Holland, A. L. 1975. Language therapy for children: Some thoughts on context and content. J. Speech Hear. Disorders 40:514–523.

Irwin, J. V., and Marge, M. 1972. Principles of Childhood Language Disabilities. Prentice-Hall, Englewood Cliffs, N.J.

Jakobson, R. 1967. Child Language, Aphasia and Phonological Universals. Mouton and Company, The Hague, The Netherlands.

Jakobson, R., Fant, C. G., and Halle, M. 1967. Preliminaries to Speech Analysis. The M.I.T. Press, Cambridge, Mass.

Kanner, L. 1943. Autistic disturbances of affective contact. Nervous Child 2:217–250.

Klinger, H. 1976. Precision fluency training. Lecture to Sigma Alpha Eta. October 20, 1976. Brooklyn College, New York.

Lenneberg, E. H. 1967. Biological Foundations of Language. John Wiley and Sons, Inc., New York.

Liberman, A. M., Cooper, F. S., Harris, K. S., and MacNeilage, P. F. 1962. A Motor Theory of Speech Perception. Haskins Laboratories, New York.

Lovaas, I., Berberich, B., Perloff, B., and Schaeffer, B. 1966. Acquisition of imitative speech in schizophrenic children. Science 151:705–708.

Lowe, A. D., and Campbell, R. A. 1965. Temporal discrimination in aphasoid and normal children. J. Speech Hear. Research 8:313–314.

McGinnis, M., Kleffner, F., and Goldstein, R. 1956. Teaching aphasic children. Volta Review 58:239–244.

McNeill, D. 1966. Developmental psycholinguistics. In F. Smith and G. A. Miller (eds.), The Genesis of Language, pp. 7–84. The M.I.T. Press, Cambridge, Mass.

McReynolds, L. V., and Huston, K. 1971. A distinctive feature analysis of children's misarticulations. J. Speech Hear. Disorders 36:155–166.

Martin, R. R., and Siegel, G. M. 1966a. The effects of response contingent shock on stuttering. J. Speech Hear. Research 9:340–352.

Martin, R. R., and Siegel, G. M. 1966b. The effects of simultaneously punishing stuttering and rewarding fluency. J. Speech Hear. Research 9:466–475.

Mattingly, I. G. 1972. Reading, the linguistic process and linguistic awareness. In J. F. Kavanagh and I. G. Mattingly (eds.), Language by Ear and by Eye: The Relationship Between Speech and Reading, pp. 133–146. The M.I.T. Press, Cambridge, Mass.

Mayberry, R. 1976. If a chimp can learn sign language, surely my nonverbal client can too. Asha 18:223–228.

Moll, K. L. 1960. Cinefluorographic techniques in speech research. J. Speech Hear. Research 3:227–241.

Moore, P. 1971. Organic Voice Disorders. Prentice-Hall, Englewood Cliffs, N.J.

Morris, L. 1962. Communication skills of children with cleft lips and palates. J. Speech Hear. Research 5:79–90.

Mueller, H. 1972. Facilitating feeding and prespeech. In P. H. Pearson and C. E. Williams (eds.), Physical Therapy Services in Developmental Disabilities, pp. 283–310. Charles C Thomas, Springfield, Ill.

Myklebust, H. 1973. Developmental Disorders of Written Language. Grune and Stratton, New York.

Mysak, E. 1968. Neuroevolutional Approach to Cerebral Palsy and Speech. Teachers College Press, Columbia University, New York.

Nazarova, L. K. 1952. The role of speech kinesthesias in writing. Sovet Pedag. 6.

Paden, E. P. 1975. ASHA in retrospect—fiftieth anniversary reflections. Asha 17:831.

Perkins, W. H. 1973a. Replacement of stuttering with normal speech: I Rationale. J. Speech Hear. Disorders 38:283–294.

Perkins, W. H. 1973b. Replacement of stuttering with normal speech: II Clinical procedures. J. Speech Hear. Disorders 38:295–303.

Philips, B. J., and Harrison, R. 1969. Language skills of preschool cleft palate children. Cleft Palate J. 6:108–119.

Piaget, J. 1963. The Language and Thought of the Child. Meridian Books, New York.

Rimland, B. 1964. Infantile Autism. Appleton-Century-Crofts, New York.

Ruder, K. F., Smith, M. D., and Herman, P. 1974. Effect of verbal imitation and comprehension on verbal production of lexical items. ASHA Monograph 18:15–30.

Schuell, H., Jenkins, J. J., Jiménez-Pabón, E. 1967. Aphasia in Adults. Harper and Row, New York.

Shankweiler, D. 1968. Disorders of reading. In J. F. Kavanagh (ed.), Communicating by Language: The Reading Process, pp. 202–211. U.S. Dept. of Health, Education and Welfare, Bethesda, Md.

Sheehan, J. 1958. Conflict theory of stuttering. In J. Eisenson (ed.), Stuttering: A Symposium, pp. 121–166. Harper and Row, New York.

Shipley, E., Smith, C., and Gleitman, L. 1969. A study in the acquisition of language: Free responses to commands. Language 45:322–342.

Smith, R., and McWilliams, B. J. 1968. Psycholinguistic abilities of children with clefts. Cleft Palate J. 5:239–249.

Soderberg, G. A. 1969. Delayed auditory feedback and the speech of stutterers: A review of the studies. J. Speech Hear. Disorders 34:20–29.

Stark, J. 1975. Reading failure: A language-based problem. Asha 17:832–834.

Stremel, K., and Waryas, C. 1974. A behavioral-psycholinguistic approach to language training. ASHA Monograph 18:96–130.

Tallal, P. 1976. Rapid auditory processing in normal and disordered language development. J. Speech Hear. Research 19:561–572.

Travis, L. E. 1931. Speech Pathology. Appleton-Century-Crofts, New York.

Vanderheiden, G. C., and Grilley, K. 1976. Non-vocal Communication Techniques and Aids for the Severely Physically Handicapped. University Park Press, Baltimore.

Van Riper, C. 1973. The Treatment of Stuttering. Prentice-Hall, Englewood Cliffs, N.J.

von Luden, H. 1961. The electronic synchron-stroboscope. Annals Otol. Rhin. and Laryngology 70:881–893.

West, R. 1958. An agnostic's speculations about stuttering. *In* J. Eisenson (ed.), Stuttering: A Symposium, pp. 122–167. Harper and Row, New York.

West, R., and Ansberry, M. 1968. The Rehabilitation of Speech. Harper and Row, New York.

Wischner, G. J. 1950. Stuttering behavior and learning: A preliminary theoretical formulation. J. Speech Hear. Disorders 15:324–335.

Wolf, E., and Ruttenberg, B. 1967. Communication therapy for the autistic child. J. Speech Hear. Disorders 32:331–335.

THERAPEUTIC RECREATION

David C. Park
and Viki S. Annand

One of the newer professional disciplines providing services to handicapped individuals is the discipline of therapeutic recreation. The emergence of this field as a professional service dates back to the mid-1940s when hospitals and institutions began hiring full-time personnel to provide recreation services for residents and patients. Since that time, the field has become established as a recognized professional discipline with a unique service to provide to the education and rehabilitation of ill, handicapped, and disabled persons.

In general, the field has become identified as that part of the overall recreation profession that is concerned with provision of services for handicapped persons, much as special education is related to the overall education field. It is true that recreation is a basic need for all individuals and is as important for handicapped persons as it is for nondisabled people. A careful delineation, however, must be made between recreation services and therapeutic recreation services because the latter involves more than the provision of recreation opportunities for disabled people. Recreation is generally seen as an activity that is engaged in as an end in itself. The primary purpose of the activity is the fun and enjoyment of having participated in it. Therapeutic recreation, on the other hand, implies the utilization of the recreation experience for larger goals that generally relate to the correction, remediation, or modification of some behavior.

This interrelatedness and this differentiation between the overall recreation field and therapeutic recreation are important in order to understand the goals, purposes, and functions of therapeutic recreation.

PROFESSIONAL PURPOSES AND GOALS

Therapeutic recreation is a special service within the broad area of recreation services (Committee of Participants, 1969). An understanding of the scope of this service requires a basic understanding of the nature of the larger service, recreation, of which it is a part. The values inherent in both services are the same and lead many people to comment that all recreation is therapeutic.

Recreation

Recreation services are often referred to as leisure services, as if recreation and leisure were synonomous. Some philosophers and sociologists would argue with this concept, stating that recreation is a measurable activity whereas leisure is a state of mind. Others regard leisure as a period of time, time when man is free from obligations. Regardless of whether the concepts of leisure and recreation are interchangeable, whether one is a generic part of the other, or whether both have numerable and varied meanings, there are some basic concepts about recreation that must be accepted in order to define and delimit elements of this professional service.

Practitioners and philosophers tend to regard recreation as an experience, a diversion, an activity, and a state-of-being. Webster defines it as a period for "re-creation," a period of rest and restoration from toil. Meyers (1962, p. 23) has compared it to the "glide" phase of the physiological concept of the harmonious performance of body functions. During the "stroke" phase individuals accomplish their work, i.e., their maintenance activities and their vocational pursuits. It is during recreation, or the "glide" phase, that people recover from stress caused during the stroke phase and experience refreshment of mind, body, and spirit.

Another important aspect of recreation is that individuals engage in it voluntarily. It is the time when they are free to pursue those activities in which they are interested. They are free to choose what they wish to do without expecting others to structure their experience.

Recreation provides the participant with satisfaction. This is an important concept to consider in understanding why people voluntarily pursue the activities they do. While people are probably not aware of it, they choose their recreation to meet their own needs. Recreation brings them a feeling of well-being, of fun. There are a variety of needs that are met through recreative experiences. These needs vary from person to person and, even for the same person, from time to time.

Many recreation professionals, sociologists, and philosophers include other elements in the concept of recreation. For example, some say that recreation must be comprised of socially acceptable activities. Others state that the activities must make constructive use of leisure time. Some people feel that the satisfaction derived from the activity must be immediate and others believe that no monetary reward for the activity is an important element of recreation. Basically, recreation can be viewed as a leisure experience engaged in voluntarily and providing satisfaction to the participant.

Values of Recreation

In view of the above concepts, some of the values that may be derived from recreation can be identified. Because recreation is voluntary, it allows people to have authority over their destiny. This concept of *freedom* is very important, because there is perhaps no other sphere in a person's life where he/she has such control. During leisure, individuals are free to choose what they wish to do and to what extent they wish to do it. As a result of this freedom to choose the activity, they are much more likely to experience *mastery* and *achievement*. The ability to succeed at something affects both how others view them, which brings *recognition,* and how they feel about themselves, which contributes to *self-concept.* It is recognized that the development of self-respect and a good self-concept are important in the healthy growth and development of every individual.

Recreation provides a variety of means for need satisfaction. It may take the form of a physical activity, a creative expression, a social experience, an exciting activity, a challenging opportunity, and/or a learning experience. Because of its diversity, recreation allows the expression of *individuality.* In this day of mass production and computerization, recreation offers some individuals the opportunities for self-identity and the development of a sense of worth and pride that they miss in their vocational lives.

Participation in physical recreational pursuits is important for maintaining a healthy physical well-being. Physical activity also can be helpful in reducing and controlling tension and anxiety. Physical health is adversely affected by contemporary life-styles, which are often sedentary, rushed, and demanding; recreation can counterbalance the ill effects on both *physical* and *mental health* of anxiety and tension.

Just as mass production can reduce the opportunities for an individual to take pride in work, it also can reduce the chances for creative expression. Recreational activities, while providing an outlet for *creative expression,* provide opportunities for *excitement* and *challenge.* In the humdrum existence of the conveyor belt, in a world in which the new frontiers are space exploration, medical research, and scientific advancement, these needs may only be met vocationally for a select few who are highly educated. Nevertheless, everyone experiences the need for excitement and challenge. Recreation may provide the means for making challenging and exciting experiences available to everyone.

The values derived from *social experiences* are perhaps most often linked with recreation. The need for acceptance and association with others is basic as identified in Maslow's hierarchy of needs. Recreation offers an abundance of opportunities for socialization, group identification, and group acceptance.

All of the preceding values of recreation contribute to the maximal growth of an individual. These experiences may meet basic needs of some individuals or may be the avenue to self-actualization for others. As people continually strive toward growth, recreation is an integral and important aspect of their lives.

Therapeutic Recreation

Access to recreational experiences is a basic right of all people, including those with handicapping conditions. Therapeutic recreation, however, is more than ensuring that handicapped individuals have the opportunity for participation in the same recreational programs, activities, and facilities that nonhandicapped citizens enjoy. Therapeutic recreation deals with meeting the special needs of handicapped individuals.

A 1969 Task Force of the National Therapeutic Recreation Society has defined therapeutic recreation as a "process which utilizes recreation services for purposive intervention in some physical, emotional and/or social behavior to bring about a desired change in that behavior and to promote the growth and development of the individual" (Committee of Participants, 1969). While recreation is of great value to the general population, it may be even more important to persons with disabilities. For some individuals who have had impairments since birth and have not had a normal opportunity to grow and develop, planned recreational experiences can offer the necessary opportunity for growth and development. For those individuals who became disabled later in life, therapeutic recreation offers a medium for strengthening weakened conditions, ameliorating inabilities, and learning adaptive skills. Basically, the goals of therapeutic recreation are the same as the rehabilitative goals of the agency or institution in which it takes place. That is, the therapeutic recreation program is related to the reason why the person is at the agency or in the institution.

This is not to suggest that all persons with handicapping conditions need therapeutic recreation. Just as there are people in the general population functioning at a variety of levels, persons with disabilities present a similar variety of functional levels. Therapeutic recreation is needed only for those individuals who are not functioning at/near their potential or for those individuals who, because of their disability, are unable to assume responsibility for their own leisure activities. Therapeutic recreation is a process that requires meeting individuals at their level of functioning and helping them move toward greater independence and growth.

A Continuum of Service

To effectively meet the needs of individuals at different functional levels and to help move them toward higher levels of functioning, a variety of service delivery systems are used. These varying services fall along a continuum and are best described by Frye's and Peters' (1972, p. 43) therapeutic recreation continuum (see Figure 1).

At the one end of the continuum are individuals who are unable to meet their own needs in recreation. These individuals require a good deal of structure and support from the therapeutic recreator. Individuals at progressive points along the continuum require less and less structure and are able to exert greater and greater independence in their leisure functioning. Individuals at the other end of the continuum are characterized by autonomous functioning and by an independent leisure life-style.

Just because therapeutic recreation is purposeful and/or prescribed, the potential of the recreation activity to provide a pleasurable, fun experience for the participant is not negated. Wherever possible, the therapist uses activities of interest to the participant as motivation. It is perhaps because of this element of fun that recreation as a treatment modality can be so valuable. Furthermore, not all recreation should be therapeutic for people functioning at levels requiring behavior change. Because all people need the "recreative" aspect of recreation, there must be opportunities for handicapped as well as nonhandicapped persons to voluntarily participate in activities for whatever satisfaction they may derive.

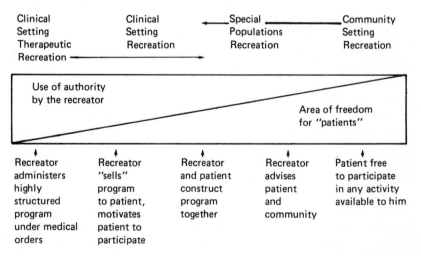

Figure 1.   Therapeutic Recreation—A Continuum. (Reprinted with permission from Frye and Peters, 1972, as taken from: Cynthia Bertholf, James Brademus, Laura Jarvis, Cheryl Reeves, "Therapeutic Recreation—A Continuum," unpublished paper, 1969. Adaptation of concept and diagram of change of authority and freedom based upon Robert Tannenbaum and Warren H. Schmidt, "How to Choose a Leadership Pattern," *Harvard Business Review,* Vol. 36, No. 2 (March–April, 1958). pp. 95–101.)

NATURE OF CLIENTS FOR WHOM SERVICES ARE APPROPRIATE

Recreation is a basic need from early childhood until death. It may be used with anyone for whom a purposeful change in behavior and planned growth and development are desired or with the person who, because of some limitation, is unable to function in a regular program. Some people regard therapeutic recreation as a service only for people with disabling conditions. Other people would broaden this concept to include any population for whom the objective is habilitation or rehabilitation.

At the present time, therapeutic recreation services are provided to people with mental illness and emotional disturbances, mental retardation, and physical disabilities including deafness, blindness, cerebral palsy, muscular dystrophy, multiple sclerosis, cardiac problems, and various orthopaedic conditions. Therapeutic recreation is also used with the aging, the socially disadvantaged, and persons in correctional facilities.

TYPE OF INSTITUTIONS FROM WHICH SERVICES ARE OBTAINED

Service delivery systems providing various types of recreational services differ from one end of the therapeutic recreation continuum to the other. For the person functioning at the extreme end of the continuum where therapeutic recreation might be most warranted, the setting would be a treatment, habilitation, or rehabilitation agency or institution. Grouping would be segregated, and programming may be on a one-to-one basis. Toward the middle of the continuum, the service delivery system would be halfway services. This setting might either be a treatment agency or a community recreation agency. The emphasis at these agencies would be on the provision of more normal recreation opportunities. Efforts would be made to help the participant function along side people in the general program. Selective integration of handicapped individuals into regular programs would be done with support, but, for the most part, actual activities would be segregated. The setting for the delivery of services to clients who function independently during their leisure time would be any of the public or private recreation services available to the general public.

Within any one of the above settings, individuals may function at various levels of independence. Keeping this in mind, some of the specific facilities where therapeutic recreation is provided include: institutions and residential schools for specific types of disabilities, nursing homes and long term care facilities, hospitals, rehabilitation centers, community rehabilitation agencies and sheltered workshops, voluntary health agencies, and quasi-public and public recreation agencies. Therapeutic recreation services also can be found in prisons and detention homes.

SPECIALIZED TECHNIQUES, APPARATUS, AND LANGUAGE

The medium used for therapeutic recreation is recreation or activities. *Activities* include but are not limited to: creative arts (arts, arts and crafts, dance, drama, movement, and music), physical activities (aquatics, low organized games, physical fitness activities, individual and dual sports, and team sports), camping and outdoor recreation, hobbies, excursions, horticultural activities, and social recreation.

The process of therapeutic recreation uses several techniques to effect the goal of behavior change. A variety of terms, discussed below, are used to describe these techniques.

Evaluation

Evaluation is a systematic process used to determine an individual's functional level or abilities in a specified area. Methods used include observation of behavior, self-report, behavior scales, and standardized tests. Evaluation is an important aspect of therapeutic recreation and includes assessing an individual's abilities, determining treatment goals, and measuring change.

Goal Planning

Goal planning (also called diagnostic/prescriptive programming and/or individualized programming) is a process that utilizes knowledge of an individual's abilities or functional level to develop specific behavioral goals for that individual. Knowledge of an individual's goals are needed to effectively plan programs.

Activity Analysis

Activity analysis is a systematic examination of an activity and its various aspects to understand the inherent qualities, participation factors, or possible outcomes. It is further used to structure that activity so that it is presented at an individual's functional level, thereby increasing the opportunity for achievement of the individual's goals as developed in goal planning.

It is the interrelationship of these three processes (evaluation, goal planning, and activity analysis) that structures and defines the therapeutic recreation process. In addition, several other leisure delivery services are used in therapeutic recreation including the following five techniques.

Diversional Recreation

Diversional recreation refers to those recreation programs established for the purpose of providing pleasure and satisfaction. In a treatment setting, it is important that individuals be free to satisfy their natural recreative needs.

This type of program provides normalizing experiences while helping to reduce the dehumanizing effects of institutionalization.

Adapted or Modified Activities

Adapted or modified activities are activities that have been changed in some manner to make it possible for an individual to participate in them. Changes may include: the use of slower movement, a new technique for accomplishing the activity, the use of aids to accomplish the activity, modified equipment, or a change in rules and procedures for the activity.

Transitional Programming

Transitional programming is specifically related to the patient's move from the institution to the community. In therapeutic recreation, the objective is to help an individual to become independent in leisure functioning. Some of the ways therapeutic recreation programs attempt to accomplish this are: skill development in activities with carry-over value, trips into the community, the provision of information about community recreation programs, leisure education and leisure counseling, and assistance in developing specific "halfway" programs in the community.

Leisure Education

Leisure education is a process to increase self-awareness and development of leisure attitudes, values, beliefs, knowledge, and skills. It may involve the development of planning and problem-solving skills.

Leisure Counseling

Leisure counseling is a helping process that utilizes specific verbal facilitation techniques to promote awareness, understanding, and clarification of the individual's self (attitudes, beliefs, values, personal resources) based upon the client's felt difficulty about leisure (such as guilt, obligation, anxiety, fear, social isolation, procrastination, boredom, uncertainty, or compulsion).

PROFESSIONAL PREPARATION

As roles and functions of therapeutic recreation personnel have become more clearly defined and as new roles have emerged, professional training requirements have changed and expanded. At the present time, therapeutic recreation career possibilities include training at the paraprofessional level, the two-year college level, the baccalaureate degree level, the master's degree level, and the doctoral level.

Historically, therapeutic recreation specialists came into the profession through a variety of interrelated routes. Some early therapeutic recreation specialists were recreation leaders who found employment in hospital set-tings. Others were physical education specialists who began developing physical activity programs in hospitals and institutions. Others were social workers who began using activities as a tool in treatment. Still others were occupational therapists who began providing diversional occupational therapy.

As the need for more and more full-time personnel in the field increased, attempts were made to organize the body of knowledge needed to perform the duties of a therapeutic recreation specialist and to develop specific training programs. The first major impetus for the growth and development of therapeutic recreation professional preparation came from the Vocational Rehabilitation Administration of the U.S. Department of Health, Education and Welfare in the early 1960s. At that time, through the Vocational Rehabilitation Act (VRA), funds were made available for the development of master's degree training programs in the area of "recreation for the ill and handicapped." During that decade, approximately 10 colleges and universities developed such programs with VRA funds that provided faculty support and student traineeships.

In the late 1960s, the Education for Handicapped Children's Act also provided training funds for the area of recreation services to handicapped children and youth as a part of the total education of handicapped children. Initially, these programs, administered by the Bureau of Education for the Handicapped (BEH) of the U.S. Office of Education, were for master's level training and provided faculty support and student traineeships. In the past few years, the numbers of specialists trained at the master's degree level has increased, and BEH has begun funding programs at the bacca-laureate level, the two-year level, and the paraprofessional level. The Bureau is currently placing increased emphasis on inservice training opportunities.

In the early 1970s, the National Therapeutic Recreation Society, the national professional organization for the therapeutic recreation field, became concerned with specific training opportunities for parapro-fessionals. In 1971, they approved a 750 clock hour training program for aides and assistants that can be provided as either a preservice or an inservice training program.

As a result of the increasing demand for therapeutic recreation person-nel and the success of the training programs identified above, many colleges and universities across the country have initiated curricula at various levels. A recent survey of colleges and universities providing training in therapeutic recreation indicated a total of approximately 100 programs at the bacca-laureate level. Approximately half of these also have programs at the master's degree level; there are an increasing number of programs at the two-year level. Currently, three universities have been approved by the National Therapeutic Recreation Society to offer the 750 clock hour program for therapeutic recreation technicians. Also, because of the increase in training programs and the need for qualitative research in the field, a number of recreation and leisure studies departments now are providing doctoral training with a special emphasis in therapeutic recreation.

Although exact roles in the field are still emerging and undoubtedly will be altered as the entire field of services to handicapped individuals changes, the following roles and the levels of training needed to perform these roles seems to be developing as follows:

Roles	Level of Training
Therapeutic Recreation Aide or Assistant	Informal inservice education or 750 clock hour program
Therapeutic Recreation Technician	750 hour program or two-year degree
Therapeutic Recreation Leader	Baccalaureate degree
Therapeutic Recreation Supervisor (master clinician)	Master's degree
Therapeutic Recreation Consultant	Master's degree/Doctorate
Therapeutic Recreation Researcher	Master's degree/Doctorate
Therapeutic Recreation Educator	Master's degree/Doctorate

LICENSURE AND CERTIFICATION

The current method for accrediting professional personnel in the therapeutic recreation field is through the National Voluntary Registration Program administered by the National Therapeutic Recreation Society (NTRS). This program was established in 1953 by three national organizations that were concerned with the development of recreation services for disabled individuals. In the absence of one single professional organization at that time, the Council for the Advancement of Hospital Recreation was created and given the authority to develop and implement a national registration program. At the time of its inception, the registration process related solely to services performed in hospitals and institutions and carried the terminology of hospital recreation.

In 1966, the program came under the direction of the newly formed NTRS, which was established for the purpose of becoming the central professional organization in the field. At that time, new standards were developed that more accurately mirrored the professional preparation programs in existence. New terminology of therapeutic recreation was adopted to reflect not only hospital services but also recreation services provided to handicapped individuals in nonhospital settings.

Since 1966, much progress has been made in the national acceptance of this registration program as the official means of being professionally recognized for employment in the field of therapeutic recreation. The number of professionally registered personnel has grown from 300 in 1966 to over 2,000 in 1977, and the applications for consideration are continuing to increase.

Even though the program is still essentially a voluntary one, it is recognized by some national standard setting agencies as the means of certifying professionally competent personnel. For example, the standards for recreation services in residential facilities for the mentally retarded conform to the requirements of the NTRS registration program. The conditions of participation for activity program directors in extended and intermediate care facilities refer specifically to the NTRS registration program. In addition, some individual state personnel requirements for departments of mental health and mental retardation require registration for therapeutic recreation personnel with the NTRS.

Some individual state professional organizations operate state registration programs that, for the most part, are patterned after the national one. In fact, some states simply require national registration with NTRS in order to qualify for state registration. Other states have developed state registration requirements that, depending on the supply of trained manpower in that particular state, are either more or less restrictive than the national program.

At the present time, the criteria for professional registration at the national level are based on academic preparation and experience in the therapeutic recreation field. No formal written examination is required. Six levels of registration, dependent upon education and experience, have been identified, and criteria have been established for qualification at each level. The six levels and evaluative criteria are as follows:

1. Therapeutic Recreation Assistant
   a. Two years of successful full-time paid experience in the therapeutic field, or
   b. Two hundred clock hours inservice training in the therapeutic recreation field, or
   c. A combination of a and b
2. Therapeutic Recreation Technician I
   Successful completion of NTRS-approved 750 hour Training Program for Therapeutic Recreation Technician I
3. Therapeutic Recreation Technician II
   a. Associate of Arts degree from an accredited college or university with an emphasis in therapeutic recreation, or
   b. Certification or other proof of satisfactory completion of two

academic years of study in recreation with an emphasis or option in therapeutic and current employment in therapeutic recreation, or

c. Certification or other proof of satisfactory completion of two academic years of study in a skills area (e.g., physical education, arts and crafts, art, dance, music) and two years of professional work experience in therapeutic recreation

4. Therapeutic Recreation Leader
   a. (Provisional) Baccalaureate degree from an accredited college or university with a major in recreation or
   b. (Registered) Baccalaureate degree from an accredited college or university with a major in recreation and an option or emphasis in therapeutic recreation, or
   c. (Registered) Baccalaureate degree from an accredited college or university with a major in recreation and one year of professional work experience in therapeutic recreation

5. Therapeutic Recreation Specialist
   a. Master's degree from an accredited college or university with a major in recreation and an option or emphasis in therapeutic recreation, or
   b. Master's degree from an accredited college or university with a major in recreation and one year of professional work experience in therapeutic recreation, or
   c. Baccalaureate degree from an accredited college or university with a major in recreation and an option or emphasis in therapeutic recreation and three years of professional work experience in therapeutic recreation, or
   d. Baccalaureate degree from an accredited college or university with a major in recreation and four years of professional work experience in therapeutic recreation

6. Master Therapeutic Recreation Specialist
   a. Master's degree from an accredited college or university with a major in recreation and an option or emphasis in therapeutic recreation plus two years of professional work experience plus two years of professional work experience in therapeutic recreation, or
   b. Master's degree from an accredited college or university with a major in recreation and three years of professional work experience in therapeutic recreation, or
   c. Baccalaureate degree from an accredited college or university with a major in recreation and an option or emphasis in therapeutic recreation and six graduate credits in therapeutic recreation plus five years of professional work experience in therapeutic recreation, or

d. Baccalaureate degree from an accredited college or university with a major in recreation and 12 graduate credits in therapeutic recreation plus six years of professional work experience in therapeutic recreation. (National Recreation and Park Association, n.d.)

Current trends in service delivery for allied health disciplines will most likely continue to require more restrictive standards for services and for personnel. As the therapeutic recreation field continues to expand and develop and as more and more professionally trained individuals become available, more restrictive standards and procedures will likely emerge, and the field will probably move closer and closer to legal licensure. The state certification procedures of California and New Jersey, which utilize a written examination, may be pointing the way toward the ultimate direction of the national program.

RESEARCH NEEDS

As with any relatively new professional discipline, the research needs in therapeutic recreation are immense. Even though recreation services have been provided for many years, concern for a coordinated effort to conduct research in the field has not been expressed until recently. Empirical data to substantiate the philosophical rationale is being demanded as therapeutic recreation develops as a professional discipline. The U.S. Department of Health, Education and Welfare has promoted empirical research through the Rehabilitation Services Administration and the Bureau of Education for the Handicapped.

It was stated earlier that the Rehabilitation Services Administration was the first federal agency to recognize the value of recreation in the rehabilitation of ill and handicapped persons. In the 1960s, at the same time that training programs in recreation were initiated, some research projects were funded. The primary purpose of these projects, which were mainly of a demonstration nature, was to determine the most appropriate methods of providing recreation services in rehabilitation facilities. Under the 1973 Rehabilitation Act, money was made available for demonstration efforts designed to make recreation areas and facilities accessible to handicapped persons. In addition, other research studies conducted by rehabilitation personnel have indicated that, in many instances, needed recreation services are not being provided handicapped persons.

Since the late 1960s, the Bureau of Education for the Handicapped (BEH) has been involved with research concerning the recreation and leisure needs of handicapped children. In 1969, BEH funded a national study conference on research and demonstration needs in the areas of physical education and recreation for handicapped children. This conference attempted to identify and place in order of priority research needs in the area of recreation to guide BEH in its funding of future research projects and to stimulate the research efforts of the field. This conference was followed, in 1974, by a BEH-funded conference specifically related to research needs in the area of leisure activity participation for handicapped populations. This conference focused on the provision of therapeutic recreation services for and leisure time participation of handicapped children. The conference participants identified five priority areas in which specific research efforts are needed. These areas are:

1. *Social psychology and leisure behavior.* One of the significant barriers to leisure participation for handicapped persons is the area of attitudes toward leisure participation. Other factors requiring research are achievement motivation in leisure activities, role of competition in growth and development, impact of mainstreaming in recreation programs, and methods of providing services.

2. *Leisure activity analysis and programming.* Efforts are under way to systematically analyze the components of a whole variety of activities in order to understand the skills, attitudes, and action required for successful participation. With this kind of knowledge, more effective recreation planning can take place, and activities can be prescribed that have a better potential for achieving specified objectives for handicapped clients.

3. *Barrier reduction and environmental design.* Much effort has been expended toward the development of standards and criteria for making buildings and facilities accessible to handicapped persons. These same efforts need to be extended into outdoor recreation areas and facilities and into the area of equipment design to enable handicapped persons to participate in leisure activities.

4. *Dissemination and utilization.* While many innovative programs and needed research activities are completed, they often are not adequately disseminated and thus cannot be utilized by others. The result is wasted effort and duplication of activities. Better methods of dissemination and utilization are needed to maximize the impact of research efforts.

5. *Service delivery.* There are many methods and modalities for delivering therapeutic recreation services. Oftentimes, the desired effect of an activity or program may not be realized because of problems in the service delivery method chosen. Research is needed to determine the most effective delivery methods in relationship to specified goals and objectives (National Recreation and Park Association, 1976).

In short, research needs in therapeutic recreation are enormous. Significant efforts have been made, but much more needs to be done. It has been argued for years that participation in recreation activities has specific impact on the growth and development, education, and rehabilitation of individuals. As in any area of social research, it is difficult to empirically prove impact with any degree of specificity. It is imperative, however, that efforts to better quantify the impact of these services continue.

INTERDISCIPLINARY COOPERATION

Therapeutic recreation is provided primarily in hospitals, institutions, and rehabilitation facilities where a therapeutic recreation specialist is one member of an interdisciplinary team approach to treatment. Because of this, it is imperative that concepts of interdisciplinary cooperation and interaction be addressed and clarified. Health care accountability trends currently demand that efforts be made to eliminate duplication of services and to provide specific accountability for services rendered. The therapeutic recreation field and other disciplines must constantly strive for increased cooperation to ensure the best quality service for patients or clients.

Perhaps the most significant problem for therapeutic recreation relates to the apparent overlapping of services with other disciplines. When therapeutic recreation first emerged as a professional service, it was concerned with the provision of a wide range of activities, employed previously for diversional purposes. As the profession developed, activities were used not only for diversion but for specifically identified treatment goals. In recent years, other disciplines have emerged that utilize a single modality for corrective and remedial purposes. Some of these disciplines are art therapy, dance therapy, music therapy, and horticultural therapy. The question of overlapping services arises when one ponders the difference between art, music, or dance provided as a treatment modality by an art therapist, dance therapist, or music therapist, and those same modalities when utilized, as part of a treatment program, by a therapeutic recreation specialist.

The answer to this question lies in the recognition of two basic facts. First of all, impact upon the cognitive, affective, and psychomotor functions of patients and clients is not the sole domain of any one particular discipline. The three domains are inextricably interrelated, and, consequently, any member of the treatment team working with the total person will influence, to some degree, all three domains. Second, even though there is some overlap in the use of specific modalities (e.g., art, music, and dance), therapists generally have different objectives in mind which, while related, are secondary to the primary goals established by the treatment team. Considering the similarities, however, that exist in the services provided by various disciplines, it is imperative that greater communication and cooperation be achieved so that the client will receive the best possible treatment without the confusion, interference, and expense of overlapping and duplicated services.

TIME AND COST

Therapeutic recreation specialists are typically full-time staff persons of a treatment or rehabilitation facility. They are responsible for providing activities and services throughout the day to meet the treatment goals of the institution and to meet the leisure time needs of the residents or patients. In most facilities, particularly residential facilities, this necessitates a staff of therapeutic recreators who cover programming from early in the morning until bedtime. Frequently, the programs and activities of the therapeutic recreation program will be conducted on weekends, evenings, and holidays when the services of other treatment disciplines are not being offered. The time of the therapeutic recreator is divided into activity leadership, record keeping, team meetings, staffings, assessment, and evaluation.

Unlike other disciplines, it is difficult to determine the specific hourly cost of therapeutic recreator service because of its broad scope. The professional service of therapeutic recreation is recognized by Medicare regulations for extended care facilities, intermediate care facilities, and psychiatric facilities, but it is usually listed as a covered service as opposed to a reimbursable one. The difference between the two types of services lies in the distinction that covered services are general services provided as routine services to those residents for whom it is deemed appropriate. Conditions of participation for Medicare payments in inpatient psychiatric facilities indicate the eligibility of therapeutic recreation as a reimbursable service only if it is provided under a very specific treatment-oriented program and under the supervision of a physician.

While this is not standard practice, attempts are being made by individual therapeutic recreation specialists to receive third party payments from health insurance carriers for services rendered. In some of these instances, professionals are prescribing specific treatment through therapeutic recreation. Some health insurance carriers are covering therapeutic recreation services on an hourly basis. At the present time, the National Therapeutic Recreation Society is studying these isolated occurrences in an effort to promote reimbursement on a national basis.

PROFESSIONAL ORGANIZATIONS

American Alliance for Health, Physical Education, and Recreation, 1201 16th Street, N.W., Washington, D.C. 20036

National Consortium on Physical Education and Recreation for Handicapped Children and Youth,

National Education Association, Suite 610A, 1201 16th Street, N.W., Washington, D.C. 20036

National Therapeutic Recreation Society, 1601 North Kent Street, Arlington, Virginia 22209

The National Therapeutic Recreation Society is the professional association of therapeutic recreators and is a branch of the National Recreation and Park Association. This is the national standard-setting organization for the therapeutic recreation professsion. It sponsors professional development conferences and workshops and publishes the professional journal, *The Therapeutic Recreation Journal.*

Within the American Alliance for Health, Physical Education, and Recreation is a unit on Programs for the Handicapped. This unit provides consultation, information, and technical assistance in the areas of recreation and physical education for handicapped individuals. Services of this unit have included the sponsorship of the Information and Research Utilization Center on Physical Education and Recreation for the Handicapped.

The National Consortium is a newly formed organization that brings together physical educators and recreation specialists concerned with delivery of services primarily to children and youth. Of specific concern to the Consortium are the programs and services administered by the Bureau of Education for the Handicapped of the U.S. Office of Education.

REFERENCES

Committee of Participants. 1969. Ninth Southern Regional Institute of Therapeutic Recreation. Unpublished paper, University of North Carolina, Chapel Hill.

Frye, V., and Peters, M. 1972. Therapeutic Recreation: Its Theory and Practice. Stackpole Publishers, Harrisburg, Pa.

Meyers, M. W. 1962. The rationale of recreation as therapy. Recreation in Treatment Centers 1:23.

National Recreation and Park Association. n.d. Information Regarding Voluntary Registration with the National Therapeutic Recreation Society. National Recreation and Park Association, Arlington, Va.

National Recreation and Park Association. 1976. Leisure Activity Participation and Handicapped Populations: Assessment of Research Needs. National Recreation and Park Association, Arlington, Va.

SUGGESTED READINGS

Avedon, E. M. 1974. Therapeutic Recreation Service: An Applied Behavioral Science Approach. Prentice-Hall, Englewood Cliffs, N.J.

Avedon, E. M., and Arje, F. B. 1964. Socio-recreative Programming for the Retarded: A Handbook for Sponsoring Groups. Bureau of Publications, Teachers College Press, New York.

Geddes, D. 1974. Physical Activities for Individuals with Handicapping Conditions. The C.V. Mosby Company, St. Louis.

Haun, P. 1965. Recreation: A Medical Viewpoint. Bureau of Publications, Teachers College Press, New York.

Hunt, V. V., 1955. Recreation for the Handicapped. Prentice-Hall, Englewood Cliffs, N.J.

Kraus, R. 1973. Therapeutic Recreation Services: Principles and Practice. W. B. Saunders Company, Philadelphia.

National Recreation and Park Association. 1967–present. Therapeutic Recreation Journal. National Recreation and Park Association, Arlington, Va.

Nesbitt, J. A., Murphy, J. F., and Brown, P. D. (eds.). 1970. Recreation and Leisure Services for the Disadvantaged. Lea and Febiger, Philadelphia.

O'Morrow, G. S. 1976. Therapeutic Recreation: A Helping Profession. Reston Publishing Company, Inc., Reston, Va.

Pomeroy, J. 1964. Recreation for the Physically Handicapped. Macmillan, New York.

Rathbone, J., and Lucas, C. 1970. Recreation in Total Rehabilitation. Charles C Thomas, Springfield, Ill.

Stein, T. A., and Sessoms, D. (eds.), 1973. Recreation and Special Populations. Holbrook Press, Inc., Boston.

Shivers, J. S., and Fait, H. F. 1975. Therapeutic and Adapted Recreation Services. Lea and Febiger, Philadelphia.

Index